Sex, Cells, and Same-Sex Desire: The Biology of Sexual Preference

Sex, Cells, and Same-Sex Desire: The Biology of Sexual Preference

John P. De Cecco, PhD
David Allen Parker, MA
Editors

Sex, Cells, and Same-Sex Desire: The Biology of Sexual Preference, edited by John P. De Cecco and David Allen Parker, was simultaneously issued by The Haworth Press, Inc., under the same title, as special issues of *Journal of Homosexuality*, Volume 28, Numbers 1/2 and 3/4 1995, John P. De Cecco, Editor.

Harrington Park Press
An Imprint of
The Haworth Press, Inc.
New York • London • Norwood (Australia)

ISBN 1-56023-060-6

Published by

Harrington Park Press, 10 Alice St., Binghamton, NY 13904-1580

Harrington Park Press is an Imprint of The Haworth Press, Inc., 10 Alice Street, Binghamton, NY 13904-1580 USA

Sex, Cells, and Same-Sex Desire: The Biology of Sexual Preference has also been published as *Journal of Homosexuality*, Volume 28, Numbers 1/2 and 3/4, 1995.

The development, preparation, and publication of this work has been undertaken with great care. However, the publisher, employees, editors, and agents of The Haworth Press and all imprints of The Haworth Press, Inc., including The Haworth Medical Press and Pharmaceutical Products Press, are not responsible for any errors contained herein or for consequences that may ensue from use of materials or information contained in this work. Opinions expressed by the author(s) are not necessarily those of The Haworth Press, Inc.

Library of Congress Cataloging-in-Publication Data

Sex, cells, and same-sex desire : the biology of sexual preference / John P. De Cecco, David Allen Parker, editors.
　　p. cm.
　　Includes bibliographical references and index.
　　ISBN 1-56024-700-2 . – ISBN 1-56023-060-6
　　1. Homosexuality–Physiological aspects. I. De Cecco, John P. II. Parker, David Allen.
QP81.6.S48 1995
306.76'6–dc20   95-6140
　　　　　　　　　　　　NWST   CIP
　　　　　　　　　　　AJC 6854

INDEXING & ABSTRACTING

Contributions to this publication are selectively indexed or abstracted in print, electronic, online, or CD-ROM version(s) of the reference tools and information services listed below. This list is current as of the copyright date of this publication. See the end of this section for additional notes.

- *Abstracts in Anthropology*, Baywood Publishing Company, 26 Austin Avenue, P.O. Box 337, Amityville, NY 11701

- *Abstracts of Research in Pastoral Care & Counseling*, Loyola College, 7135 Minstrel Way, Suite 101, Columbia, MD 21045

- *Academic Abstracts/CD-ROM*, EBSCO Publishing, P.O. Box 2250, Peabody, MA 01960-7250

- *Applied Social Sciences Index & Abstracts (ASSIA) (Online: ASSI via Data-Star) (CD Rom: ASSIA Plus)*, Bowker- Saur Limited, Maypole House, Maypole Road, East Grinstead, West Sussex RH19 1HH England

- *Book Review Index,* Gale Research, Inc., P.O. Box 2867, Detroit, MI 48231

- *Cambridge Scientific Abstracts*, *Risk Abstracts*, Cambridge Information Group, 7200 Wisconsin Avenue, #601, Bethesda, MD 20814

- *Criminal Justice Abstracts*, Willow Tree Press, 15 Washington Street, 4th Floor, Newark NJ 07102

- *Criminology, Penology and Police Science Abstracts*, Kugler Publications, P.O. Box 11188, 1001 GD-Amsterdam, The Netherlands

- *Current Contents: Clinical Medicine/Life Sciences (CC:CM/LS) (weekly Table of Contents Service),* and *Social Science Citation Index.* Articles also searchable through *Social SciSearch,* ISI's online database and in *ISI's Research Alert* current awareness service, Institute for Scientific Information, 3501 Market Street, Philadelphia, PA 19104-3302

- *Digest of Neurology and Psychiatry,* The Institute of Living, 400 Washington Street, Hartford, CT 06106

(continued)

- *Excerpta Medica/Secondary Publishing Division*, Elsevier Science, Inc./Secondary Publishing Division, 655 Avenue of the Americas, New York, NY 10010

- *Expanded Academic Index*, Information Access Company, 362 Lakeside Drive, Forest City, CA 94404

- *Family Life Educator "Abstracts Section,"* ETR Associates, P.O. Box 1830, Santa Cruz, CA 95061-1830

- *Family Violence & Sexual Assault Bulletin*, Family Violence & Sexual Assault Institute, 1310 Clinic Drive, Tyler, TX 75701

- *Index Medicus/MEDLINE*, National Library of Medicine, 8600 Rockville Pike, Bethesda, MD 20894

- *Index to Periodical Articles Related to Law*, University of Texas, 727 East 26th Street, Austin, TX 78705

- *INFO-SOUTH Abstracts: contemporary social, political, and economic information on Latin America; available on-line,* North-South Center Consortium, University of Miami, Miami, FL 33124

- *Inventory of Marriage and Family Literature (online and hard copy)*, National Council on Family Relations, 3989 Central Avenue NE, Suite 550, Minneapolis, MN 55421

- *Leeds Medical Information,* University of Leeds, Leeds LS2 9JT, United Kingdom

- *Mental Health Abstracts (online through DIALOG)*, IFI/Plenum Data Company, 3202 Kirkwood Highway, Wilmington, DE 19808

- *MLA International Bibliography,* Modern Language Association of America, 10 Astor Place, New York, NY 10003

- *PASCAL International Bibliography T205: Sciences de l'information Documentation*, INIST/CNRS-Service Gestion des Documents Primaires, 2, allée du Parc de Brabois, F-54514 Vandoeuvre-les-Nancy, Cedex, France

- *Periodical Abstracts, Research 1 (general and basic reference indexing and abstracting data-base from University Microfilms International (UMI), 300 North Zeeb Road, P.O. Box 1346, Ann Arbor, MI 48106-1346)*, UMI Data Courier, P.O. Box 32770, Louisville, KY 40232-2770

(continued)

- *Periodical Abstracts, Research II (broad coverage indexing and abstracting data-base from University Microfilms International (UMI), 300 North Zeeb Road, P.O. Box 1346, Ann Arbor, MI 48106-1346)*, UMI Data Courier, P.O. Box 32770, Louisville, KY 40232-2770

- *PsychNet*, PsychNet Inc., P.O. Box 470250 Aurora, CO 80047-0250

- *Psychological Abstracts (PsycINFO)*, American Psychological Association, P.O. Box 91600, Washington, DC 20090-1600

- *Public Affairs Information Bulletin (PAIS)*, Public Affairs Information Service, Inc., 521 West 43rd Street, New York, NY 10036-4396

- *Religion Index One: Periodicals*, American Theological Library Association, 820 Church Street, 3rd Floor, Evanston, IL 60201

- *Sage Family Studies Abstracts (SFSA)*, Sage Publications, Inc., 2455 Teller Road, Newbury Park, CA 91320

- *Social Planning/Policy & Development Abstracts (SOPODA)*, Sociological Abstracts, Inc., P.O. Box 22206, San Diego, CA 92192-0206

- *Social Sciences Index (from Volume 1 & continuing)*, The H.W. Wilson Company, 950 University Avenue, Bronx, NY 10452

- *Social Work Abstracts*, National Association of Social Workers, 750 First Street NW, 8th Floor, Washington, DC 20002

- *Sociological Abstracts (SA)*, Sociological Abstracts, Inc., P.O. Box 22206, San Diego, CA 92192-0206

- *Studies on Women Abstracts*, Carfax Publishing Company, P.O. Box 25, Abingdon, Oxfordshire OXI4 3UE, United Kingdom

Book reviews are selectively excerpted by the Guide to Professional Literature of the Journal of Academic Librarianship.

SPECIAL BIBLIOGRAPHIC NOTES

related to special journal issues (separates)
and indexing/abstracting

❏ indexing/abstracting services in this list will also cover material in any "separate" that is co-published simultaneously with Haworth's special thematic journal issue or DocuSerial. Indexing/abstracting usually covers material at the article/chapter level.

❏ monographic co-editions are intended for either non-subscribers or libraries which intend to purchase a second copy for their circulating collections.

❏ monographic co-editions are reported to all jobbers/wholesalers/approval plans. The source journal is listed as the "series" to assist the prevention of duplicate purchasing in the same manner utilized for books-in-series.

❏ to facilitate user/access services all indexing/abstracting services are encouraged to utilize the co-indexing entry note indicated at the bottom of the first page of each article/chapter/contribution.

❏ this is intended to assist a library user of any reference tool (whether print, electronic, online, or CD-ROM) to locate the monographic version if the library has purchased this version but not a subscription to the source journal.

❏ individual articles/chapters in any Haworth publication are also available through the Haworth Document Delivery Services (HDDS).

CONTENTS

ABOUT THE EDITORS

John P. De Cecco is Professor of Psychology and Director of Human Sexuality Studies at San Francisco State University, where he also serves as the coordinator of the new Bisexual, Lesbian, and Gay minor program. He has been editor of the *Journal of Homosexuality* since 1977. He has had a long-standing interest in the biology of sexual preference and recently edited with John Elia, *If You Seduce a Straight Person, Can You Make Them Gay?* (1993). He is a member of the International Academy of Sex Research, the Society for the Scientific Study of Sex, and the recipient of the Magnus Hirschfeld Medal (1992) for outstanding contributions to sexology.

David Allen Parker holds a Master of Arts degree in Social Psychology from San Francisco State University, and is a Research Associate of the Center for Research and Education in Sexuality, San Francisco.

Preface

Since its inception in 1974, the *Journal of Homosexuality* has published relatively few articles on the biology of sexual preference. In retrospect this appears to have been the unwitting result of the fact that the most rapid expansion of lesbian, gay, and bisexual studies has occurred in the social sciences, the humanities, and the arts. Even psychology, the discipline that sometimes bridges between biology and the social sciences, in recent years has played a relatively minor role in gay studies, except for research on homophobia and occasional studies on identity formation and relationships. Most psychologists, along with most other social scientists who might have pursued studies on these and related topics, turned instead to research on the personal and social impact of the AIDS epidemic and how to prevent its continued devastation.

While lesbian, gay, and bisexual studies was laying down a path of its own, the biological studies of sexual preference continued on a course set in the nineteenth century by Karl Heinrich Ulrichs and Magnus Hirschfeld. The biological research preserved as axiomatic the interlocking assumptions that, in nature, the purpose of sexuality was reproduction and that biological femaleness and maleness exist as primary, dichotomous, and opposed states that provide the cross-cultural and transhistorical foundation for gender differences and thereby the perpetuation of the species. In the meantime, gay studies was documenting the great variety of gender and sexual expressions that have existed over time and cultures and how their meanings derived from the historical and cultural contexts in which they have occurred. What this present work attempts to do, there-

[Haworth co-indexing entry note]: "Preface." De Cecco, John P., and David Allen Parker. Co-published simultaneously in *Journal of Homosexuality* (The Haworth Press, Inc.) Vol. 28, No. 1/2, 1995, pp. xxi-xxiii; and: *Sex, Cells, and Same-Sex Desire: The Biology of Sexual Preference* (ed: John P. De Cecco, and David Allen Parker) The Haworth Press, Inc., 1995, pp. xiii-xv. Multiple copies of this article/chapter may be purchased from The Haworth Document Delivery Center [1-800-3-HAWORTH; 9:00 a.m. - 5:00 p.m. (EST)].

xiii

fore, is to report, review, and, where appropriate, question the recent biological research on sexual preference from two vantage points: (a) that of scientists who have knowledge of the biological processes and structures in question and the relevant methodologies for investigating them; (b) that of scholars in the social sciences and humanities who represent the emerging field of gay studies.

We have tried to demystify the biological research on sexual preference by making it as accessible as possible to readers unfamiliar with biological and medical research and terminology. Where appropriate the introductions to the various sections lay out central concepts for the articles that follow. Technical terms are usually defined where they occur in the articles and again in the glossary. There are figures to assist the understanding of those parts of the reproductive and endocrinal systems and of the brain that are the particular foci of the research to which the articles refer.

In the process of undertaking a project of such vast interdisciplinary scope we needed and have had the assistance of many scholars. First of all we are deeply grateful to our several contributors from Europe and the United States, many of whom have rarely published in a journal outside of their parent disciplines, who kindly accepted our invitation to prepare their articles and gracefully shouldered, with only occasional pique, successive rounds of manuscript editing. Not all of the individuals to whom we extended invitations were able to accept, especially at a time when they and their research reports were hot on the media circuit.

Among our several contributors we are particularly grateful to Dr. William Byne, who not only prepared his own seminal article dealing with the brain, but also, at our request, perused the figures depicting the brain, the introductions to the various sections, and the glossary, and made many invaluable suggestions. We want to express our thanks to Professors Martin Duberman and Randolph Trumbach of the Center for Gay and Lesbian Studies (CLAGS) in the Graduate Center of the City University of New York, Dr. Gert Hekma of the University of Amsterdam, and Drs. Theo van der Meer of the Free University, Amsterdam, for recommending to us some of our contributors and encouraging their contributions. We wish to thank our colleagues in the International Academy of Sex Research for making it possible for three of our authors (including one of the editors of this collection) to present a critique of the biological research at its 1993 meeting in Asilomar, California.

There are several individuals who helped with the graphics and to whom we express our gratitude: to Terry C. P. Lynch, MD, of the University of California San Francisco Medical Center at Mt. Zion Hospital for the photograph (MRI) of the brain, and to Eric Kalabacos, Craig Barnes, and Thom Howard for the computer graphics involved in reproducing the figures dealing with the brain (Figures 1-4, pp. 278-280). We also wish to thank Ron Enriquez, MD, of the University of California San Francisco Medical Center for guiding us to the reference material in medical books and journals.

Finally we thank our colleague and friend, John Patrick Elia, who was willing to listen to all of our complaints, real and contrived, over the two-year period this project was underway, supplying when needed a sobering word of advice and many words of encouragement.

John P. De Cecco, PhD
David Allen Parker, MA
San Francisco

SECTION I: INTRODUCTION

The Biology of Homosexuality:
Sexual Orientation or Sexual Preference?

John P. De Cecco, PhD
David Allen Parker, MA

SUMMARY. This paper begins with a summary of the biological research on homosexuality that occurred in the late 1980s and early 1990s. It then summarizes the treatment of this research chiefly by the print media. It then adumbrates the presuppositions about sexuality and gender upon which the reports were based. It is argued that the presuppositions, which are asserted without being examined, date back to the nineteenth century. They ignore the historical, sociocultural, and humanistic research of the last two decades that collectively comprise the field of gay, lesbian, and bisexual studies. The discussion of the issue of choice follows and it recognizes the various constraints on choice without eliminating it as an element of sexual expression. Finally, the paper sets forth a general conception

Correspondence may be addressed to the authors at the Center for Research and Education in Sexuality (CERES), San Francisco State University, San Francisco, CA 94132.

[Haworth co-indexing entry note]: "The Biology of Homosexuality: Sexual Orientation or Sexual Preference." De Cecco, John P., and David Allen Parker. Co-published simultaneously in *Journal of Homosexuality* (The Haworth Press, Inc.) Vol. 28, No. 1/2, 1995, pp. 1-27; and: *Sex, Cells, and Same-Sex Desire: The Biology of Sexual Preference* (ed: John P. De Cecco, and David Allen Parker) The Haworth Press, Inc., 1995, pp. 1-27. Multiple copies of this article/chapter may be purchased from The Haworth Document Delivery Center [1-800-3-HAWORTH; 9:00 a.m. - 5:00 p.m. (EST)].

1

of homosexuality that includes its psychological and socio-cultural
dimensions along with the biological.

This collection of papers on the biological antecedents of homosexuality has been occasioned by the spate of reports that have
recently appeared in scientific journals, most of which have received widespread attention in the media. Over the last decade
homosexuality has been a focal public interest that arose in part
from the success of the Lesbian and Gay Liberation movement in
gaining a place on the national political agenda and the popular
association of homosexuality with the AIDS epidemic.

Although research on the biology of homosexuality is over one
hundred years old (Herrn, this volume), publication of reports in
scientific journals gathered momentum in the 1980s and the 1990s.
This followed the official declaration of the American Psychological Association in 1973 that homosexuality "per se" would no
longer be classified as a mental illness. This action had the effect of
relegating psychological and psychiatric explanations of homosexuality to history but left the way clear for biological speculations
and research.[1] The friendly receptivity with which scientific and
medical journals have greeted the biological studies of the last two
decades is extraordinary, particularly in light of the early skepticism
of the distinguished biologist of homosexuality, Alfred Kinsey. In
1941 Kinsey (p. 428) wrote:

> Any hormonal or other explanation of the homosexual must
> allow . . . that the picture is one of endless integration between
> every combination of homosexuality and heterosexuality; . . .
> that both homosexual and heterosexual activities may occur
> coincidentally in a single period in the life of a single individu-
> al; and that the exclusive activities of any one type, may be
> exchanged, in the brief span of a few days or a few weeks, for
> an exclusive pattern of the other type, or into a combination
> pattern that embraces the two types.

The individual who pioneered the current wave of biological
investigations is Günter Dörner, the director of the Institute of Experimental Endocrinology at Humboldt University in Berlin. He

came to public attention in the United States with an article entitled "Sexual Destinies," published in *Omni* magazine in 1987. Appearing above the article's title was the bold assertion, "Homosexuals are born, not made, claims one physician [i.e., Dörner] who says he has proof positive that sexual orientation is sealed in the womb." In that article Dörner stated that the notion that homosexuality had a biological basis first occurred to him in the late 1960s while he was watching the Vienna ballet on television. He recalled that "there were some homosexual dancers with typical female behavior . . . gestures that *couldn't* (our emphasis) be performed by heterosexual males" (Murray, 1987, p. 100).

He assumed that the dancers were homosexual because he "knew" that most male ballet dancers are homosexual. In the case of such males, the biological cause of their putative homosexuality is a hormonal abnormality that occurs during pregnancy and leaves lasting marks on the brain. The particular hormone was androgen, which he called the "masculinizing" hormone, and the particular region of the brain was the hypothalamus, a region of the lower brain. According to Dörner, since the hypothalamus of homosexual men was structured like that of heterosexual women, both had similar reactions to injections of the so-called "female" hormone, estrogen (Gooren, this volume; Banks & Gartrell, this volume).

Almost all of Dörner's research has been conducted on rats. His first published research on homosexual men appeared in 1975 (Dörner, Rohde, Stall, Krell, & Massius, 1975). For almost a decade this study remained unreplicated, although Dörner continued to press its conclusions. The first attempt to replicate Dörner's research was made in the United States in 1984 (Gladue, Green, & Hellman, 1984). That study, which claimed to support Dörner's findings, was published in *Science,* a journal that commands an authoritative voice for the disciplines it serves, including biology. Its appearance attracted considerable media attention (including the article on Dörner that was published in *Omni*) and paved the way for reports that appeared later in the decade and at the beginning of the nineties, each claiming to have discovered "new" biological markers for homosexuality.

In the late eighties the focus of biomedical research on homosexuality shifted in emphasis from hormones to genes. In 1986,

Richard Pillard, a gay psychiatrist, and James Weinrich, a gay sociobiologist, published a study that concluded that male homosexuality runs in families–that it was much more likely that brothers of gay men would be homosexual than it was for brothers of straight men (Pillard & Weinrich, 1986). Their article was published in the premiere research journal for psychiatry, *Archives of Psychiatry.* Five years earlier Pillard and his colleagues (Pillard, Poumadere, & Caretta, 1981) had published a review article in that same journal that speculated on possible genetic markers for homosexuality. Since *Archives* enjoys within its discipline the prestige that *Science* has within the natural sciences, the familial study of 1986 received considerable media attention.

Shortly after the publication of the report by Pillard and Weinrich (1986), there appeared in *Brain Research,* another prestigious scientific journal, reports of studies exploring possible links between homosexuality and the structure of the hypothalamus. This is the region of the lower brain that, on basis of his research on rats, Dörner had claimed was the area within which lay the essential differences between females and males in reproduction, gender roles, and sexual preference (see Figure 4, p. 280). The research on the hypothalamus was conducted at the Netherlands Institute for Brain Research under the leadership of Professor D. F. Swaab, a professor of neurobiology at the University of Amsterdam (Swaab & Hofman, 1988, 1990; Swaab, Gooren, & Hofman, this volume). Earlier, in 1985, Swaab and Fliers had published a report in *Science* claiming that a particular region of the hypothalamus was "sexually dimorphic," that is, showing different structures in females and males. In brain research, reports of studies claiming to have found new areas of "sexual dimorphism" often precede reports claiming to have identified new markers for homosexuality. Indeed, in 1990, Swaab and Hofman claimed that they had found a particular nucleus (i.e., the suprachiasmatic nucleus) in the hypothalamus that was larger and contained more cells in gay than in straight men. This study stirred more interest in Europe than in the United States and kindled considerable controversy over its implied biological determinism in the Dutch press.

By the end of the eighties the search for biological markers of homosexuality included three major areas of biological investigation: hormonal, genetic, and brain research. Psychodynamic explanations of homosexuality, such as those proposed by Freud and his followers, were virtually abandoned, except by a small group of psychoanalysts, many of whom, in 1973, had opposed the declassification of homosexuality as a mental illness.

During the summer of 1991, *Science* published a report on the hypothalamus by a gay neuroscientist, Simon LeVay. LeVay was new to the field of biological research on homosexuality; his previous research had been on a distinctly different region of the brain known as the visual cortex. LeVay carried out his study at the Salk Institute for Biological Studies, named after the renowned scientist, Jonas Salk. LeVay claimed that he had found a nucleus in the hypothalamus INAH 3 (see Figure 4, p. 280) that had twice the volume in heterosexual than in homosexual men. This was a different nucleus than that described by Swaab and Hofman (1990; Swaab, Gooren, & Hofman, this volume). LeVay claimed to have found no corresponding difference in the size of the nucleus identified by Swaab.

At the end of 1991, while LeVay was still on the media circuit, a "twins" study was published by Michael Bailey, a clinical psychologist at Northwestern University, and Richard Pillard (Bailey & Pillard, 1991). In that same year Bailey, as a member of two different research teams, also published reports that concluded that homosexuality was "strongly familial" and that mothers of "effeminate" boys were more "stress-prone" than other mothers (Buhrich, Bailey, & Martin, 1991; Bailey, Willerman, & Parks, 1991). In their twin study, Bailey and Pillard (1991) concluded that the rate of homosexuality was higher in twins than in the twins' adopted siblings and higher still in twins who issued from one fertilized egg (i.e., monozygotic or identical twins) than those who emerged from two different eggs (i.e., dizygotic or fraternal twins). Their conclusion was that there is a "substantial inheritability" of male homosexuality. In a later report, also published in *Archives of General Psychiatry,* the same claim was made for female homosexuality (Bailey, Pillard, Neale, & Agyei, 1993).

The tide of research for biological markers of homosexuality continued to rise in 1992, when interest moved back to the brain. In that year two neurobiologists, Laura Allen, a post-doctoral student, and Roger Gorsky, a professor in the Department of Anatomy and

Cell Biology and in the Laboratory of Neuroendocrinology at the University of California at Los Angeles, reported in the *Proceedings of the National Academy of Sciences,* that they had found a new area of the brain that differed in size between heterosexual and homosexual men. That area was the anterior commissure, a group of fibers lying adjacent to the hypothalamus and interconnecting the temporal lobes of the brain (see Figures 1, 3, & 4, pp. 278-280). Their report claimed that this structure was larger in heterosexual women than in heterosexual men and larger in homosexual than in heterosexual men. In an interview with the *Advocate,* Allen stated that her study suggests "the [entire] brain is organized differently [in gay men] not just the region that affects sexual behavior." The implication was that gay men physically are like straight women as well as behaving like them in sharing their attraction to men (Gallagher, 1992). In their report, Allen and Gorski speculated that further research is likely to find that the *global* (i.e., the entire) brain structure of homosexual males differs from that of heterosexuals.

Finally, in July, 1993, in what appeared to be the *coup de maitre* of the biological search for the causes of homosexuality, *Science* published a study that claimed to have discovered genetic markers on the X-chromosome that "influenced" a homosexual orientation in males (Hamer, Hu, Magnuson, Hu, & Pattatucci, 1993). The research team worked in the Laboratory of Biochemistry in the National Cancer Institute in Bethesda, Maryland, where they had been studying the development of cancers in persons infected with HIV. The study, based on "pedigree analysis," involved drawing blood samples from men who identified themselves as homosexuals. They also took blood samples from their male relatives, including brothers, uncles, and cousins. They identified a gene "on the long arm of the X-chromosome" that they claimed correlated with self-reports of homosexuality. Hamer and his colleagues concluded that homosexuality was more likely transmitted genetically through mothers rather than through fathers since males derive their single X-chromosome from their mothers.

TREATMENT OF THE REPORTS IN THE MEDIA

We have confined our discussion to investigators who have recently published in scientific journals and whose reports have attracted considerable attention in the mass media. Among the journals, *Science* published three of the reports (Gladue et al., 1984; LeVay, 1991; and Hamer et al., 1993); *Archives for Psychiatry* published two (Pillard & Weinrich, 1986; Bailey and Pillard, 1991); and *Brain Research* (Swaab & Hofman, 1990) and *Proceedings of the National Academy of Science* (Allen & Gorski, 1992) published one each. All four journals contribute to the biomedical canon as represented by textbooks in their fields.

The report by LeVay made the biggest media splash. The *New York Times* gave it front page coverage (August 20, 1991): "Zone of Brain Linked to Men's Sexual Orientation." The *Wall Street Journal* covered the report on the front page of its "Marketplace" section under the banner, "Study Raises Issue of Biological Basis of Homosexuality" (Winslow, 1991, p. B2). *Newsweek* signed in with "What Causes People to be Homosexual?" (Sept. 9, 1991). *Time* mentioned it on its cover and ran an article under the title, "Are Gay Men Born That Way?" (Gorman, 1991). In the *San Francisco Chronicle* the report was hailed as "Brain Cell Study Finds Link to Homosexuality: Tissues Differ between Gay and Straight Men" (Perlman, 1991, p. A1). It was the subject of broadcasts on *Nightline,* the nightly news analysis program of the American Broadcasting System, and on the *MacNeil/Lehrer NewsHour* of the Public Broadcasting Service. LeVay appeared on several talk shows, including *Donahue* and *Oprah.* LeVay's report also attracted attention in the national gay press, particularly the *Advocate* and *10 Percent Magazine* (Gallagher, 1991; Cohn, 1992).

Some of this interest was fostered by the editors of *Science,* who regularly authorize press releases for forthcoming issues. The entire front page of its press release for the issue in which LeVay's research appeared was devoted to that report and linked it to previously published articles on gender differences in the brain, a topic also popular with *Science* (Gallagher, 1991). In that same issue of *Science,* there appeared three additional articles prepared by staff writers. One raised the question about the biological basis of homosexuality (Barinaga, 1991). Although sounding a cautionary note about this brain research, the author quotes several investigators who were optimistic that future studies would find the cause of homosexuality in the brain. The article ends with Swaab's assertion that the difference between heterosexuals and homosexuals is "in the brain, not in the heart" (Barinaga, 1991, p. 957).

The second article dealt specifically with purported differences between the female and male brain (Gibbons, 1991). Claims were made that there were differences in three areas of the brain, each of which lie outside the cerebral cortex–the hypothalamus, the corpus callosum, and the anterior commissure (see Figures 1, 3, & 4, pp. 278-280). There was confident speculation, however, that sex differences would be found throughout the brain. The third article dealt with the political implications of the search for cognitive differences in females and males, such as differences in verbal expression, spatial ability, quantitative reasoning, and scientific thinking (Holden, 1991). One researcher questioned the very existence of such phenomena, while another insisted that the biological differences were irrefutable.

The LeVay report achieved notoriety for reasons beyond the authoritative aura lent to it by *Science* and the Salk Institute and by the scientific mystique that surrounds brain research. LeVay, who was born and partly educated in England, used the report's publication as the occasion for "coming out" and, in the process, revealed that the cause of the recent death of his American "lover" was HIV infection (Zamichow, 1991). The latter revelation fortuitously linked his research to the AIDS epidemic which, because of its association with gay men, may be what had garnered some of the media and popular interest in biological studies of homosexuality in the first place. Personal disclosures by a gay brain researcher, laying claim to notable academic and professional affiliations, and emerging fresh from his bereavement, offered too much of a spectacle to be ignored by television and the press.

About one year later, *Science,* perhaps in response to the criticism it received in publishing this study, arranged for a staff writer to do a follow-up article that questioned the degree to which LeVay's personal convictions affected his research (Marshall, 1992). LeVay was described as believing that "he sees no need to create special barriers between his role as advocate and his work as a scientist" (Marshall, 1992, p. 621). The conviction in question was LeVay's repeated assertion that the discovery of the biological causes of homosexuality would win tolerance for gay people since it would show that they had no choice but to be gay.

Other authors of these biological reports, albeit less flamboyantly, could not resist sounding the same political notes in defense of their research conclusions. Most of them asserted the belief that the discovery of the biological basis of homosexuality would protect homosexuals from discrimination. With unintentional irony, Bailey and Pillard (1991) referred to a 1989 survey that showed that there was more "tolerance" for homosexuals who were born gay than for those who chose or learned to be homosexual. Dr. Hamer, in a statement that was at once a plea for open-mindedness and a foreclosure of counter arguments and research findings expressed his belief that homosexuality is basically biological: "I'm perfectly aware there are many people who are not interested in the facts, who have their own deeply-held beliefs, which I respect, that will not be swayed by science . . . but I am optimistic that the majority of Americans are willing to listen to the facts" *(Wall Street Journal,* August 12, 1993, p. A4).

PRESUPPOSITIONS OF THE RESEARCH REPORTS

There have been three decades of gay and lesbian studies dealing with historical and cultural forms of homosexuality, including the century-old history of attempts to identify its biological markers (see Herrn; Dickemann, this volume), that the biological studies have ignored. As this collection demonstrates, even biological scientists pointed out the methodological flaws, among others, in sample selection, measurement procedures, and utilization of earlier research as well as the practice of scientific journals in reporting studies before they had been properly replicated (Byne; Fausto-Sterling; Haynes; and McGuire, this volume). Both the scholars and scientists questioned the reports' underlying conceptualizations of homosexuality and gender differences and the political claims made by their authors either in the reports themselves or in their press comments following publication.

The research reports we have reviewed are based on a number of preconceptions about homosexuality that, as Haumann (this volume) points out, represent the transformation of social ideologies into physical realities. First, at the most general level sexuality is viewed as basically physical and behavioral, a material entity that is bequeathed by nature, something given rather than learned, achieved, and institutionalized. From this physical perspective, sexuality resides in the body, the genes, the glands, and the subcortical brain. Behaviorally it resides in copulatory activity involving the genitals.

In this view sexual behavior is mechanically driven by its physical underpinnings. Elements of motivation, unconsciousness, intention, perception, interpretation, and choice, as well as influences of time, society, and culture spice the sexual and gender cake but do not constitute their basic ingredients. Thus the term "sexual preference," with its connotations of learned and evolving taste and acquired discretion, becomes "sexual orientation," a biological mechanism that steers our sexual behavior toward one gender and away from the other (De Cecco & Elia, 1993).

The belief that homosexuality inheres in the body led the biological investigators to be cavalier in the identification and selection of subjects since one "specimen" was essentially equal to all others. In the brain studies, particularly those of Swaab and LeVay, the researchers never knew their subjects. All they had was a collection of disembodied brains. Their subjects' homosexuality was asserted on the basis of their medical histories, which presumably recorded that the subject was homosexual or bisexual. Whether these labels were applied by the subjects to themselves while alive or were merely conjectures of attending medical personnel cannot be ascertained from the published reports. If neither the homosexual nor bisexual designation appeared in the patients' records, the researchers apparently assumed the subjects were heterosexual.

In the case of living subjects, other investigators largely relied on various forms of self-identification and sometimes on their self-identified gay subjects' opinions of the sexual proclivities of their relatives (see McGuire, this volume). Self-identification could range merely from the subject's disclosure that he was gay or his rating himself from 2 to 6 on the Kinsey (1948) heterosexual-homosexual (0 to 6) rating scale. What could be construed as "bisexuality," for the most part was conceptually and methodologically subsumed under homosexuality (see Van Wyk & Geist, this volume).

Only if one presupposes that sexual preference is biologically mandated could one believe that a single label or number, even if self-applied, could adequately represent the range, variation, and nuance of an individual's sexual expression and experience over a lifetime.

This mechanistic assumption, particularly true of genetic studies, was spoofed in an op ed letter to the *New York Times,* by a writer, Daniel Mendelsohn (1993), who, in mock response to a piece in a fictional scientific journal, *Nurture,* that claimed that conservatism is inherited, observed:

> Biologists have long suspected that conservatism is inherited. 'After all,' said one author of the *Nurture* article, 'it is quite common for a Republican to have a brother or sister who is Republican.' The finding has been greeted with relief by parents and friends of Republicans, who tended to blame themselves for the political views of otherwise loveable people– their children, friends, and unindicted co-conspirators.

The second and related assumption of these research reports was that homosexuality, as a biological given, existed as the antithesis of heterosexuality. Over the past two decades, however, gay and lesbian scholarship has documented the fact that the notion that individuals exist as two distinct species, one exclusively heterosexual, the other exclusively homosexual, is of fairly recent origin, born in the eighteenth and nineteenth centuries and institutionalized in 19th century medicine (Foucault, 1976; Weeks, 1991; Trumbach, 1991). In several historical periods and in many cultures, past and present, no such antithesis has existed. Almost anyone who engaged in homosexual practice was believed to be capable also of heterosexual practice. Nor was it thought that homosexual practice, especially in youth, in any way precluded adult heterosexuality (e.g., Dover, 1978; Herdt, 1981; Blackwood, 1985).

Several writers, some from the scientific community, raised questions about the researchers' purified conceptions of homosexuality. In an op ed piece in the *New York Times* that appeared after the publication of the study by Hamer and his colleagues, Ruth Hubbard (1993), a Harvard biologist, commented:

Studies of human biology cannot explain the wide range of human behavior. Such efforts fail to acknowledge that sexual attraction depends on personal experience and cultural values and that desire is too complex, varied and interesting to be reduced to genes.

William Rasberry (1993), in the *Washington Post,* in a similar vein, voiced his objections to the biological preconceptions:

Science may yet prove me wrong, but it seems fairly clear to me that homosexuality and heterosexuality exist not as absolutes but as points on a continuum. Few people strike me as either perfectly straight or perfectly gay. If what I observe as a common sense observation is true, it follows that sexuality involves at least some volition–more, no doubt, for some than for others.

Darell Rist (1992, p. 428), the co-founder of the Gay and Lesbian Alliance Against Defamation, believed that the scientific studies were motivated by the "terrified recognition that the subversive kernel of same-sex love, like murder and mayhem and every other sin, lies waiting to bloom in all of us, under proper watering."

Because homosexuality as both desire and behavior rears its head when it shouldn't, the necessity to distinguish the real article from frivolous lapses of locker room playfulness dates back to its earliest conceptualizations. Almost from the beginning of its medicalization in the nineteenth century, a distinction has been drawn between "congenital" or innate and "acquired" homosexuality. The "real" indelible form was that predestined at birth. Krafft-Ebing (1886/ 1906), for example, differentiated between homosexuality that is passed down the family tree as a "hereditary taint" and that acquired through habitual masturbation and heterosexual debauchery. In later discussions there has been the distinction between *obligatory* homosexuality, the equivalent of Krafft-Ebing's inherited form, and *facultative* homosexuality that is "situational" or "opportunistic" (e.g., Money & Ehrhardt, 1972; Money & Tucker, 1975). In the obligatory form, choice for the afflicted individuals never existed because they are obliged to be homosexual due to an innate biological constitution. In the facultative form the individual engages in homosexual behavior only when he has no opportunity for hetero-sexual intercourse, as is the case in prison and other sex-segregated social settings.

It is the so-called inherited or obligated form of homosexuality that is unwittingly the focus of interest for most of the biological research. When the researchers state that their findings may not apply to *all* homosexuals, they believe that at least they apply to those whose homosexuality is biologically mandated–those who have no choice but to be gay or lesbian.

One major difficulty with the distinction between innate and acquired homosexuality is that human sexual behavior is always situational or circumstantial to some extent. That is, it involves a particular person, and either a fantasized or real partner and it occurs at a particular time and in a specific location and culture. Only if one believes in an innate human sexuality that is so biologi-cally driven that it demands expression regardless of circumstances and available partners, does the distinction between an innate and an acquired homosexuality have meaning.

A third presupposition of the biological research is that homo-sexuality in its "true" form is invariably associated with feminine behavior and appearance in men and masculine behavior and ap-pearance in women (Oudshoorn; Gooren, this volume). The first bald assertion that homosexuality was a cross-gendered biological phenomenon was made by Karl Heinrich Ulrichs in the 1860s even before the term homosexuality was invented (Kennedy, 1988). Ul-richs believed that homosexuals existed as a "third sex," a unique form of psychological and spiritual androgyny that reflected the physical hermaphroditism that began to preoccupy medicine in the eighteenth century (Jones & Stalltbrass, 1991; Trumbach, 1991). In fact, in the biological research, the degree to which an individual departs from the sex role stereotypes is taken as an indication of the strength of genetic determination.

As we have noted, this presupposition that homosexuality is a cross-gendered phenomenon has been fairly explicit in the brain research where the purported discovery of new physical factors associated with homosexuality are in some way or another linked to characteristics that typically occur in the opposite sex. It has also been embedded in the genetic research. The recent research report on the chromosomal basis of homosexuality (Hamer et al., 1993) avoids the association between male homosexuality and femininity at least at the level of presupposition, but ends up linking it to a physical characteristic of the opposite-sex parent, the mother.

Even family and twins studies are not immune to the assumption that homosexuals are cross-gendered. Recall Bailey's studies of "effeminate" boys (Buhrich et al., 1991; Bailey et al., 1991). Through questionnaire data, many of the studies have tried to verify retrospectively the prevalence of "gender nonconformity" in their subjects' early childhood, that is, to identify the proto-homosexuals, the sissy boys and the tom-boy girls, in order to shore up the contention that such children are born to fulfill an adult homosexual destiny.

A lingering subtext of the cross-sex assumption is the belief that when nature has its head together it produces heterosexuals. When it produces homosexuals something has gone wrong. It does this by producing sexually "dimorphic" females and males, that is men and women whose anatomical and physiological *differences* are more decisive in determining their sexual and social destinies than their *similarities* (De Cecco, 1990 a,b). The central ingredient of a heterosexual destiny is reproduction. For purposes of procreation the biological characteristics of males and females, as ordained by nature, are therefore not only distinct but also complementary.

For those who accept sexual dimorphism and reproduction as the foundation of human sexuality, homosexual behavior constitutes a singularly serious anomaly, one that cries out for explanation. It compromises the basic duality of the two sexes by one individual absurdly attempting to couple with another who possesses the same equipment. It precludes reproduction, thereby threatening the survival of the human race. Such tacit but entrenched beliefs are why the biological explanations of homosexuality always hover at the edge of pathology, although, in the era of the lesbian/gay civil liberties movement, the language within which they are clothed has become more circumspect–*atypicality* and *exceptionality* have replaced *abnormality* and *disorder.*

Here too the biological research has displayed a woeful ignorance of historical and cultural studies that have discovered various alignments of gender roles and homosexuality. In several tribal societies there have existed masculinization rituals in which the semen of adult men was imparted to or ingested by young boys so that the latter would develop into warriors (Herdt, 1981). In Greek pederasty, the older men played the role of mentor in the sexual and civic development of the adolescent boy into full manhood (Dover, 1978). In aristocratic and court circles of seventeenth-century England, men who bore the reputation of womanizers were known for their elegant dress and elegant manners, characteristics that today many would consider to be "effeminate" (Trumbach, 1991). In fact the gender boundaries for feminine and masculine appearance, voice, gesture, movement, speech, and habit have often been so distinctly cultural and historical, that it can confidently be asserted that the biological research hopelessly conflates homosexuality and gender.

The fourth assumption of the biological researchers (to which we referred when discussing LeVay) is that such studies will inevitably lead to lesbian and gay emancipation since no society would be irrational and irresponsible enough to oppress or insist on altering homosexuals who have no other choice but to be who they are. That is not what Herrn (this volume) found in investigating the history of that research nor what Magnus Hirschfeld, the originator of this aspiration, faced when the Nazis, shortly after coming into power in 1933, raided his Berlin institute and burned the books. Since the Age of Reason, we have become bitterly aware of the irrational sources that lay dormant in individuals and societies from which racism, sexism, nationalism, and, indeed, homophobia spring. Lillian Faderman (Angier, 1991), a historian of nineteenth and twentieth century lesbianism, noted that the biological studies had their origin in the nineteenth century. They appeal today to self-identified homosexuals because they keep their parents off their backs and demonstrate the foolishness of laws against homosexuality. Faderman, however, points out that biological studies invariably have led to attempts to eradicate homosexuality.

Since tolerance is a social virtue, the argument for tolerance of individuals whose sexual preferences are not exclusively heterosexual is more securely grounded in principles of individual liberty and social justice than in biology (Nardi, 1993). In fact, it appears more patronizing than genuinely tolerant to accept a homosexual preference because the persons so possessed cannot help themselves. The "tolerance" of the biologists of homosexuality betrays the wistful hope that everyone would be fortunate enough to be born heterosexual. Genuine tolerance would be based on the moral conviction that a person with a homosexual preference should enjoy the same respect and sexual freedom as a person with a heterosexual preference, regardless of the origin and nature of either choice.

THE ISSUE OF CHOICE

The most fundamental of the biological presuppositions is that the general contours of sexual expression are permanently established by biology and that experience and culture serve only to fill in the details. As biological explanations of the homosexual preference have gained ascendancy over the past two decades, we have noted that there has been a corresponding shift in conceptualization away from sexual *preference* toward sexual *orientation,* a term that presupposes the existence of a congenital steering mechanism that inexorably drives the individual toward one biological sex and away from the other.

By favoring "orientation" over "preference" the biological theorists of homosexuality hope to eliminate or minimize choice. In their minds choice is associated with complete volition and full responsibility for ensuing consequences. Choosing to be homosexual is to risk social disapproval and persecution. Even today there are evangelical religious leaders who, invoking the Old Testament, condemn homosexual behavior as nothing less than an *abomination.* Undoubtedly some biological theorists hope that by substituting a biological drive that is entirely involuntary for the entirely voluntary act of choice, gay men and lesbians can be spared such moral opprobrium and the justification it provides for the continued intolerance of them. As stated previously, the biological rationale as a political strategy has failed in the past (Herrn, this volume; Tsang, this volume). It has failed to convince large numbers of people who continue to believe that our sexual needs and behavior are subject to traditional ethical restraints even if the alternative to the practice of the forbidden behavior is total sexual abstinence. There are also those, even among sexologists, who believe that homosexual behavior is indeed biological, but it's a biology that has gone awry, producing degenerates who contaminate the human genetic pool from which "gay" genes should be banished.

The moral trepidations and solicitousness of the biological theorists should not discourage inquiry into what constitutes sexual preference and choice in our lives and how the awareness of options and choice can be important ingredients of change. In modern usage, the word *preference* implies choice–to favor one entity over another. *Choices are seldom if ever entirely volitional nor can their consequences always be fully anticipated.* Here we shall summarize factors and circumstances that always make them contingent decisions.

First, choices are influenced by our character. According to the philosopher Bernard Williams (1985), when we say that an individual freely chooses we are asserting that that person (1) did indeed choose, (2) knew what he or she was choosing, and (3) intended the particular consequences of the choice. Here the focus is almost entirely on the act of choosing. What this formulation omits is the actor. We do not ask whether as a person the individual could have chosen to be someone of different tastes and attitudes, though we know that character and personality broadly influence and restrict the likely choices.

Second, sexual choice does not occur in a social or cultural vacuum. Gay and lesbian studies remind us that sexual preferences and behavior are not immune to the social and cultural contexts within which they emerge (Foucault, 1976; Weeks, 1991). Preferences and behavior are part of character and personality, which in turn, as the cultural anthropologists have shown, are products of social institutions such as gender, race, and class (Mead, 1968; Roscoe, 1988).

Third, the existence of an option does not require that it be chosen. Discussing the option of being a lesbian, Claudia Card (1992) has pointed out that the word choice has two meanings: (a) whether an option exists and (b) whether someone actually chooses it. Heterosexual women who are unaware of the lesbian option in their lives do not feel that they have any choice but to be heterosexual. As Card (p. 41) states, "lesbians are more likely to have exercised choice in becoming lesbians than heterosexual women are to have exercised choice in becoming heterosexual."

Fourth, choices are not necessarily mutually exclusive, that is, the choice of one option does not necessarily preclude the future or contemporaneous possibility of choosing another related one. This is even clearer in the realm of sexual preference, where, for example, to prefer people of one gender does not require an enduring antipathy to those of the other. In fact, human beings have the almost irascible ability of synthesizing options into quite unanticipated choices.

Fifth, all choices have general consequences for our lives including those pertaining to sexual preference. Either a heterosexual or homosexual choice is part of an individual's life and therefore affects and is shaped by other aspects of that life. Sexual preferences, for example, are linked to gender; they are, in fact, the choice of one gender over the other. Since men and women continue to be culturally assigned different roles in society, relationships between individuals of the same gender may take forms quite distinct from heterosexual relationships, for example, in the matter of partner dependency. A relationship between two men may considerably differ from a relationship between two women in its restrictions or opportunities for multiple sexual partners. In the heterosexual relationships there is usually the responsibility for children, which endures even after the parental relationship ends. Heterosexual relationships have legal obligations to be met and privileges to enjoy that are for the most part absent in homosexual relationships. Issues over the custody rights of gay and lesbian parents to children, either those who are biologically linked or those adopted, are being painfully resolved in the courts. Within the nexus of such relationships perceptions, feelings, intuitions, sensitivities, expectations, understandings, satisfactions, hopes, and even an ethic emerge or are forged that are intricately connected to each partner's whole personality and character.

Given these several constraints on free choice, can a man or woman whose preferences have been heterosexual change them to homosexual if they try hard enough? Card's (1992, p. 45) answer is "not necessarily," certainly no easier than giving up smoking, eating meat, masturbating, or being lazy. Because our early sexual choices are so intimately tied to the rest of our lives (though we often are aware that an option had existed only in retrospect), they may in practice become irrevocable or be modified only to the extent that the individual is willing and able piecemeal to change other things of her or his life. Because heterosexual preferences are imbedded in the habits, perceptions, and domiciled feelings of past experience and shored up by social norms, law, and tradition hardly means that they are biologically ordained. Surely the life histories of individuals who have substituted a homosexual for a heterosexual choice or combined the two choices amply demonstrate that such a change is possible.

A GENERAL CONCEPTION OF HOMOSEXUALITY

In its late nineteenth-century avatar homosexuality was a psychological and medical phenomenon with pathological mental and physical underpinnings. From the turn of the century, Freudian psychology and American psychoanalysis portrayed it as a mental state caused by early childhood trauma, one that led to the individual's failure to achieve adult genital heterosexuality. With the advent of gay, lesbian, and bisexual studies, particularly in the last two decades, homosexuality has been investigated as a historical, political, social, and cultural phenomenon. More recently, as seen in the articles in this collection, it has been revisited as a biological state.

Our present knowledge of homosexuality therefore, is drawn from several disciplines and theoretical perspectives. An adequate conception of homosexuality must embrace all of its known or purported aspects: the biological, the psychological, and the sociocultural. Beyond the anatomy and physiology of the genitals, the biological features should include the material aspects of the body that are the biological investigators' present focus of attention, namely the genes, the endocrine system, and the brain. Beyond genital behavior, the psychological dimensions should encompass all the relevant mental processes, including individual perception, motivation, and the ingredients from which personal meaning and understanding derive, such as learning, cognition, and language. Beyond conditioned responses to a fixed environment, the sociocultural parameters of homosexuality should embrace the institutions and traditions that, over time, have shaped its expression and meaning and, in turn, have been modified by it.

Each of these categories–the biological, psychological, and socio-cultural–constitutes a level of description and analysis that is suitable only for phenomena that lie within its methodological and explanatory reach. However, research on homosexuality is rife with repeated attempts to treat aspects borrowed from one level of discourse within the methodological and conceptual constraints of another level. Biology, which should be employed to describe only the corporeal aspects of homosexuality, if such exist, has attempted to explain homosexuality as human behavior and imagination, which are essentially psychological, or as self-announced gay or lesbian identity, an idea that derives from a historical and socio-political context. Psychological theory, which should be employed to describe only individual mental, emotional, and behavioral aspects of homosexuality, has been employed for building models of personal development that purport to mark the steps in an individual's progression toward a mature and egosyntonic gay or lesbian identity. The embracing and disclosing of such an identity, however, is best understood as a political phenomenon occurring in a historical period during which identity politics has become a consuming preoccupation. Socio-cultural explanations, prevalent in gay and lesbian history and biography, have viewed gay men and lesbians as trans-historical biological entities of mixed gender, a heretofore unrecognized "third sex" that has somehow shaped history while avoiding any basic transformation by it.

All such efforts to account for phenomena belonging to one level of discourse in terms of another level are based on fallacies of reductionism and determinism (De Cecco & Elia, 1993). By *reductionism* we refer to any conceptualization of homosexuality that ignores one or more of its parameters, that is, shrinks it back to a less complex phenomenon than is warranted by our knowledge. By *determinism* we refer to the assigning of primacy to one level of discourse and the subordination of the other levels.

The determinism and reductionism that have undermined modern research on homosexuality are classic examples of the blind man and the elephant, except, in some cases, one wonders if there *is* any elephant at all. Most of the research develops out of disciplinary perspectives with which the investigator is most familiar. Rarely are investigators aware of information discovered in other disciplines. As this collection of papers will show, the biological theorists have little if any knowledge of the psychological, social, cultural, and historical studies of homosexuality. Their knowledge of the non-biological research is of a few social science studies that were based on the presupposition that homosexuality is basically a biological phenomenon. Such intellectual parochialism has led the biological theorists to adopt very simplistic concepts of homosexuality as dependent variables, more often expressed as a measurement technique, for example, a numerical rating on the Kinsey heterosexual-homosexual rating scale, than as a theory. The historical, cultural, and humane corpus of knowledge and its evolving theory, what has come to be known as gay, lesbian, and bisexual studies, for most biologists, is *terra incognita*.

The other source of determinism and reductionism is found in both the biological and socio-cultural studies. It is the reification of the notion of gay and lesbian identity. In the biological studies, as we have noted, a subject's self-identification as gay or lesbian is accepted as *prima facie* evidence that the individual is a flesh and blood exemplar of the species in which he or she claims membership. Within vaguely defined population boundaries, one exemplar is as good as any other since together they are biological equivalents. Some authors of the socio-cultural studies, after almost two decades of gay and lesbian studies that refute the idea of a timeless gay or lesbian inclination, identity, spirit, or cross-gender behavior have difficulty giving up the quest for some universal attribute that fuses the homosexuality of the past and of divergent cultures with that of the present. The fact that such concepts are offshoots of modern identity politics that reduce the personal to the political appears to elude them. In our view homosexuality is an aspect of life of a person, a part of that person's whole life. This life consists of biological, psychological, and socio-cultural ingredients. Each category of ingredients is also an aspect of the person's homosexuality.

Is there a conception of homosexuality that avoids the various forms of reductionism and determinism and encompasses the many facets identified in the research of the past two decades? In our opinion a broad conception would have to meet at least two criteria: it would anchor sexuality in the individual and it would assign primacy to the individual over society. To tie sexuality to the individual is to treat it as an aspect of a person's life but not the whole of it. That life provides a psychological context within which homosexuality is felt, expressed, and understood. Despite the regimentation of sexuality that seems to occur in modern society, for many it is still desirable to experience it as something intimate and private, something for which we would invent rules rather than follow those of others. Most people still probably cherish the opportunity to enjoy sexuality in their own fashion and at their own pace, in ways that are uniquely, perhaps even strangely and opaquely congenial. Sexuality may be one of few areas of personal autonomy and indulgence that escapes the standardization that has swept over modern society.

In addition, we believe in the primacy of the individual and that the uniqueness of personality and character should serve as the basis of purpose and sexual expression. Whatever may be the biological or socio-cultural constraints on sexual expression, to some degree they must be embedded in the attitudes and propensities of the individual who enacts them. Sexual violence and abuse, for example, exist in a society largely to the extent that they have become parts of the personality and character of those who engage in them. Similarly, the enjoyment of sexuality relatively free of the guilt and fears of the past cannot occur by social prescription but requires the personal incorporation of new, accepting attitudes.

The idea of a gay and lesbian sexual identity has been formulated over the last two decades. Historically it is the product of the gay and lesbian liberation movement which, itself, grew out of the Black civil rights and women's liberation movements of the fifties and sixties. Like ethnic identities, sexual identity assigns individuals to membership in a group, the lesbian and gay community. Although sexual identity has become a group identity, its historical antecedents can be traced to the nineteenth-century notion that homosexual men and women, each a representative of a newly discovered biological specimen, represented a "third sex." Homosexuality, which had been conceived primarily as an act was thereby transformed into an actor (De Cecco, 1990b). Once actors had been created it was possible to assign them a group identity. Once a person became a member of a group, particularly one that has been stigmatized and marginal, identity as an individual was easily subsumed under group identity.

As this brief history reveals, the idea of the gay and lesbian sexual identity conflates sexuality and gender as well as the individual and the group. To conceive of gay men and lesbians as a third sex is to assign them a gender category. However, the assumption is that those who occupy that category are sexually attracted to those of their own gender. In the biological studies that have used the Kinsey heterosexual-homosexual rating scale, subjects that are assumed to belong to a gay and lesbian cross-gender phenotype are indeed identified by self-reports of their sexual fantasies and behavior.

There is also the conflation of the individual and the group. The word identity has been used in psychology to describe the personal identification within various historical and cultural contexts (Gleason, 1983). In its psychological dimension, identity is often equated with self. To know oneself is to have achieved a personal identity. The early psychological models of the gay and lesbian identity, for example, made the awareness of one's erotic feelings the pivotal step in achieving that identity. The psychological, however, is easily conflated with the cultural. For a person to assert that he or she has a Jewish or Italian temperament is at once a self-description and also an identification with a group or culture. To believe that white people think and act differently than black people is at once a personification of a culture and an assignment of personal membership in it.

Such amalgamation of meanings, in the politics of sexual identity, has served two purposes. It has been a source of great emotional strength for those who have participated in the gay and lesbian liberation movement, particularly during the last two decades, and has sustained them through several confrontations with political and religious leaders who fight any attempt to erode the link between sexuality and procreation. It has generated an enormous amount of research on homosexuality in many disciplines, including the biological research described in this volume. Much of this research in fact has been done by men and women who publicly assumed a gay identity and thereby have become political actors.

Regarding identity politics, the Oxford historian Eric Hobshawn (1993, p. 62) had this to say:

> Myth and invention are essential to the politics of identity by which groups of people today, defining themselves by ethnicity, religion, or the past or present borders of states, try to find some certainty in an uncertain and shaking world by saying, 'We are different from and better than the Others.'. . . It is very important for historians to remember their task is, above all, to stand aside from the passions of identity politics–even if they also feel them. After all, we are human beings too.

Of relevance to this collection of papers is the danger of having the search for scientific facts compromised by the political ideologies of the investigators. In the case of historical research there have been egregious examples of anachronism in the search for the gay men and lesbians of the past and the attribution of the gay identity to the biblical David and Naomi, to Julius Caesar and Alexander the Great, to the temple priests of classical Greece, and to medieval witches. By taking on the conflated notion of sexual identity, the biological research, in its search for physical markers that distinguish heterosexuals from homosexuals, has unwittingly enlisted itself in the politics of sexual identity.

NOTE

1. The understandable joy with which the gay and lesbian psychiatrists and psychologists greeted the decision of the American Psychiatric Association in 1973 to "declassify" homosexuality as a mental illness obscured the fact (1) it was merely being reclassified, first as "sexual orientation disturbance" and, still later, as "egodystonic homosexuality," and (2) that the groundwork for conceptualizing it as a physical condition was being laid, in some cases by their very supporters among the straight psychiatrists. In the third revision of the *Diagnostic and Statistical Manual* (1980), the gay lobby managed to eliminate all references to homosexuality as a psychological disorder. However, it was in the decade that immediately followed the reclassification that the biological research on homosexuality gathered momentum, media attention, and public visibility. In the meantime, under the heading "Psychosexual Disorders," the *Manual* still lists "gender

disorder," and includes "transsexualism" and "gender identity disorder of child-hood." "Transvestism" appears under "paraphilias," the latter term an attempt to detoxify the older term, "sexual deviations." For a fuller discussion of the politics of the reclassification and its hidden biological agenda, see De Cecco (1987a) and De Cecco (1990b).

REFERENCES

Allen, L. S., & Gorski, R. A. (1992). Sexual orientation and the size of the anterior commissure in the human brain. *Proceedings of the National Academy of Science, 89,* 7199-7202.

American Psychiatric Association (1980). *Diagnostic and Statistical Manual of Mental Disorders, 3rd edition.*

Angier, N. (1991, September 1). The biology of what it means to be gay. Will a new scientific study further homosexual rights or homophobia. *New York Times,* sec. 4, pp. 1-4.

Bailey, J. M., & Pillard, R. C., Neale, M. C., & Agyei, Y. (1993). Heritable factors influence sexual orientation in women. *Archives of General Psychiatry, 50,* 217-223.

Bailey, J. M. & Pillard, R. C. (1991). A genetic study of male sexual orientation. *Archives of General Psychiatry, 48,* 1089-1096.

Bailey, J. M., Willerman, L., & Parks, C. (1991). A test of the maternal stress theory of human male homosexuality. *Archives of Sexual Behavior, 20,* 277-293.

Barinaga, M. (1991). Is homosexuality biological? *Science, 253,* 956-957.

Blackwood, E. (Ed.). (1985). Anthropology and homosexual behavior. *Journal of Homosexuality, 11*(3/4), combined issues.

Buhrich, N., Bailey, J. M., & Martin, N. G. (1991). Sexual orientation, sexual identity, and sex-dimorphic behaviors in male twins. *Behavior Genetics, 21*(1), 75-96.

Card, C. (1992) Lesbianism and choice. *Journal of Homosexuality, 23*(3), 39-52.

Cohn, M. (1992). Dr. Simon LeVay explains lesbians, the roots of desire and his new-found activism. *10 Percent,* 35-39 et seq.

De Cecco, J. P. (1987a). Homosexuality's brief recovery: From sickness to health and back again. *Journal of Sex Research, 23*(1), 106-129.

De Cecco, J. P. (1987b). The two reviews of Meyer-Bahlburg: A rejoinder. *Journal of Sex Research 23* (1), 123-127.

De Cecco, J. P. (1990a). Homosexual as act or person. In L. R. Mass (Ed.), *Dialogues of the sexual revolution: Homosexuality as behavior and identity,* vol. II, 132-169.

De Cecco, J. P. (1990b). Confusing the actor with the act: Muddled notions about homosexuality. *Archives of Sexual Behavior, 19*(4), 409-412.

De Cecco, J. P., & Elia, J. P. (1993). A Critique and synthesis of biological essentialism and social constructionist views of sexuality and gender. *Journal of Homosexuality, 24*(3/4), 1-26.

Dörner, G., Rohde, W., Stahl, F., Krell, L., & Masius, W. G. (1975). A neuroendocrine predisposition for homosexuality in men. *Archives of Sexual Behavior, 4,*
1-8.

Dover, K. J. (1978). *Greek homosexuality.* New York: Vintage Books.

Faderman, L. (1993, July 18). *New York Times,* p. 13.

Foucault, M. (1976). *Volenté de savoir.* Paris: Editions Gallimard.

Gallagher, J. (1991, October 8). Hypothalamus study and coverage of it attracts
many barbs. *Advocate,* pp. 14-15.

Gibbons, A. (1991). The brain as "sexual organ." *Science, 253,* 957-959.

Gladue, B. A., Green, R., & Hellman, R. E. (1984). Neuroendocrine response to
estrogen and sexual orientation. *Science, 225,* 1496-1499.

Gleason, P. (1983). Identifying identity: A semantic history. *The Journal of American History, 69(4),* 910-931.

Gorman, C. (1991, September 9). Are gay men born that way? *Time,* pp. 60-61.

Hamer, D. H., Hu, S., Magnuson, V. L., Hu, N., & Pattatucci, A. M. L. (1993). A
linkage between DNA markers on the X chromosome and male sexual orientation. *Science, 261,* 321-327.

Herdt, G. H. (1981). *Guardians of the flutes: Idioms of masculinity: A study of
ritualized homosexual behavior.* New York: McGraw-Hill.

Hobshawn, E. (1993, December 16). The new threat to history. *The New York
Review of Books,* pp. 62-64.

Holden, C. (1991). Is the "gender gap" narrowing? *Science, 253,* 956-957.

Hubbard, R. (1993, August 2). False genetic markers. *New York Times,* p. 5 (op
ed).

Jones, A. R., & Stalltbrass, P. (1991). Constructing the hermaphrodite in Renaissance Europe. In J. Epstein & K. Straub (Eds.), *Body guards: The cultural
politics of gender ambiguity.* London: Routledge, pp. 80-111.

Kennedy, H. (1988). *Ulrichs: The life and works of Karl Heinrich Ulrichs.* Boston: Alyson Publications.

Kinsey, A. F. (1941). Homosexuality: Criteria for a hormonal explanation of the
homosexual. *Journal of Clinical Endrocrinology, 1,* 424-428.

Kinsey, A. F., Pomeroy, W. B., & Martin, C. E. (1948). *Sexual behavior in the
human male.* New York: W. B. Saunders.

Krafft-Ebing, R. von (1906). *Psychopathia sexualis: With special reference to the
antipathetic sexual instinct.* F. J. Rebman, trans. Brooklyn, NY: Physicians and
Surgeons Book Company. [Originally published in 1886.]

LeVay, S. (1991). A difference in hypothalamic structure between heterosexual
and homosexual men. *Science, 253,* 1034-1037.

Marshall, E. (1992). When does intellectual passion become conflict of interest:
Sex on the brain. *Science, 257,* 620-621.

Mead, M. (1968). *Sex and temperament in three primitive societies.* New York:
Dell. [Originally published in 1935.]

Mendelsohn, D. (1993, July 26). Republicans can be cured: A new study links
genetics to conservatism. *New York Times,* p. 5 (op ed).

Money, J., & Ehrhardt, A. (1972). *Man & woman, boy & girl: The differentiation* and dimorphism of gender identity from conception to maturity. Baltimore: Johns Hopkins.

Money, J., & Tucker, P. (1975). *Sexual signatures: On being a man or woman.* Boston: Little Brown.

Murray, L. (1987). Sexual destinies: Homosexuals are born, not made, claims one physician, who says he has proof positive that sexual orientation is sealed in the womb. *Omni,* 100-103 et seq.

Nardi, P. M. (1993). Gays should lean on justice, not science. *Los Angeles Times,* August 6, p. B7.

Perlman, D. (1991, August 30). Brain cell study finds link to homosexuality. *The San Francisco Chronicle,* p. A1 et seq.

Pillard, R. C., & Weinrich, J. D. (1986). Evidence of familial nature of male homosexuality. *Archives of General Psychiatry, 43,* 808-812.

Pillard, R. C., Poumadere, J., & Caretta, R. A. S. (1981). Is homosexuality familial? A review, some data, and a suggestion. *Archives of Sexual Behavior, 10,* 465-475.

Rasberry, W. (1993, August 26). Genetics and sexual orientation. *The Times* (San Mateo), p. A8.

Rist, D. Y. (1992, October 19). Are homosexuals born that way? *The Nation,* 424-429.

Roscoe, W. (Ed.). (1988). *Living the spirit: A Gay American Indian anthology.* New York: St. Martin's.

Socarides, C. W. (1978). *Homosexuality.* New York: Jason Aronson.

Swaab, D. F., & Hofman, M. A. (1990). An enlarged suprachiasmatic nucleus in homosexual men. *Brain Research, 537,* 141-148.

Swaab, D. F., & Fliers, E. (1985). A sexually dimorphic nucleus in the human brain. *Science, 228,* 1112-1115.

Trumbach, R. (1991). London sapphists: From three sexes to four genders in the making of modern culture. In J. Epstein & K. Straub (Eds.), *Body guards: The cultural politics of gender ambiguity.* London: Routledge, pp. 112-141.

Weeks, J. (1991). *Against nature: Essays on history, sexuality, and identity.* London: Rivers Oram Press.

Williams, B. (1985). *Ethics and the limits of philosophy.* Cambridge: Harvard University Press.

Winslow, R. (1991, August 30). Study raises issue of biological basis of homosexuality. *Wall Street Journal,* p. B 1.

Zamichow, N. (1991, September 9). Scientist finds solace, therapy in research on gays. *Los Angeles Times,* p. B5.

SECTION II: HISTORICAL AND CONCEPTUAL BACKGROUND

Introduction

In preparing this volume, we have tried to explore all of the aspects of biological theories of sexual preference. The issues involved have a vibrant history, are wide-ranging, and remain the objects of much controversy. In our first section, we start with discussions of the history of the biological theories and sociocultural concepts of gender and sexuality. The next three sections deal with three specialized areas of biological science and related issues: genetics and evolution, hormones and the endocrine system, and brain physiology and structure. A final section deals with social stigma, science, and medicine. Each of these sections is briefly introduced by an explanation of the key concepts and terms that you will find in that section. In addition, we have included a glossary at the end of the volume.

[Haworth co-indexing entry note]: "Introduction." Co-published simultaneously in *Journal of Homosexuality* (The Haworth Press, Inc.) Vol. 28, No. 1/2, 1995, p. 29; and: *Sex, Cells, and Same-Sex Desire: The Biology of Sexual Preference* (ed: John P. De Cecco, and David Allen Parker) The Haworth Press, Inc., 1995, p. 29. Multiple copies of this article/chapter may be purchased from The Haworth Document Delivery Center [1-800-3-HAWORTH; 9:00 a.m. - 5:00 p.m. (EST)].

On the History of Biological Theories of Homosexuality

Rainer Herrn, PhD

Magnus-Hirschfeld-Gesellschaft, Berlin

SUMMARY. Biological theories of homosexuality fit into the discourse on reproduction and sexuality that began in the nineteenth century. They arose in the context of the early homosexual rights movement, with its claim for natural rights, and the psychiatric discussions about sexual perversions. With the classification of homosexuality as a distinct category, homosexuals were excluded from the "normal." Biological theories of homosexuality were attempts not only to explain its causes, but also to maintain the exclusion of homosexuals as the "other." Biological explanations can be categorized as genetic, constitutional, endocrinological, and ethological. On the one hand, biological theories were used in the struggle for homosexual rights. On the other hand, they were used to "cure" homosexuals. Every theory led to a specific therapy. This paper points out

Dr. Rainer Herrn studied at the Karl-Marx University in Leipzig (1978-1983), where he received his PhD in Behavior Genetics (1986) and was appointed Research Fellow (1986-1989). He was a Research Fellow at Humboldt University in Berlin (1989-1991), where he investigated theories of homosexuality. He is presently Research Fellow, Magnus-Hirschfeld-Gesellschaft, and Head of the Research Department on the History of Sexual Science (Forschungsstelle zur Geschichte der Sexualwissenschaft) in Berlin. His current research is on the Institute for Sexual Science in Berlin (Institut für Sexualwissenschaft Berlin), 1919-1933.

Correspondence may be addressed to: Lychener Strasse 64 SF, 10437 Berlin, Germany.

[Haworth co-indexing entry note]: "On the History of Biological Theories of Homosexuality." Herrn, Rainer. Co-published simultaneously in *Journal of Homosexuality* (The Haworth Press, Inc.) Vol. 28, No. 1/2, 1995, pp. 31-56; and: *Sex, Cells, and Same-Sex Desire: The Biology of Sexual Preference* (ed: John P. De Cecco, and David Allen Parker) The Haworth Press, Inc., 1995, pp. 31-56 Multiple copies of this article/chapter may be purchased from The Haworth Document Delivery Center [1-800-3-HAWORTH; 9:00 a.m. - 5:00 p.m. (EST)].

31

the roots of this thinking, traces the development of various theories, and shows the utilization of biological theories in treating homosexuality.

In the popular and scientific cultures of today, any behavior that is considered "abnormal" requires an explanation. To meet this requirement, biological explanations have been widely accepted over the last century. It is the intent of this paper to review the traditional acceptance of these explanations. The presuppositions of biological explanations of homosexuality and their disciplinary ramifications will be discussed briefly.

The belief that biology can explain homosexuality must be reexamined. With few exceptions, biological theories of homosexuality are vague speculations about its causes. They were developed historically by adopting very diverse then-contemporary biological theories and scientific methods, which were often taken completely out of context. These explanations generally lacked definitional clarity. For instance, the term "homosexuality" might refer to either physical contact or the affectional bond between individuals of the same sex. Frequently, the definitions implied that homosexuality could be reduced to same-sex sexual behavior. Other definitions conflated the behavior with the individual. Most biological explanations scarcely differentiate between male and female homosexuality. When homosexuality in women is described at all, it is considered to be the reverse of that in men. Biological explanations are not objective science, but rather the products of discussions of naturalness, degeneration, and pathology; self-explanation, separation, and rejection; emancipation, decriminalization, proscription, persecution, and therapy.

The search for biological explanations began around 1865, when Ulrichs considered homosexuals "female" souls in "male" bodies (Ulrichs, 1898, "Inclusa"). But how is it that the soul and the love-drive in *Urninge* (later "homosexual men") was designated as "female" and that of the *Urninden* (later "homosexual women") as "male"? The historical documents confirm that the dichotomization of the sexual characteristics that occurred in the eighteenth century and the social construction of two biological sexes manifestly led to the biological theories of homosexuality. The important social, political, economic, and epistemological dimensions of the discourse on what is commonly viewed as male and female has long since been pointed out, among others, by Thomas Laqueur (1990), Karin Hausen (1976), and Claudia Honegger (1991). Between the seventeenth and the nineteenth centuries the one-sex model, in which male was the only sex socially defined, was changed to a two-sex model that is still held today. The one-sex model conceived the sexual organs of a woman as atrophied forms of those of a man—the vagina as inner penis, the labia as foreskin, the uterus as scrotum, and the ovaries as testicles. The later two-sex model conceived the genitals as entirely distinct organs, from which biological sex was derived. The differences between the sexes were no longer understood as graduated differences in the same thing, but rather as two separate things. With the dichotomization of woman and man they became completely distinct beings with regard to sex, body, sexuality, and their abilities.

In the nineteenth century, researchers began studying homosexuality. It was conceived as a combination of the dichotomous "female" and "male." Psychiatrists were among the first to seek the origins of homosexuality. At first the psychiatric gaze was directed to sexual excesses, to the masturbation of children (who were thought to be asexual), and then to the sexual perversions, in which same-sex sexuality was included. Perhaps this was due to the conception that for some reason same-sex sexuality lay outside of both maleness and femaleness and was incompatible with the two-sex model directed toward reproduction. To reconcile this, it was assigned its own category.

The first biological explanations of homosexuality arose in the late nineteenth century and were built upon the scientific principles of the Enlightenment. The majority of these principles come from a materialistic theory, according to which every function of the human being has a specific purpose and that psychological functioning is one. This materialistic determinism often leads to a biological reductionism. This is partly due to the principle of analogy, which allows anatomic/physiologic comparisons as well as comparisons between human behavior and that of animals. Even before its application to homosexuality, animal-human analogies were employed in the discussion of human functions, including reproduction and sexuality in woman (Laqueur, 1990; Hausen, 1976; Honegger, 1991). Making scientific the difference between people, e.g., between the sexes or between nations, is just as much a precondition as the research of the "other," under which not only the geographic "other" was understood, but also those who do not behave "normally" in one's own culture, e.g., the insane, the criminal, and the perverse (cf. Moravia, 1980; Honegger, 1991).

The first ideas about the "nature" of *Uranismus* (later "homosexuality"), drawn from medicine and biology, were presented between 1862 and 1879 in the letters and works of Karl Heinrich Ulrichs (1898, 1899), a jurist and early courageous fighter for the recognition of the rights of those whose sexual behavior was with their own sex. As a jurist, he sought above all the decriminalization of Uranismus. His advocacy was based on his understanding of "naturalness." He believed that the whole range of sexual attributes considered male and female was natural. Similarly, he based his theory of Uranismus in nature, calling it psychic hermaphroditism, which he considered a naturally occurring combination of male and female. His so-called scientific theory conceived "homosexual men" as biological males with female psyches. His assumption that "male homosexuals" have female characteristics and "female homosexuals" male characteristics was an attempt to naturalize what is held to be "against nature." The scientific as well as the political dimension of his works founded a tradition which became the central thesis of later biological theories of homosexuality.[1]

The reasons that led him to associate same-sex sexuality with its naturalness were common in the biological thinking of the nineteenth century. The natural sciences, with their discoveries and successes, were widening their influence beyond their own borders in attempting to explain human behavior. Scientific findings were given immediate credibility. These biological explanations were widely accepted by the general public (cf. Mann, 1973). Following this trend, Ulrichs, although very isolated in the beginning with his theory, founded a tradition based on the belief that homosexuality was biological and therefore "natural."

The specific traits that Ulrichs believed evidenced naturalness were taken over by researchers from various disciplines, first by the psychiatrists Carl Westphal (1869) and, later, Richard von Krafft-

Ebing (1903). Both, however, considered such traits to be pathological. Later, around 1896, Ulrichs's theory was adopted by the reformer Magnus Hirschfeld (1896), who revised it and applied it to the emancipation movement.

The following classification of the research into four premises is possible, since the available works derive from four independent scientific disciplines: genetics, constitutional biology, endocrinology, and behavioral research It should also be added that the premises relate to and complement one another.

HEREDITY

There have been hereditary models of homosexuality for 120 years. They were employed by forensic medicine, psychiatry, and almost at the same time in the emancipatory discussion concerning the decriminalization of same-sex sexuality. Since then they have been brought up to date and today are still present in both traditions. Hereditary premises start from the position that homosexuality is a universal attribute that may be determined by bodily peculiarities of homosexuals, and that this peculiarity is genetically determined.

In the eighteenth and nineteenth centuries the starting point for the hereditary model of homosexuality postulated an innate sexual drive and a natural dichotomy between male and female sexuality. The French physician Moreau de Tours (1859) described sexual drive as an autonomous "sense," which, like the other senses, can become sick (Wettley, 1959).

In the discourse on the regulation of population in the nineteenth century a superior role was held by sexual selection as presented by Darwin. The individual was measured by his "useful" contribution to the reproduction of the population. Non-reproducing individuals were designated as "unfit." Together with the cultural pessimism, the reception of Darwinian theories in psychiatry led to the construction of degeneration theory. Degeneration theory held that characteristics that represented evolutionary "throw-backs" occasionally occurred in humans. According to this theory mental and physical degeneration leads to the downfall of families and even nations. Same-sex sexuality was designated by psychiatry as a form of degeneration. There have been several attempts to uncover the hereditary origins of homosexuality.

Until about 1850 the pederast was held to be a casual perpetrator and the pederastic act (anal intercourse) as morally reprehensible and juridically punishable. With an Enlightenment view, on the basis of "true observation of nature," the Berlin forensic doctor Johann Ludwig Casper in 1852 expressed doubts about the traditional views concerning the signs of the pederastic act on the anus and penis, and the supposed devastating effects of this act on health (Casper, 1852, 1863). On the basis of his own forensic activity he investigated eleven cases. He found neither wounds on the anus, nor disease as consequences. Rather, he observed what he called "feminine outward appearance." He conjectured: "The sexual attraction of man to man is in many unfortunates–but I suspect in the minority–innate" (1852, p. 62). With this supposition the scientific gaze shifted from seeking evidence of a criminal act to diagnosing mental illness in a person.

Psychiatry, which had been traditionally occupied with the sexual aberrations, took over the power of defining homosexuality as a perversion in the period following. It listed, classified, and evaluated the so-called perversions. Influential representatives of German psychiatry, like Wilhelm Griesinger, Carl Westphal, and Richard von Krafft-Ebing, gave credibility to the view of homosexuality as a perversion. Corresponding to the various theories ranging from the biological to the psychological, there were differing views on the origins of homosexuality. Theories ranged from exclusively inherited, which Westphal (1869) represented, to exclusively acquired, which Albert von Schrenk-Notzing (1892) advocated.[2]

Ulrichs played an essential role in anchoring homosexuality to biology. The starting point of his theory is the assumption that homosexuality is innate and therefore natural. Homosexual males and homosexual females were different, but not sick. His belief was that the sex of the human embryo cannot be differentiated in the first weeks of life. He combined this with a "kernel" theory, whereby there are various kernels for body, gender, sexuality, and psyche, which were formed in the male or female direction. On the basis of a modified nature, there arises Uranismus (homosexuality) and other forms of sexual variation (sexual intermediates). In Urninge (male homosexuals) and Urninden (female homosexuals) the "love drive"–which had its seat in the brain–and the psyche developed in a direction opposite to the genital sex. In males the love-drive is directed to men, and in females to women. Ulrichs understands Uranismus as an innate "species of hermaphroditism" that is part of the natural order.

The political aspects of his work consisted of demands for decriminalization and equalization of Urninge and Urninden based on the argument that what is natural should not be punished.

Notwithstanding the argument in psychiatry over heredity versus environment, the further discussion about the valuation of innateness of same-sex sexuality, naturalness versus pathological disposition, occurred in the following period in the field between psychiatry and the rising reform movement, in particular in the Scientific Humanitarian Committee, of which the physician Magnus Hirschfeld was a co-founder. A separation of the theories into psychiatric and reformist does not occur. The positions become clear in their valuation. The Darwinian interpretation formulated by psychiatry was negatively represented, e.g., by the American psychiatrist James G. Kiernan (1884), who saw homosexuality as an atavism, i.e., a throw-back to evolutionarily "lower," hermaphroditic animal forms, or by the French physician Julien Chevalier (1893), who interpreted it as an evolutionarily faulty development. The reformers, e.g., Hirschfeld (1914), understood it, to be sure, as a malformation, like hare-lip or cleft palate, but applied these interpretations positively, as proofs of naturalness.

The theories based on heredity were formulated first by Ulrichs (1898, "Memnon") and later by Krafft-Ebing (1903).[3] Ulrichs understood homosexuality as natural, but Krafft-Ebing considered it pathological. Hirschfeld, in his first work *Sappho und Sokrates* in 1896 until about 1916, subscribed to a genetic theory. In his article "Heredität und Homosexualität" (Heredity and Homosexuality, 1903b) he attempts to remove pathology from the hereditary hypotheses. He writes that "there must be a family disposition to homosexuality, but not a pathological disposition. This fact is [buttressed by] the relatively large occurrence of homosexual brothers and sisters. Among 100 Urninge are found on the average 8 whose brother or sister is likewise homosexual . . . In 20-25% of homosexuals where hereditary taint is present . . . were signs of degeneration, which were independent of homosexuality as such" (Hirschfeld, 1903b, p. 140). Important, too, is the fact that Hirschfeld used August Weißmann's theory of the inheritance of latent characteristics to explain the heritability of homosexuality. In every child characteristics of the father and mother are inborn, but need not appear. Thus peculiarities of ancestors are latently passed on. This theory was important to the explanation of an interrupted genealogical series (Hirschfeld, 1914, pp. 362-363).

The final explanation that Hirschfeld employed to support the theory goes back to the Berlin geneticist Richard Goldschmidt (1916), who carried out cross-breeding on butterflies. Through the hybridization of various subspecies, he created male animals with female chromosomes. He named them "Umwandlungsmännchen" (transformed males) and speculated about an analogy to homosexuality. According to him, male homosexuals are genetically female, and female homosexuals, genetically male. He asserted that hormonal causes are responsible for the expression of this so-called "faulty development." Hirschfeld was so fascinated by this scientific explanation that he set up butterfly breeding in his Institute for Sexual Science in Berlin to verify the result.[4] This theory was only disproved in the 1950s through a chromosomal analysis (Pare, 1956).

Around 1900 the eugenic discussion began in Germany. It represented an economic valuation of human beings based on biology. Homosexuality was drawn into this discussion though it played a minor role. In 1904 the psychiatrist and eugenicist Ernst Rüdin, who later, under Heinrich Himmler (early Nazi director of propaganda and later chief of the Gestapo), co-authored the Nazi sterilization law of 1933, wrote an article "Zur Rolle der Homosexuellen im Lebensprozeß der Rasse" (On the Role of Homosexuals in the Life Process of the Race). His central question was: "Is the uncomplicated homosexual disposition a formation that serves a goal of the race?" And his answer: "The life and work of homosexuals offers us . . . nothing that is not and could not be produced by psychically and bodily harmoniously formed true maleness and femaleness . . . Already in the first case (uncomplicated homosexuality) there remains the uncompensated inability to reproduce, which adds harm to the race, and this is sharpened in the second case through a genuinely pathological deficiency" (Rüdin, 1904, pp. 104-106). He concluded that homosexuals should neither marry, since they robbed the nation of a reproductively perfect partner, nor should they reproduce, so as not to pass on their pathological disposition. Through the close connection of sexology and eugenics, it is no wonder that reformers such as Hirschfeld (1903a, 1918a) advocated these restrictions.

The assumption of power by the Nazis in Germany in 1933 meant the end of the sexual reform movement and an increased persecution of homosexuals; means were sought to eradicate homosexuality. To that end genetic, endocrinologic, psychiatric, and psychoanalytic theories were pressed into service. The psychiatrist R. Lemke (1940) asserted that homosexuality is inherited in a dominant-recessive process following Mendelian rules. According to his conception, homozygotic (with an identical pair of genes) homosexuals would in every case be homosexual. Heterozygotic (with a mixed pair of genes) homosexuals would be homosexual only under "unfavorable" circumstances. Carriers of the disposition could be determined diagnostically. In an attempt to eliminate homosexuality, Lemke proposed that homosexuals be prohibited from any sexual acts; and furthermore, that the noncompliant be taken into custody or, with their consent, castrated. Though Lemke's theory played only a marginal role in the canon of disciplinary punishment and suppression of homosexuality, it exemplifies how medicine can be used as a political instrument of oppression and how apparently harmless scientific theories can become ideologies.

The premise of a specific genetic determinative was now the one that was further pursued after 1945. Already in the 1930s, but strengthened from 1950, the twins method, which was applied in the research into intelligence and schizophrenia, was used for the proof of the inheritance of homosexuality (Lewontin, Rose, & Kamin, 1982, 1988). In 1952, Franz Kallmann, a pupil of Rüdin who had emigrated from Germany to the United States in 1935, conducted a research project to compare monozygotic with dizygotic twins. The very premise of his method was strongly criticized. What could any results have said about heredity, if the twins were reared in the same environment? These criticisms were also applied to the work of Sanders (1934), Habel (1950), and Rainer, Mesnikoff, Kolb, and Carr (1960). There was also criticism of what the researchers meant by "separate environments." It was frequently a short period of time or a small distance that separated the twins.

To date, all attempts to find the origins of homosexuality in genes have failed. Because of these insufficiencies, critics of the genetic-reductionist premise Lewontin, Rose, and Kamin (1988) summarize: "The story is completely made up." In spite of repeated criticisms, research on twins is used to explain purported differences between homosexuality and heterosexuality.

CONSTITUTIONAL BIOLOGY

Beginning with the assumption that every function of the body is bound to a somatic correlate, one can, even if somewhat arbitrarily, divide constitutional-biological explanations into two directions: (1) The neuroanatomic direction: the assumption of a sexual drive in the brain. The causes of homosexuality, as a deviant sexual drive, are sought in the brain. (2) The physiometric direction: the bodily differences of homosexuals from heterosexuals. Beginning with the observation that homosexuals appear different, one sought to verify the scattered signs by bodily measurements and comparisons.

As early as the eighteenth century psychiatry was occupied with the functioning and malfunctioning of the brain. This conception originates from the psychiatrist and anatomist Franz Joseph Gall (1791), who is considered the founder of phrenology, the theory of localization of personality attributes in the brain (cf. Ackerknecht, 1984; Wettley, 1959, pp. 15-20). He believed that different parts of the brain were arranged for distinct mental functions. Thus the brain is not a single organ, but rather a number of organs that are sensitive to distinct influences and thereby preset for distinct tasks. In his conception, the organs can be located anatomically by the shape of the skull. He also asserted that the sex drive is present at birth. It is latent in the first years of life, develops during puberty, and reaches completion by the age of 45. The argument that had established itself at that time–whether women had a sexuality at all or only one more weakly imprinted than that of men–which according to Laqueur (1990) had come about through the discovery of the independence of orgasm and fertilization, also found its outcome in Gall's speculative phrenology. Since men have a more strongly pronounced cerebellum than women, they were also believed to have a more strongly pronounced sexual drive.

Although Gall's phrenological theory was controversial and rejected in its extreme form, the concept of localized mental activity, the senses, and their illnesses were not. Psychiatry occupied itself with the sexual perversions, one of which they considered homosexuality. Speculations about its localization in the brain also arose.

Ulrichs's conception that the Urning is a psychic hermaphrodite (i.e., a bodily man with a female soul and love drive) was of far-reaching importance for the formation of localization theories. The American psychiatrist Kiernan built on Ulrichs's thesis and concluded: "It becomes necessary in the course of enquiry to ascertain whether the brain which determines the action of the mind can be so transposed that the feminine brain shall occupy the body of a male and vice versa" (Kiernan, 1884, p. 281). For the Viennese psychiatrist Krafft-Ebing this went too far; he wrote in the posthumously published 12th edition of his *Psychopathia sexualis* (1903): "One does not have to imagine . . . 'a female soul in a male brain' or vice versa, . . . but rather only a female psycho-sexual center in a male brain, or vice versa" (p. 248). Of course there was no empirical evidence for this theory, but nonetheless it was believed.

At this time, another localization theory was put forth by the Italian anthropologist Paolo Mantegazza. He believed that the "true" homosexuals were sexually passive and that anal intercourse was their preferred practice. Male homosexuals are to be explained, in his words, as "an anatomical anomaly [that] sometimes leads the final branches of nerves to the rectum; therefore its stimulation causes for the *patici* (the passives) that genital excitement that in ordinary cases can be caused only through the genitals" (Mantegazza, 1886, p. 106).

Localization in the brain also played a role in the endocrinological research on the causes of homosexuality. According to the Viennese physiologist Eugen Steinach, the sexual object choice is determined by the proportion of the secretion of male and female hormones. In his theory, male homosexuals over-produce female sexual hormones (Steinach, 1919a). The Steinach tradition of research into causes was passed on to his co-worker Walter Hohlweg and by the latter to his pupil Günter Dörner.[5] Since about 1967 Dörner has investigated the purported hormonal causes of homosexuality. His research is based on the assumption that a sexual center in the brain is sexually undifferentiated in the embryo, but is hormonally differentiated before birth. Dörner believes that due to an excess of male sexual hormones during pregnancy the sexual center of the female embryo is programmed in a male direction; and through a surplus of female sexual hormones, that of the male is programmed in a female direction. Based on his research on rats he concluded: "Neuroendocrinologically determined male homosexuality can be brought to far-reaching regression [reversal] in adult animals through surgical lesions of a female erotic center localized in the central hypothalamus" (Dörner, 1972, p. 195). West German psychosurgeons, calling on this theory, burned out the alleged sexual center of homosexual men.[6] This led to severe personality disturbances in those so altered. Only on the basis of strong protests, such as that of the sexologist Volkmar Sigusch (1977), were these inhuman practices halted.

Just as the variations between the sexes were researched on all levels in comparative anatomy and physiology from the eighteenth century, attention being directed at difference, in the nineteenth century this discovery of difference concerned above all people of other nations. They were defined by "racial" difference. Especially at the beginning of the twentieth century constitutional biology received, by way of racial hygiene, great attention; "races" were measured, compared, and evaluated. It is therefore not surprising that the measuring rod was also applied to homosexuals.

As explained earlier, the assumption that *Urninge* (homosexual men) are physically different from *Dioninge* (heterosexual men) originally can be found already in Ulrichs. Later Hirschfeld adopted this view. He classified sexual intermediates employing endocrinology. The formation of the sexual organs, the body, the psyche, and sexuality were directed by the gonads, or rather their products. The formation of intermediates was dependent on a critical period of hormonal influence (Hirschfeld, 1918b, pp. 79-82). Hirschfeld believed that homosexuals are physically different from heterosexuals with regard to "voice and speech," "hairiness," "pelvis and figure," as well as "body integument and muscle, skin, and fat tissue" (Hirschfeld, 1914, p. 125-147). Hirschfeld's pupil Arthur Weil, therefore, set out to prove this empirically; the results of his first empirical investigation were published in the work "Die Körpermaße der Homosexuellen als Ausdrucksform ihrer besonderen sexuellen Veranlagung" (1921, The bodily measurements of homosexuals as an expression of their particular sexual disposition). Weil employed Gall's phrenological theory in an attempt to prove the supposed difference between homosexuals and heterosexuals. He stated: "Above all there are two relationships that are independent of the activity of the [gonads]: the relation between lower and upper body . . . and the relation of shoulder width to hip width." And he found that "95% of all male homosexuals investigated . . . deviated from the heterosexual average." From this Weil drew the conclusion: "The least that we must now assume is [that there is] a particular bodily disposition, a certain constitution that distinguishes the homosexual man from the normal average, and indeed we can now assume as the essence of this disposition, that the [gonads], as a result of some kind of inhibition of their internal secretory activity, were not able to transform the body to the pure male type" (Weil, 1921, pp. 116-118). Hirschfeld was elated with these results which lent his theories credibility. But Weil's work was strongly attacked on the basis of methodology (cf. Mair & Zutt, 1922; Wortis, 1936). He had not contrasted comparable samples of homosexuals and heterosexuals. The literature on the constitutional premise is very extensive; some works support Weil's statements, others do not. Thus Allen (1958) ascertained that there are no bodily differences between heterosexuals and homosexuals (p. 43). In the 1950s, the most comprehensive constitutional biological investigation was carried out at the Prague Institute for Sexual Science (Freund, 1963, pp. 156-166). They compared weight, stature, length of trunk, shoulder and hip width, size of the skeleton and the muscular apparatus, the laying on of fat, as well as hairiness on the four regions of the body. The diameter of the areola of nipple was noted and the prostate examined by hand and classified. In addition the length of the flaccid penis and the longitudinal axis of the testicles were measured. Even the voice and the vocal apparatus were evaluated. Those tested were divided into three groups: feminine homosexuals, non-feminine homosexuals, and heterosexuals. This exhaustive investigation concluded that no differences in the bodily measures could be found among the three groups. What was established was merely that homosexuals are somewhat lighter and have a significantly "larger penis" than heterosexuals. If we ignore the possible implication of the longer penis, then it becomes clear that there were obviously no constitutional differences. Since then the premise has not been pursued further; the theory of bodily differences between homosexuals and heterosexuals has finally been abandoned.

ENDOCRINOLOGY

Endocrinology began to develop around the turn of the century as a subfield of physiology, particularly from neurophysiological investigations on vertebrates (Biedl, 1913). Though the sexually specific effects of gonadal secretions on the body were already known by Charles Edouard Brown-Séquard around 1890, the sexual hormones that are of interest here were able to be described in their chemical structure and isolated only in the 1930s. Following the "discovery" of anatomical and physiological "differences" between the sexes, central importance was attributed to hormonal differences. The Viennese physiologist and pathologist Eugen Steinach, building on earlier theories of hormonal causes of homosexuality, laid claim to a complete biological determination. According to his theory, the endocrine system regulated the growth of the body as well as the whole personality, including psychological attributes such as "masculinity" and "femininity," "direction of eroticism," and "sexual mentality" (Steinach & Loebel, 1938, pp. 15-20). Inspired by a work on the physiology of the genitalia in frogs, he began to work on sexual physiology. At first he carried out research on castration and re-implantation of gonads in frogs, later in guinea pigs, rats, and goats (Steinach, 1912).

Steinach observed that the effects of the gonads began in puberty and influenced the observable sex. Therefore he named these structures "puberty glands" (*Pubertätsdrüse*). The basic assumption of his theory was that these puberty glands, in every animal and human, corresponded to the embryonic sexual condition of being undifferentiated.

Steinach based his theory on animal research in which female gonads were implanted in males, and male gonads in females. Animals with such cross-sexed gonadal assignment showed sexual characteristics and behaviors that corresponded to the implanted gonads. He believed that homosexuality was such a cross-sexed disorder of the puberty glands. His theory distinguished between homosexuals "with periodic attacks of the homosexual drive" and those with "constant homosexuality" (Steinach, 1919a, p. 141). The former, like the experimentally produced animals, had puberty glands which alternately produced male and female hormones influencing the choice of sexual object. In the case of "constant" homosexuals he asserted that, after the development of the sexual organs, the male puberty glands degenerate and the female puberty glands replace them. Such cross-sexed hormonal production supposedly caused the "constant" homosexual. Steinach believed he had proven that "the question of the biological basis of homosexuality has been definitively solved" (Steinach, 1919a, p. 141).

Steinach then attempted to replicate his research in homosexual men. He searched for "female tissue" in their testicles. Lichtenstern and Steinach reported that they found, especially in older homosexuals, signs of degeneration of the testicles and complete atrophy of the glands (Steinach, 1919b). Besides Leydig's cells (which he called M-cells), which produce the male hormone, Steinach identified cells that produce the female hormone (which he called F-cells). These F-cells were the cause of "constant" homosexuality and were assumed to be suppressed in the heterosexual man by the M-cells.

Though many criticized Steinach's research (e.g., the psychiatrist Albert Moll, 1921), Magnus Hirschfeld quickly added it to his arsenal of "proofs" for innateness because his theory of the naturalness of homosexuality lacked an empirical basis. Already in 1912 he was of the opinion that the hormones he called "Andrin" and "Gynäcin" were the essential fluids that allowed sexual characteristics to mature. Hirschfeld not only took over Steinach's theory, but he also sought to support it through his own research.[7]

One of Steinach's critics, the endocrinologist C. Benda (1921), disagreed with his theory, stating: "Indeed the fundamental morphological method of proof of Steinach, from which he infers the decisive importance of his so-called puberty glands for the development of the secondary sexual characteristics, rests on an untenable basis" (p. 30). He himself investigated the testicles of homosexuals under the microscope and came to the following conclusion: "Likewise untenable from the morphological standpoint are his statements about the 'puberty glands' of homosexual human testicles . . . The expert easily recognizes in his 'F-cells' typical Leydig's cells" (p. 31). "My findings on the testicles of four investigated cases of homosexuals . . . showed outstandingly lively spermiogenesis" (p. 37).

Steinach's theory was already clearly and unambiguously disproved before the castration experiments were fully underway. According to Steinach's theory, homosexuals lacked the proper puberty glands. He advised therefore the castration of the puberty glands of homosexuals and the implantation of testicles from heterosexuals. The Viennese surgeon Lichtenstern was the first to attempt this procedure. By 1920 he had operated on seven homosexuals (Steinach & Lichtenstern, 1918). The Berlin physician Richard Mühsam (1920, 1921) "treated" four more homosexuals. At first the success of treatment was euphorically reported, the inclination toward men in homosexuals dissolved according to the statements of the "operating surgeons" and the heterosexual inclination appeared. According to Mühsam, Hirschfeld had referred homosexuals for the "operation" in at least two cases, something Hirschfeld never mentioned.[8] In 1923 these operations were stopped because they had changed nothing in the sexual orientation.

The surgeon E. Kreuter, at first a follower of the Steinach-Lichtenstern views, stated that in one case, two years after an implantation, he himself could "no longer detect with the microscope the traces of the transplanted testicle" (Kreuter, 1922, pp. 538-539). He surpassed his colleagues in scientific zeal. He implanted in an "originally heterosexually experiencing man, a bilateral castrate, . . . a testicle of a heavy genuine homosexual." "After the transplantation not even a hint of a homosexual attitude appeared." Richard Mühsam (1926), too, ceased his operations. Without retracting his theory Steinach wrote in 1938: "To be sure, the ultimate reason why one individual becomes a physical hermaphrodite and another merely a psychic intermediate grade [i.e., homosexual] is still in darkness" (Steinach & Loebel, 1938, p. 119). He never mentioned the attempts on homosexuals undertaken in his name. "They sacrificed their testicles to scientific thinking," stated Gunter Schmidt (1988, cf. 1984) in retrospect.

The Nazis employed all available theories on the etiology of homosexuality in an attempt to eradicate it. In the 1930s, testosterone (the so-called male sexual hormone) was first isolated. The Danish physician Carl Vaernet, who advised Heinrich Himmler, believed that homosexual men had a deficit of male sexual hormones (Schoppmann, 1991, pp. 157-162). Through the implantation of hormone pellets into the inguinal (groin) region he believed he could transform them into heterosexuals. In 1944 Vaernet began his research on homosexuals by castrating prisoners in the Buchenwald concentration camp. He too reported "success." The extent of his research on humans is hard to reconstruct. From various sources it appears that there were 13-15 persons, two of whom died as a consequence of the operation.

The Steinach practice was continued by the Berlin endocrinologist Günter Dörner, who to this day does research on pre-natal sexual hormone imbalances in an attempt to explain homosexuality.[9] Like Steinach, most of his research was performed on rats and based on the conception of homosexuality as the feminine in the homosexual man and the masculine in the homosexual woman. He proceeds from the assumption that there is a sexually neutral sexual center that up to the third month of pregnancy is able to be steered toward either a "heterosexual" or "homosexual" orientation. Like Steinach, Dörner (1972) also made suggestions for therapy, this time in the form of pre-natal injections of hormones to correct the imbalances. He would like to allow women to "decide" whether they would prefer a homosexual or a heterosexual child.

BEHAVIOR

Ulrichs (1898, "Memnon") reported, under the heading "Uranismus in the animal and plant world": "In free-swimming water plants, . . . e.g., Valisneria, a certain approach of individual male plants to [other] male plants may be observed" (p. 134). Since he also believed he could show homosexuality in higher animals, he came to the conclusion that "Uranismus, as a law of nature, *goes right through the whole animal and plant kingdoms.*" From today's perspective, Ulrichs had subscribed to the anthropomorphization that is common in medicine and biology.

Around 1890, in conjunction with a discussion about whether sexual perversions were innate or acquired, ethological references also became popular in the psychiatric literature. The well-known Berlin psychiatrist and sexual perversions theorist Albert Moll, in two of his works presented evidence of the universality and pathology of homosexuality (Moll, 1898, pp. 276, 368-407, 492-494; 1899, pp. 35, 368-410). He described, among others, dogs and rabbits who rub against one another until ejaculation. In his conception, homosexuality was an arrested development caused by a psychological deficiency. Contrary to Ulrichs's concept of an inherited disposition, Moll asserted that rearing and environment are essential influences in the development of homosexuality. He further argued that homosexuality is therefore treatable.

The first systematic work on homosexuality in the animal kingdom was presented by the Berlin zoologist Ferdinand Karsch in 1900. His work was an attempt to refute the assertion of the forensic doctor Casper, that "such a thing occurs never and nowhere in the whole animal kingdom in male or female animals" (p. 34). Karsch's work is constructed strictly phylogenetically. Using the then new concept of homosexuality, it is described in mammals (e.g., monkeys and rodents), then in birds, and finally in insects and spiders. A certain arbitrariness was shown in attributing meaning to animal behavior. One must remember that these works hardly played a role in psychiatry's debate about sexual perversions. The psychiatrist Emil Kraepelin (1918) wrote: "To compare the animal and plant world, which is done by Hirschfeld, is not recommended because of the incomparability of the relations" (p. 118).

In order to lend credibility to such research, two limitations were imposed on the definition of homosexuality: (1) So as to make certain what is homosexual, those ways of behaving were selected that count as homosexual: mutual manipulation of the sexual organs in the case of female individuals and anal penetration in the case of male individuals. (2) So as to weaken the criticisms against those who make analogies in the behavior of lower animals and humans, observations above all on higher animals, especially the primates, were brought out as evidence. The principle of analogy formation remained the same.

Over the last forty years several works have built upon this comparison (Ford & Beach, 1951; Klimmer, 1965; Weinrich, 1987; Sommer, 1990). These works are inspired by an attempt to legitimate homosexuality as something universal and natural. Rather than criticize these works on the basis of their data, one should consider the underlying assumptions in which same-sex behavior, wherever it occurs, is equated with homosexuality. One must therefore ask what use a category is if it includes such diverse behavior. It would be fascinating to place same-sex behavior in the animal kingdom in its respective social context. Perhaps then one would come to the conclusion that it fills definite functions, not comparable to human homosexuality, and is a matter of independent phenomena of the specific animal species under study.

CONCLUSION

If one starts out with homosexuality as more than sexual acts between individuals of the same sex, if one holds firm to homosexuality as a phenomenon whose cultural, social, and psychic dimensions are not specific transformations of an omnipresent biology, then biological explanations, however they are worded, are insufficient.

Such explanations are to be understood only in a scientific-historic and social-historic context. The nineteenth-century conception of homosexuals established them as different from "normal." The belief in distinct anatomies and psychologies in homosexuals provided this. Subsequent works continue to today, inspired by the attempt to constantly confirm that the homosexual is still the "other." And this attempt is reinforced by the media as "new results" about biological causes make headlines.

The thrust of these works is a search for masculinity in the homosexual woman and femininity in the homosexual man. The supposed femininity of homosexual men was presumed to be in the chromosomes, in the brain, in the body structure, or in the hormones. The conception of homosexuality as a phenomenon dividing the sexes is a basis of its enduring interest.

As was shown in this article, the interpretation of biological theories is always dependent on the standpoint of the observer and on the social climate. Gay men and lesbians as well as representatives of the gay movement who seize upon these explanations today thereby perpetuate the natural scientific and social separation. As a sexual-political instrument, biological explanations of homosexuality promise an advantage only because natural scientific hypotheses, presented as "hard facts," are given more credence than social scientific explanations. Only when "scientific explanations" are made into instruments of medical intervention does their danger to homosexuals become palpable. Until now every theory about the supposed causes of homosexuality has brought forth specific attempts at cure or prevention. The Enlightenment motto of Hirschfeld, "Through science to justice," has not only proved to be an illusion, but is also dangerous. The social acceptance of homosexuality is not to be found in science.

NOTES

1. For the sexual-political dimensions of Ulrichs's work and its place in the literature, see Kennedy, 1990.

2. In Westphal's important article of 1869 the "contrary sexual feeling" is conceptualized psychiatrically for the first time. Westphal understands it as "innate perversion of the sexual feeling with the knowledge of the morbidity of this phenomenon" (p. 73).

3. As evidence for the assumption of innateness, which already contains an idea of heredity, Ulrichs (1898, "Memnon") writes: "In individual families we see Uranismus repeat itself in various, sometimes numerous persons. A great number of such families could be pointed out.

"In particular, it occurs that there are two, even three, Urning brothers, even if they grew up separated from one another" (p. 133).

Like many of his contemporaries, Krafft-Ebing conceived of homosexuality as degeneration. For him it was, besides other "bodily" and "psychic" degenerations, a symptom of deterioration. He had "designated this peculiar sexual feeling as a functional sign of degeneration and as the partial appearance of a neuro(psycho)pathic, mostly hereditarily determined condition." "In almost all cases where an inquiry into the bodily-psychic condition of ancestors and blood relatives was available, neuroses, psychoses, signs of degeneration, etc. were found in the families concerned" (Krafft-Ebing, 1903, pp. 242-243).

4. Richard Goldschmidt (1916) believed that the genetic basis effected a hormonal malformation in homosexuals, that "it is entirely thinkable that intersexualism [such as homosexuality] can be 'healed' through treating with gonad extracts or, better still, through transplantation of normal gonads . . . It is perhaps possible to try such methods of treatment without any danger on, say, adolescent pseudohermaphrodites or strong homosexuals" (p. 14).

In the report of the first year of the Institute, whose director was Hirschfeld, may be read: "The rearing of exotic silk-moths . . . with the goal of hybridization and gaining of intersexual variants through cross-breeding . . . was successfully begun" ("Bericht," 1920, p. 66).

5. The chemist Walter Hohlweg worked from 1926 to 1928 as an endocrinologist in the Physiological Department of the Biological Research Station of the Academy of Sciences in Vienna, whose director was Eugen Steinach. The two researchers published jointly. From 1928 Hohlweg worked in Berlin in the Shering Drug Company. In 1952 the Institute for Experimental Endocrinology (Institut für experimentelle Endokrinologie) was founded at the Charité in Berlin. From the beginning Hohlweg was the director of the Institute. His pupil and successor was the endocrinologist Günter Dörner. Hohlweg's research concerns the specificity of sex hormones. He discovered the estrogen-feedback effect, which Dörner believed he could prove to be different for homosexuals and heterosexuals (cf. Gooren, 1988).

6. There were three psychosurgery teams in West Germany: in Hamburg (D. Müller), in Göttingen (F. D. Roeder), and in Homburg (G. Dieckmann). In 1962 the first psychosurgical "treatment" was carried out by Roeder on a man labeled as paedophile-homosexual. In 1979, Schorch and Schmidt estimated that, up to that time, operations had been performed on approximately 70 men labeled as sexually abnormal. The results of animal experiments, especially those using white laboratory rats, of the endocrinologist Günter Dörner served as the scientific basis for these operations (Müller, Orthner, Roeder, König, & Bosse, 1974).

In 1972 Dörner organized an International Symposium on the Endocrinology of Sex in Berlin. The psychosurgeons took part and reported on the scientific basis as well as the results of their operations. Of the scientific basis, Müller et al. said:

> Dörner (1969) concluded from his extensive experiments with rats, that the CAJALsche nucleus in the hypothalamus is a 'center of female eroticization' and that the 'center of male eroticization' can be localized within the area preoptica directly in front of the ventromedial nucleus . . . On the basis of this experimental research we surgically switched off the CAJALsche nucleus in our patients with homosexual behavior. (Müller et al., 1974, p. 82)

In the discussion of the paper Dörner said: "We were very much impressed when Roeder and Müller described an inhibition of homosexual behavior in men following lesions in the ventromedial nucleus, since we had published independently at the same time a similar effect in homosexual male rats after lesions in just the same hypothalamic region" (p. 105). And the operations continued (Müller, 1974).

The sexual scientists Eberhard Schorch and Gunter Schmidt of the Department of Sexual Research of the University of Hamburg Psychiatric Clinic (Abteilung Sexualforschung der Psychiatrischen Universitätsklinik Hamburg) and Volkmar Sigusch and Martin Dannecker of the Department for Sexual Science of the Clinic of the University of Frankfurt a.M. (Abteilung Sexualwissenschaft des Klinikums der Universität Frankfurt a.M.) protested against not only the inadmissible transfer to humans of the results of animal experiments, but also the surgery itself on the grounds that it deformed the personality of the patients (Schorch & Schmidt, 1979; Sigusch, 1977).

7. "I myself, along with several colleagues, have had occasion in my Institute to investigate under the microscope the testicles of homosexuals in *seven cases . . .* The entire result is the following: In all the testicles we have conditions, which must be understood at least as *striking deviations* from typical testicle conditions" (Hirschfeld, 1921, p. 174). How Hirschfeld came by his specimens remains unmentioned.

8. Magnus Hirschfeld referred at least three or four homosexual patients to the surgeon Richard Mühsam, who castrated one testicle and implanted slices of so-called heterosexual testicles in each of them. According to Mühsam: "The well-known connection between periodical dipsomania with increased homosexual sensation and inclination led me to castrate a 39-year-old police officer. That man and the patient mentioned earlier had been referred to me by my colleague Magnus Hirschfeld" (Mühsam, 1926, p. 454). "The second patient was referred to me by Magnus Hirschfeld in order to remove the patient's bisexual sensation . . . The third case concerned a 27-year-old physician. I thank Magnus Hirschfeld for also referring him to me" (Mühsam, 1921, p. 824).

9. The theory is, if with modifications, represented by Dörner today in spite of harsh inner- and interdisciplinary criticisms (see Pfäfflin, 1990; Schmidt & Clement, 1990; Gooren, 1988). An extensive presentation of the theory will therefore be dispensed with.

REFERENCES

Ackerknecht, E. H. (1984). *Kurze Geschichte der Psychiatrie*, 3rd ed. Stuttgart.

Allen, C. (1958). *Homosexuality*. London.

Benda, C. (1921). Bemerkungen zur normalen und pathologischen Histologie der Zwischenzellen des Menschen und der Säugetiere. *Archiv für Frauenkunde und Eugenik*, Vol. 7, No. 1: 30-40.

Bericht über das erste Tätigkeitsjahr (1. Juli 1919 bis 30. Juni 1920) des Instituts für Sexualwissenschaft. (1920). *Jahrbuch für sexuelle Zwischenstufen*, Vol. 20, Nos. 1/2.

Biedl, A. (1913). *Innere Sekretion*, Vols. 1 & 2, 2nd ed. Wien/Berlin.

Casper, J. L. (1852). Ueber Nothzucht und Päderastie und deren Ermitelung seitens des Gerichtsarztes. Nach eigenen Beobachtungen. *Vierteljahresschrift für gerichtliche und öffentliche Medizin*, Vol. 1: 21-78.

Casper, J. L. (1863). Zweite Novelle. Zur Lehre von der Päderastie. *Klinische Novellen zur gerichtlichen Medizin*, Vol. 1: 33-45.

Chevalier, J. (1893). *Inversion sexuelle*. Paris. Quoted in Wettley (1959).

Dörner, G. (1972). *Sexualhormonabhängige Gehirndifferenzierung und Sexualität*. Wien/New York.

Ford, C. S., & Beach, F. A. (1951). *Patterns of sexual behavior*. New York.

Freund, K. (1963). *Die Homosexualität beim Mann*. Leipzig.

Gall, F. J. (1791). *Philosophisch-medicinische Untersuchungen über Natur u. Kunst im kranken u. gesunden Zustande des Menschen*.

Goldschmidt, R. (1916). Die biologischen Grundlagen der konträren Sexualität und des Hermaphroditismus beim Menschen. *Archiv für Rassen- und Gesellschafts-Biologie*, Vol. 12: 1-14.

Gooren, L. J. G. (1988). Biomedizinische Theorien zur Entstehung der Homosexualität. Eine Kritik. *Zeitschrift für Sexualforschung*, Vol. 1, No. 2: 132-145.

Hausen, K. (1976). Die Polarisierung der "Geschlechtscharaktere". Eine Spiegelung der Dissoziation von Erwerbs- und Familienleben. In W. Conze (Ed.), *Sozialgeschichte der Familie in der Neuzeit Europas* (pp. 367-393). Stuttgart.

Habel, H. (1950). Zwillingsuntersuchungen an Homosexuellen. *Zeitschrift für Sexualforschung*, Vol. 1, No. 2: 168-180.

Hirschfeld, H. (pseudonym, Th. Ramien). (1896). *Sappho und Sokrates. Wie erklärt sich die Liebe der Männer und Frauen zu Personen des eigenen Geschlechts?* Leipzig.

Hirschfeld, H. (1903a). Das Harmonische der urnischen Persönlichkeit. *Jahrbuch für sexuelle Zwischenstufen*, Vol. 5, No. 1: 67-104.

Hirschfeld, H. (1903b). Heredität und Homosexualität. *Jahrbuch für sexuelle Zwischenstufen*, Vol. 5, No. 1: 138-159.

Hirschfeld, H. (1914). *Die Homosexualität des Mannes und des Weibes*. Berlin.

Hirschfeld, H. (1918a). Ist die Homosexualität körperlich oder seelisch bedingt? *Münchener medizinische Wochenschrift*, Vol. 65, No. 11: 298-300.

Hirschfeld, H. (1918b). *Sexualpathologie. II. Teil, Sexuelle Zwischenstufen. Das männliche Weib und der weibliche Mann*. Bonn.

Hirschfeld, H. (1921). Hodenbefunde bei intersexuellen Varianten. *Archiv für Frauenkunde und Eugenik, Sexualbiologie und Vererbungslehre*, Vol. 7, No. 2, Sexualwissenschaftliches Beiheft: 173-174.

Honegger, C. (1991). *Die Ordnung der Geschlechter. Die Wissenschaft vom Menschen und das Weib, 1750-1850*. Frankfurt.

Kallmann, F. J. (1952a). Comparative twin study on the genetic aspects of male homosexuality. *Journal of Nervous and Mental Disease*, Vol. 15, No. 4: 283-298.

Kallmann, F. J. (1952b). Twin and sibship study of overt male homosexuality. *American Journal of Human Genetics*, Vol. 4, No. 2: 136-146.

Karsch, F. (1900). Päderastie und Triebadie bei den Tieren auf Grund der Literatur. *Jahrbuch für sexuelle Zwischenstufen*, Vol. 2: 126-155.

Kennedy, H. (1990). *Karl Heinrich Ulrichs. Sein Leben und sein Werk*. Beiträge zur Sexualforschung, Vol. 65. M. Folkerts (Trans.). Stuttgart. Original publication: *Ulrichs: The life and works of Karl Heinrich Ulrichs, pioneer of the modern gay movement* (1988). Boston.

Kiernan, J. G. (1884). Original communications. Insanity. Lecture XXVI.–Sexual Perversions. *Detroit Lancet*, Vol. 7, No. 11: 481-487.

Klimmer, R. (1965). *Die Homosexualität*, 3rd ed. Hamburg.

Kraepelin, E. (1918). Geschlechtliche Verirrungen und Volksvermehrung. *Münchener medizinische Wochenschrift*, Vol. 65, No. 5.

Krafft-Ebing, R. von. (1903). *Psychopathia sexualis*, 12th ed. Stuttgart.

Kreuter, E. (1922). Hodentransplantation und Homosexualität. *Zentralblatt für Chirurgie*, No. 16: 538-540.

Laqueur, Th. (1990). *Making sex: Body and gender from the Greeks to Freud.* Cambridge, MA.

Lemke, R. (1940). *Uber Ursache und strafrechtliche Beurteilung der Homosexualität.* Jena.

Lewontin, R. C., Rose, S., & Kamin, L. J. (1982). *Not in our genes.* New York.

Lewontin, R. C., Rose, S., & Kamin, L. J. (1988). *Die Gene sind es nicht . . . Biologie, Ideologie und menschliche Natur*, H. Skrowronek & K. Juhl (Trans.). München. (Originally published 1982).

Mair, R., & Zutt, J. (1922). Zur Frage des Zusammenhanges zwischen Homosexualität und Körperbau. *Monatsschrift für Psychiatrie und Neurologie*, Vol. 72: 54-63.

Mann, G. (Ed.). (1973). *Biologismus im 19. Jahrhundert.* Stuttgart.

Mantegazza, P. (1886). *Die Geschlechtsverhältnisse des Menschen.* Berlin.

Moll, A. (1898). *Untersuchungen über die Libido sexualis.* Vol. 1. Berlin.

Moll, A. (1899). *Die konträre Sexualempfindung.* Berlin.

Moll, A. (1921). *Behandlung der Homosexualität: biochemisch oder psychisch?* Bonn.

Moravia, S. (1980). The Enlightenment and the sciences of men. *History of Science*, Vol. 18: 247-288.

Moreau de Tours, J. H. (1859). *La psychologie morbide dans ses rapports avec la philosophie de l'histoire.* Paris.

Mühsam, R. (1920). Ueber die Beeinflussung des Geschlechtslebens durch freie Hodenüberpflanzung. *Deutsche medizinische Wochenschrift*, Vol. 46, No. 29: 823-825.

Mühsam, R. (1921). Weitere Mitteilungen über Hodenüberpflanzung. *Deutsche medizinische Wochenschrift*, Vol. 47, No. 13: 354-355.

Mühsam, R. (1926). Chirurgische Eingriffe bei Anomalien des Sexuallebens. *Therapie der Gegenwart*, Vol. 67: 451-455.

Müller, D. (1974). Die Ergebnisse stereotaktischer Eingriffe im Gehirn bei Sexualtriebstörungen. Vortrag auf der Jahrestagung der Bundesarbeitsgemeinschaft der Ärzte und Psychologen in der Straffälligenhilfe am 21.6.74.

Müller, D., Orthner, H., Roeder, F., König, A., & Bosse, K. (1974). Einfluß von Hypothalamusläsionen auf Sexualverhalten und gonadotrope Funktion beim Menschen. Bericht über 23 Fälle (Influence of Hypothalamus Lesions on

Sexual Behaviour and Gonadotropic Function in Man. Report on 23 Cases). In G. Dörner (Ed.), *Endocrinology of sex* (pp. 80-105). Leipzig.

Pare, C. M. B. (1956). Homosexuality and chromosomal sex. *Journal of Psychosomatic Research*, Vol. 1: 247-251.

Pfäfflin, F. (1990). Neuroendokrinologische Forschungsergebnisse und Sexualwissenschaft. Zur Vorgeschichte eines Konflikts. *Zeitschrift für Sexualwissenschaft*, Vol. 3, No. 1: 54-74.

Rainer, J. D., Mesnikoff, A., Kolb, L. C., & Carr, A. (1960). Homosexuality and heterosexuality in identical twins. *Psychosomatic Medicine*, Vol. 22, No. 4: 251-259.

Rüdin, E. (1904). Zur Rolle der Homosexuellen im Lebensprozeß der Rasse. *Archiv für Rassen- und Gesellschafts-Biologie*, Vol. 1, No. 1: 99-109.

Sanders, J. (1934). Homosexuelle Zwillinge. *Genetica*, Vol. 16: 401-434.

Schmidt, G. (1984). Helfer und Verfolger. Die Rolle von Wissenschaft und Medizin in der Homosexuellenfrage. *Mitteilungen der Magnus-Hirschfeld-Gesellschaft*, Vol. 3: 21-33.

Schmidt, G. (1988). *Das große Der Die Das. Über das Sexuelle.* Hamburg.

Schmidt, G., & Clement, U. (1990). Does peace prevent homosexuality? *Archives of Sexual Behavior*, Vol. 19, No. 2: 183-187.

Schoppmann, C. (1991). *Nationalsozialistische Sexualpolitik und weibliche Homosexualität.* Pfaffenweiler.

Schorch, E., & Schmidt, G. (1979). Hypothalamotomie bei sexuellen Abweichungen. Eine Kritik aus sexualwissenschaftlicher Sicht. *Nervenarzt*, Vol. 50: 689-699.

Schrenk-Notzing, A. von. (1892). *Die Suggestionstherapie bei krankhaften Erscheinungen des Geschlechtssinns.* Stuttgart.

Sigusch, V. (1977). Medizinische Experimente am Menschen. Das Beispiel Psychochirurgie. *Jahrbuch für kritische Medizin*, Beilage 17.

Sommer, V. (1990). *Wider die Natur?* München.

Steinach, E. (1912). Willkürliche Umwandlung von Säugetier-Männchen in Tiere mit ausgeprägt weiblichen Geschlechtscharakteren und weiblicher Psyche. *Pflüger's Archiv für Physiologie*, Vol. 144: 71-108.

Steinach, E. (1919a). Mitteilungen aus der biologischen Versuchsanstalt der Akademie der Wissenschaften in Wien (Physiologische Abteilung; Vorstand: E. Steinach). Nr. 38. Experimentelle und histologische Beweise für den ursächlichen Zusammenhang von Homosexualität und Zwitterdrüse. *Anzeiger der Wiener Akademie, Mathematisch-naturwiss. Klasse*, Vol. 56, No. 11: 138-141.

Steinach, E. (1919b). Mitteilungen aus der biologischen Versuchsanstalt der Akademie der Wissenschaften in Wien (Physiologische Abteilung; Vorstand: E. Steinach). Nr. 39. Histologische Beschaffenheit der Keimdrüse bei homosexuellen Männern. *Anzeiger der Wiener Akademie, Mathematisch-naturwiss. Klasse*, Vol. 56, No. 11: 142-147.

Steinach, E., & Lichtenstern, R. (1918). Originalien. Umstimmung der Homosexualität durch Austausch der Pubertätsdrüsen. *Münchener medizinische Wochenschrift*, Vol. 65, No. 6: 145-148.

Steinach, E., & Loebel, J. (1938). *Sex and life.* London.

Ulrichs, K. H. (1898). *Forschungen über das Rätsel der mannmännlichen Liebe,* 2nd ed., Magnus Hirschfeld (Ed.). Leipzig. Contains: "Vindex" (1864), "Inclusa" (1864), "Vindicta" (1965), "Formatrix" (1865), "Ara spei" (1865), "Gladius Furens" (1868), "Memnon" (1868), "Incubus" (1869), "Argonauticus" (1869), "Prometheus" (1870), "Araxes" (1870), "Critische Pfeile" (1879).

Ulrichs, K. H. (1899). Vier Briefe. *Jahrbuch für sexuelle Zwischenstufen,* Vol. 1: 36-70.

Weil, A. (1921). Die Körpermaße der Homosexuellen als Ausdrucksform ihrer besonderen Veranlagung. *Jahrbuch für sexuelle Zwischenstufen,* Vol. 21, Nos. 3/4: 113-120.

Weinrich, J. D. (1987). *Sexual landscape: Why we are what we are, why we love whom we love.* New York.

Westphal, C. (1869). Die conträre Sexualempfindung. *Archiv für Psychiatrie und Nervenkrankheiten,* Vol. 2, No. 1: 73-108.

Wettley, A. (1959). *Von der "Psychopathia sexualis" zur Sexualwissenschaft.* Beiträge zur Sexualforschung, Vol. 17. Stuttgart.

Wortis, J. (1936). A note on the body build of the male homosexual. *American Journal of Psychiatry,* Vol. 93: 1121-1125.

Homosexuality, Biology, and Ideology

Günter Haumann, PhD

SUMMARY. This paper critically examines the complex relationships and interdependencies between biological theories on homosexuality and sociosexual ideologies. It challenges the privileged status of biology as the ultimate authority on homosexuality. This status is based on the belief that biology is a value-free science. On the contrary, this essay shows how unacknowledged assumptions and culturally bound patterns of thinking about sexuality taint biological research. Sociosexual ideologies are defined as principles that organize the ways we express our sexualities and the way we theorize about them in biology. The following ideologies are identified: (1) sexuality-as-heterosexuality, (2) sexuality-as-reproduction, (3) sexual dualism (male vs. female), and (4) the view that homosexuality is a sexual inversion. The process by which these ideologies are incorporated into biology is two-fold: (1) as a projective act from society onto nature and (2) as a reflective act from nature back into society. It is further argued that biological knowledge of homosexuality resulting from that process can be used for diverse political interests. Finally, it is proposed that since biological theories on homosexuality are inseparable from the context of their paradigmatic origin, it is possible that new theories could be derived from new ideologies.

Over the past hundred years the biological sciences have produced a large body of theories on sexuality. Traditionally, the "nat-

Günter Haumann has studied biology and philosophy at the University of Graz, Austria, and sexual science at the Universities of Amsterdam and Utrecht, The Netherlands.

Correspondence may be addressed: Lomanstraat 90/4, NL-1075 RG Amsterdam, The Netherlands.

[Haworth co-indexing entry note]: "Homosexuality, Biology, and Ideology." Haumann, Günter. Co-published simultaneously in *Journal of Homosexuality* (The Haworth Press, Inc.) Vol. 28, No. 1/2, 1995, pp. 57-77; and: *Sex, Cells, and Same-Sex Desire: The Biology of Sexual Preference* (ed: John P. De Cecco, and David Allen Parker) The Haworth Press, Inc., 1995, pp. 57-77. Multiple copies of this article/chapter may be purchased from The Haworth Document Delivery Center [1-800-3-HAWORTH; 9:00 a.m. - 5:00 p.m. (EST)].

uralist" holds that human sexuality is part of the natural order, whereas the "environmentalist" argues that human sexuality is part of the social order (cf. Stein, 1990). Claiming that homosexuality has a biological basis, biological sex research strives to explain it as either a common and normal aspect of the natural order (e.g., sociobiology) or as a disturbance of it (e.g., endocrinology, brain research). Despite the array of different biological theories on homosexuality and the fact that they are often incompatible, they still enjoy a high level of interest. Like all natural sciences, biology is a highly respected discipline. The enormous progress that it has made and the knowledge it has produced has deeply influenced our understanding of the natural world. This has strengthened the conviction that biology has important contributions to make to our understanding of all aspects of human sexuality. Biological theories on sexuality are generally considered to be more accurate and reliable than psychological or sociological theories.

Recently, this attitude towards biological research could be recognized again when a genetic study by Hamer, Hu, Magnuson, Hu, and Pattatucci (1993) was published suggesting that at least one subtype of male homosexuality is genetically influenced. Though the study does not at all allow definitive conclusions about the origin of homosexuality, it gained enormous and largely uncritical publicity.

There are two main reasons for the belief that ultimate truth resides in biological theories of sexuality. One reason is that the use of naturalistic categories in biological sex-research seduces us into thinking that biology is dealing with purely natural entities. Terms such as *instinct, drive, excitement, reproduction, masculine,* and *feminine* seem to be a neutral and direct naming of phenomena. Actually, they are only representations of the way we perceive and think about nature. That is to say, such terms have a conceptual history through which they have derived specific meanings (Tiefer, 1991).

The second reason why biology is believed to produce the truth about sexuality has to do with its claim to be an "objective" science. The natural sciences are traditionally seen as producing knowledge that is independent of culture, ideology, and prejudice. The adherence to epistemological and methodological rules supposedly guarantees the objectivity of the scientific process. The theories resulting from this scientific process are believed to reflect nature as it really is (Hempel, 1966; Popper, 1962; but see also Feyerabend, 1975).

This objectivist notion of science is also prevalent in most of the biological studies on homosexuality. For this reason biological theories on homosexuality attract great attention and receive immediate credibility. Biology is still considered to be the ultimate authority on homosexuality for a large part of the scientific community as well as for the general public.

In this article, I will challenge the notion that biological research on homosexuality is an autonomous enterprise carried out by ideologically independent scientists. In particular, I will point out that their background assumptions and culturally bound patterns of thinking about sexuality *do* play a crucial role in biological studies on homosexuality. I will describe the most powerful ideologies and demonstrate how they affect every level of the research process, from the definition of the problem to the findings produced. I also will look at how ideologies and the theories based on them work both within science (i.e., epistemologically) and outside of science (i.e., politically) (Haumann, 1992a; Salamun, 1988). The political aspect is of considerable social relevance because it touches the question of the legitimating and normative functions that biological theories can exercise.

Criticizing the scientific enterprise is always a tricky venture, especially when the focus is as respectable as biology and as sensitive an issue as homosexuality. One always risks being misunderstood. Therefore, I want to stress that I do not intend to denigrate biology as a whole, nor do I mean to say that biology cannot make contributions to the understanding of homosexuality. My aim is to show that biology, like all other scientific approaches to homosexuality, is not immune to the cultural and political context within which it takes place.

THE MAKING OF THE HOMOSEXUAL BODY

The conviction that biological research is an appropriate way to study and understand homosexuality relies on several assumptions about the essential nature of homosexuality. In particular, it is presumed that homosexual behavior and desire are determined by biological factors, be they genes, hormone levels, or brain structures. Homosexuality is not conceived as a social or psychological phenomenon shaped by cultural space or historical age, but a natural universal, expressed variously in different cultures and ages. This assumption entails more than the general claim that homosexuality is a natural potential of all human beings. It implies that homosexuality has a *specific* biological causation and manifestation which is typical only for some individuals–the so-called homosexuals.

The second implication of every biological approach to homosexuality is the belief in biological differences between homosexual and heterosexual individuals. Such differences are sought at anatomical, genetic, endocrinological, or behavioral levels. The corresponding biological disciplines–each claims that the particular level of organization with which it deals is the adequate base to look for the manifest signs of homosexuality–are specifically anatomy/morphology, genetics, endocrinology, and ethology. Their basic assumption is, as Leonore Tiefer (1990, p. 312) notes, "that the body comes before everything else; it is the original source of action, experience, knowledge, and meaning for the species and for the individual."

The attempts to find homosexual features were introduced in the beginning of the nineteenth century when forensic doctors began to examine the anus and penis of men who had engaged in anal intercourse. They claimed that men who engaged in receptive intercourse had funnel-shaped anuses with smooth skin around them whereas men who had insertive anal intercourse had thin and tapering penises. The real purpose of their examinations, however, was not to enlarge knowledge about sex but to provide "scientific" arguments for criminal trials of sodomy (cf. Hekma, 1987; Müller, 1991). As soon as the early sexologists, most of whom were physicians, had created a sexological category of homosexuality, systematic studies began to search for distinct physical characteristics in homosexuals (Foucault, 1978; Hekma, 1987; Katz, 1983; Müller, 1991).

Attempts to locate physical signs of homosexuality have not ceased in spite of their failure. As new biological subdisciplines develop and diversify, they repeatedly create the expectation that *they* are the right tool with which to grasp the biological essence of homosexuality. Historically, each is abandoned and replaced with new theories. (For critical reviews of current biological theories on homosexuality see Byne & Parsons, 1993; Friedman & Downey, 1993). Although many of the old theories appear as unacceptable or even ridiculous to us now, we must not forget that they fit into the intellectual and scientific context of their time.

BIOLOGY APPROACHES HOMOSEXUALITY

Which biological subdiscipline is best suited to study homosexuality? In spite of a general account of biological bases of homosexuality, there appears to be competition among subdisciplines for the priority of knowledge. It is remarkable, for instance, that neuroendocrinological and sociobiological research programs on homosexuality hardly address one another, let alone try to develop an integrated biological theory of homosexuality. Endocrinologists show little interest in evolution; sociobiologists have only a passing interest in hormones. Such intradisciplinary separatism does not heighten the credibility of biology as the basis for understanding homosexuality.

Biology is commonly held to be an objective enterprise that produces objective knowledge, free of social values and ideologies. Values and ideologies that affect the research process presumably are excluded by methodology. This notion of biology has been challenged by feminist biologists and theorists in a number of areas of biological research on sexuality (see, e.g., Birke, 1986; Bleier, 1984; Fausto-Sterling, 1985; Harding, 1986; Harding & O'Barr, 1987). These critics convincingly show that scientific inquiry cannot adequately be understood without considering their contexts. To view them as pure knowledge of the natural world would ignore the role of ideologies in shaping science. Therefore we do better to perceive "science as social knowledge" (Longino, 1990).

Given this conception of science, one wonders how social ideologies become incorporated into biological research on homosexuality. Actually, every step of the scientific process can be affected. Even before starting with the research, the investigator has certain beliefs about the essential nature of homosexuality that never are questioned.

To define homosexuality as an object of biological concern places it within the paradigm of the natural sciences. A paradigm is not merely a framework of terms and theories within which the inquiry occurs; it also prescribes how the object is to be viewed, which methodological procedure will be chosen, and which results count as acceptable knowledge about the object (Kuhn, 1970).

The questions that are most important in biology are questions of causation. There are two types of causation questions concerning homosexuality (Weinrich, 1987). The first one asks how an individual becomes homosexual. This search for causation is the approach taken by neuroendocrinological and brain researchers. Such studies primarily focus on the etiology of homosexuality, and not on the etiology of heterosexuality. They regard homosexuality as a biological aberration calling for explanation. The second type of causation asks why certain individuals become homosexual. It is concerned with the evolutionary mechanisms that have led to the development of homosexuality. Homosexuality in this sociobiological understanding is seen as a natural strategy of genes and not as an aberration.

Causal explanations epitomize the problem of reductionism. At least two kinds of reductionism can be distinguished in science: methodological and epistemological. "Methodologically, reductionism is the practice of characterizing a system or process in terms of its smallest functional units" (Longino, 1990, p. 226). Living organisms are too complex to understand as a whole. Therefore in the search for the biological basis of homosexuality, it is considered to be legitimate and necessary to observe the smallest organizational units.

"Ontological reductionism argues that those smallest functional units are what is real and that all causal processes can ultimately be understood as a function of interactions among these least bits" (Longino, 1990, p. 226). This second form of reductionism is precisely what lies at the heart of every essentialist position. It assumes that homosexuality is produced by a basic biological process and that homosexual identity, desire, and behavior are its natural and direct results. Ontological reductionism as a mode of explanation in

biological research on sexuality leads to an impoverished understanding of the natural world (Birke, 1986). To define complex
sexual systems (e.g., individuals or cultures) in terms of biological
units suggests that they are qualitatively little more than the totality
of those units.

When homosexuality is reduced to a solely biological phenomenon, such things as desire and attraction are merely functions of
biological circumstances. The traditional but questionable distinction between explaining and understanding as two different ways of
knowing, with explaining assumed to be specific to the natural
sciences, understanding specific to the humanities (Wright, 1971),
is still perpetuated in biological research on homosexuality (Haumann, 1992b). As long as this remains unchanged, a truly interdisciplinary approach to homosexuality will not be possible.

Reductionism always implies a high degree of determinism (see,
e.g., Barnett, 1988). All behavioral, individual, and cultural expressions of homosexuality are thought to be more or less determined
by biological factors. To contend that they are not directly determined, but rather predisposed by biology is no less deterministic.
Central to determinism is a linear model of causality which insists
on chains of causes running from molecular events right up to
human behavior and social organization (cf. Birke, 1981, 1986;
Doell & Longino, 1988; Ruse, 1988). By that means, determinism
can serve as a very powerful instrument in ideological discussions
(Lewontin, Rose, & Kamin, 1984).

The final point in the research process at which ideologies play a
crucial role is evidential reasoning. This is the cognitive practice in
science that mediates between data and hypotheses. Helen Longino
(1990) points out,

> that evidential reasoning is always context-dependent, that
> data are evidence for a hypothesis only in light of background
> assumptions that assert a connection between the sorts of thing
> or event the data are and the processes or states of affairs
> described by the hypotheses. Background assumptions can
> also lead us to highlight certain aspects of a phenomenon over
> others, thus determining the way it is described and the kind of
> data it provides. Background assumptions are the means by

which contextual values and ideology are incorporated into scientific inquiry. (pp. 215-216)

To sum up, we have to recognize that even strict adherence to the rules of scientific procedure does not nullify the impact of ideologies on scientific research.

IDEOLOGIES: FROM SOCIETY TO NATURE AND BACK AGAIN

Science, as a system of knowledge production, is a social practice inseparable from its specific historical and cultural surroundings. Ideologies influence the scientific process from its very beginning and shape the theories resulting from it. Biological studies on homosexuality, in particular, are heavily influenced by ideologies. These are powerful, unreflected patterns of looking at and thinking about sexuality that are bound to culture and interests.

There is a basic ideological mechanism which propagates mutual dependency between science and society–a process of projection and reflection (cf. Topitsch, 1988). When studying supposedly natural phenomena like homosexuality, the natural world with its confusing complexity is never viewed in a "neutral" way but only through the perspective of a specific culture. Even the description of the unknown and new is always made in terms of the known and common. The ideologies which organize and structure our sexuality in society also organize our view of sexuality in the natural world.

This means that the way we customarily see sexuality in society is the basis of an interpretative pattern for sexuality in nature. Constitutive elements of that sociosexual order are, for instance, the dualistic concepts of sex and gender. Their application as descriptive and interpretative categories to natural matters implies that the natural order is identical to the social order. The very way we look at nature is a culturally constrained act. Only by imposing social ideologies onto nature, can biologists speak of "gay genes," "homosexual rats," or "male" and "female" sex hormones. Natural sexuality is constructed through "sociomorphous interpretations" (Topitsch, 1988) of nature, that is, through a projection from society to nature.

This is one part of the ideological mechanism. The second can be called reflection. Having claimed, for example, that nature herself is differentiated into male and female or that animals can be homosexual, it can be further asserted that human sexuality is largely grounded in biology. This reflection from nature back to society is informed by "biomorphous interpretations" (Topitsch, 1988) of the social organization. Such appeals to a natural state can be, and in fact are, used to reinforce or legitimate the social and ideological *status quo.*

PROJECTIONS:
THE SOCIOMORPHOUS VIEW OF NATURE

Key Concepts

The biological discourse on homosexuality commonly relies on a set of terms whose use is so widespread that their meanings are no longer questioned. These concepts are reduced to key words (Williams, 1976) that presumably have a clear-cut meaning. A closer look, however, reveals that these words have a variety of different and often contradictory meanings. Their meanings are so indeterminate that they can be used in almost any discursive context. For example, consider such words as *sexuality, homosexuality, nature, sexual drive, sexual attraction, sex, gender,* and *sexual intercourse.* Their specific meanings have to be inferred from the context in which they occur. Nevertheless, they have a strong persuasive effect in the biological discourse because they seem to have exact and unequivocal meanings.

The most problematic terms in biological research on homosexuality are *sexuality* and *homosexuality.* Sexuality has been perceived as an essential and real category. The practice of defining human beings and structuring society through "sexuality" is not a universal phenomenon but a modern one, not older than two hundred years (see, e.g., Dannecker, 1991; Davidson, 1987; Foucault, 1978; Padgug, 1979).

The use of the term "sexuality" in biology is based on two ideological notions, both of which are important for the biological conceptualization of homosexuality. The first one, I will call the sexuality-as-heterosexuality ideology. It underlies most of the research on the neuroendocrinological basis of homosexuality. Inasmuch as heterosexual behavior is supposed to be the universal, normal form of sexual expression, heterosexuality is more or less equated with sexuality. Homosexuality is conceptualized as the aberration that calls for special attention. Heterosexuality is the "natural" category which needs no biological explanation.

In his critical examination of biomedical theories of sexual orientation, Louis Gooren (1990, p. 85) concludes that, "Up to the present day, solid evidence of biological correlates of homosexuality is lacking." But even if the findings of biomedicine were as neutral as they seem to be, the underlying ideology of sexuality-as-heterosexuality retains a strong pathologizing character.

The categorical status of heterosexuality in our culture (cf. Rich, 1980; Jackson, 1989) has led to an imbalance between the treatment of heterosexuality and homosexuality. Unlike homosexuality, which has a very colorful history of construction, heterosexuality is little more than a pale negative-category. Because heterosexuality is conceived to be the norm, it is unnoticed and unmarked. "Heterosexual" plainly means "not homosexual," whereas the term "homosexual" is burdened with a host of meanings, assumptions, and theories. Biological research on homosexuality often evokes the idea that there *is* more to study about homosexuality than about heterosexuality.

The second major presupposition in biological research on homosexuality can be called the sexuality-as-reproduction ideology. It provides the paradigm for sociobiology. Sociobiologists do not distinguish between biologically normal and aberrant forms of sexuality. Instead, they try to regard every sexual expression as natural and evolved through natural selection (e.g., Rasa, Vogel, & Voland, 1989; Symons, 1979; Wilson, 1975). As Weinrich (1990, p. 127) puts it, "sociobiologists first look for what went right instead of what went wrong." Sexuality in this conception is a mere function of the reproductive urges of the genes. Homosexuality is viewed as one strategy for reproduction (see Ruse, 1981, 1988; Sommer, 1990; Weinrich, 1987). The adaptionist concept of sexuality with its reproduction ideology, although more liberal than the biomedical model, is also very questionable because of its obsession to trace every aspect of human sexuality back to nature (cf. Futuyma & Risch, 1983/1984). In this sense, it cannot escape the accusation of being deterministic, despite strenuous assertions by sociobiologists to the contrary (Weinrich, 1990).

Sexual Dualism

One of the most fundamental features of Western thought is its sexual dualism (Jordanova, 1989; Sedgwick, 1991) whereby our social world is divided into male and female, men and women, homosexuals and heterosexuals, and sexuals (adults) and asexuals (children). This dualism is one of a series of dichotomies that includes nature versus culture, reason versus emotion, public versus private, active versus passive, objective versus subjective, and so on. We tend to polarize phenomena and then regard them as mutually exclusive. Finally, hierarchical relations between the two poles are established, one being valued at the expense of the other. For instance, male is superior to female and heterosexual superior to homosexual. Differences become polarities which, in turn, become hierarchies (Jay, 1981).

This dualistic sexual system is projected onto nature and serves as a basic interpretative pattern in biology (cf. Spanier, 1991). In our everyday experience, if we view social order as sexually dimorphic, we will presume that the natural order also consists of a sexually dimorphic scheme. Hence, even biological entities below the organizational level of the individual (e.g., bacteria, genes, hormones, or brain regions) are considered as male or female. (For critical reviews see, e.g., Fausto-Sterling, 1985; Oudshoorn, 1991; Spanier, 1991; Wijngaard, 1991).

The ideology of the dualistic sexual system is rooted so deeply in our social life that we take it for granted. But there is already a lot of anthropological evidence that there have been cultures that had three, or more, sex and gender categories (cf. Blackwood, 1986; Herdt, 1987, 1990; Ortner & Whitehead, 1981; Williams, 1986). Their sexual view of nature was probably very different from ours.

But the history of Western culture also supplies examples of alternative sexual and gender systems (see Epstein & Straub, 1991). According to Randolph Trumbach (1991), the notion that there are two biological sexes began to predominate in Western culture in the eighteenth century. Before that, it was held that there are three biological sexes: man, woman, and hermaphrodite. But even the status of the categories "man" and "woman" and their relation to each other was fluid, as Thomas Laqueur (1990) has shown. Laqueur has documented how our two-sex model, woman being the opposite of man, developed out of a one-sex (male) model.

Finally, the third-sex theories by Ulrichs (1898; see also Kennedy, 1988) and Hirschfeld (1914) are examples, too, of alternative sexual systems although they never gained much popularity within the dominant culture of the time. Nevertheless, they regarded homosexuals as the *biological* representatives of a third category.

Gender Inversions

The ideology of sexual dualism, comprised of male and female as two mutually exclusive categories, is an essential part of our ideological order. The underlying idea is that only male and female can attract each other while male and male or female and female are incompatible. A sexual interaction between two individuals of the same sex is obviously a threat to such a sexual order. To repulse this threat and to preserve this order, individuals who engage in homosexual activities must be considered misrepresentative of the sex to which they seem to belong. They are believed to lack characteristics of their sex and to exhibit characteristics of the opposite sex. Such thinking lies at the heart of the concept of inversion, a powerful ideology that shapes much of the theorizing on homosexuality in biology. But homosexuality and sexual inversion are distinguishable conceptually. As C. A. Tripp (1987, p. 20) puts it, "homosexuality refers to any sexual activity between members of the same sex. Inversion, on the other hand, implies nothing about the sex of the partner; it refers to a reversal of the commonly expected gender-role of the individual, whether animal or human."

In popular understanding, homosexuality is equated with cross-gender behavior. The ideological power of gender inversion is greatest in societies with an almost total gender role separation. In Mediterranean and Latin-American countries, for example, it is cross-gender behavior, especially men acting in a "feminine" way, that is much more stigmatized socially than a same-sex interaction (see Almaguer, 1991; Dall'Orto, 1990; Parker, 1986).

Although a conceptual shift has taken place in Western society since the turn of the century "from sexual inversion to homosexuality" (Chauncey, 1982/1983), the inversion ideology still dominates biological theorizing. The idea of masculine and feminine behavior as markers of sexual orientation is also applied in animal research. The theoretical confusions and inconsistencies caused by the conflation of sexual behavior and gender choice were addressed by Beach (1979). He noted that the term *homosexual* in animal research is used with two different meanings: (1) as a description of individual animals which show a behavioral pattern typical for the opposite sex, and (2) as a description of individual animals which show heterosexual behavior but do so in response to a partner of the same sex. The first meaning is clearly an instance of the inversion ideology projected onto nature. It serves as an "ideal" model for the biological understanding of human homosexuality (Birke, 1981; Ricketts, 1984).

The notion of homosexuality as inappropriate maleness or femaleness is very often employed in the use of animal models in endocrinology. A male rat exhibiting lordosis is called homosexual, regardless of the sex of "his" partner; likewise, a female rat exhibiting mounting behavior is called homosexual, regardless of the sex of "her" partner (Dörner, 1976). Following this argument, we arrive at an absurdity that is described by Ricketts (1984) on the basis of an experiment by Dörner and Hinz (1968) as follows: "In one experiment, demasculinized, lordotic male rats were caged with androgenized, aroused female rats. The 'homosexual' females mounted the 'homosexual' males with the result that each animal managed to behave both heterosexually (by the criterion of partner choice) and homosexually (by the criterion of sexually dimorphic mating behavior) at exactly the same moment" (Ricketts, 1984, p. 85).

But often, biology projects the inversion ideology directly onto human nature, as history shows. Originating from the early, psychological theories of sexual inversion (Ellis, 1915; Freud, 1962; for review see Chauncey, 1982/1983), biomedicine soon applied the gender-based concept of homosexuality to the whole body, thereby making it a central paradigm in biological research. Jennifer Terry

(1990) critically examined studies, conducted in the 1930s, which sought to determine physical characteristics distinguishing lesbians from heterosexual women. Although the findings were inconclusive, the studies purported to support the inversion theory. The theory, moreover, was so strongly held that "any signs of 'femininity' in [lesbians] created confusion among the researchers. When these signs did appear, they were often discounted by researchers as elements of masquerade covering over more masculine essences" (Terry, 1990, p. 322).

The association of biological femininity with male homosexuality and biological masculinity with female homosexuality remains an influential presupposition (De Cecco, 1987). This is particularly true for the fields of neuroendocrinology and brain research. Dörner (1988a, 1988b) considers male homosexuality as "feminization of sexual orientation" and as "heterotypical" or "female-type sexual behavior." (A conceptual distinction between homosexual *orientation* and *behavior* is always lacking.) According to the neuroendocrinological hypothesis, homosexuals have prenatally undergone a hormonally induced, sexual differentiation of the brain that is typical for the opposite sex. Consequently, homosexual men have a "female hypothalamus" (Dörner, 1988a; Gladue, Green, & Hellman, 1984). Although subsequent researchers could not confirm this hypothesis, they did find evidence that another part of the hypothalamus, the suprachiasmatic nucleus, is larger in homosexual men than in heterosexual men and women (Swaab & Hofman, 1990; Byne, this volume). Recently, LeVay (1991) has gained notoriety with his claim that INAH 3, another area of hypothalamic nuclei, is about equal in size in homosexual men and heterosexual women, whereas it is more than twice as large in heterosexual men. As inconclusive or preliminary as these findings may be, they remain unchallenged.

Occasionally, the reference to the inversion ideology is explicit. In an article on the biological basis of homosexuality, Ellis and Ames (1987) boldly extend its applicability when they state that "inversion can involve any of the four phenotypic dimensions of sex: the genital dimension, the nongenital morphological dimension, the neurological dimension, and the behavioral dimension" (Ellis & Ames, 1987, p. 251). The notion of homosexuality as sexual and gender inversion, thus, remains a dominating explanatory pattern in the biological study of homosexuality.

REFLECTIONS:
THE BIOMORPHOUS VIEW OF SOCIETY

Ideologies which have been projected onto nature and which have become an integral element of biological knowledge are also reflected back onto society. That is, once they have acquired the status of biological facts, they serve as a reference point for further interpretations. This reflection from biology to society can best be called a biomorphic view of human sexuality. Its implicit assumption is that we first must look at the sexual order in nature in order to be able to understand the sexual order in society.

Since biological theories conceptualize homosexuality as a natural phenomenon first and foremost, they appear as totally unpolitical and socially neutral. This apolitical stance not only hides their ideological content but also renders them accessible to political abuse. By hypothesizing biological differences between homosexuals and heterosexuals, biological theories reinforce and legitimate the existing order without ever having questioned its validity. Biology, actually, produces and reproduces politics of sexual difference. As Wendell Ricketts (1984, p. 90) puts it, "No one knows exactly why heterosexuals and homosexuals ought to be different, and the blatant tautology of the hypotheses appears to have escaped careful attention: Heterosexuals and homosexuals are considered different because they can be divided into two groups on the basis of the belief that they can be divided into two groups."

But even if clear evidence for such difference could be found, there would still be the issue of the political significance ascribed to them (cf. Lewontin, Rose, & Kamin, 1984). What should follow politically from the presumption that homosexuals and heterosexuals differ in a particular biological character? The answer can only be: Nothing. Nevertheless, the temptation to commit a naturalistic fallacy is great (Sommer, 1990). Biological theories have often been used as instruments for political interests. The effort to contribute to the emancipation of gays and lesbians by scientifically "proving" their "naturalness" is illusory since the same facts can also be used to characterize homosexuality as a biological anomaly. The reliance on biology as a basis for both identity formation and political activism is a very tricky issue that warrants critical examination (Cohen, 1991). Does society require biological data in order to be tolerant of homosexuals as Ernulf, Innala, and Whitam (1989) suggest? And does the gay and lesbian movement really need biology in order to be effective?

Gay and lesbian liberation by science remains a risky, double-edged business. We must not forget that Hirschfeld's famous motto "Per scientiam ad justitiam" (through science to justice) failed to reach its aim since the political opponents in that time also used biological "facts" to enforce their reactionary program (see Jellonnek, 1990; Schmidt, 1984; Schoppmann, 1991).

The connection between homosexuality and biomedicine has a long and eventful tradition which persists to this day. Unfortunately, it has never really benefitted gays and lesbians (cf. Schmidt, 1984).

CONCLUSIONS

Like all systems for producing knowledge about homosexuality, biology is dependent on a sociocultural context. The recognition that the biological study of homosexuality is, to a great extent, culturally biased, does not simply dismiss biological research on homosexuality; nor does it impute an unavoidable link between biological explanation and political conservatism (Benton, 1984). However, biological research on homosexuality could be based on a different ideological foundation. Feminist biologists, for example, have already demonstrated in a number of works that the adoption of a critical feminist point of view can give rise to biological knowledge on sex and gender that is, indeed, different from the traditional patriarchal and masculinist theories (see, e.g., Birke, 1986; Bleier, 1984; Fausto-Sterling, 1985; Harding, 1986; Keller, 1985). Their works convincingly show that new questions lead to new answers. Feminist biology destroys the myth of pure and objective biological knowledge. It shows that a different ideological point of view can be of heuristic value, and further shows that such a point of view can have an important regulative function politically.

But what could a different point of view of research on homosexuality look like? The conventional concept of sexual inversion, for instance, relies on the belief that homosexuality has to be interpreted in terms of gender inversion and sexual dualism. However, homosexuality in the gay/lesbian culture of modern Europe and North America is much more characterized by a transformation from gender-structured relations to relations in which both partners are alike in terms of gender, behavior, identity, and age. From that cultural background it is clearly not the case that "naturally" only males and females attract each other or that reproduction is the primary natural purpose of sexual activity. Biological knowledge of homosexuality based on such a cultural background would differ from conventional theories.

The perspective taken in this paper challenges the notion that biology is politically neutral and that sexual theory and sexual ideology are totally distinct (see also Irvine, 1990). Since "nature can show us nearly everything we wish to see" (Spanier, 1991, p. 335), we should remain very cautious about the claim that biology is the foundation and rationale of the social order. Biological knowledge of homosexuality obtains its legitimacy from science and its relevance from political ideology, but we must not forget that both science *and* ideology participate in its production.

REFERENCES

Almaguer, T. (1991). Chicano men: A cartography of homosexual identity and behavior. *Differences: A Journal of Feminist Cultural Studies, 3*(2), 75-100.

Barnett, S. A. (1988). *Biology and freedom. An essay on the implications of human ethology.* Cambridge: Cambridge University Press.

Beach, F. A. (1979). Animal models for human sexuality. In R. Porter & J. Whelen (Eds.), *Sex, hormones and behavior* (pp. 113-143). Ciba Foundation Symposium, 62. Amsterdam: Excerpta Medica.

Benton, T. (1984). Biological ideas and their cultural use. In S. C. Brown (Ed.), *Objectivity and cultural divergence* (pp. 111-133). Cambridge: Cambridge University Press.

Birke, L. (1981). Is homosexuality hormonally determined? *Journal of Homosexuality, 6*(4), 35-49.

Birke, L. (1986). *Women, feminism and biology: The feminist challenge.* Brighton: Harvester.

Blackwood, E. (Ed.). (1986). *Anthropology and homosexual behavior.* New York: The Haworth Press, Inc.

Bleier, R. (1984). *Science and gender: A critique of biology and its theories on women.* New York: Pergamon Press.

Byne, W., & Parsons, B. (1993). Human sexual orientation: The biologic theories reappraised. *Archives of General Psychiatry, 50,* 228-239.

Chauncey, G. (1982/1983). From sexual inversion to homosexuality: Medicine and the changing conceptualization of female deviance. *Salmagundi, 58-59,* 114-146.

Cohen, E. (1991). Who are "we"? Gay "identity" as political (e)motion (A theoretical rumination). In D. Fuss (Ed.), *Inside/out: Lesbian theories, gay theories* (pp. 71-92). New York: Routledge.

Dall'Orto, G. (1990). Mediterranean homosexuality. In W. R. Dynes (Ed.), *Encyclopedia of homosexuality* (pp. 796-798). New York: Garland.

Dannecker, M. (1991). Sexualität als Gegenstand der Sexualforschung. *Zeitschrift für Sexualforschung, 4,* 281-293.

Davidson, A. (1987). Sex and the emergence of sexuality. *Critical Inquiry, 14,* 16-48.

De Cecco, J. (1987). Homosexuality's brief recovery: From sickness to health and back again. *Journal of Sex Research, 23*(1), 106-114.

Doell, R. G., & Longino, H. E. (1988). Sex hormones and human behavior: A critique of the linear model. *Journal of Homosexuality, 15*(3/4), 55-78.

Dörner, G. (1976). *Hormones and brain differentiation.* Amsterdam: Elsevier.

Dörner, G. (1988a). Neuroendocrine response to estrogen and brain differentiation in heterosexuals, homosexuals, and transsexuals. *Archives of Sexual Behavior, 17*(1), 57-75.

Dörner, G. (1988b). Sexual endocrinology and terminology in sexology. *Experimental and Clinical Endocrinology, 91,* 129-134.

Dörner, G., & Hinz, G. (1968). Induction and prevention of male homosexuality by androgen. *Journal of Endocrinology, 40,* 387-388.

Ellis, H. (1915). *Sexual Inversion* (3rd ed.). Studies in the psychology of sex, vol. 2. Philadelphia: Davis.

Ellis, L., & Ames, M. A. (1987). Neurohormonal functioning and sexual orientation: A theory of homosexuality-heterosexuality. *Psychological Bulletin, 101,* 233-258.

Epstein, J., & Straub, K. (Eds.). (1991). *Body guards: The cultural politics of gender ambiguity.* New York: Routledge.

Ernulf, K. E., Innala, S. M., & Whitam, F. L. (1989). Biological explanation, psychological explanation, and tolerance of homosexuals: A cross-national analysis of beliefs and attitudes. *Psychological Reports, 65,* 1003-1010.

Fausto-Sterling, A. (1985). *Myths of gender: Biological theories about women and men.* New York: Basic Books.

Feyerabend, P. (1975). *Against method: Outline of an anarchistic theory of knowledge.* London: New Left Books.

Foucault, M. (1978). *The history of sexuality: Vol. 1. An introduction.* New York: Pantheon.

Freud, S. (1962). *Three essays on the theory of sexuality.* New York: Basic Books. (Originally published 1905.)

Friedman, R. C., & Downey, J. (1993). Neurobiology and sexual orientation: Current relationships. *The Journal of Neuropsychiatry and Clinical Neurosciences, 5,* 131-153.

Futuyma, D. J., & Risch, S. J. (1983/1984). Sexual orientation, sociobiology, and evolution. *Journal of Homosexuality, 9(2/3),* 157-168.

Gladue, B. A., Green, R., & Hellman, R. E. (1984). Neuroendocrine response to estrogen and sexual orientation. *Science, 225,* 1496-1499.

Gooren, L. (1990). Biomedical theories of sexual orientation: A critical examination. In D. P. McWhirter, S. A. Sanders, & J. M. Reinisch (Eds.), *Homosexuality/heterosexuality: Concepts of sexual orientation* (pp. 71-87). New York: Oxford University Press.

Hamer, D. H., Hu, S., Magnuson, V. L., Hu, N., & Pattatucci, A. M. L. (1993). A linkage between DNA markers on the X chromosome and male sexual orientation. *Science, 261,* 321-327.

Harding, S. (1986). *The science question in feminism.* Ithaca: Cornell University Press.

Harding, S., & O'Barr, J. F. (Eds.). (1987). *Sex and scientific inquiry.* Chicago: University of Chicago Press.

Haumann, G. (1992a, July). *Ideologiekritik und Ethik sexualwissenschaftlicher Erkenntnis.* Paper presented at the IV. International Berlin Conference for Sexology, Berlin, FRG.

Haumann, G. (1992b). Paradigmenwechsel oder Theorienpluralismus? Tendenzen der Homosexualitätsforschung. *Sexus, 1/2,* pp. 4-13.

Hekma, G. (1987). *Homoseksualiteit, een medische reputatie: De uitdoktering van de homoseksueel in negentiende-eeuws Nederland.* Amsterdam: SUA.

Hempel, C. G. (1966). *Philosophy of natural science.* Englewood Cliffs, NJ: Prentice-Hall.

Herdt, G. (1987). *The Sambia: Ritual and gender in New Guinea.* New York: Holt, Rinehart, & Winston.

Herdt, G. (1990). Mistaken gender: 5-alpha reductase hermaphroditism and biological reductionism in sexual identity reconsidered. *American Anthropologist, 92,* 433-446.

Hirschfeld, M. (1914). *Die Homosexualität des Mannes und des Weibes.* Berlin: Louis Marcus.

Irvine, J. M. (1990). *Disorders of desire: Sex and gender in modern American sexology.* Philadelphia: Temple University Press.

Jackson, M. (1989). "Facts of life" or the erotization of women's oppression? Sexology and the social construction of heterosexuality. In P. Caplan (Ed.), *The cultural construction of sexuality* (pp. 52-81). London: Routledge.

Jay, N. (1981). Gender and dichotomy. *Feminist Studies, 7(1),* 38-56.

Jellonnek, B. (1990). *Homosexuelle unter dem Hakenkreuz: Die Verfolgung von Homosexuellen im Dritten Reich.* Paderborn: Schöningh.

Jordanova, L. (1989). *Sexual visions: Images of gender in science and medicine between the eighteenth and twentieth centuries.* New York: Harvester Wheatsheaf.

Katz, J. N. (1983). *Gay/lesbian almanac*. New York: Harper & Row.

Keller, E. F. (1985). *Reflections on gender and science*. New Haven: Yale University Press.

Kennedy, H. (1988). *Ulrichs: The life and works of Karl Heinrich Ulrichs, pioneer of the modern gay movement*. Boston: Alyson.

Kuhn, T. S. (1970). *The structure of scientific revolutions* (2nd ed.). Chicago: University of Chicago Press.

Laqueur, T. (1990). *Making sex: Body and gender from the Greeks to Freud*. Cambridge: Harvard University Press.

LeVay, S. (1991). A difference in hypothalamic structure between heterosexual and homosexual men. *Science, 253*, 1034-1037.

Lewontin, R. C., Rose, S., & Kamin, L. J. (1984). *Not in our genes: Biology, ideology, and human nature*. New York: Pantheon.

Longino, H. E. (1990). *Science as social knowledge: Values and objectivity in scientific inquiry*. Princeton, NJ: Princeton University Press.

Müller, K. (1991). *Aber in meinem Herzen sprach eine Stimme so laut: Homosexuelle Autobiographien und medizinische Pathographien im neunzehnten Jahrhundert*. Berlin: rosa Winkel.

Ortner, S., & Whitehead, H. (Eds.). (1981). *Sexual meanings*. New York: Cambridge University Press.

Oudshoorn, N. (1991). *The making of the hormonal body: A conceptual history of the study of sex hormones 1923-1940*. Enschede: Alfa.

Padgug, R. (1979). Sexual matters: On conceptualizing sexuality in history. *Radical History Review, 20*, 3-23.

Parker, R. (1986). Masculinity, femininity, and homosexuality. In E. Blackwood (Ed.), *Anthropology and homosexual behavior* (pp. 155-163). New York: The Haworth Press, Inc.

Popper, K. R. (1962). *Conjectures and refutations*. London: Routledge & Kegan Paul.

Rasa, A. E., Vogel, C., & Voland, E. (Eds.). (1989). *The sociobiology of sexual and reproductive strategies*. London: Chapman & Hall.

Rich, A. (1980). Compulsory heterosexuality and lesbian existence. *Signs: Journal of Women in Culture and Society, 5*, 631-660.

Ricketts, W. (1984). Biological research on homosexuality: Ansell's cow or Occam's razor? *Journal of Homosexuality, 9*(4), 65-93.

Ruse, M. (1981). Are there gay genes? Sociobiology and homosexuality. *Journal of Homosexuality, 6*(4), 5-34.

Ruse, M. (1988). *Homosexuality: A philosophical inquiry*. New York: Basic Blackwell.

Salamun, K. (1988). *Ideologie und Aufklärung: Weltanschauungstheorie und Politik*. Vienna: Böhlau.

Schmidt, G. (1984). Allies and persecutors: Science and medicine in the homosexuality issue. *Journal of Homosexuality, 10*(3/4), 127-140.

Schoppmann, C. (1991). *Nationalsozialistische Sexualpolitik und weibliche Homosexualität*. Pfaffenweiler: Centaurus.

Sedgwick, E. K. (1991). *Epistemology of the closet.* New York: Harvester Wheatsheaf.

Sommer, V. (1990). *Wider die Natur? Homosexualität und Evolution.* Munich: C. H. Beck.

Spanier, B. B. (1991). "Lessons" from "nature": Gender ideology and sexual ambiguity in biology. In J. Epstein & K. Straub (Eds.), *Body guards: The cultural politics of gender ambiguity* (pp. 329-350). New York: Routledge.

Stein, E. (Ed.). (1990). *Forms of desire: Sexual orientation and the social construction controversy.* New York: Garland.

Swaab, D. F., & Hofman, M. A. (1990). An enlarged suprachiasmatic nucleus in homosexual men. *Brain Research, 537,* 141-148.

Symons, D. (1979). *The evolution of human sexuality.* New York: Oxford University Press.

Terry, J. (1990). Lesbians under the medical gaze: Scientists search for remarkable differences. *The Journal of Sex Research, 27*(3), 317-339.

Tiefer, L. (1990). Social constructionism and the study of human sexuality. In E. Stein (Ed.), *Forms of desire: Sexual orientation and the social construction controversy* (pp. 295-324). New York: Garland.

Tiefer, L. (1991). Sexualwissenschaft und die Beschwörung des Natürlichen. *Zeitschrift für Sexualforschung, 4,* 97-108.

Topitsch, E. (1988). *Erkenntnis und Illusion: Grundstrukturen unserer Weltauffassung* (2nd, rev. ed.). Tübingen: Mohr.

Tripp, C. A. (1987). *The homosexual matrix* (2nd ed.). New York: Meridian.

Trumbach, R. (1991). London's sapphists: From three sexes to four genders in the making of modern culture. In J. Epstein & K. Straub (Eds.), *Body guards: The cultural politics of gender ambiguity* (pp. 112-141). New York: Routledge.

Ulrichs, K. H. (1898). *Forschungen über das Rätsel der mannmännlichen Liebe,* ed. M. Hirschfeld. Leipzig: Spohr. (Reprint New York: Arno Press, 1975.)

Weinrich, J. D. (1987). *Sexual landscapes: Why we are what we are, why we love whom we love.* New York: Charles Scribner's Sons.

Weinrich, J. D. (1990). The Kinsey scale in biology, with a note on Kinsey as a biologist. In D. P. McWhirter, S. A. Sanders, & J. M. Reinisch (Eds.), *Homosexuality/heterosexuality: Concepts of sexual orientation* (pp. 115-137). New York: Oxford University Press.

Wijngaard, M. van den (1991). *Reinventing the sexes: Feminism and biomedical construction of femininity and masculinity 1959-1985.* Delft: Eburon.

Williams, R. (1976). *Keywords: A vocabulary of culture and society.* New York: Oxford University Press.

Williams, W. (1986). *The spirit and the flesh: Sexual diversity in American Indian culture.* Boston: Beacon Press.

Wilson, E. O. (1975). *Sociobiology: The new synthesis.* Cambridge, MA: Harvard University Press.

Wright, G. H. von (1971). *Explanation and understanding.* Ithaca: Cornell University Press.

Female or Male:
The Classification
of Homosexuality and Gender

Nelly Oudshoorn, PhD

University of Amsterdam

SUMMARY. During this century the issue of homosexuality has been a recurrent theme on the research agenda of biologists. Historically, the life sciences have conceptualized homosexuals as persons with characteristics of the opposite sex. This paper discusses how the discourse on homosexuality became entangled with the discourse on gender.

Why should it not be conceivable that nature, in its variability, takes a different approach in some individuals so that, with regard to the body, it lets the male 'anlage' develop but not the

Nelly Oudshoorn is Assistant Professor of Science and Technology Studies at the University of Amsterdam.

Correspondence may be addressed: University of Amsterdam, Department of Science and Technology Dynamics, Nieuwe Achtergracht 166, 1018 WV Amsterdam, The Netherlands.

A more extended version of this paper has been published in *Die Experimentalisierung des Lebens. Experimentalsysteme in den biologischen Wissenschaften 1850/1950,* ed. Hans-Jörg Reinberger & Michael Hagner (Berlin: Akademie Verlag, 1993).

[Haworth co-indexing entry note]: "Female or Male: The Classification of Homosexuality and Gender." Oudshoorn, Nelly. Co-published simultaneously in *Journal of Homosexuality* (The Haworth Press, Inc.) Vol. 28, No. 1/2, 1995, pp. 79-86; and: *Sex, Cells, and Same-Sex Desire: The Biology of Sexual Preference* (ed: John P. De Cecco, and David Allen Parker) The Haworth Press, Inc., 1995, pp. 79-86. Multiple copies of this article/chapter may be purchased from The Haworth Document Delivery Center [1-800-3-HAWORTH; 9:00 a.m. - 5:00 p.m. (EST)].

female 'anlage' while, with regard to the mind, it lets the female 'anlage' develop in all its tendencies but not the male 'anlage,' thus allowing the 'anlage' of femininity to develop in terms of softness of character, occupational interests, mannerisms, and particularly, the direction of the sexual love drive toward men? (Ulrichs, 1862)

During this century, homosexuality has been a recurrent theme of biomedical researchers. The biomedical discourse on homosexuality can be traced back to the last decades of the nineteenth century. Remarkably, the idea that homosexuality is biological does not originate with biologists or physicians; rather, it was first introduced by a lawyer, Carl Heinrich Ulrichs, in the 1860s. Ulrichs suggested that homosexuality might be understood in terms of a duality between the body and the mind (i.e., a female soul in a male body) (Meyer-Bahlburg,1984).[1]

Biologists translated Ulrichs's idea into a concept of sexual duality that is biologically based. Homosexuals were conceptualized as persons with characteristics of the opposite sex. This idea has been the concept guiding the research on homosexuality in the biomedical sciences since the turn of this century. The search for cross-sexed characteristics initially centered on external physical attributes (e.g., the shape of the chest and muscles, and the breadth of the shoulders and pelvis). Characteristics that were considered typically masculine or feminine were measured and categorized, but no evidence could be found to support the notion that homosexuals have such cross-sexed attributes (Meyer-Bahlburg,1984).

Following the emergence of the new research fields of genetics and endocrinology, the medical researchers began studying internal parts of the body. Their search for biological bases of homosexuality focussed on sex chromosomes and sex hormones. The most recent biological theory locates homosexuality in the brain: homosexual men are described as having a "female" brain and homosexual women, a "male" brain (Dörner, 1976). The debate on homosexuality by lawyers and sexologists and the categorization of gender by sex endocrinologists in the early decades of this century are crucial points in the history of the biomedical sciences for understanding how the classification systems of homosexuality and gender became entangled.

THE CLASSIFICATION OF HOMOSEXUALITY

In the late nineteenth century lawyers and sexologists campaigned against a section of the German penal code that made homosexual acts punishable by law, arguing that homosexuality was biologically based and should not be illegal.[2] Influential sexologists, such as Richard v. Krafft-Ebing, Havelock Ellis, and Magnus Hirschfeld, classified homosexuality as congenital and suggested that "nobody can be morally blamed for having such a disposition" (Hirschfeld, 1899). Prior to the approach of these sexologists, psychiatrists classified homosexuality as a pathological state of moral depravity that could be traced to childhood sexual abuse. Sexologists refuted these claims and turned to the life sciences to describe homosexuality.

The sexologists' reliance on the life sciences was, however, not politically successful. Their argument for legal equality for homosexuals was based on the claims that the bases of sexual preference are biological. A minority of progressive German politicians supported their position, but were not successful in changing the penal code. The majority opposed the change, arguing that homosexuality could not be natural "since otherwise Nature would have put homosexuality to the service of procreation and the maintenance of the species" (Deutscher Reichstag, 1905).

Early sexologists were more successful in the scientific arena. They developed criteria that became the building blocks of the life sciences' classification of homosexuality for more than eight decades. Elaborating on Ulrichs's ideas of homosexuality, Magnus Hirschfeld proposed a theory which conceptualized homosexuals as an intermediate gender state between the extremes of complete maleness and complete femaleness. According to this theory, homosexual men and women were physically male or female, but had sexual and emotional attributes of the opposite sex. Hirschfeld's theory classified homosexuals as a third gender and gave rise to a classification system of homosexuality that was intertwined with the classification of gender.

THE CLASSIFICATION OF GENDER

In 1916, Eugen Steinach, a Viennese anatomist, reported that he produced hermaphroditic animals by transplanting gonads from one to the other gender. Steinach referred to Hirschfeld when reflecting on his animal experiments, stating: "Homosexuality can also be ascribed to the existence of a hermaphrodite pubertal gland, just as Hirschfeld rightly postulated when he talked about the congenital disposition of the homosexual" (Steinach, 1916). Steinach suggested that the testicles of homosexual males contained "deviated cells" which he called "F-cells" and which had a "feminizing or homosexual-making" effect (Lichtenstern, 1920). Steinach's experiments did not remain restricted to animals. He performed the first surgical operation in which testicular tissue was transplanted from a heterosexual into a homosexual man. Medical records indicate that at least 11 men underwent the "Steinach operation" between 1916 and 1921 (Schmidt, 1984). Hirschfeld actually collaborated by referring some of his patients to surgeons who performed this operation.

These experiments inextricably linked the classification system of homosexuality with the classification of gender and launched the life sciences' search for biological markers of femininity and masculinity in homosexuals. The then emerging field of sex endocrinology introduced the concept of male and female sex hormones as chemical agents that control masculinity and femininity. This concept of sex hormones led to important changes in classification practices and to a shift from a primarily descriptive to a more experimental approach. As a function of hormonal levels, gender could be measured, quantified, and manipulated by means of laboratory techniques. This made it possible to abandon the rigorous dualistic classification of gender in favor of one in which all organisms can have feminine as well as masculine characteristics.[3]

With this quantitative theory, the endocrinologists introduced a new classification of gender. In the earlier definitions, individuals could be classified into one of the three categories on the basis of their genitals: (1) as male, (2) as female, or (3) as hermaphrodite. With this model, endocrinologists constructed a classification of gender in which individuals could vary from "a virile to effeminate male" or from "a masculine to a feminine female" as Robert Frank (1929) described it. The Dutch research group led by Laqueur described gender as follows: "The occurrence of the female hormone in the male body gives rise to many fantastic reflections . . . It is now proved that in each man there is something present that is inherent in the female sex. Whether we will succeed in determining the individual ratio of each man, in terms of a given percentage femininity, we don't know" (Borchardt et al., 1928).

TESTS FOR HOMOSEXUALITY

Early Laboratory Tests for Homosexuality in Animals

Sex endocrinologists also introduced laboratory tests to measure maleness and femaleness in animals. The female factor was measured with the vaginal smear test; the male factor with the comb test.[4]

The vaginal smear test traced cellular changes in ovariectomized mice induced by administration of female sex hormones. This test was considered to be revolutionary because it enabled researchers to infer what was happening in the internal reproductive organs without having to perform surgery. The changes in the vagina could be determined by examining smears of easily accessible cells under the microscope. Compared with other tests, the vaginal smear test had the advantage of being rapid and inexpensive. Other methods used in endocrinological research were based on time-consuming surgical interventions in experimental animals and were expensive because each experiment required a new animal (Frank, 1929).

The comb test for male homosexuality consisted of measuring comb size in castrated roosters before and after hormonal treatments. Laqueur and his co-workers at the University of Amsterdam introduced this method in which the silhouette of the comb was photographed and measured (Frank, 1929). Comb size was expected to increase in response to the administration of testosterone (a male hormone) or decrease with estrogen (a female hormone). The very choice of this test was one of the reasons why research on male sex hormones did not become current as fast as research on female sex hormones. It can easily be imagined that the keeping of roosters is inconvenient, particularly since most laboratories at the time had only limited space. Despite this disadvantage, the comb test was considered to be a rather convenient method because the test animals could be used several times and changes in comb size could easily be detected (Tausk, 1932).

Early Laboratory Tests for Homosexuality in Humans

In the 1930s, experimental techniques had advanced sufficiently to study hormones in humans. Early sex endocrinologists claimed that homosexuality was due to an endocrine imbalance. In 1935, Clifford Wright, a general practitioner in Los Angeles, described this conception of homosexuality as follows:

> All individuals are part male and part female, or bisexual, and this fact is substantiated by hormone assays in the urine. The urine of the normal man or woman shows the presence of hormones of both the male and female types (. . .) In the normal male, the male hormone predominates; in the normal female, the female hormone predominates. This, in my opinion, is the cause of normal sex attraction. In the homosexual the dominance is reversed. In the man there is a predominance of the female element and in the homosexual woman a dominance of the male factor. (Wright, 1938)

Sex endocrinologists now claimed to possess a scientific test to measure the "biological markers" of homosexuality.

These researchers classified homosexuality as a pathological condition that had to be "cured" by medical interventions. Soon after the first sex hormones were identified and synthesized, physicians began treating homosexuals with "sex appropriate" hormones in an attempt to make them heterosexual (Meyer-Bahlburg, 1984). In the 1930s and 1940s, there were numerous experiments in which male homosexuals were given male sex hormones. More recently (in the 1960s and 1970s) German neuro-surgeons claimed to be able to induce heterosexuality in homosexuals by removing parts of the hypothalamus which they called the "female sex center" (Schmidt, 1984).

CONCLUSIONS

A review of experimental practices enables us to understand how the discourse on homosexuality became entangled with the discourse on gender. Laboratory techniques tied together two different classification practices: that of the laboratory and that of sexologists. The introduction of laboratory tests in the early decades of this century resulted in a shift from a descriptive to an experimental model of homosexuality that was, and remains to this day, intertwined with gender.

NOTES

1. Historically, theories and research on homosexuality have focussed mainly on homosexual men rather than women.

2. For an extensive analysis of this episode, see Schmidt, 1984.

3. Following the debate on the sexually specific origin and function of sex hormones, that took place in the 1920s, sex endocrinologists had replaced their original assumption, that each gender could be recognized by its own sex hormone, by a model in which male and female sex hormones are present and functional in both genders. For a detailed analysis of this debate, see Oudshoorn, 1990.

4. These tests were accepted as standards at the Conferences on the Standardization of Sex Hormones that took place in London in the 1930s (Dale 1935a,1935b).

REFERENCES

Borchardt, E., Dingemanse, E., Jongh, S. E. de, Laqueur, E. (1928). Over het vrouwelijk geslachtshormoon Menformon, in het bijzonder over de anti-masculine werking. *Ned. Tijdschr. Geneesk.*: 1028.

Dale, H. H. (1935a). Conference on the Standardisation of Sex Hormones held at London on July 30th and August 1st 1932. *Quarterly Bulletin of the Health Organisation of the League of Nations, 4*, 121-128.

Dale, H. H. (1935b). Report of the Second Conference on the Standardisation of

Sex Hormones, held in London July 15th to 17th 1935. *Quarterly Bulletin of the Health Organisation of the League of Nations, 4*, 618-630.

Deutscher Reichstag (1905). Protokoll der Verhandlung, betreffend Änderung des Paragraphen 175 des Strafgesetzbuchs, vom 31. Mai 1905. (Reprinted in *Jahrbuch für sexuelle Zwischenstufen, 7*, 971-1037.)

Dörner, G. (1976). *Hormones and brain differentiation*. Amsterdam: Elsevier.

Frank, R. T. (1929). *The female sex hormone*. Springfield, IL, Baltimore, MD: Charles C Thomas Publishers.

Hirschfeld, M. (1899). Petition an die gesetzgebenden Körperschaften des Deutschen Reiches behufs Änderung des Paragraphen 175 des R.-Str.-G.-B. und die sich daran anschliessenden Reichstagsverhandlungen. *Jahrbuch für sexuelle Zwischenstufen, 1*, 239-280.

Lichtenstern, R. (1920). Bisherige Erfolge der Hodentransplantation beim Menschen. *Jahreskurse für ärtzliche Fortbildung, 11, Heft 4*, 8-11.

Meyer-Bahlburg, H. F. L. (1984). Psychoendocrine research on sexual orientation. Current status and future options. *Progress in Brain Research, 61*, 375-399.

Oudshoorn, N. (1990). Endocrinologists and the conceptualization of sex, 1920-1940. *Journal of the History of Biology, 23, no. 2*, 163-186.

Schmidt, G. (1984). Allies and persecutors: Science and medicine in the homosexuality issue. *Journal of Homosexuality, 10* (3/4), 127-141.

Steinach, E. (1916) Pubertätsdrüsen und Zwitterbildung. *Archiv für Entwicklungsdynamik, 42*, 307-332.

Tausk, M. (1932). Over een mannelijk geslachtshormoon. *Het Hormoon, 1*(7), 49-54.

Ulrichs, C. H. (1862). Fourth letter to his relatives, written on December 23, 1862. Quoted from Hirschfeld (1906).

Wright C. A. (1938). Further studies of endocrine aspects of homosexuality. *Medical Records*, May 18.

SECTION III: IS SEXUAL PREFERENCE DETERMINED BY HEREDITY?

Introduction

DNA is the basic substance that carries the hereditary information that directs the way in which an organism grows and develops. DNA stands for *d*eoxyribo*n*ucleic *a*cid. It is a long chain-like molecule formed of variously ordered repetitions of links called bases which are chemically connected to molecules of phosphoric acid. These acid molecules give the whole DNA molecule the properties of an acid. Other elements in this molecule include carbon, oxygen, hydrogen, and nitrogen. In the process of cell division the DNA reproduces itself so that each new cell contains the same genetic information as the original cell.

In addition to cell division, cells also engage in protein synthesis. Proteins are made up of 20 different substances called amino acids that are linked together in various amounts and sequences. It is the sequence of amino acids that gives each protein its unique characteristics—whether it serves as an element of structure or as an enzyme involved in metabolism.

Groups of three bases linked together in a particular order in the

[Haworth co-indexing entry note]: "Introduction." Co-published simultaneously in *Journal of Homosexuality* (The Haworth Press, Inc.) Vol. 28, No. 1/2, 1995, pp. 87-90; and: *Sex, Cells, and Same-Sex Desire: The Biology of Sexual Preference* (ed: John P. De Cecco, and David Allen Parker) The Haworth Press, Inc., 1995, pp. 87-90. Multiple copies of this article/chapter may be purchased from The Haworth Document Delivery Center [1-800-3-HAWORTH; 9:00 a.m. - 5:00 p.m. (EST)].

DNA chain specify a particular amino acid. Thus, the order in which the bases are arranged in DNA determines the sequence of amino acids in proteins. A *gene* is a stretch of DNA that codes for the production of a single protein. The production of a protein from the DNA template is a complex process that involves the formation of an intermediate called messenger RNA. *RNA* stands for *ribonucleic acid*. In addition to messenger RNA, other forms of RNA and various enzymes participate in the formation of a protein.

Chromosomes consist of double strands of DNA arranged in the shape of a double helix, and of proteins that are believed to serve regulatory functions. For the purposes of this discussion, one can imagine that genes are arranged on chromosomes like beads on a string. In between the genes are base sequences that may serve no known function or that may participate in regulating the activity of other genes.

With the exception of the sperm and ova that contain unpaired chromosomes, human cells contain 23 pairs of chromosomes. When an egg and sperm unite they form a *zygote*, with the full complement of 23 pairs. Twenty-two of these pairs are referred to as autosomes, while the last pair is the sex chromosomes. Female mammals possess paired X chromosomes, one inherited from the father and one inherited from the mother. Males possess one X which was inherited from the mother and one Y chromosome from the father. Thus sex is determined by whether the sperm that fertilizes the egg carries an X or a Y chromosome.

Specific genes occupy specific sites or loci on the chromosomes. A gene may have a number of different variations which are known as *alleles*. If an individual inherits the same allele for a particular locus from each parent, that individual is said to be *heterozygous* for that particular allele. The effect that a particular allele has on a given trait often depends on whether the individual is *homozygous* or heterozygous for that allele. The expression of a particular allele may also depend on the effects of genes at other loci.

EVOLUTION

Over generations organisms can change (or *adapt*) to best suit their environments and to maximize their chances of survival. Some of these changes are caused by natural and random variations in the genetic make-up of the organism (called *mutation*). Evolutionary theories assume that genetic components are maintained in a species if they are beneficial to its survival and that those that are not beneficial may be lost. *Natural selection* refers to the interaction between organisms and their environment which determines their subsequent success in reproduction. Those that do reproduce successfully pass on what will be the genetic material of future generations (which is called *reproductive success*).

TWIN STUDIES

The genetic makeup of an individual is called the *genotype*. The observable expression of the genotype is called the *phenotype*. Environmental influences may cause individuals with the same genotype to have different phenotypes. Twins are often studied in an attempt to sort out the effects of genes versus those of the environment. Identical twins arise from the same single cell or zygote formed by the union of a sperm and egg and share all of their genetic material. Because they developed from the same zygote, such twins are called *monozygotic*. Fraternal twins develop from different zygotes and thus share only half of their genetic material as do nontwin siblings. Because they developed from two different zygotes, they are called *dizygotic*.

Twin studies are of two sorts. The most useful in distinguishing genetic from environmental effects involves identical twins who were separated at birth and reared in different environments. If a given trait tends to be shared by identical twins even when they were reared in different environments, it is often assumed to be genetically determined. To date, studies of sexual orientation in identical twins reared apart provide only anecdotal evidence because none has included more than a few pairs.

The second type of twin study involves comparing the *concordance* for a particular trait in identical and fraternal twins. In this design in which the twins were reared together, their environments are assumed to have been equal. Because identical twins share all of their genetic material while fraternal twins share only half, a higher concordance in the identical twins is taken as evidence for a genetic effect. Interpretation of such studies is limited with respect to sexual orientation because the assumption of equal environments has not been validated.

A Critique of the Possibility of Genetic Inheritance of Homosexual Orientation

James D. Haynes, PhD

State University of New York, College at Buffalo

SUMMARY. Many workers in human sexuality have tried to discover causes of sexual orientation. No one theory has proved to be satisfactory. Studies of monozygotic and dizygotic twins, some of whom have been reared separately and some together, suggest that there may be an inherited component of homosexuality. Other studies, particularly those concerned with the evolution of human sexuality, question such a possibility. A further question arises because a large part of the human population is neither exclusively homosexual nor exclusively heterosexual. This paper will examine the evidence for genetic inheritance presented by twin and family studies. It will explore ways in which a gene favoring a homosexual orientation but not reproduction could continue to exist in a population. The importance of defining terms that refer to sexual orientation will be discussed in the context of determining exactly what may be inherited. Finally, the effects of accepting genetic inheritance as the cause of sexual orientation will be discussed.

One of the strongest of human attractions is the sexual. When men and women began trying to understand sexual attraction, it

---

James D. Haynes is Professor of Biology at the State University of New York, College at Buffalo.

Correspondence may be addressed: State University College, Department of Biology, 1300 Elmwood Avenue, Buffalo, NY 14222.

[Haworth co-indexing entry note]: "A Critique of the Possibility of Genetic Inheritance of Homosexual Orientation." Haynes, James D. Co-published simultaneously in *Journal of Homosexuality* (The Haworth Press, Inc.) Vol. 28, No. 1/2, 1995, pp. 91-113; and: *Sex, Cells, and Same-Sex Desire: The Biology of Sexual Preference* (ed: John P. De Cecco, and David Allen Parker) The Haworth Press, Inc., 1995, pp. 91-113. Multiple copies of this article/chapter may be purchased from The Haworth Document Delivery Center [1-800-3-HAWORTH; 9:00 a.m. - 5:00 p.m. (EST)].

quickly became evident that it takes many forms. These variations were widespread throughout the ancient cultures (Bullough, 1976; Dynes, 1990). It is highly probable that such variations existed even before the written record. Particular forms of expression were accepted by some cultures but were rejected, sometimes in brutal and violent fashion, by others (Bullough & Bullough, 1977). Various kinds of sexual behavior were incorporated into religious myths.

It was not until the middle 1800s when Charles Darwin and Alfred Wallace began to postulate evolution by natural selection, and when Gregor Mendel published his monumental work on genetic inheritance, that the biological tools became available to explore why human beings are the way they are (Arms & Camp, 1987). In 1886 Richard von Krafft-Ebing attempted to show a genetic basis for homosexuality, contending that homosexuals had multiple hereditary flaws (see Krafft-Ebing, 1965). Sigmund Freud (Allgeier & Allgeier, 1991) and Magnus Hirschfeld (Schmidt, 1984) began to examine sexual behaviors at the turn of the century, basing their theories on psychology and biology. Kallmann's (1952a,b) study of identical twins used genetics to look for the hereditary bases of homosexual behavior. The interest in the causes of sexual behavior, particularly those behaviors that some people would judge to be "abnormal," continues to the present time. Although sexual behavior has been studied from various perspectives–mythological, psychological, sociological, and biological–the question continues to be: Is sexual behavior the result of genetically inherited characteristics over which we have no control (*nature*) or is it a choice that is determined by the environmental conditions of the individual, consciously made and consciously changed (*nurture*)? Perhaps neither nature nor nurture alone can adequately explain sexual orientation, but both play roles.

BIOLOGICAL INHERITANCE

It is simplistic to say that all human characteristics are inherited (or are "biological"), although a case can be made for that argument. For example, the ability of a person to react to a physical stimulus, regardless of the source, is biological. The perception of the stimulus through the sensory organs (sight, touch, smell, hearing, and taste) is certainly biological and the reaction may be physical, mental, or emotional, all of which are under control of the hormonal and nervous systems. Because biological systems are genetically inherited and since behavior cannot occur without them, all human behavior is biological and influenced by genetics. However, neither physically inherited characteristics nor reactions to environmental stimuli are immutable, although some are much more difficult to change than others (Money, 1988).

The terms *male* and *female* are biologically defined by the way in which the individuals act in the process of procreation (Money, 1988). That is, the male is the individual who produces the sperm that fertilizes the egg which is produced by the female. In human beings, the male has a 46,XY chromosomal pattern, the female a 46,XX; each is expected to have a particular set of sex organs, internal and external; both possess certain secondary sex characteristics particular to their genetic sex; and each sex is also defined by certain kinds of behaviors. It would seem, therefore, that the two sexes are well-defined and the social expectations for each should be predictable because the genotype (the total genetic make-up of an individual; often refers to only one or a few gene pairs) controls the inheritance of the physical characteristics (the phenotype, which is the physical expression of the genotype) that react to environmental stimuli.

However, both observational and experimental evidence point to a contrary conclusion. Although the genotypes differ dramatically, the anatomical structures of the two sexes start from an undifferentiated set of organs composed of two gonads, two sets of genital ducts (the Mullerian and Wolffian ducts), and a urogenital sinus (Figure 1). These appear about the 5th or 6th week of pregnancy. The two sexes differentiate under the influence of the *testis determining gene* on the Y chromosome. The sex organs of the male and female are homologues of each other (Katchadourian, 1989; Masters, Johnson, & Kolodny, 1988). Thus, there are many similarities between the two sexes.

An individual inherits an X chromosome from the mother and either an X or a Y chromosome from the father. In the case of the male, the testis-determining-gene on the Y chromosome acts on the

FIGURE 1. Internal undifferentiated sex organs at 5-6 weeks.

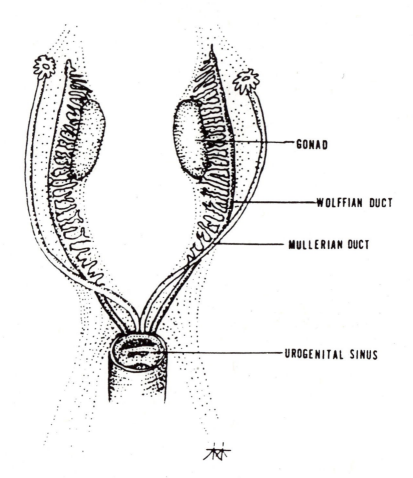

undifferentiated gonad and causes it to become an embryological testis which then begins to produce testosterone and Mullerian regression hormones. The testosterone causes the Wolffian ducts to differentiate into the epididymus, vas deferens, and seminal vesicle and stimulates the development of the external male genitalia (Figure 2). The Mullerian regression hormone inhibits the differentiation of the Mullerian ducts. In the absence of a Y chromosome, the gonad will develop into an ovary, the Mullerian ducts will

FIGURE 2. Internal and external male sex organs after differentiation and maturation. The external genitalia are on the left; the internal on the right.

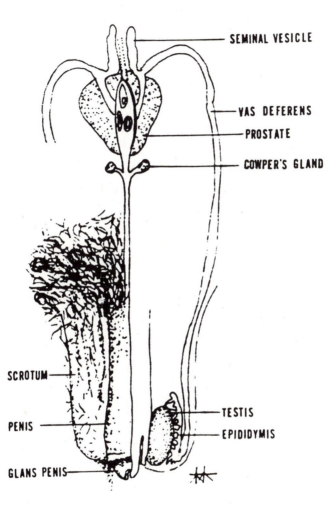

produce the fallopian tubes, uterus, and the upper part of the vagina and external female genitalia will develop (Figure 3).

In summary, it seems that the genital system of human beings is destined to become female unless there is the active intervention of the testis determining gene carried by the Y chromosome. It would

FIGURE 3. Internal and external female sex organs after differentiation and maturation. The external genitalia are on the left; the internal on the right.

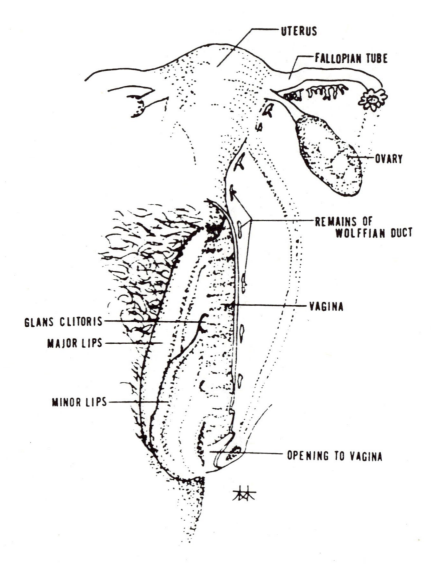

seem from this brief overview of embryological development that the formation of the sexual structures in human beings is determined by a specific factor, develops in well-defined ways, is predictable, and generally immutable.

Although this is true in the vast majority of cases, enough exceptions exist to cast doubt on the immutability of the genetic inheritance of sexual characteristics. There are many examples of ways in which the genetic sex of an individual does not fully determine sexual expression. A number of these are discussed in Money's work (1988) and general textbooks (e.g., Levitan & Montagu, 1977; Mange & Mange, 1990; Masters, Johnson, & Kolodny, 1988). Three examples will illustrate that genetic sex does not *absolutely* determine the other aspects of sexuality.

COMPLETE ANDROGEN INSENSITIVITY SYNDROME

Complete androgen insensitivity syndrome occurs in individuals who are 46,XY, who have undescended testicular gonads (and are sterile), the usual levels of androgens (e.g., testosterone) in the blood, but look like females at puberty and have a shallow vagina that looks normal from the outside. Although the testes function inside the abdomen, there are no male structures developed. The Mullerian inhibiting hormone inhibits the development of female structures from the Mullerian ducts. This condition occurs at a frequency of about 1 per 65,000 genetic males and is inherited as an X-linked recessive characteristic which renders all of the body cells incapable of utilizing testosterone. Therefore, the body fails to masculinize because of the testicular estrogen that circulates in the blood of all males. The vulva appears normal but because the cells are unable to respond to testosterone, pubic and underarm hair is either absent or sparse. The breasts develop at puberty and the body takes on the shape of a female (Masica, Ehrhardt, & Money, 1971). These individuals can live as heterosexual females in their adult lives although they are chromosomal males.

ADRENOGENITAL SYNDROME

Adrenogenital syndrome is a common cause of female pseudo-hermaphroditism. The individual is a 46,XX with the usual internal female genitalia. However, because of a recessive genetic factor, the adrenal cortex produces an excess of testosterone which induces the masculinization of the external genitalia. In extreme cases, the clitoris enlarges to the size of a normal penis, the clitoral hood becomes a foreskin, and the labia majora fuse forming an empty scrotum. To all outward appearances, the individual is a male with undescended testes. They are often classified as males until they reach about ten years of age when the testes are expected to have descended into the scrotum. By the time the true condition is discovered, the individual has learned to live as a boy, and can continue to live quite well as a man in his adult life although he has a female chromosomal pattern (Money & Dalery, 1976).

TRANSSEXUALISM

Transsexualism is a condition in which individuals feel alienated from their bodies and gender and wish to change them to look like the opposite sex. They believe they are trapped in the body of the wrong sex. The condition has been widely studied (Benjamin, 1966; Goodman et al., 1985; Hoenig, 1985; Sorensen & Hertoft, 1982; Stoller, 1982; and others) but there has been no agreement on cause. Although there are no reliable statistics on the numbers of transsexuals in the population, The American Psychiatric Association (1980) reported that there are many more men than women who seek help and sex reassignment at gender identity clinics. In 1953, George Jorgensen, a private in the U. S. Army, underwent surgery that made her genital sex compatible with her perceptions of herself as female. She took the name Christine Jorgensen (1967), and became the first internationally known person who underwent the male-to-female genital change. In 1953, this surgery was not available in the United States so Jorgensen had the operation in Copenhagen, Denmark. Since Jorgensen, thousands of people in the United States and other western countries have undergone what may be called a "sex change operation" because they believe that the anatomical sex with which they were born should be "corrected" to match their "real" sex. Most male-to-female transsexuals live as heterosexual women and may marry men and, through adoption, rear children (Money, 1988). Most female-to-male transsexuals live as heterosexual men and establish families (Money, 1988). Thus most transsexuals settle into their newly assigned roles after sex-reassignment surgery. Some male-to-female transsexuals identify themselves as lesbians and seek a woman as their love object. This author is acquainted with a man who fathered four children in a heterosexual marriage, but for as long as he could remember had thought that he should be a female. Finally, at age 54, he underwent surgery and had his genital and hormonal sex changed to match what he believed was his real sex. As a transsexual, this person identified herself as a lesbian and continues (15 years later) to live that lifestyle. Although the process of undergoing sex modification can be extremely difficult physically, emotionally, socially, culturally, and financially, the motivation is so great that it overcomes these obstacles. These three examples show that one's biological sex or genotype is not the sole determiner of one's sexuality. In most cases, the genotype is immutable and the results are predictable. However, the exceptions demonstrate there is variability even in what was long considered to be biologically predetermined. It is known that among other animals the expression of a genotype can be modified by environmental factors. For example sex determination among sea turtles (Standora & Spotila, 1985) is dependent upon the temperature during the incubation of the eggs. Eggs incubated under higher temperatures produce mainly females while those incubated under cooler conditions produce mainly males. Thus, throughout the animal kingdom, the plasticity of the genotype provides the mechanism for sexual variation.

THE INFLUENCE OF THE KINSEY SCALE

The famous scale devised by Alfred Kinsey has received wide recognition since its original publication (Kinsey, Pomeroy, & Martin, 1948). Although controversial, it continues to be prominent in describing the relationship between homosexuality and heterosexuality. It may be comforting to some to be able to view behavior as either homosexual or heterosexual. Such a dichotomy is possible only if individuals are attracted exclusively to their own sex or to the opposite sex. The Kinsey scale provides a continuum of psychosexual and overt sexual behavior between the two extremes. Although criticized by many scholars, the general opinion of researchers is that it is still useful. Suggested improvements included separate scales for fantasy, love, self-identification, and sexual attraction (Reinisch, 1990).

The Kinsey scale rates human psychosexual (ideation) and behavioral response from 0 to 6. Although each rating has lengthy definitions, for the purposes of this discussion the following simplifications, which fall within the original definitions, will be used. The individual is rated as 0, if he/she is exclusively heterosexual; 1, if largely heterosexual, but with incidental homosexual experience; 2, if largely heterosexual, but with distinct homosexual experience; 3, if heterosexual and homosexual experiences are equal; 4, if largely homosexual, but with distinct heterosexual experience; 5, if largely homosexual, but with incidental heterosexual experience; and 6, if exclusively homosexual (Kinsey, Pomeroy, Martin, & Gebhard, 1953).

The Kinsey 0's and 6's fit the need to have two entirely separate groups of heterosexuals and homosexuals. Individuals are rated as 0's if all of their psychosexual fantasies and overt sexual activities are directed toward persons of the opposite sex. They are rated as 6's if all of their activities are directed toward persons of the same sex. It is the Kinsey 1 through 5's that present the real problems of definition, especially when discussing the possibility of genetic inheritance of sexual orientation, because their behavior may be either homosexual or heterosexual concurrently or sequentially (Money, 1988).

The term bisexual is often used behaviorally to describe the Kinsey 1 through 5's. The Kinsey numbers represent a ratio of homosexual to heterosexual behavior with 50:50 being the Kinsey 3. The Kinsey 3 connotes "true" bisexual behavior, where sexual encounters with the same or opposite sex occur equally. The term *bisexual* in biology means being of both sexes or having both male and female organs, thus making it equivalent to hermaphroditism. Its social use is confusing for it sometimes refers to a person's sexual politics. The confusion surrounding the use of the term has been recognized by other workers (Blumstein & Schwartz, 1976, 1977) who have suggested the substitution of the term *ambisexual,* which recognizes the ability for a person to be sexually attracted to both genders.

The term ambisexual was used by Masters and Johnson (1979) to describe a group of men and women who had frequent sexual interaction with members of both sexes but who reported no exclusive preference for one gender over the other. Sexual interaction was viewed as simply a matter of sexual release. After about eight months of a national search in 1968, only 6 men and 6 women were found who fit these criteria. Anyone who has been sexually active, at least in the homosexual milieu, knows people who take advantage of any opportunity for sexual release regardless of gender. Careful follow-up studies need to be done to determine just how long individuals remain in that category. Money (1988) uses the term to mean characteristics shared by both sexes, making it also equivalent to hermaphroditism. Katchadourian (1989) further complicates the issue by equating the terms bisexual and ambisexual.

For the purposes of this study, the term *ambisexual* will be used in the general sense to describe all five of the intermediate Kinsey ratings. The term *bisexual* will be used to describe only the Kinsey 3. The use of genetic inheritance to explain sexual orientation must take the behavioral continuum into account and also explain how an individual may occupy one or more levels concurrently or sequentially (Money, 1988).

TWIN STUDIES

The study of twins and their familial relationships has provided ways of comparing the influence of genetic inheritance with environmental factors on the phenotype (the observable expression of the interaction of the genotype and the environment of an organism; some genes are recessive and may not be immediately expressed) of the individual. *Monozygotic twins* (MZ) are those who develop from the splitting of a single zygote (fertilized egg) within the first two weeks of development. *Dizygotic twins* (DZ) result from the fertilization of two separate eggs by two separate sperm (Maxson & Daugherty, 1989). Both kinds of twins experience the same general environment while they are in the uterus, but from the moment of conception are subjected to a multiplicity of intrauterine environmental factors which are capable of affecting the influence of the genes.

Some of these prenatal factors are the age of the father or mother, maternal emotions that may affect hormonal changes, drugs, radiation, and, finally, conditions in the uterus such as temperature, pressure, and characteristics of the amniotic fluid (Levitan & Montagu, 1977). The twins may be enclosed in the same outer embryonic membrane (which is only true for MZ twins) or separate ones (which can be either MZ or DZ). Whether MZ or DZ, each embryo may produce its own placenta, or they may fuse if implantation takes place close to each other (Mange & Mange, 1990). Therefore, there are many factors that can act upon MZ or DZ twins prenatally so that the uterine environment of each twin may be different.

It is usually assumed that MZ twins are genetically identical. While in most cases this may be true, chromosomal changes brought about by the differences in the uterine environment may occur in one twin and not in the other. Genes always interact with the environment, which includes other genes within the genotype. Therefore, MZ twins are not necessarily "identical," and it has been suggested that the use of that term be dropped (Levitan & Montagu, 1977). DZ twins are no more closely related than any other siblings. Thus, while they may share some traits, it is unlikely that their phenotypes would be very similar. Twins are said to be *concordant* for a specific trait if they both have that trait, and *discordant* if one does not (Mange & Mange, 1990).

Farber (1981) also questions the similarity of genetic identity in MZ pairs. While she recognizes the value of studying MZ twins, she points out that it rests on two assumptions: (a) MZ twins share an identical genotype, and (b) concordance of traits is linked to genetic factors while discordance is linked to environmental influences. However, she insists,"No trait is independent of hereditary or environmental agents. Certain environmental conditions are necessary before a genetic potential becomes expressed (or, conversely, inhibited), while the genetic endowment of any individual is certain to influence the way he perceives, experiences, or processes environmental stimuli" (p. 5). She goes on to point out causes of differentiation in MZ pairs (e.g., mutation and chromosomal damage). She also discusses other influences, including fetal blood supply, and the possibility that some overriding environmental condition such as prematurity, atypical birth experiences, or low socioeconomic class might limit the expression of the phenotype. The effects of such environmental conditions could mistakenly be attributed to the genotype. She sets up a list of five criteria that fulfill experimental requirements (p. 30), but recognizes that studies rarely meet them:

1. Selection of genetically identical individuals (MZ twins).
2. Random selection of subjects.
3. Random assignment to rearing conditions.
4. Selection of pairs that are reared separately as single individuals.
5. No organic and nongenetic features (such as prematurity) should exist within pairs which might artificially inflate or deflate heritability estimates.

Because so few studies meet these requirements, the results of such studies must be considered unreliable. "No conclusion from twin-reared-apart data as they now exist is generalizable" (p. 300). Her criteria should be applied to any twin studies espousing a genetic basis for inheritance of sexual orientation.

THRESHOLD TRAITS

Threshold traits are conditions that may appear in individuals and are discontinuous (either present or absent, but not along a continuum), appear to have a genetic component, and do not show Mendelian inheritance. Four of these have been studied for their concordance in both DZ and MZ twins: (1) Cleft lip/cleft palate, DZ (5%), MZ (35%); (2) Schizophrenia, DZ (15%), MZ (45%); (3) Diabetes mellitus Type 1, DZ (5%), MZ (50%); and (4) Diabetes mellitus Type 2, DZ (25%), MZ (95%) (Mange & Mange, 1990). Although concordance of these traits is higher among MZ twins, factors other than genetic inheritance must be at work because the percentage of concordance is never 100 and DZ twins show some degree of concordance for each of the traits.

Kallmann (1952a,b) studied 45 DZ and 40 MZ twin pairs. Of his

DZ pairs, 26 cases could be examined because they had co-twins who survived beyond the age of 18 years. Of these, concordance for homosexual behavior varied from 11.5 to 42.3% depending on whether the rates were related to the Kinsey 5-6 or to the total range of Kinsey's 0-6. He found 100% concordance for homosexuality among the MZ twin pairs, none of whom ranked below a 3 on the Kinsey scale. If Kallmann's findings could be confirmed, they would present strong, but not indisputable evidence of genetic inheritance of the homosexual orientation.

No study has been able to replicate Kallmann's 100% concordance rate. Kallmann's study is flawed in several ways. First, his subjects do not represent a random sample. They were chosen "with the aid of psychiatric, correctional, and charitable agencies [and] also through direct contacts with the clandestine homosexual world" (Kallmann, 1952a, p. 287). This sample bias is what allows him to later say: "the urgency of such additional work with respect to the genetic aspects of homosexual behavior is underscored by the ominous fact that adult homosexuality continues to be an inexhaustible source of unhappiness, discontent, and a distorted sense of human values" (1952a, p. 296). Second, although he indicates that not all members of his DZ pairs were available for examination, he is silent about the availability of his MZ pairs. One is led to assume that all were available, a highly unlikely event. Third, there is no indication that the members of the MZ twin pairs were reared separately. Thus, there is no reliable way to separate the effects of the environment from those of the genotype. Fourth, there is no indication how he determined the placement of the subjects on the Kinsey scale. Fifth, he did not indicate how he judged whether the twins were MZ or DZ. Sixth, he reported that only 18 of his subjects were emotionally and socially adjusted, a bias enforced by the first weakness of the study, and again underscoring the need for a random sample.

Although any genetic study of inheritance of the homosexual orientation must address the criticisms listed above, one can agree with Kallmann in two areas. He recognized the difficulty of investigating the sex habits of a group of people who feel themselves ostracized by society and who feel the need for self-protection. Therefore, the question of genetic mechanisms in homosexual development "may still be regarded as entirely unsettled" (Kallmann, 1952a, p. 286). There are also the obstacles of retrospective investigation by subjects who must trust to their memories. Everything considered, the researcher is faced with a formidable set of obstacles in determining both sexual orientation and familial relationships that could reveal patterns of inheritance.

Although Kallmann did not believe in the healthy homosexual, his views were not as negative as one of his predecessors (Lang, 1940), whom Kallmann cites extensively. Thomas Lang tried to find a genetic basis for homosexual orientation because he felt that the inherited weakness could be eliminated by execution, a position consistent with the Nazis' idea of developing a superior race (Lang, 1940).

The literature reports many cases of MZ co-twins that are discordant for homosexuality (Farber, 1981; Davison, Brierley, & Smith, 1971; Money, 1980; Heston & Shields, 1968). Davison, Brierley, and Smith (1971) report the case of a MZ pair that was discordant. In this case, the use of aversion therapy to alter the orientation of the homosexual twin was reported as a "success." The individual still claimed to be "free" from homosexual desire after two years. Money (1988) doubts the permanence of such change and compares such efforts to trying to change the handedness of a person. The result is poor writing. Indeed, in the latter case the individual apparently had trouble establishing relationships with females, and was judged to be changed only by what he told his therapist. However, Davison, Brierley, and Smith (1971) attribute the patient's homosexuality to "over-mothering" that resulted from the near-death in infancy of the co-twin. Therefore, because environmentally induced behaviors may be more easily changed than genetically inherited ones, aversion therapy may have been more effective than expected.

Heston and Shields (1968) report on a family composed of mother, father, and 14 siblings, among which were three sets of MZ twins. One set of the twins was concordant for heterosexuality; the other two sets concordant for homosexuality. The familial history and the relationships between and among the twin pairs make it impossible to differentiate between genetic and environmental influences. The authors concluded that their evidence "will not support either genetic or environmental determinism as an explanation of the homosexuality of the twin pairs" (p. 156).

A recent report that proposes a genetic basis for homosexuality, one that led to the media's claim that the "cause" had been discovered, was conducted by Bailey and Pillard (1991). Their study reported that 52% (29/56) of MZ co-twins, 22% (12/54) of DZ co-twins, and 11% (6/57) of adoptive brothers were homosexual. They asserted that these results "suggest that genetic factors are important in determining individual differences in sexual orientation" (p. 1093).

The subjects were recruited from advertisements placed in gay publications in the Midwest and Southwest. The co-twins were reared in the same environments, identified their own sexual orientation, and were asked what they believed their relatives' orientation to be. In determining rates of homosexuality, the general categories of homosexual/gay, heterosexual, or bisexual were used. Homosexual/gay and bisexual were later combined under the category of homosexual.

The major distinction upon which their conclusions are based was the distinction between heterosexual and nonheterosexual relatives. That is, they lumped together heterosexual and "other." The assumption that because all of the siblings were reared together they were reared in the same environment was also unwarranted. Macroenvironmental and microenvironmental differences do occur (Davison, Brierley, & Smith, 1971; Money, 1988; Heston & Shields, 1968; Farber, 1981).

Studies of MZ and DZ twins and their familial relationships have provided no reliable data for supporting the idea of inheritance of sexual orientation, either heterosexual or homosexual. Because of ethical considerations, no rigorously scientific protocol (Farber, 1981) can be used. Without such a protocol, it is difficult to understand how we will ever know the exact contributions of the genotype to sexual orientation. MZ pairs may not be "identical" and the uterine environment of each twin may be slightly different, thus providing a prenatal environmental variation. Although reared in the same place, the social environment can vary and render impossible the separation of genetic and environmental influences on behavior. Environments may not vary even when the MZ pairs are separated because twin pairs are more likely to be adopted by other family members such as aunts, uncles, and cousins or by people of the same social class.

RETENTION OF HOMOSEXUAL GENETIC COMPONENTS

One of the arguments against genetically inherited homosexual orientation is that a gene controlling such inheritance would be lost from the population because of the lack of reproduction resulting from homosexual acts. While offspring are not produced in same-sex encounters (although lesbians can be impregnated by donated sperm and men can donate their sperm to a surrogate), homosexual men and women can and do have children of their own. Homosexual orientation does not preclude the ability to reproduce.

The application of biological principles, particularly genetic and evolutionary ones, to human social behavior is called sociobiology. This controversial approach has been described by Wilson (1975) and used by Ruse (1981) as a method to explain the genetic determination of sexual orientation. Ruse discusses four hypotheses although he recognizes that the evidence to support them is inconclusive.

The first of these is the *Balanced Superior Heterozygote Fitness* hypothesis (Hutchinson, 1959). This hypothesis presumes the existence of a recessive gene for homosexuality and a dominant one for heterosexuality. The individuals possessing either two genes for homosexuality (Kinsey 6) or for heterosexuality (Kinsey 0) would be homozygous. Persons possessing one gene for each trait would be heterozygous and heterosexual. If the heterozygotes were better able to survive and reproduce than either of the homozygotes, their offspring would maintain the homosexual gene in the population. The same sort of mechanism works with sickle-cell anemia in which individuals (the heterozygotes) with a recessive gene for the trait are better able to live in their environment than either of the homozygotes because the heterozygous condition makes them resistant to malaria.

Assuming that the postulated homosexual gene is expressed in some altruistic way leads to hypotheses of *Kin Selection* (Hamilton, 1964a,b) and *Parental Manipulation* (Trivers, 1974). In both of these cases the homosexuals are not expending energy in the production of their own offspring and therefore can use that energy to increase their siblings' chances for reproduction by helping them to rear their children. The homosexuals are, in effect, "sacrificing" their reproductive capacity to the greater good of the social order and their family. It could be further postulated that the nonreproductive behavior of homosexual acts limits the population and therefore reduces the competition for resources, jobs, and mates. Thus, in terms of Darwinian evolution, there is survival value for the retention of the homosexual gene.

The fourth hypothesis is called *Homosexuality as a By-Product.* It speculates that homosexuality, at least in male homosexuals, is a by-product of the propensity for boys to masturbate. Since boys are denied intercourse with females until long after puberty, some of them become fixated on their own penis and come to prefer penises to vaginas. This idea is certainly not new. One of the early reasons for condemning masturbation was that it was believed that the practice would lead to homosexual behavior.

It should come as no surprise to anyone who has followed these sociobiological arguments, that their validity has been severely questioned. Futuyma and Risch (1984) have evaluated the first three hypotheses for their *scientific* content and have found them lacking (they do not deal with the fourth, presumably because even Ruse calls it speculation). They argue that evolutionary explanations of homosexuality assume *a priori* that orientation must have a genetic basis. Because they do not believe there is any reliable evidence to support that assumption, they do not accept the sociobiological arguments.

CONCLUSIONS

Although there is no reliable evidence that sexual orientation is genetically inherited, neither is there evidence for the conclusion by Hoult (1984) that it is the result of social-learning. The available evidence forces one to consider that neither nature nor nurture provides the sole answer to the cause of sexual orientation, either heterosexual or homosexual. One may consider that genetic material (nature) is acted upon during a critical period by environmental influences (nurture) or, in a more general sense, that neither influence can act without the other. Human beings are born with the potential for sexual behavior. The particular kind of behavior depends upon the interaction of the environment (opportunity) and the genotype. Money (1988) uses the analogy that human beings have the mental ability to use language. The particular language is determined by the social order within which the individual is reared.

If nature and nurture acted consistently, the result would be immutable orientation. However, only the Kinsey 0's and 6's appear to have an immutable sexual orientation, and then only if it is defined solely by sexual behavior. The immutability of orientation is particularly questionable when one considers that ambisexuality is so widespread.

Any attempt to demonstrate genetic inheritance of sexual orientation must explain how a continuum of ambisexual behaviors could exist. It is possible to postulate a polygenetic inheritance such as occurs in skin color (Mange & Mange, 1990) or body height (Levitan & Montagu, 1977), but no evidence exists to support this notion.

Definitions of human sexuality are often arbitrary and often represent social and cultural stereotypes. Attempts to categorize individuals as male or female, masculine or feminine, homosexual or heterosexual, ambisexual, bisexual, or transsexual immediately confront difficulties of definition. All of these terms appeal to the desire to stuff behavior into neat pigeonholes.

Even characteristics that have been shown to be determined by genetic inheritance and that are usually predictable are somewhat plastic if there is a change in a chromosome or gene. These occur with the Complete Androgen Insensitive Syndrome and the Adrenogenital Syndrome. These two syndromes along with transsexualism demonstrate that genetic sex does not always determine gender and further undermines the idea of immutability of genetic inheritance. Sexual behavior has been recognized by many researchers as progressing along a continuum from heterosexuality to homosexuality and not distributed as discrete categories. If factors other than behavior are considered, the categories become even more diffused.

Aside from the fact that human beings are curious and have always sought to explain their existence and behavior, there is no necessity for knowing why an individual has a particular sexual orientation. Until fairly recently, all research into the area has been in search of a "cure" or behavioral change. The concepts of "sin" or "perversion" provided the motivation for the search.

When it was recognized that homosexual orientation was no more explainable than a heterosexual one, people began to accept it as natural and to look for a "natural biological" or "scientific" explanation. If homosexual behavior, it was reasoned, could be found to be caused by some force not in control of the individual, then the individual could be "excused" or become more "acceptable" because his behavior was beyond his control. Some writers believed that a biological explanation would further the cause of gay liberation. Such views have been voiced in the popular media such as *Newsweek* (1992) and even in some of the gay press (*Advocate,* 1992). Others in the same articles voiced concerns about where this type of research could lead.

Such caution is well deserved. There is no reason to assume that because something is "natural" or "normal" that it should not be changed. It is natural that certain genetic conditions produce a cleft palate or Down's syndrome, yet no one would suggest that those conditions not be treated for the betterment of the individual. It was normal for people to die with smallpox or polio, but scientists worked hard to overcome those diseases, just as they are working to overcome the natural results of infection with HIV. Biological processes, except in the long evolutionary run, are not benevolent. We often try to change them because we perceive them as detrimental to happy, productive lives.

If the homosexual orientation is perceived as detrimental to the social order, then there is no "natural" or "normal" biological process that dictates that it should not be changed. There is a long history in which people try to use scientific knowledge to further their social agenda. Lang (1940) used his knowledge to argue for the elimination of the "weakness" of homosexuality from Nazi Germany by killing the homosexuals. Hirschfeld (Schmidt, 1984) tried to use his knowledge to promote sexual liberation for the homosexual, but he was persecuted and his work was turned against his cause. Dörner (1983) uses his research to correct "abnormal" brain conditions and to prevent the intrauterine development of homosexuality. Thus scientific research offers no guarantees for gay liberation.

All available scientific evidence points to the conclusion that sexual orientation, be it heterosexual, ambisexual, or homosexual, is a result of the interaction of genotype and environment. People are born with the innate ability to perform sexually, but the focus of that performance is no more immutable than language skills. Further, there is evidently great plasticity in orientation, as one moves from one point on the sexual continuum to another, for differing lengths of time, and at different periods of one's life. The constraints placed by the social order on particular orientations have no basis in biology. Thus homosexuals should seek their liberation through political and social efforts rather than biological research.

REFERENCES

Advocate. (1992, March 24). Raiders of the gay gene, pp. 60-62.

American Psychiatric Association. (1980). *Diagnostic and statistical manual of mental disorders* (3rd ed.). (DSM-III). Washington, DC: American Psychiatric Association.

Allgeier, E. R., & Allgeier, A. R. (1991). *Sexual interactions* (3rd ed.). Lexington, MA: D. C. Heath.

Arms, C. P., & Camp, P. (1987). *Biology* (3rd ed.). Philadelphia, PA: Saunders.

Bailey, J. M., & Pillard, R. C. (1991). A genetic study of male sexual orientation. *Archives of General Psychiatry, 48*, 1089-1096.

Benjamin, H. (1966). *The transsexual phenomenon.* New York, NY: Julian Press.

Blumstein, P., & Schwartz, P. (1976). Bisexuality in men. *Urban Life, 5*(4), 339-358.

Blumstein, P., & Schwartz, P. (1977). Bisexuality: Some social psychological issues. *Journal of Social Issues, 33*(2), 30-45.

Bullough, V. L. (1976). *Sexual variance in society and history.* New York, NY: Wiley-Interscience.

Bullough, V. L., & Bullough, B. (1977). *Sin, sickness, and sanity: A history of sexual attitudes.* New York, NY: Garland.

Davison, K., Brierley, H., & Smith, G. (1971). A male monozygotic twinship discordant for homosexuality: A repertory grid study. *The British Journal of Psychiatry, 18*, 675-682.

Dörner, G. (1983). Letter to the editor. *Archives of Sexual Behavior, 12*, 577-582.

Dynes, W. R. (Ed.). (1990). *Encyclopedia of homosexuality.* New York, NY: Garland.

Farber, S. L. (1981). *Identical twins reared apart: A reanalysis.* New York, NY: Basic Books, Inc.

Futuyma, D. J., & Risch, S. J. (1984). Sexual orientation, sociobiology, and evolution. *Journal of Homosexuality, 9*(2/3), 157-168.

Goodman, R. E., Anderson, D. C., Bullock, D. E., Sheffield, B., Lynch, S. S., & Butt, W. R. (1985). Study of the effects of estradiol on gonadotropin levels in untreated male-to-female transsexuals. *Archives of Sexual Behavior, 14*, 141-147.

Hamilton, W. D. (1964a). The genetical theory of social behavior. I. *Journal of Theoretical Biology, 7*, 1-16.

Hamilton, W. D. (1964b). The genetical theory of social behavior. II. *Journal of Theoretical Biology, 7*, 17-32.

Heston, L., & Shields, J. (1968). Homosexuality in twins. *Archives of General Psychiatry, 18*, 149-160.

Hoenig, J. (1985). Etiology of transsexualism. In B. W. Steiner (Ed.), *Gender dysphoria: Development, research, and management.* New York, NY: Plenum.

Hoult, T. F. (1984). Human sexuality in biological perspective: Theoretical and methodological considerations. *Journal of Homosexuality, 9*(2/3), 137-155.

Hutchinson, G. E. (1959). A speculative consideration of certain possible forms of sexual selection in man. *American Naturalist, 93*(869), 81-91.

Jorgensen, C. (1967). *Christine Jorgensen: A personal autobiography.* New York, NY: Paul S. Eriksson.

Kallmann, F. J. (1952a). Comparative twin study on the genetic aspects of male homosexuality. *The Journal of Nervous and Mental Disease, 115*(4), 283-298.

Kallmann, F. J. (1952b). Twin and sibship study of overt male homosexuality. *The American Journal of Human Genetics, 4*(2), 136-147.

Katchadourian, H. A. (1989). *Fundamentals of human sexuality* (5th ed.). Fort Worth, TX: Holt, Rinehart and Winston.

Kinsey, A. C., Pomeroy, W., & Martin, C. (1948). *Sexual behavior in the human male.* Philadelphia, PA: Saunders.

Kinsey, A. C., Pomeroy, W., Martin, C., & Gebhard, P. (1953). *Sexual behavior in the human female.* Philadelphia, PA: Saunders.

Krafft-Ebing, R. V. (1965). *Psychopathia sexualis.* New York, NY: Paperback Library.

Lang, T. (1940). Studies on the genetic determination of homosexuality. *Journal of Nervous and Mental Disease, 92*, 55-64.

Levitan, M., & Montagu, A. (1977). *Textbook of human genetics* (2nd ed.). New York, NY: Oxford University Press.

Mange, A. P., & Mange, E. J. (1990). *Genetics: Human aspects* (2nd ed.). Sunderland, MA: Sinauer Associates Inc.

Masica, D. N., Ehrhardt, A. A., & Money, J. (1971). Fetal feminization and female gender identity in the testicular feminizing syndrome of androgen insensitivity. *Archives of Sexual Behavior, 1*, 131-142.

Masters, W. H., & Johnson, V. E. (1979). *Homosexuality in perspective.* Boston, MA: Little, Brown.

Masters, W. H., Johnson, V. E., & Kolodny, R. C. (1988). *Human sexuality* (3rd ed.). Glenview, IL: Scott, Foresman.

Maxson, L. R., & Daugherty, C. H. (1989). *Genetics: A human perspective.* Dubuque, IA: W. C. Brown.

Money, J. (1980). *Love and love sickness: The science of sex, gender difference and pairbonding.* Baltimore: Johns Hopkins University Press.

Money, J. (1988). *Gay, straight, and in-between.* New York, NY: Oxford University Press.

Money, J., & Dalery, J. (1976). Iatrogenic homosexuality: Gender identity in seven 46,XX chromosomal females with hyperadrenocortical hermaphroditism born with a penis, three reared as boys, four reared as girls. *Journal of Homosexuality, 1*, 357-371.

Newsweek. (1992, February 24). Born or bred? pp. 46-53.

Reinisch, J. M. (1990). *The Kinsey Institute new report on sex.* New York, NY: St. Martin's Press.

Ruse, M. (1981). Are there gay genes? Sociobiology and homosexuality. *Journal of Homosexuality, 6*(4), 5-33.

Schmidt, G. (1984). Allies and persecutors: Science and medicine in the homosexuality issue. *Journal of Homosexuality, 10*(3/4), 127-140.

Sorensen, T., & Hertoft, P. (1982). Male and female transsexualism: The Danish experience with 37 patients. *Archives of Sexual Behavior, 11*(2), 133-155.

Standora, E. A., & Spotila, J. R. (1985). Temperature dependent sex determination in sea turtles. *Copeia* (3), 711-722.

Stoller, R. J. (1982). Transvestism in women. *Archives of Sexual Behavior, 2*, 99-115.

Trivers, R. L. (1974). Parent-offspring conflict. *American Zoologist, 14*, 249-264.

Wilson, E. O. (1975). *Sociobiology: The new synthesis.* Cambridge, MA: Harvard University Press.

Is Homosexuality Genetic?
A Critical Review and Some Suggestions

Terry R. McGuire, PhD

Rutgers University

SUMMARY. Genetic analysis of behavioral differences among human beings requires both careful experimental design and appropriate genetic models. Any genetic study must use (1) valid and precise measures of individual differences, (2) appropriate methods to ascertain biological relationships, (3) research subjects who have been randomly recruited, (4) appropriate sample sizes, and (5) appropriate genetic models to interpret the data. In addition, the researchers must exercise caution in interpreting biosocial effects from the observed phenotypic correlations. To date, all studies of the genetic basis of sexual orientation of men and women have failed to meet one or more or any of the above criteria.

In the past few years there have been a number of studies of the familial nature of homosexuality with heavy emphasis on possible genetic origins. These studies have been carried out for a number of reasons. Bailey and Pillard (1991), for example, suggested that the search for biological explanations for homosexuality (1) reflects the failure of social and psychological explanations, (2) looks instead to neurohormonal mechanisms, and (3) could be politically useful.

Terry R. McGuire is Associate Professor of Biological Sciences.
Correspondence may be addressed: Department of Biological Sciences, Nelson Biological Laboratories, Rutgers University, Piscataway, NJ 08855-1059.

[Haworth co-indexing entry note]: "Is Homosexuality Genetic? A Critical Review and Some Suggestions." McGuire, Terry R. Co-published simultaneously in *Journal of Homosexuality* (The Haworth Press, Inc.) Vol. 28, No. 1/2, 1995, pp. 115-145; and: *Sex, Cells, and Same-Sex Desire: The Biology of Sexual Preference* (ed: John P. De Cecco, and David Allen Parker) The Haworth Press, Inc., 1995, pp. 115-145. Multiple copies of this article/chapter may be purchased from The Haworth Document Delivery Center [1-800-3-HAWORTH; 9:00 a.m. - 5:00 p.m. (EST)].

They write, "A final factor that has increased interest in biological explanations of sexual orientation is the continuing tension between those who view homosexuality as an illness or a sign of moral weakness, and those who see it simply as an alternative phenotype, without moral or pathological implications. It appears that one's etiological theory of homosexuality may contribute importantly to one's views on this larger issue" (p. 1089). These behavior-genetic studies have been widely reported in the popular press although the press often makes claims far beyond those intended by the investigators. For example, Wheeler (1992) reported that one scientist found the Bailey and Pillard (1991) evidence so compelling that he intended to search for the gene or genes that may cause homosexuality. Despite the "hype" of popular press articles, just how compelling is the evidence for a genetic factor in homosexuality?

I have worked extensively with insect behavior genetics. This allows a level of certainty since the implications of my research apply mostly to laboratory-reared insects. Still, I must be careful to use appropriate experimental designs, have adequate sample sizes and control groups, and use suitable genetic models. Even when all of these criteria have been met, in drawing conclusions I must be extremely cautious in generalizing from research on one strain of insects to other strains of the same species.

Genetic analyses of human behavioral differences also require careful experimental design and appropriate genetic models. Any behavior-genetic study must use (1) valid and precise measures of individual differences, (2) appropriate methods to ascertain biological relationships, (3) research subjects that have been randomly recruited, (4) appropriate sample sizes, and (5) appropriate genetic models to interpret the data. In addition, the experimenters must exercise caution in attributing biosocial effects to the observed genetic and phenotypic correlations.

THE PHENOTYPE: HOMOSEXUALITY, HETEROSEXUALITY, AND BISEXUALITY

One of the most important aspects of a behavior-genetic study is to accurately and reliably measure individual differences. In experimental behavior genetics we identify *behavior in terms of physical description* (Hinde, 1959). Animals are observed in the field or in the laboratory and experimenters record the duration and frequency of "discrete units of behavior." These units are then described in sufficient detail so that other experimenters studying the same animal can replicate the original observations. For example, if a male fruit fly, *Drosophila melanogaster,* is placed with a virgin female, the experimenter might record such physical activities as bouts of wing vibration, orientation to and following of the female, bouts of genital licking, and attempted and completed copulations. Because the above activities result in reproduction, they can be categorized as *courtship.* The term *courtship* is used to identify discrete physical units of behavior or as a *description in terms of consequences. Description in terms of consequences* is particularly useful for comparing disparate physical descriptions across species.

Human behavior-geneticists generally study *behaviors in terms of consequences* rather than studying physical units of behavior. For example, two individuals might obtain identical IQ scores even though they had different responses to particular questions and used entirely different problem-solving strategies. Similarly, sexual orientation is generally described in terms of gender of the sexual partner, sexual feelings, or fantasies without reference to any physical behavior.

Kinsey, Pomeroy, & Martin (1948) defined homosexuality in a way that it would be suitable for genetic studies and be *"applicable to all persons who have ever had any homosexual experience"* (p. 662; italics mine). They insisted that homosexuality should be determined only after a complete sexual history had been obtained. The Kinsey group was particularly critical of research which used the reports of relatives or relied on suspicion, gossip, or accidental public disclosure. They believed that neither marriage nor evidence of sexual relations with the opposite gender was a suitable criterion for assuming heterosexuality. Finally, they believed that a balance between heterosexuality and homosexuality exists in most individuals. The seven-point Kinsey scale was originally developed because they wanted to demonstrate that an artificial dichotomy of homosexuality and heterosexuality did not exist. An individual's position on the scale was based on both overt sexual activity and on psychological responses to members of both genders. Furthermore, they believed that a person's position on the scale was not static but changed over a person's lifetime. Due to these reasons, the group was adamant that homosexuality could only be accurately assessed through face-to-face interviews.

Other researchers used the Kinsey scale, a comparative, descriptive tool, as a measurement instrument (e.g., Kallman 1952a,b). Pillard and Weinrich (1986) attribute powerful assessment capabilities to the Kinsey scale, stating that "the predominant homosexual and the predominant orientation are personality traits that can be reliably and objectively defined using the Kinsey scale, and that they appear to be relatively enduring characteristics of the individual" (p. 809). In their study, subjects were asked to rate themselves on the Kinsey scale along three dimensions: "fantasy-behavior rating in adolescence, combined fantasy-behavior rating in adulthood, and age at first homosexual experience" (p. 809). Buhrich, Bailey, and Martin (1991) had subjects give themselves a percentage score based on items "concerning same-sex sexual orientation, attraction and contact," which they describe "as defining features of a homosexual orientation and highly intercorrelated" (p. 80). Bailey and Pillard (1991) assigned Kinsey ratings using 5 questions. In the case of Pillard and Weinrich, the questions were essentially a self-rating Kinsey scale.

Obtaining accurate Kinsey ratings may be extremely difficult. Questionnaire studies probably underestimate the occurrence of homosexuality. Gebhard (1972) has stated that "Obtaining truthful responses on a subject as taboo as homosexuality requires winning the trust of, and [establishing] rapport with, the respondent and also probing rather than accepting the initial reply at face value. Without this personal and probing element, a questionnaire survey will always produce low incidence figures for taboo behavior." The Kinsey scale is continuous in ranking. Position assignments, however, are more difficult to make in the middle than at the extremes of the scale. If one has never had a heterosexual contact it would be easy to rate oneself as a 6. If one has had both heterosexual and homosexual contacts, one could rate oneself anywhere from 1 to 5. Determining the exact balance between homosexual and heterosexual activity and fantasy might be easier for an experienced sex researcher than for the untutored respondent. This difficulty might, in fact, explain the infrequent reports of bisexuals in many studies that use self-rating techniques. Much worse than self-ratings are ratings assigned by the "relatives" of the individuals that refused to answer the questionnaire.

ASSESSMENT OF GENETIC RELATEDNESS

It is essential to know the genetic relatedness of individuals in a behavior-genetic study. This is true whether one is assessing the types of twins (see below) or inferring family relationships. *Genetic relatedness* is a statistical term that depends on the average number of genes that two family members have in common. In addition, family members might share interactions that arise between genes. Genetic relatedness can only be ascertained by the appropriate biological methods. It cannot be determined by questionnaire studies nor observed family social arrangements.[1]

Many investigators use questionnaires to assess twin zygosity. Zygosity refers to whether the twins come from two eggs or one egg. Two-egg twins are dizygotic (DZ) or "fraternal"; one-egg twins are monozygotic (MZ) or "identical." Such questionnaires might be fairly accurate (90-95%) if they are answered by both twins (Nichols & Bilbro, 1966; Ooki, Yamada, & Hayakawa, 1990). However, this means that 10% are *inaccurate*. Furthermore, Carter-Saltzman and Scarr (1977) showed that the diagnosis of zygosity might be as much as 40% inaccurate depending on the characteristics one is studying. At a minimum, researchers should check on the accuracy of questionnaire data by assessing the zygosity of a subsample with biological methods.

The inaccuracy of questionnaire studies of zygosity favor genetic theories. Similar DZ twins who share physical or behavioral characteristics may be diagnosed as MZ and dissimilar MZ twins as DZ. This is particularly true if the trait being studied is used to determine zygosity. For example, one could never use physical appearance for classification if the study was on the genetics of height. Similarly, homosexual DZ twins might use their homosexuality to decide that they are, in fact, MZ twins. MZ twins that do not share a sexual preference might decide that they are DZ because of the common belief that homosexuality is inherited. Nichols and Bilbro

(1966) developed their questionnaire when zygosity testing was an art and MZ twins were ascertained by exclusion. If twins did not match on any single blood group test they were diagnosed as DZ twins. That is, twins with no discrepancies were considered to be MZ. At that time, the available tests were only about 90% accurate and required fairly sophisticated analyses. There are now available many other genetic tests for zygosity (e.g., HLA blood groups, electrophoretic protein variation, and DNA fingerprints). Zygosity can now be ascertained with more than a 99% rate of accuracy. No credible geneticist would consider publishing an animal study in which 10% of the relationships were unknown, or worse, biased in the direction that the investigator desires. Human behavior geneticists should require the same degree of accuracy.

RECRUITMENT OF SAMPLE

The results of a behavior-genetic study should be applicable to the wider population. Ideally, subjects should be randomly recruited from the population, but it is probably impossible for financial as well as ethical reasons. Not only would it be difficult to obtain an adequate sample size for rare behaviors but also human subjects can not be compelled to participate in a study. One is then left to recruit subjects non-randomly. For example, homosexual subjects are often recruited through gay and lesbian publications even though the readers of such publications are not representative of the entire homosexual population. In family studies, one might recruit a subject but then fail to obtain the cooperation of other family members. Family members that agree to participate might be very different from those that do not.

Recruitment bias is even more pronounced in twin studies. The proportionally greater participation of women and MZ twins is so pronounced that it has been given the name of the "rule of two-thirds" (see Lykken, McGue & Tellegen, 1987). It is very likely that twins showing striking differences will be the most likely to refuse participation. At a minimum, as Lykken and colleagues state, one could show that "the dependent variable has a larger variance in the twin sample [than in] the reference population" (p. 358). Alternatively, one could show that the means and variances of the MZ and

DZ twins are identical. If a representative sample is not possible, the behavior-genetic researcher must attempt to assess the effects of non-random recruitment and report how they limit the generalizability of the results.

SAMPLE SIZE

Sample size is important not only for assigning standard errors to estimates of traits (something seldom calculated) but also for determining the complexity of the genetic model that one can test. Klein, DeFries, and Finkbeiner (1973, p. 356) have stated that "In the estimation of population parameters such as heritability and genetic correlation, a major consideration must be that of the statistical significance of possible results. Unless the resulting estimates can be demonstrated to be statistically significant, the question of practical or scientific significance cannot be raised."

The Kinsey group believed that several hundred siblings were required in genetic studies of homosexuality to achieve statistical significance although this may be too conservative. To estimate heritability (see below) the minimum sample size for a family study is 400 families of 4 members each (Klein et al., 1973; Klein, 1974). If one wants to compare two populations for heritability, the minimum sample size is 400 families of 4 members in each population. Twin studies also require large sample sizes. Eaves (1972) suggested that it might be necessary to measure as many as 2500 pairs of twins and siblings. Even such an ambitious study would not adequately address complex genetic models.

BIOLOGICAL, GENETIC, AND INHERITED TRAITS

Before I continue with my review of genetic studies of homosexuality, I will discuss a few genetic terms and concepts that may be unfamiliar to non-geneticists.

The fundamental unit of heredity is the gene which is made up of DNA. Humans inherit one half of their genes from each parent. The complement of genes that comes from each parent is called one's *genotype*. Our genotype is our only inheritance; it is the only way genetically that we can resemble a parent. The genotype, however, is not one's *genetic constitution* or *genetic architecture*. These latter terms refer not only to genes but also to genetic interactions.

In a speech before the Animal Behavior Society, Aubrey Manning (1975) stated that the fundamental goal of behavior genetics "was to discover how behavioral potential is encoded in the genome and expressed during the course of development." The geneticist must understand how differences at the level of macromolecules (e.g., DNA) are manifested as differences in complex behaviors at the level of the whole organism. Manning proposed that the immensity of the question was matched by the inaccessibility of the answer. Although he was speaking somewhat facetiously, he was correct in asserting that the correlation of gene differences with behavioral differences requires careful analyses at all levels of organization (e.g., biochemical, physiological, and anatomical).

The processes of biological development are largely unknown. The information encoded in the DNA of a single cell directs the formation of a complex organism with, in the case of humans, over a 100 trillion cells. If genes acted linearly, there would not be enough genes in the DNA to produce a human being. There are no equations for producing human beings. Genes not only make specific products, but they also interact with other genes to produce what are called emergent interactions. These interactions shape development. Genes may be active only once during development or many times. At each period the phenotype of the gene might change in response to the surrounding cells or other genes. Even after a gene has had its particular effect, it may continue to influence other genes by its role in complex gene-to-gene or tissue-to-tissue interactions.

The amazing thing about biological development is that it works so efficiently. At birth most people are basically normal although even minor fluctuations in gene composition or environment can cause large changes in complex systems such as animal and human behavior. Identical genotypes in identical environments may show large differences in a number of phenotypes (see Storrs and Williams, 1968, on monozygotic armadillos). At birth, individuals can be genetically identical but biologically different because of idiosyncratic developmental events. These differences become part of the *permanent phenotype* of the individual. Most people's understanding of genetics is based on the inheritance of genes of major influence (e.g., white vs. red eyes in the fruit fly *Drosophila melanogaster*), which exert more-or-less the same effect in all individuals. Genes of modest effect and those affecting normal differences in behavior are much more difficult to detect within the rich nexus of genetic interactions.

Genetics is concerned with differences. Only about 30% of all human genes show detectable variation. The other 70% are highly invariant in all members of the human species. The vast majority of our human characteristics are genetic but invariant. These characteristics distinguish us from other species but are of little interest to a geneticist. Geneticists are concerned only with the 30% of genes that do vary within a species.

During development, interactions arise within a gene and among genes. Humans possess two alternate forms of a gene called *alleles*. The effect of one allele depends to some extent on the other allele present. Thus, the effect of an allele A_1 largely depends on whether the other allele of the same gene is A_1, A_2, or A_3. This type of within-gene interaction is called *dominance*. Your resemblance to your mother depends, in part, on your father's genes. The effect of alleles of one gene may depend on pairs of alleles of other genes. These are called *epistatic* interactions. Epistatic interactions arise within an individual and cannot be inherited by offspring. As the number of genes increases arithmetically, the number of epistatic interactions increases geometrically. Epistatic interactions are genetic, but they contribute nothing to the resemblance between parents and offspring, or between relatives such as half-siblings (who share only one parent in common). Epistatic interactions contribute to the resemblance between full sibs and are extremely important in determining the resemblance of monozygotic twins. Epistatic interactions are interesting to a geneticist but are not what most people consider to be genetic since they cannot be inherited.

In addition to genes and interactions, in humans (and mammals in general), the genes from the father are treated differently from the genes from the mother (Rodgers, 1992). Paternal genes are tagged with methyl groups that identify them as your father's contribution. We are just beginning to understand this function.

BREEDING VALUE (ADDITIVE GENETIC VALUE) AND HERITABILITY

Individual differences in complex traits are generally influenced by differences in the alleles of three or more genes. These complex traits are called *polygenic traits* or *quantitative traits*. It is convenient to treat polygenic traits *as if* each allele adds a certain quantitative increment to a metric trait. A metric trait is one showing a continuous distribution such as height or weight. For example, we might invent a genetic system wherein each allele "adds" 2 liters of milk for a cow, or 1 inch of height for a human. The effect of any quantitative gene is measured in terms of gene frequencies and in terms of some theoretical parameters. The gene frequency is the proportional representation of an allele in the population. For example, if 60% of the alleles of the A gene are A_1 alleles then the gene frequency of A_1 is 0.60. The theoretical parameters are based on the phenotypic values of the two homozygotes (two identical alleles) and the heterozygote (two different alleles) for each gene. The phenotypic values for the homozygote and heterozygote are generally unknowable. If both gene frequencies and the theoretical values are known, then one can calculate the *breeding value* or *additive genetic value* for any individual in the population. The additive genetic value describes the deviation of a single individual's offspring from the average individual in the population. If these values are not known, we can estimate the net breeding value across all genes by careful breeding studies. For example, in dairy cows we might mate 10 bulls each to 5 cows and look at the milk yield of 5 calves of each of those females. We could then partition out the breeding value of each bull. Such analyses are not possible for humans. The additive genetic value is a *populational descriptor* and is accurate only for the gene frequencies described and the environment in which it is measured.

We cannot measure the additive genetic value of any individual human subject. Instead we look at the phenotypic variance of a trait and then attempt to subdivide that variance. Starting with the simple (and nonsensical) nature-nurture equation that the *phenotype = the environment* plus *the genotype* (P = G + E), we can partition the variance using the following equation:

Equation 1: $V_p = V_g + V_e + 2Cov_{(ge)}$

That is, the phenotypic variance (V_p) is a function of the genotypic variance (V_g), the environmental variance (V_e), and the genotype-environmental covariance ($2Cov_{[ge]}$). The genotype-environment covariance becomes important if genotypes are not randomly distributed across environments. Covariance is relatively easy to eliminate in the lab, but it is very important for humans. Parents with abundant financial resources can provide their children with rich environments. For example, they will provide expensive art lessons for children with artistic talent. Later in life, individuals will select environments in which they are most comfortable. In practice, most researchers ignore the covariance since it is nearly impossible to measure in human populations. In doing so they overestimate genetic variance and heritability.

Just as total phenotypic variance can be formulated as a linear equation, total genotypic variance (V_g) can be subdivided into *additive genetic variance* (V_a), *dominance deviation variance* (V_d), and different types of *epistatic genetic variances,* which can be summarized as (V_i).

Equation 2: $V_g = V_a + V_d + V_i$

The above terms are all *populational descriptors*. They describe the partitioning of variance in a particular population with a particular gene frequency. In a different population, the values of the variance change. The additive genetic variance is the variation in breeding value and the portion of the variation that can be inherited. In practice, many researchers assume that dominance deviation and the epistatic variance are zero. They, therefore, estimate only the additive genetic variance. Dominance and epistatic variance are nearly impossible to measure but they cannot merely be discarded. My own work with relatively simple behaviors in flies indicates that epistatic variance is much more important than additive genetic variance (McGuire, 1992; McGuire & Tully, 1986, 1987).

Other researchers subdivide the environmental variance into *within family variance*, variance that makes family members differ among themselves, and *between family variance*, variance that makes one family different from another. The equation for phenotypic variance (ignoring all possible genotype-environment covariances) is hereby expanded to:

Equation 3: $V_p = V_a + V_d + V_i + V_{ew} + V_{eb}$

In agricultural science, researchers can predict the results of selective breeding in particular agricultural environments if they know the ratio of additive genetic variance to total phenotypic variance (V_a/V_p). This ratio is called *narrow heritability* (h^2). Narrow heritability is used for economic purposes to compare the efficacy of selective breeding with that of environmental modification. Narrow heritability is *not* a function of a trait. It is a populational descriptor. Its value depends on gene frequencies and environmental variance. It is most certainly not a nature/nurture ratio. A trait might be 100% genetic yet have no genetic variance – the classical description of an instinct. That is, the narrow heritability of instinct would be zero. Heritability for a trait can be estimated in a specified human population only under certain conditions where there is no genotype-environment covariance, no dominance deviation variance, and no epistatic genetic variance. The heritability estimate, however, is only valid for the conditions under which it is measured. It cannot be applied to other populations nor even to the same population reared under different environmental conditions. In any case, heritability applies only to variance and not to individuals. It cannot be used to comprehend the etiology of a trait. Heritability estimates, however, are often used for the sole purpose of human behavior-genetics studies.

GENETIC MODELS

There is nothing mysterious or magical about genetic models. They are essentially sophisticated guesses about a particular set of phenotypes. Mathematical models are constructed using specific genetic theories. For example, researchers working with animal or plant genetics construct models based on expected Mendelian ratios. They breed organisms of known genotype and measure the distribution of phenotypes among the progeny of many different generations. Then they compare observed phenotypic distributions with expected phenotypic distributions for goodness of fit. The complexity of the models they test depends on the number of generations sampled and the sample size (Mather & Jinks, 1982). Researchers working with humans might measure a trait in multigenerational families and then propose various models to explain the observed patterns of inheritance in a family tree. Such procedures are successful only if the phenotype can be unambiguously measured and only if a few genes contribute to the differences.

If phenotypic differences involve many genes of small effect, then the effects of those genes might be statistically estimated using highly structured breeding designs. Such designs are not ethically permissible for humans. Studies of quantitative traits in men and women are generally limited to the estimation of heritability. That is, one studies the variance in the trait but not the trait itself.

Recent attention has focused on model fitting that is based on path analyses or path models (Wright, 1968). Path models use variance-covariance matrices to estimate genetic and environmental parameters. The underlying assumption of path models is that the resemblance between any two relatives is a linear sum of genetic and environmental variables. The models are generally quite simple but they require many presuppositions. For example, it is assumed that MZ and DZ twins have experienced equal environments (Heath, Neale, Hewitt, Eaves, & Fulker, 1989) and have been randomly selected. It is further assumed that the behavior of interest is either continuously or dichotomously variable. If the latter, it is assumed that the behavior must represent an underlying normal distribution. Generally only additive genetic values can be estimated. Genetic dominance, for example, cannot be estimated unless other parameters are removed. Complex interactions such as epistasis or effects of assortative mating can not be represented in the model. Experimenters assign numerical weights to the parameters of the model and see how well their guesses explain the observed correlations. Alternate models are evaluated using goodness-of-fit procedures (usually Chi-square [χ^2]) (Neale, Hewitt, Eaves, &

Fulker, 1989, p. 44). Even a good fit to the data does not prove that the model is correct. As Neale et al. (p. 46) have stated, "On the contrary, the model could be completely and utterly false yet give a good account of the observed data." Researchers also often evaluate alternative models without actually determining if any of the parameters of that model are significantly different from zero. Exploring biometrical genetic models as a first step can be quite interesting. They are extremely limited, however, and one must be cautious in interpreting the results.

BEHAVIOR GENETICS STUDIES OF HOMOSEXUALITY

There are three methods available for human behavior genetics: family studies, twin studies, and adoption studies. Only the first two have been attempted with homosexuality. All of these studies share common problems, including non-random recruitment and small sample size.

Family Studies

The underlying presupposition of family studies is that behavioral resemblance between relatives should be a function of the number of genes (and interactions) that the relatives share. For example, parents and offspring share 1/2 of their genes but none of their genetic interactions. Full sibs share 1/2 of their genes as well as 1/4 of their dominance and some of their epistatic interactions. Half sibs share 1/4 of their genes in common but no genetic interactions. Researchers look at the correlations between many kinds of relatives and estimate various genetic and environmental parameters, including heritability.

In a family study it is extremely important that family members have been reared in equivalent environments and that the same behavior is measured at the same age with the same tests. Determining equivalency of environments is especially difficult in multigenerational studies. Measuring all family members at the same age with the same test is nearly impossible for multigenerational studies and awkward for sibling studies. If one uses different tests, then it is difficult to interpret any correlations. Using individuals of different ages may or may not affect the results depending on the particular behavior studied. In family studies of homosexuality it is inappropriate to compare adults to adolescents.

There have been few systematic family studies of homosexuality; most are anecdotal. For example, Dank (1971) described six homosexual siblings who had a very abusive, alcoholic father. His findings paralleled those of Heston and Shields (1968), who studied a family of 14 siblings, with two sets of MZ twins who were both homosexual. Their family resembled Dank's family in the descriptions of the father and mother. These two reports, however, were case studies, not family studies. Henry (1948) studied family trees for a number of homosexuals. He collected his information from the subjects and lumped a variety of traits (e.g., artistic ability, venereal disease, alcoholism, psychopathology, homosexuality, promiscuity, and bisexuality). As such, his family trees are essentially useless.

Parent-offspring studies of homosexuality are difficult, since many homosexuals do not have children and since those who do are hard to recruit for a family study (e.g., Kallman, 1952a,b). Kallman studied 112 male non-twin singletons and 85 male twin pairs. Among this group there were found only 5 offspring. He was unable to verify paternity for any of the five. Kallman had information on 88 fathers of homosexual men. Only 2 of these had court records that substantiated homosexual activity. Kenyon (1968) reported more homosexuals in the families of lesbian subjects as compared to heterosexual controls. Kenyon believed that his figures were too disparate to make any meaningful statistical comparisons. His results most likely reflected differential shared information (more open discussion of sexual orientation) than differential homosexuality. Pillard, Poumadere, and Carretta (1981) summarized their research on 35 male homosexuals. They reported no increase in lesbian sisters but a large increase in homosexual and bisexual brothers (12/45). Few details about recruitment, ascertainment of subject homosexuality, or procedures for rating relatives were presented.

Pillard, Poumadere, and Carretta (1981) and Pillard and Weinrich (1986) have presented the most extensive family study to date. They will be discussed together since they used many of the same subjects. Subjects were recruited through advertisements appearing in three general interest newspapers, a gay newspaper, and a radio station in the Boston area. This was a highly selected sample of educated Caucasian males. Almost all of the gay subjects were recruited through the advertisements in the gay newspaper and there was a great deal of self-selection. Two hundred ninety-five men initially answered the message (N = 295). One hundred four men did not meet eligibility requirements (N = 191). An additional 80 men either refused to participate or failed to show up for the inter-view (N = 111). Another 11 men were dropped because they "were of ambiguous sexual orientation or revealed an inconsistency be-tween their sexual fantasies and their sexual behavior" (p. 515). Another 5 were dropped because they were adopted or had adopted siblings and one more was dropped for a language barrier (N = 100). These 100 males had 238 brothers and sisters over the age of 20. Ten of the index cases refused to allow one or more of their siblings to be contacted (Sibling N = 221). Eight siblings could not be contacted (Sibling N = 213). Thirty-six others declined to partic-ipate (Sibling N = 177) and one sibling had incomplete data (Sib-ling N = 176). The number of index cases entirely eliminated, since no siblings participated, was not given.

As previously discussed, it is absolutely essential that all mem-bers of the group be measured in the same way. Pillard et al. (1981) rated their index cases using personal interviews and assigned four separate Kinsey ratings (0 to 6) of fantasy and behavior over their lifetime and for the past year. These four ratings were then used to get a "consensus rating" (Pillard & Weinrich, 1986, p. 809). This was unnecessary since they state (p. 809) that "in most cases there was no conflict among the four ratings" and they had already elimi-nated those subjects with inconsistent scores. When there was con-flict, they either used current ratings or averaged the fantasy and behavioral ratings and rounded off toward the higher Kinsey num-ber.

While one might argue with their choice of methods, the inexpli-cable part of the studies concerns their use of Kinsey ratings. Kinsey et al. (1948) devised the scale to demonstrate a continuum of sexual orientation. That is, humans were not dichotomized into homosexual/heterosexual with bisexuals being some insignificant group. After assigning Kinsey ratings, however, Pillard and Weinrich dichotomized the index cases into homosexual (4-6) and heterosexual (0-2). They identified no bisexuals, asserting the old notion that bisexuals are rare.

Sibling sexual orientation was rated four different ways. Pillard et al. (1981) asked the index cases about the sexual orientation of their siblings. They ranked their siblings as probably or possibly heterosexual or homosexual. Pillard and Weinrich divided siblings into three categories: 123 siblings answered three questions on a questionnaire; 39 completed a face to face interview; and 15 completed a telephone interview. Nineteen siblings completed both a personal interview and a questionnaire. Since all 19 were heterosexual this procedure does not validate their questionnaire. Some siblings were included, even if they refused to participate, if the information provided by the index subject was verified by another sibling or by the experimenter's observations (e.g., talking to a spouse was evidence for heterosexuality). The use of four different methods seriously compromises the study.

A still more serious problem is their conflicting definitions of sexual orientation (see Table 1). An individual who rated 2 on the Kinsey scale must be confused about his sexual identity! If he was an index case, he was a heterosexual. If he was a sibling of an index case, then he was a bisexual, on page 810, and a homosexual, on page 811. An index case and his sibling with identical sexual orientations (Kinsey rating 2) would be classified as different! There is no legitimate reason, empirically or statistically, to force

TABLE 1. Conflicting definitions of sexual orientation—Pillard and Weinrich (1986).

	Index Cases (p. 809)	Siblings (p. 810)	Siblings (p. 811)
Heterosexual	0-2	0-1	0-1
Bisexual	3	2-4	
Homosexual	4-6	5-6	2-6

subjects into a dichotomous rating. Although the experimenters give lip service to the Kinsey scale, if they really used it as it was originally intended, they would present the raw distributions for all ratings. It might subsequently be necessary to combine ratings in order to meet the minimum assumptions for Chi-square tests but this should be done only after the distribution has been presented.

Recently, Hamer, Hu, Magnuson, Hu, and Pattatucci (1993) claimed to have found a maternal inheritance for male homosexuality. In addition, they state that they found five markers on the X-chromosome that are linked to homosexuality. These results suggest that there is an X-linked "gene" for homosexuality. This research was widely reported in the popular press and on television. Despite all of this attention, these are very preliminary results. I have to agree with King (1993) that "Were virtually any other trait involved, the paper would have received little public notice until the results had been independently replicated" (p. 288).

Hamer et al. undertook this research because of the compelling "evidence" for genetic and neuroanatomical factors in male homosexuality. I will not review their introduction in detail. I invite the reader to compare their superficial acceptance of most genetics-of-homosexuality papers with the serious criticisms in this paper. Similarly, the reader should compare their easy acceptance of neuroanatomical studies of homosexual men with Byne's (this volume) careful critiques.

The Hamer et al. study shares many of the problems of other studies of homosexuality. The populations studied are not representative of the general population. One of their populations, for example, consisted of 76 men from an HIV clinic. It was difficult to obtain family data for these men. Only twenty-six of these men had one or more of their relatives agree to participate. The second sample consisted of 38 pairs of homosexual brothers who were recruited through advertisements in homophile publications (two pairs were added later). Respondents to the ads were rejected if they had a homosexual father or son or more than one lesbian sister. Assessment of homosexuality was by either interview or questionnaire. In general, respondents placed themselves on the Kinsey scale. Although the probands reported a wide range of sexual behaviors, identities, and fantasies, the experimenters divided the men into homosexual or heterosexual. The relatives were assigned sexuality orientations by the probands. This method has surface validity. If heterosexuals make up 98% of the population (as the experimenters suggest) then one can obtain a high rate of reliability by always guessing heterosexual. In addition, this method might be fairly accurate in determining homosexuals who have come out to their families. Thus one might get good agreement between the guess of the proband and the admitted sexual orientation of a relative, but such methods are probably not accurate in assessing the wide range of human sexual orientation.

The researchers report an excess of homosexual maternal male relatives over homosexual paternal male relatives for men from the HIV clinic. This conclusion is based on multiple Chi-square comparisons of the observed frequencies of each class of relatives to a hypothetical 2% populational frequency. These are inappropriate tests. In every case, the expected frequency of homosexual relatives is less than 5. Such small samples mean that one often rejects the null hypothesis when there is, in fact, no difference. I have reanalyzed the data from Table X using a contingency Chi-square test for independence. The contingency Chi-square test is not so affected by small sample sizes. Using the more appropriate test, I compared similar pairs of relatives (maternal vs. paternal uncles; maternal cousins from uncles, and aunts, and paternal cousins from uncles and aunts). In none of these three cases did I find a significant difference. That is, there was no evidence for a maternal effect.

There were also problems with the methodology and the data in the linkage study. There were no differences in rates of homosexuality between maternal and paternal uncles (contingency Chi-square test) despite the fact that this sample had been "enriched" for "genes" on the X chromosome. There was a slight difference between maternal cousins from uncles and from aunts (prob. between .01 and .05). This might be significant but it is difficult to imagine a genetic system that failed to affect uncles but affected more distantly related cousins.

The researchers attempted to find co-occurrences of homosexuality and markers on the X-chromosome. They looked at 22 X-chromosome markers (repeated sequences and Restriction Fragment Length Polymorphisms) in 40 pairs of homosexual brothers. If any of these markers were near the putative "homosexual gene" then most or all of the homosexual brothers should share those marker alleles as "identical-by-descent." That is, the alleles would be meiotic copies. In an ideal situation, the mother would give the homosexual "gene" to half of her sons and the "heterosexual" gene to the other half. This would be detected by the fact that the homosexual pairs would have the same linked markers. This assumes that the mother is heterozygous for all the markers linked to the putative "gene." If she is homozygous for these markers, then the brothers could have the same marker genotype but not the same "homosexual" gene. At a minimum then, one must test all of the brothers and all of the mothers. It would certainly be desirable to test all members of the pedigree.

Despite the necessity of testing all the mothers, the researchers have complete data on only 14 of 40 mothers. The researchers report that 33 out of 40 pairs of brothers were concordant on 5 linked markers (a probability they calculate as better than .001). This number is misleading. The majority of the concordances come from 21 pairs of siblings where the mother was not tested. These brothers are concordant at many loci, not just the five of interest. This result suggests that the mothers were homozygous at many loci. The brothers are concordant but might be either identical by descent or alike in kind. Only the first case provides evidence for a linked gene. If these 21 cases are excluded from the analyses, the differences (12 vs 7) are not nearly so impressive.

Until these results are replicated with better recruitment procedures, accurate, reliable, and consistent assessment of sexual orientation, sufficient sample sizes, appropriate statistics, and rigorous testing of all members of the pedigrees, they should be viewed with extreme skepticism.

Twin Studies

At first glance, using twins seem to be the ideal method of studying human behavior genetics. Price (1950, p. 293) has stated that "monozygotic twins are 'experiments' which nature has conducted for us, starting in each case with identical sets of genes and varying environmental factors." There are two ways of conducting twin studies. One is to find monozygotic twins (also called MZ twins, one-egg twins, or identical twins) who have been separated at birth. If they are MZ twins and they had been randomly placed into families, then the behavioral trait for which they correlate is genetic. This is the direction taken by Bouchard and colleagues (Bouchard, Heston, Eckert, Keyes, & Resnick, 1981). The other twin method compares sets of MZ twins to sets of dizygotic twins (also known as DZ twins, two-egg twins, and fraternal twins). If MZ and DZ twins experience equal environments, and one makes a number of simplifying assumptions, then heritability can be estimated. Such heritability estimates are often the only goal of twin studies, including those of homosexuality.

Twin studies are often used to calculate heritability (h^2). MZ twins share all of their additive genetic variance (V_a), all of their dominance genetic variance (V_d), and all of their epistatic interaction variance (for only two genes V_{aa}, V_{ad}, V_{dd}). The usual method of calculating heritability is to calculate the intraclass correlations for MZ twins and DZ twins. If one assumes equal environments, no dominance variance, and no interaction variance, then the difference between the MZ and DZ correlations equals $1/2$ h^2 (Falconer, 1981). If there is dominance and epistasis, the estimate of h^2 is widely biased. The heritability estimate includes not only additive variance, if any, but $3/2$ V_d and $3/2$ V_{aa} + $7/4$ V_{ad} + $15/8$ V_{dd}. Even modest amounts of V_d, V_{aa}, V_{ad}, or V_{dd} would vastly overestimate the genetic contribution *even if there were absolutely no additive genetic variance.* In most models, the contribution of the environmental effects depend on the accurate estimate of heritability. Inflating the heritability term must necessarily deflate the environmental terms (see Haviland, McGuire, & Rothbaum, 1983, p. 638).

Twin Studies of Homosexuality

Most twin studies of homosexuality are anecdotal accounts of concordant (both twins are homosexual) or discordant (only one twin is homosexual) twin pairs. For example, Pardes, Steinberg, and Simon (1967) presented a case study of a lesbian twin pair who had mutual sexual contact. Perkins (1973) described a pair of lesbian MZ twins but limited her analysis (somewhat inexplicably) to an analysis of their chromosomes (both had a normal female complement). Other researchers studied discordant twins. Parker (1964),

Klintworth (1962), Zuger (1976), and McConaghy and Blaszczyn- ski (1980) studied six pairs of discordant male MZ twins. Rainier, Mesnikoff, Kolb, and Carr (1960) reported on one pair of male and one pair of female MZ twins whom they described as discordant. The female twins, however, had never engaged in sexual activity. Finally, Dank (1971) and Heston and Shields (1968) discussed a total of 4 twin pairs within their highly dysfunctional families (see above). The male DZ twin pair reported by Dank (1971) was dis- cordant. Two of the three male MZ twin pairs reported by Heston and Shields (1968) were concordant for homosexuality while the third pair was concordant for heterosexuality.

There is only one study of homosexual MZ twins reared apart (Eckert, Bouchard, Bohlen, & Heston, 1986). It reported on 6 pairs of twins (2 male and 4 female) with at least one member of the pair describing himself/herself as homosexual. One of the male pairs was concordant for homosexuality. The other male pair (age 35) had one member who had been exclusively homosexual since age 19 and another member who had been exclusively heterosexual since age 20. The experimenters were willing to "forgive" the adolescent heterosexual affairs of twin A and labeled him as homo- sexual. However, the 15 years of exclusive heterosexual activity of twin B with his wife was not persuasive enough for the experiment- ers to diagnose his sexual orientation. They concluded that "the male pairs tend to confirm earlier studies of twins and twin families; the concordance rate for sexual orientation among MZ pairs is consistently above that of DZ pairs, and despite all problems of ascertainment and diagnosis, it is hard to deny genetic factors as an aetiological role" (p. 424). Three of the female twin pairs were definitely discordant for homosexuality. The fourth pair had one member who had extensive homosexual affairs until her second marriage at age 29 and had been exclusively heterosexual for 19 years. The other sister was homosexual. The experimenters con- cluded that homosexuality was "acquired after conception, most likely after birth, but before menarche" (p. 424). None of these conclusions, however, followed from their data.

There have been few formal studies of homosexuality using MZ and DZ twins: Kallman (1952a,b), Heston and Shields (1968), Buh- rich, Bailey, and Martin (1991), Bailey and Pillard (1991), and King and McDonald (1992). Since four of these five studies are often cited as "proving" the biological basis of homosexuality, I will examine them here.

Kallman (1952a,b) recruited a total of 85 MZ and DZ twins from contacts within psychiatric, correctional, and charitable organizations and through "direct contacts with the clandestine homosexual world" (p. 287). He identified homosexuals as having ratings from 3 to 6 on the Kinsey scale. Kallman claimed that all co-twins of his MZ index cases were homosexual–100% concordance, while the DZ twins showed only moderate concordance. Kallman (1960) later acknowledged that the 100% concordance was only a statistical artifact.

Heston and Shields (1968) studied a few male twins included in the Maudsley twin study who were acknowledged homosexuals. They had 12 twin pairs (5 MZ and 7 DZ). At least one of the twins in each pair had been referred to the Maudsley hospital for psychiatric counseling. The authors acknowledged that these men were not a representative sample. Zygosity was diagnosed by blood testing. The subjects were classified as either homosexual or heterosexual without any use of Kinsey ratings. Two of five pairs of MZ twins were concordant for homosexuality and one of seven pairs of DZ twins was concordant. Obviously, the sample size is too small to draw inferences about genetic influences on homosexuality.

Buhrich, Bailey, and Martin (1991) studied sexual identity and sexual orientation in 95 pairs of MZ and 63 pairs of DZ male twins, a highly selected sample. Questionnaires were mailed to 303 twin pairs. In only 162 of the pairs did both members return the questionnaire. One pair had to be eliminated since the data was incomplete. The median age was 25 (ranging 19-40). Thus, the researchers were combining data from adolescent twins (ages of maximal sexual flexibility) and adults who are more likely to be stable in their sexual identity. Zygosity was determined by questionnaire.

The method used by Buhrich group to determine sexual orientation is suspect. Subjects provided a percentage rating in response to three questions pertaining to adult sexual orientation. The percentages were then averaged and turned into modified Kinsey ratings (1 to 6 instead of 0 to 6). The questions were never pretested for reliability (p. 80).

The authors reported proportionally more homosexual MZ than DZ twins. They inappropriately used a t-test of means for nominal data. A Chi-square was done on only *part* of the data. I reanalyzed the data using the entire distribution and found no differences between the two groups (Contingency $\chi^2 = 5.7$; N.S. at .05 level, df = 3. The last three categories were combined to meet the assumptions of χ^2 testing). The rest of the paper was devoted to fitting correlations into complex path models. They reported a familial connection to homosexuality, which could be attributed to either genetics or environment. With a small sample size and non-random sampling it is difficult to interpret the significance of their results.

Bailey and Pillard's (1991) study was widely reported in the popular press. As with other studies, Bailey and Pillard (1991) had the problem of non-random recruitment of subjects and uneven cooperation of family members. All subject recruitment was through gay publications in the Midwest and Southwest. They obtained 115 twins and 46 subjects with an adoptive brother. Subjects were interviewed either in person or by telephone. These 161 subjects had 174 qualified relatives. Permission was granted to contact only 135 of the relatives. Of these only 127 relatives returned the questionnaires. They also used the reports of the subject to identify the sexual orientation of their relatives (113 co-twins and 57 adoptive brothers). In addition, twin subjects were asked about non-twin brothers, although the latter were not contacted.

The researchers relied heavily on questionnaires. Zygosity was based entirely on a questionnaire. The relatives answered 5 questionnaire items about sexual preference. Two questions requested self-assigned Kinsey ratings. Four different instruments were used to measure homosexuality: (1) personal interviews of index cases, (2) telephone interviews, (3) questionnaire answers, and (4) rating by co-twin. Kinsey ratings for relatives were not presented although the investigators categorized them as homosexual, bisexual, and heterosexual. It is impossible to reanalyze their data since they do not report the proportion of heterosexual, bisexual, and homosexual individuals in each group. However, they assert that 29 out of 56 MZ co-twins were bisexual or homosexual (bisexuals were grouped with homosexuals, combined to one term of homosexuality) while 12 out of 54 DZ co-twins were homosexual. In addition, 6 out of 57 adopted brothers were homosexual. Using ratings derived from questionnaire responses, the concordance rates of MZ twins was 50% (25 out of 50), DZ twins was 24% (11 out of 46), and adopted brothers was 19% (6 out of 31). Adopted brothers were not significantly different from DZ twins. Bailey and Pillard attributed this result to sampling error. That is, heterosexual adoptive brothers were not allowed to be contacted. Of non-twin biological brothers (13 out of 142), 9.2% were reported to be homosexual, a percentage no greater than that for adopted brothers.

Such results are problematic. The greater MZ vs. DZ correlations could be due to differential environmental effects, recruitment bias, substantially shared environments, additive genetic effects, or substantial non-additive genetic effects. The fact that biological brothers and adopted brothers show the same incidence of homosexuality strongly suggests that it is entirely environmental in origin. Bailey and Pillard downplay this comparison which seriously weakens their biological argument, by invoking the Pillard and Weinrich (1986) study. I have already shown that study has profound problems of its own and its results cannot rescue the weak results of this subsequent study.

Bailey and Pillard (1991) estimate heritability using tetrachoric correlations and model fitting. No standard errors of the heritability estimates are reported. It is quite possible that the heritability estimates are not significantly different from either zero or one since very large numbers of twins must be tested to get an accurate estimate. Rather than estimating heritability directly, Bailey and Pillard use model fitting. That is, they found an estimate of heritability that made their particular model work. However, it is inappropriate to try to fit alternative models without evaluating the significance of each parameter contained within that model.

King and McDonald (1992) investigated factors within a twin pair that might lead to homosexuality. They recruited 46 homosexual men and women who were twins through advertisements in local and national gay publications in Britain. These subjects completed a questionnaire about themselves and their co-twin. In addition, they answered questions about sexual attraction toward, and sexual interaction with, their co-twin. Information was not confirmed by the co-twins. Zygosity was determined by asking the subjects if they were monozygotic or dizygotic twins. This study shares all of the problems of the previous four twin studies.

King and McDonald did not find any evidence for a genetic basis of homosexuality. Only 9 of the co-twins were rated as homosexual or bisexual (5 out of 15 MZ twins and 3 out of 22 DZ twins). The researchers also reported that 7 of the twins (6 MZ, 1 DZ) had had sexual contact with their same-sex twin. In five of these seven cases, however, the co-twin was regarded as heterosexual. Obviously, the data in this study are no stronger than the data in the other four studies. King and McDonald suggest, however, that it is time to look at the dynamics of the twin relationship. They state a "more detailed exploration of the sexual relationships between twins and their later development may cast more light on the origins of sexuality than a narrow search for genetic factors" (p. 409).

SOCIAL IMPLICATIONS OF GENETIC MODELS

Research on humans is often used for political or social purposes. For example, some people want homosexuality to be biological or genetic because they then believe that because homosexuals are "born that way" they will somehow be tolerated. Others advocate environmental explanations since this justifies their belief that individuals "chose a gay lifestyle." I am all too conscious of the sordid history of eugenics in the United States where pseudogenetics has been used as an instrument of oppression. For example, studies of poor Southern whites who were characterized as "shiftless lazy white trash" tried to show that their behavior was genetic. We now know that their lethargy was due to chronic hookworm infection (Chase, 1980). More recently, people advocated incarcerating XYY males at birth because they were destined to become violent criminals (Reilly, 1977, pp. 238-248). The political decision to back a genetic explanation for homosexuality is a two-edged sword; it can alleviate discrimination or it might lead to another round of eugenics.

CONCLUSIONS

The evidence for a genetic component for homosexuality is hardly overwhelming. Numerous studies that purport to prove the existence of a genetic aspect to homosexuality are either anecdotal or seriously flawed. Homosexuality is often poorly defined and researchers use a variety of behavioral measures. The sample sizes are too small and recruitment of subjects is biased. As a result, only the simplest possible genetic models can be applied. At best, there might be a modest familial effect to account for populational variance, although the significance of such an effect is impossible to assess. It is very difficult to determine whether a hypothesized familial factor is due to additive genetic, emergent genetic, environmental, or random effects.

If researchers continue to pursue this type of investigation of homosexuality, then, at a minimum, they should be expected to adhere to scientific standards. The "glamour" of working on controversial behaviors must not be a substitute for scientific rigor. Researchers working with traits that are stigmatized must be even more rigorous in their methodology and extremely careful in generalizing their data.

Even if one could design a human-behavior genetic study that met all of the requisite criteria, one could ask, "What do you intend to learn from twin and family studies of homosexuality?" Partitioning the variance of a population tells us nothing about an individual's sexual orientation or about the etiology of any particular trait. There is no compelling reason to estimate heritability unless one is going to selectively breed for the trait. Heritability will not lead one to discover its etiology.[2]

As a culture, the West is obsessed with causality and dichotomy. Just as many researchers persist in asserting a homosexual/heterosexual dichotomy, most people want to have homosexuality attributed either to a genetic or an environmental factor. At best, they wish to know *how much* of the trait is genetic and how much is environmental. This nature-nurture dichotomy can never be resolved because it is false. Genetically identical animals reared in identical laboratory environments are often very different. Such variation is generally attributed to unseen environmental differences (Fausto-Sterling, this volume). The variation, could just as easily be due to differences in the timing of developmental events. The process of growing from a single cell to a functional adult is chaotic and dynamic (Gleik, 1988). Even if we knew absolutely everything about genes and absolutely everything about environments, we still could not predict the final phenotype of any individual. It is very likely that behavior, in general, and sexual identity, in particular, are results of idiosyncratic processes. Minor events can be amplified to have major effects. The nature-nurture dichotomy should be retired once and for all.

NOTES

1. Non-biological methods might be extremely misleading. For example, Johnson (1974) studied the inheritance of fingerprint patterns in 212 families. He obtained blood group information on 38 of those families. In 5 of the 38 families (13%), there was one child or more that could not be assigned to at least one parent, which could be the result of infidelity and unreported adoptions. Phillip (1973) reported that 30% of English husbands in his study of over 200 families had to be disqualified as biological parents of their children. After statistical adjustment, Ashton (1980) reported a mismatch rate of 2.3% in his study of 1748 Hawaiian families. Sharfetter (1978) briefly summarized studies on parent-offspring mismatches and suggested that the percentage of mismatches varies across ethnic groups. In most cases, it is not known. Accurate information on biological relationships is critical if one is going to draw biological conclusions.

2. I will illustrate this point with a medical example. Tuberculosis is a bacterial disease. Kallman and Reisner (1943) reported a correlation for TB of 87.3 for MZ twins and a correlation of 30.2 for same-sex DZ twins. Similar correlations occur in families. From these data the heritability of TB would be extremely high. Work on the causes and treatment of TB, however, came out of the disciplines of microbiology, physiology, and chemistry. Knowing something of the genetic aspect of populational variance did not contribute to understanding the disease. Similarly, even if some researcher ultimately measures the narrow heritability of homosexuality in a particular population, we will have learned nothing about the development of sexual identity. Understanding of sexual identity will come from other disciplines such as psychology or sociology.

REFERENCES

Ashton, G. C. (1980). Mismatches in genetic markers in a large family study. *American Journal of Human Genetics, 32*, 601-613.
Bailey, J. M., & Pillard, R. C. (1991). A genetic study of male sexual orientation. *Archives of General Psychiatry, 48*, 1089-1096.
Bouchard, T. J., Heston, L. L., Eckert, E., Keyes, M., & Resnick, S. (1981). The Minnesota study of twins reared apart: Project description and sample results in the developmental domain. In L. Gedda, P. Parisi, & W. E. Nance (Eds.),

Twin research 3, intelligence, personality and development (pp. 227-233). New York: Alan R. Liss.

Buhrich, N., Bailey, J. M., & Martin, N. G. (1991). Sexual orientation, sexual identity, and sex-dimorphic behaviors in male twins. *Behavior Genetics, 21,* 75-96.

Carter-Saltzman, L., & Scarr, S. (1977). MZ or DZ? Only your blood grouping laboratory knows for sure. *Behavior Genetics, 7,* 273-280.

Chase, A. (1980). *The legacy of Malthus.* Urbana: University of Illinois Press.

Dank, B. M. (1971). Six homosexual siblings. *Archives of Sexual Behavior, 1,* 193-204.

Eaves, L. J. (1972). Computer simulation of sample size and experimental design in human psychogenetics. *Psychological Bulletin, 77,* 144-152.

Eckert, E. D., Bouchard, T. J., Bohlen, J., & Heston, L. L. (1986). *British Journal of Psychiatry, 148,* 421-425.

Falconer, D. S. (1981). *Introduction to quantitative genetics.* London: Longman.

Gebhard, P. H. (1972). Incidence of overt homosexuality in the United States and Western Europe. *National Institute of Mental Health Task Force on Homosexuality: Final Report and Background Papers,* pp. 22-29.

Gleik, J. (1988). *Chaos, making of a new science.* New York: Viking.

Hamer, D. H., Hu, S., Magnuson, V. L., Hu, N., & Pattatucci, A. M. L. (1993). A linkage between DNA markers on the X chromosome and male sexual orientation. *Science, 261,* 321-327.

Haviland, J. M., McGuire, T. R., & Rothbaum, P. A. (1983). A critique of Plomin and Foch's "A twin study of objectively assessed personality in childhood." *Journal of Social and Personality Psychology, 45,* 663-640.

Heath, A. C., Neale, N. C., Hewitt, J. K., Eaves, L. J., & Fulker, D. W. (1989). Testing Structural equation models for twin data using LISREL. *Behavior Genetics, 19,* 9-35.

Henry, G. W. (1948). *Sex variants: A study of homosexual patterns.* New York: Hoeber, Inc.

Heston, L. L., & Shields, J. (1968). Homosexuality in twins. *Archives of General Psychiatry, 18,* 149-160.

Hinde, R. A. (1959). Some recent trends in ethology. In S. Koch (Ed.), *Psychology: A study of science. Vol 2* (pp. 561-610). New York: McGraw-Hill.

Johnson, R. P. (1974). Phenotypic variation, fingerprints, and human behavior: An application of the family pedigree paradigm. *Dissertation Abstracts International, 35,* 546-B.

Kallman, F. J. (1952a). Comparative twin study on the genetic aspects of male homosexuality. *The Journal of Nervous and Mental Disease, 115,* 283-298.

Kallman, F. J. (1952b). Twin and sibship study of overt male homosexuality. *American Journal of Human Genetics, 4,* 136-146.

Kallman, F. J. (1960). Discussion of Rainier, J. D., Mesnikoff, M. D., Kolb, L. C., & Carr, A., Homosexuality and heterosexuality in identical twins. *Psychosomatic Medicine, 22,* 258-259.

Kallman, F. J., & Reisner, D. (1943). Twin studies on genetic variation in resistance to tuberculosis. *Journal of Heredity, 34*, 269-276, 293-301.

Kenyon, F. E. (1968). Studies in female homosexuality. V. Sexual development, attitudes and experience. *British Journal of Psychiatry, 114*, 1343-1350.

King, M., & McDonald, E. (1992). Homosexuals who are twins. A study of 46 probands. *British Journal of Psychiatry, 160*, 407-409.

King, M. (1993). Sexual orientation and the X. *Nature, 364*, 288-289.

Kinsey, A. C., Pomeroy, W. B., & Martin, C. E. (1948). *Sexual behavior in the human male.* Philadelphia: Saunders.

Klein, T. W. (1974). Heritability and genetic correlation: Statistical power, population comparisons, and sample size. *Behavior Genetics, 4*, 171-189.

Klein, T. W., DeFries, J. C., & Finkbeiner, C. T. (1973). Heritability and genetic correlation: Standard errors of estimates and sample size. *Behavior Genetics, 3*, 355-364.

Klintworth, G. K. (1962). A pair of male monozygotic twins discordant for homosexuality. *Journal of Nervous and Mental Disease, 135*, 113-125.

Lykken, D. T., McGue, M., & Tellegen, A. (1987). Recruitment bias in twin research: The role of two-thirds reconsidered. *Behavior Genetics, 17*, 343-362.

Manning, A. (1975, May). *Future directions for behavior genetics.* Paper presented at the meeting of the Animal Behavior Society, Wilmington, NC.

Mather, K., & Jinks, J. L. (1982). *Biometrical genetics: The study of continuous variation.* Cambridge: Cambridge University Press.

McConaghy, N., & Blaszczynski, M. A. (1980). A pair of monozygotic twins discordant for homosexuality: Sex-dimorphic behavior and penile volume responses. *Archives of Sexual Behavior, 9*, 123-131.

McGuire, T. R. (1992). A biometrical genetic approach to chromosome analyses in *Drosophila*: Detection of epistatic interaction in geotaxis. *Behavior Genetics, 22*, 453-467.

McGuire, T. R., & Tully, T. (1986). Food search behavior and its relation to the central excitatory state (CES) in the genetic analysis of the blow fly *Phormia regina. Journal of Comparative Physiology, 100*, 52-58.

McGuire, T. R., & Tully, T. (1987). Characterization of genes involved with classical conditioning produce differences between bidirectionally selected strains of the blow fly *Phormia regina. Behavior Genetics, 17*, 97-107.

Neale, N. C., Heath, A. C., Hewitt, J. K., Eaves, L. J., & Fulker, D. W. (1989). Fitting genetic models with LISREL: Hypothesis testing. *Behavior Genetics, 19*, 35-49.

Nichols, R. C., & Bilbro, W. C. (1966) The diagnosis of twin zygosity. *Acta Genetica, 16*, 265-275.

Ooki, S., Yamada, K., & Hayakawa, K. (1990). Zygosity of twins by questionnaire. *Acta Genet Med Gemmellol, 39*, 109-115.

Pardes, H., Steinberg, J., & Simon, R. C. (1967). A rare case of overt and mutual homosexuality in female identical twins. *The Psychiatric Quarterly, 41*, 108-133.

Parker, N. (1964). Homosexuality in twins: A report on three discordant pairs. *British Journal of Psychiatry, 110*, 489-495.

Perkins, M. W. (1973). Homosexuality in female monozygotic twins. *Behavior Genetics, 3*, 387-388.

Phillip, E. E. (1973). Discussion in *Law and Ethics of A.I.D. and Embryo Transfer.* Ciba Foundation Symposium. Amsterdam: Elsevier, Excerpta Medica, North-Holland.

Pillard, R. C., Poumadere, J., & Carretta, R. A. (1981). Is homosexuality familial? A review, some data, and a suggestion. *Archives of Sexual Behavior, 10*, 465-475.

Pillard, R. C., & Weinrich, J. D. (1986). Evidence of Familial Nature of Male Homosexuality. *Archives of General Psychiatry, 43*, 808-812.

Price, B. (1950). Primary biases in twin studies. A review of prenatal and natal difference-producing factors in monozygotic pairs. *American Journal of Human Genetics, 2*, 293-352.

Rainier, J. D., Mesnikoff, M. D., Kolb, L. C., & Carr, A. (1960). Homosexuality and heterosexuality in identical twins. *Psychosomatic Medicine, 22*, 251-258.

Reilly, P. (1977). *Genetics, law, and social policy,* Cambridge, MA: Harvard University Press.

Rodgers, J. (1992). Mechanisms Mendel never knew. *Mosaic, 22*, 2-11.

Scharfetter, C. (1978). Alleged vs biological paternity. *Behavior Genetics, 8*, 383-384.

Storrs, E. E., & Williams. R. J. (1968). A study of monozygous quadruplet armadillos in relation to mammalian inheritance. *Proceedings of the National Academy of Sciences, U.S.A., 60*, 910-914.

Wheeler, D. L. (1992). Studies linking homosexuality to genes draw criticism from researchers. *Chronicle of Higher Education, 38*, A7-A9.

Wright, S. (1968). *Evolution and the genetics of populations. Vol. 1.* Chicago: University of Chicago Press.

Zuger, B. (1976). Monozygotic twins discordant for homosexuality: Report of a pair and significance of the phenomenon. *Comprehensive Psychiatry, 17*, 661-669.

Wilson's Panchreston:
The Inclusive Fitness Hypothesis
of Sociobiology Re-Examined

Mildred Dickemann, PhD

Richmond, California

SUMMARY. Of several hypotheses proposed by sociobiologists to explain "homosexuality," the most widely discussed is the inclusive fitness hypothesis, which is examined here in the work of the primary sociobiological proponents, E. O. Wilson, Michael Ruse, and James Weinrich. After reviewing the basic evolutionary concepts of natural selection, adaptation, and inclusive fitness/kin selection, I analyze the inclusive fitness hypothesis of homosexuality, taking as an exemplar the initial statement of E. O. Wilson. The implicit assumptions in this hypothesis are identified: that "homosexuality" is a unitary phenomenon, of direct genetic origin, occurring at similar frequencies across societies and through time, without direct reproductive gain, which therefore must be of genetic advantage to relatives. Each of these implicit assumptions is discussed and assessed in turn. The inclusive fitness hypothesis, derived primarily from current stereotypes about homosexuals in Western society, is found to be misconceived and without scientific merit. A general discussion of the nature-nurture, or essentialist–social-constructionist, controversy as it involves this hypothesis concludes the essay.

Mildred Dickemann is Professor Emerita of Anthropology, Sonoma State University.

Correspondence may be addressed: 2901 Humphrey Ave., Richmond, CA 94804.

[Haworth co-indexing entry note]: "Wilson's Panchreston: The Inclusive Fitness Hypothesis of Sociobiology Re-Examined." Dickemann, Mildred. Co-published simultaneously in *Journal of Homosexuality* (The Haworth Press, Inc.) Vol. 28, No. 1/2, 1995, pp. 147-183; and: *Sex, Cells, and Same-Sex Desire: The Biology of Sexual Preference* (ed: John P. De Cecco, and David Allen Parker) The Haworth Press, Inc., 1995, pp. 147-183. Multiple copies of this article/chapter may be purchased from The Haworth Document Delivery Center [1-800-3-HAWORTH; 9:00 a.m. - 5:00 p.m. (EST)].

147

I have been speculating last night what makes a man a discoverer of undiscovered things; and a most perplexing problem it is . . . As far as I can conjecture the art consists of habitually searching for the causes and meaning of everything that occurs. This implies sharp observation, and requires as much knowledge as possible of the subject investigated.

–Charles Darwin (cited in Bowlby, 1990, p. 412)

SCOPE OF THE ESSAY

The appearance of the body of theory and analysis termed "sociobiology" on the intellectual scene in the early 1970s resulted in several hypotheses attempting to explain "homosexuality" in its terms. Subsequent works have identified from two to eight sociobiological hypotheses. However, I limit my attention to the earliest and most widely discussed hypothesis, first proposed by R. L. Trivers (1974) and E. O. Wilson (1975, p. 555), the kin selection or inclusive fitness hypothesis. This is not so much a new formulation as a casting in evolutionary terms of a commonly held stereotype. Most discussions by both laypersons and scholars of the possible adaptive functions of homosexuality are versions of this notion. Hence it seems an advantage in clarity to deal solely with this proposition. While remarks on homosexuality may be found in passing in many evolutionary works on human behavior, I focus here on the more extended treatments of Kirsch & Rodman (1982), Ruse (1981, 1988), Weinrich (1977, 1987b), and Wilson (1975, 1978). Alternate hypotheses and briefer discussions may be found in Hutchinson (1959), Kirsch & Weinrich (1991), Ruse (1979), Trivers (1985), and Weinrich (1982, 1987a).

In evaluating this, or any, causal proposition about the origins or functions of homosexuality or any other behavior, there are three requisites: a knowledge of the scientific method of hypothesis formation and testing (though an acute sense of logic and common sense is often adequate here); a grasp of the theoretical framework being applied (in this case neo-Darwinian evolutionary theory); and lastly, some knowledge of the subject under investigation (if merely to avoid the waste of time, effort, and funds which results from the exploration of nonsensical or improbable hypotheses). As will be seen, one or more of these ingredients is problematic in the works reviewed here. Yet this body of work must be approached with tolerance. Some of it has been produced by individuals only self-trained in the theory, or by those with no initial familiarity with the diversity of human psyches and behaviors, or with homosexuality per se, other than the convenient myths supplied by their own society, which then become the "subject" of the explanatory hypothesis. And it has taken time for those working in this field to identify and explore the many implications for behavior of Darwinian theory. Most importantly, the new fields of gender, sexuality, and gay studies have undergone an explosion simultaneous with developments in Darwinian behavioral studies. It is not surprising, then, that those doing evolutionary analyses of human behavior (including myself) have often found it difficult to maintain competence in, and adequately integrate, these two large, interdisciplinary, expanding fields. Yet in the perhaps biased view of this gay Darwinian anthropologist, lack of knowledge of the subject under discussion seems to be the weakness most salient in the work under consideration.

WHAT IS SOCIOBIOLOGY?

Natural Selection, Adaptation, and Reproductive Success

To understand the theoretical approach termed "sociobiology," a brief lesson in the history of biology is more enlightening than a dissertation on genetics or evolution. The theory of biological evolution, or inherited change in species through time, was a well-known though unpopular idea among early nineteenth-century Western scientists. Darwin supplied a mass of evidence demonstrating its occurrence in a variety of species and, more importantly, developed an explanation of the means by which this change came about. *Natural selection* refers to the differential *reproductive success* (RS) of different organisms within a species, dependent upon individual variations in those attributes that affect, directly or indirectly, that success. Those leaving more breeding offspring to subsequent generations will, by definition, determine the attributes of the species in the future. This is reproductive success. But this change, or the success of some variants over others, occurs not only because there is always individual variation in every population (i.e., most individuals are genetically unique) but because environments vary through space and time as well. Thus it is the attributes of the environment ("nature") that determine ("select") which organismic variants will be most "fit" (i.e., reproductively capable). Darwin did not know *how* these variations were inherited; he did know that their inheritance was essential to his theory.

In the years since the publication of Darwin's *Origin* in 1859, and the subsequent construction of modern genetics, the basic proposition of evolution by natural selection has been confirmed and endlessly reconfirmed. Darwin's natural selection is the primary, though not the only, means by which evolutionary change comes about. Behind the assumption of selection lies the implication of *adaptation:* if organisms have been selected over time to survive and reproduce in a specific set of circumstances, they are more or less, though never perfectly, adapted to that environment in physiology, morphology, and behavior. Of course the claim of adaptation always requires proof. Too hasty assumption of "reasons" for organismic attributes can result in attractive but unproven "just so stories," which have been justly criticized. Nevertheless, the adaptationist assumption is an extremely fruitful source of working hypotheses for future testing.

One of the most difficult aspects of the theory of natural selection is that whereas laypersons conceive of individual behavior as operating for "the good of the species," Darwin emphasized the operation of this process primarily at the level of the individual. (Trivers, 1985, pp. 68-69, discusses the persistence of species-level thinking in biology.) It is individuals, not groups, that have offspring. Reducing natural selection to the level of the organism alone was not entirely satisfactory, however. Darwin himself recognized the problem of eusocial insects (those having large numbers of hive members that are sterile throughout their lives). In the honeybee, for example, great numbers of worker bees, sisters or daughters of the reigning egg-laying queen, spend their lives maintaining the hive and raising the queen's offspring. How could selection produce this arrangement? This problem, particularly plaguing to entomologists, received little attention until the 1960s, when the growth of more sophisticated subdisciplines of ecology, animal behavior, and population genetics, and the desire to include humans within the domain of evolutionary theory, resulted in a flurry of interest in "group selection" at the level of the population or species, now much qualified.

Inclusive Fitness and Kin Selection

Part of the problem of the social insects was resolved by unravelling their distinctive system of inheritance, which need not concern us here. But the more generally significant theoretical breakthrough for social organisms as a whole was the proposal of W. D. Hamilton (1964). He observed that those genes passed on to the next generation, that is, those replicated and preserved, need not be those of the individual per se, but may be identical genes in his or her close relatives. Such kin share a high proportion of the same genes, from the same ancestors. Therefore, if one aids one's close kin in ways that enhance *their* reproduction, one is in fact insuring the perpetuity of "one's own" genes. Such an act of assistance always costs something, ultimately time and energy. But if it benefits a reproducing relative sufficiently, that cost may be offset. Depending upon circumstances, one may gain more by aiding a relative than by attempting to reproduce oneself and insure the survival and reproduction of one's own offspring. We may then think of the *inclusive fitness* of an individual, including both his own direct descendants and those of his close kin.

What degree of relatedness is necessary for this process to operate? Parents are always related to each offspring by one half: half of each parent's genome (total genetic material) is present in each child. Siblings (i.e., brothers and sisters) vary from three fourths to one fourth, averaging half of their genes in common. An individual is related to her sibling's child by one fourth; half-siblings to the same degree, as are grandparents to grandchildren. First cousins share one eighth of their genes. So one gains more by helping closer relatives, all other things being equal, which of course they never are. The operation of inclusive fitness depends upon the opportunities for and constraints on all actors. Although the theory is often conceived as though the "altruist," or nonreproductive, were sacrificing her reproductive potential in order to gain better inclusive reproduction through a relative, in fact, the individual in question may have little or no reproductive capacity at all. But the equations always tell us what is the next best thing to do. The altruist must gain more from his relative's increased RS than he loses by forgoing his own reproduction. (Although the term "altruist" is used by biologists for such actors, it is clear that the "altruist" is in fact selfish. The existence and nature of true altruism in humans remains a mystery.)

The notion of inclusive fitness, and the possibility of *kin selection* that flowed from it, that is, selection at the level of the cooperating kin unit (Maynard Smith, 1964), were enormously productive in animal behavior research, especially given the large number of vertebrate species that are to some degree social. For example, these theories stimulated investigation of "kin recognition," which may be necessary for the operation of behavior based on relatedness. Similarly, much attention has been paid to the role of non-breeding "helpers at the nest" in birds and other organisms. In both cases, the result has been the discovery of far more "kin behavior" and in far more species than anyone would have suspected fifty years ago. These ideas were absorbed into an increasingly sophisticated subdiscipline of animal behavior, stimulating a return by biologists to Darwin's work and to neo-Darwinian theory.

Human Sociobiology

The consonance between this theory and what we know about humans is striking. To students of humankind, the Hamiltonian hypothesis is a genetical explanation for the universal human practice of nepotism, or the dictum: "Aid kin!" Consequently, a few social scientists found the approach very attractive as a research framework (although others found it profoundly threatening). Evolutionary ideas were applied to human behavior initially in the early 1970s (Alexander, 1974; Campbell, 1972; Fox, 1975). However, they attracted little attention from the lay public or academics outside biology until the publication of E. O. Wilson's *Sociobiology: The New Synthesis* (1975), which offered an integration of inclusive fitness, kin selection, and group selection theory with population biology and social behavior in animals, including humans. The term "sociobiology," although independently coined with a variety of meanings in the past, was made popular by this work. (For more recent introductions, see Daly & Wilson, 1983, and Trivers, 1985.)

It is important in assessing Wilson's contribution to understand what his special focus was. As an entomologist, having just completed the magisterial *Insect Societies* (1971), Wilson was intensely curious about the evolution of "eusociality," that extreme degree of social organization in which significant numbers of individual organisms sacrifice their own reproduction in the interests of the group. He wished to explore the possibility of group selection across a range of species, and speculate on its relevance to humans. As an entomologist thinking about his own species, he was curious whether group or kin selection could explain the appearance of altruism in humans. Indeed, in a philosophical sense, the question of altruism may be said to be the core of the volume. However, as a researcher immersed in the study of organisms with primarily close genetical control over behavior and little flexibility or learning, he was, I believe, primarily oriented toward the search for directly genetical inheritance of social behaviors and of altruism, rather than predisposed to unravel the complex interplay of direct and indirect genetic and environmental forces that seems apparent to most social scientists and students of vertebrate behavior. (Subsequent work has convinced most evolutionary biologists that selection operates at many levels: gene, chromosome, organism, population, and species. However, in species with a majority of reproducing individuals, the individual level is primary. See Alexander & Borgia, 1978; Dawkins, 1976; Trivers, 1985.)

THE INCLUSIVE FITNESS THEORY
OF HOMOSEXUALITY

The canonical text in this corpus, probably inspiring most subsequent discussion of the hypothesis, is the proposal of E. O. Wilson (1975, p. 555):

> the influence of genetic factors toward the assumption of certain *broad* roles cannot be discounted. Consider male homo-

sexuality. The surveys of Kinsey and his coworkers showed that in the 1940s approximately 10 percent of the sexually mature males in the United States were mainly or exclusively homosexual for at least three years prior to being interviewed. Homosexuality is also exhibited by comparably high fractions of the male populations in many if not most other cultures. Kallman's twin data indicate the probable existence of a genetic predisposition toward the condition . . . An interesting . . . hypothesis has been suggested to me by Hermann T. Spieth (personal communication) and independently developed by Robert L. Trivers (1974). The homosexual members of primitive societies may have functioned as helpers, either while hunting in company with other men or in domestic occupations at the dwelling sites. Freed from the special obligations of parental duties, they could have operated with special efficiency in assisting close relatives. Genes favoring homosexuality could then be sustained at a high equilibrium by kin selection alone. It remains to be said that if such genes really exist they are almost certainly incomplete in penetrance and variable in expressivity, meaning that which bearers of the genes develop the behavioral trait and to what degree depends on the presence of modifier genes and the influence of the environment.

Unstated Assumptions

While the source of sociobiologists' interest in homosexuality is expressed above, many of the assumptions on which the hypothesis rests are not overtly stated. More explicit is philosopher Michael Ruse (1981, pp. 8-9):

> Homosexual individuals are by definition attracted to members of their own sex. Homosexual couplings . . . cannot lead to offspring. Hence, someone who is exclusively homosexual cannot have offspring and is therefore effectively sterile, that is, biologically unfit. (Obviously I exclude the relatively rare phenomenon of . . . artificial insemination.)

The logical chain of propositions which can be reconstructed from these sources is as follows:

1. "Homosexuality" (or "homosexuals") is (are) a discrete, identifiable, unitary entity, all representatives of which share the same cause or causes;
2. It is probably genetic or predominantly genetic in origin;
3. "Homosexuals" exist in all or most human societies at frequencies from two to ten percent;
4. Yet "homosexuals" never or rarely reproduce, thus failing to pass their genes on to the next generation;
5. Such a high frequency of an allele (alternate form of a gene) cannot be maintained by mutation alone for any significant period of time, as no known mutation rates are this high (cf. Weinrich, 1987b, pp. 317-318, 332). (A mutation is a change in the form of a gene, random with respect to environmental pressures, that results in a different expression in the phenotype.)
6. Therefore, the condition must be maintained either by some genetic advantage to those who possess it in dilute form, who reproduce more effectively as a result (the heterozygote advantage hypothesis, not discussed here), or it must provide some benefits to relatives of the affected individual sufficient to offset the cost of his or her birth and rearing, and greater than would have been gained by her or his own effort to reproduce (inclusive fitness hypothesis).

Note that for this proposal to be tenable, the condition must be inherited from non-homosexual parents, as Wilson indicates, thus requiring either recombination or some significant environmental cue or influence to bring it into existence in its "homosexual," nonreproducing form. Or, if only males are specified, it might be carried singly on the X or Y sex chromosome. Given the assumptions listed above, it is clear that "homosexuality" represents a puzzle for evolutionary theory, and the inclusive fitness theory of Hamilton offers the most attractive resolution. However, *all of the assumptions* listed above, with the exception of 5, regarding rates of mutation, are at best undemonstrated, and at worst conceptually or factually erroneous. I will address each one in turn. (Other critiques, partially paralleling my own, are Futuyma & Risch, 1984, and Kitcher, 1985, pp. 243-252.)

SYSTEMATICS: DO WE EXIST?

Description, Classification, and Hypothecation in Science

Despite much frothy recent theoretical discussion, the best science has consisted, for a hundred and fifty years, of a rather simple but powerful set of operations (Bowlby, 1990; Ghiselin, 1969; Levins, 1968). Usually termed the "hypothetico-deductive method," good science involves the movement of thought, both analytic and intuitive, back and forth between more abstract, generalizing levels of theory and hypothesis, on the one hand, and more particular levels of description and classification, on the other. (All description is of course low-level generalization.) Description and classification, in the curious mind, provoke theory, because they provoke questions about the nature of relationships. A hypothesis, or proposition about such relationships in the natural world, is then tested against new data or cases (not those that generated it) and modified or discarded as the outcome dictates. In the process of moving back and forth between the general and the particular, *both* undergo revision. One cannot "explain" an "event" if it is not a natural entity, but merely a construction in the mind of the viewer.

All entities in the natural world have boundaries, yet all these bounded phenomena, whether chairs or ecosystems, "bleed" into the surrounding environment. To study the external world, we must settle for "partially non-arbitrary boundaries," but the less arbitrary the better. Which boundaries we choose will depend in part on the question asked, as well as the accuracy of our description of the event. Failure to attend to the relation between the attributes (i.e., the existence and nature) of the entity under study and the explanatory hypothesis proposed is a prescription for disaster or at least nonsense. Thus, "racial/ethnic group" may be a valid category for some purposes in modern nation-states, where legal and social treatments define such classes of people. Yet for other purposes, it may be essential to distinguish between Korean-Americans, Jewish-Americans, and Turkish-Germans. For yet other purposes, even these categories will need further subdivision, by dialect, sex, social class, or generation.

Sociobiological Classifications of Homosexuality

Ironically, in his *Sociobiology,* Wilson (1975, p. 29) provides a useful discussion of biological reasoning. He warns of the dangers of *panchrestons,* global labels covering widely varying phenomena, with varying usages, which therefore explain nothing and hinder analysis. Yet this warning is not heeded in his own or subsequent work on "homosexuality." Neither the authors reviewed here nor the sources they cite agree on definitions and classifications of the presumptive phenomenon. Nor do the authors specify the relation of their chosen definitions to the hypotheses they propose. In 1987, an Amsterdam conference was entitled "Homosexuality, Which Homosexuality?" (Altman et al., 1989). These works provide no answer to the question.

A common response to the taxonomic problem is to fall back on sexual activity alone, as Kinsey did: homosexuals are those who have same-sex sexual contacts. This creates as many problems as it solves. Classic Athenian men of the citizen class, acting within approved gender boundaries, with normal marital and reproductive life histories, engaged in intergenerational and sometimes same-generational sexual and affectional relations with other men. Were they "homosexuals"? Ruse (1988, p. 138) includes them in his *Homosexuality,* stating that "[h]omosexuality as it presents itself in our society . . . is not the same as the homosexuality of Ancient Greece . . . Yet . . . there are threads linking homosexuals." They also appear in Weinrich's *Sexual Landscapes* (1987b, pp. 88-93, 331) as practicing "homosexuality," but it is hard to see how this case can mesh with the North American cross-gendered "berdache" (another panchreston?) that Weinrich proposes as a kind of primordial gay. And what of the now widely recognized pattern of masculine sex in some U. S., Latin American, and Mediterranean communities, in which casual male-male sex, usually with some marker of differential dominance, is an acceptable part of normal "heterosexuality"? Are these heterosexuals "homosexual"? Or what of individuals with sexual and affectional attraction to their own sex who are chaste? There is nothing wrong with studying sexual contacts alone, but to do so excludes gender identity, gender role, and social labelling and so has no necessary relation to categories of persons or emotions. This realization is of course fundamental to modern historical and comparative analysis of sexuality and gender, of which these authors seem blissfully unaware.

Kirsch and Rodman (1982, p. 185) take the opposite approach, excluding "situational" homosexuality as well as all sex containing aggressive, territorial, or economic motivations, leaving "an affective, often erotic interest in the same sex." Aside from the danger of classifying behaviors on the basis of presumed motives, this approach prevents any study of the forms of homosexuality without motivational testimony. Further, it fails to clarify the relation between homosexuality and friendship.

Both Ruse (1988, p. 75) and Weinrich (1977, p. 144; 1987b, p. 27) define transsexuals as individuals cross-gendered in self-identity, that is, who believe that their sexual identity does not conform to their morphogenetic sex, whether or not they undergo sex-change surgery. Weinrich (1987b, p. 317) reports that sociobiologists regard transsexuals as part of a continuum with homosexuals, but elsewhere (1987b, pp. 20-25) he proposes that they constitute a distinct "gender transposition." Ruse (1988, pp. 75-76) insists that even if "transsexualism is a form of homosexuality taken to an extreme . . . this does not mean that there are not real differences, in fact, between transsexuals and homosexuals (that is to say most homosexuals)."

Such intellectual confusion is sometimes stunning. Arguing for the universality of "gender transpositions," Weinrich (1987b, p. 106) asserts that "the better we know the cultures involved, the more various gender transposition patterns merge into and overlap each other." Therefore, "the . . . similarity of this mishmash from culture to culture is strong evidence that it is not constructed from culture alone." And, under the heading "Bad Science and Bad Societies," he states (1987b, p. 393), "If anthropologists don't know what ordinary modern lesbian women are really like–in terms of personality, sexuality, bonding and all that–how can they recognize ordinary lesbian women in other societies if lesbians happen to exist there?" This is not the only place in this corpus where the fallacy of *petitio principii* (assuming as a premise the conclusion to be proved) appears.

Weinrich devotes much space to arguing that human "homosexuality" is "natural" because "it" occurs in other organisms as well. This even larger universe of cases requires even greater definitional simplification, to same-sex acts of genital contact, stimulation, or arousal. Such a definition loses many human "homosexual" acts. But in any case, the logic is faulty. Human "naturalness" in no way depends on the occurrence of similar behaviors in other species. *Speech* is natural to humans, whatever lizards and seagulls may do. And any of Weinrich's readers who recognize the presence of evil as a "natural" component of earthly existence will scarcely be persuaded to tolerance upon learning that it is even more widespread than they had imagined.

Paradoxically, both Ruse and Weinrich recognize the problem they are confronting, however briefly. Weinrich (1987b, pp. 30-31) states: "The scientists who make up these definitions were raised in Western societies and could conceivably have been too influenced by Western notions of gender identity. The result would be a classification that merely reflects Western prejudices . . . This is the reason why cross-cultural studies are so important to gender-identity research; they help us decide whether our definitions make sense." But, as the quotation on lesbians, above, makes clear, non-Western data do not save Weinrich from the very conceptual morass that he warns against in others (see also Weinrich, 1987a, p. 44).

Similarly, Ruse (1988, pp. 137-138), commenting on genetic theories, states, "Illicitly, one is picking out certain human features, like homosexuality, giving them a real existence, and then trying to tie them in to the genes. One is reifying, in a quite unacceptable way. Homosexuality is being considered a 'thing'." This passage occurs halfway through a book titled *Homosexuality,* and the issue is nowhere raised again. Indeed, in the same passage Ruse proposes that "homosexual orientation" is "plausibly a candidate for a biological explanation" (equating biology with genetics) based on a study of male homosexuals in West European and European-dominated societies. Even the use of the singular in the title and text is a manifestation of *petitio principii:* Bell and Weinberg, disciples of Kinsey, titled their 1978 San Francisco study *Homosexualities* to underline their conviction that multiple natures and multiple origins were involved.

In discussing the "unusual sexual behaviors" of seagulls (which she does *not* term "homosexuality" or "lesbianism") and their relevance to humans, ornithologist Judith Latta Hand (1981, p. 139) observes: "these observations . . . demonstrate that *patterns* of higher vertebrate social structure and behavior, even those of birds, are not evolved entities per se. They are epiphenomena that emerge as individuals interact" (her italics). Would that these authors had pondered this fact.

Perhaps a primary source of the difficulty, for all the authors, is simply the desire to make use of existing literature, rather than beginning *de novo* with the task of description and classification. Especially in sexology, psychology, and endocrinology, contradictory and unreal taxonomies employed by many authors force a researcher attempting synthesis or overview into quicksand. Adding to this literature whatever has been said on "homosexuality" in past times and faraway places insures a resulting "mishmash" of ill-defined partially overlapping units. In such circumstances, the will-o'-the-wisps of "pure" homosexuality, heterosexuality, transsexualism, and so forth may appear over the marsh, luring the unwary traveller into the bog of pseudoscience.

Those who have attempted, over the last two decades, to comprehend the varieties of human sex and gender, even including some working from a sexological perspective, have already recognized the inadequacy of "homosexuality" and "homosexual" as terms to label reality beyond the social constructions of specific Western populations. Aware that social and historical forces have generated the rubrics under which our initial studies of deviant sex/gender began, most researchers have moved to a more descriptive program, namely the reconstruction of the history and anthropology of sexuality and gender by the accumulation of individual cases, limited in time and space, described in their own terms and categorized using expressly stated criteria. (This shift has been accompanied and perhaps in part driven by the increasing recognition of sexual and gender diversity within our gay communities, and the consequent search for new ways to describe ourselves.) Of course these descriptive efforts are accompanied by speculations, tentative and inadequate, always under revision in response to new data. That is the method of science. It does not characterize the procedures of the "sociobiologists" considered here, whatever their disciplines.

SOCIOBIOLOGY AND GENETIC DETERMINISM

Genes, Behavior, and Environment

All of the authors under review suffer to some degree from the false equation of "biology" with "genetic inheritance," an error widespread among laypersons, and reinforced by the first, semi-popular, coffee-table overview of sociobiology. The public, it seems, has accepted Mendel while rejecting Darwin, ironically, since the governing theory of all modern biology was initially developed by Darwin without assistance from genetics. One result of this misconception has been a flood of racist and sexist tracts claiming validity under the rubric of "sociobiology." Since these misconceived productions are, for most lay people, social scientists, and feminists, the primary source of information on the application of Darwinian theory to human behavior, fruitful dialogue across perspectives, even within disciplines has become difficult or impossible. (An excellent discussion of this fallacious equation is by Alexander [1987, pp. 6-12], who notes that the same process of pejoration corrupted the term "ethology," originally a neutral term for animal behavior, to refer to the search for rigid genetical controls popularized by Robert Ardrey and Konrad Lorenz.)

The search for genetic bases of behavior is certainly justified: what is indefensible is the neglect of environmental variables, and hence any serious recognition of gene-environment interaction. This neglect gives the work on homosexuality a strange bias, distinguishing it from the mass of current animal behavior literature, which focusses primarily on function, environmental context, and reproductive consequences. (See, for example, Stacey & Konig's 1990 collection, *Cooperative Breeding in Birds,* which employs the same inclusive fitness hypothesis.) A large literature on animal behavior has accumulated since the 1950s, making clear the many different routes by which behaviors and social structures are produced. Some organisms, such as invertebrates, rely heavily on narrow genetic programs with little responsiveness to environmental variation or capacity for learning (though slugs and bees do learn). Others, and especially mammals, have many behavior programs designed to produce differential responses in different environments, including varieties of learning. The consequence is that the search for genetic bases must be a *different* project, and properly a subsequent project to the initial task of description and classification of behavior, its variation within environmental contexts, and its consequences. In behavioral biology, work on behavioral genetics, while not inconsequential, has as a result moved to the back seat, while the enormous task of description, classification, and functional analysis receives most effort. It is striking how this development parallels the shift in studies of gender and sexuality mentioned above.

Phenotype and Genotype

The false equation of biology with genetics reflects a failure to understand the concept of the *phenotype*. Everything organismic that we observe, whether behavior, morphology, physiology, or neurology, is phenotypic. That is, it is a product of the *interaction* of genes with bodily and extra-bodily (internal and external) environments from the moment of conception. Only those engaged in the analysis of DNA are studying genes directly. The rest of us are merely peering *through* phenotypes, when trying to determine genetic contributions. *No gene is directly expressed.* A research design failing to take account of this is doomed to error.

Of course, some genetic programs, in humans as in other organisms, are less responsive to environmental variation than others. The expression, "direct genetic control," refers to such less malleable traits. For example, eye color, under strong genetic control and extremely stable, nevertheless does undergo change under the impact of long years of exposure and cellular aging, or as the result of traumas to the eye. Other, very plastic, traits are in fact genetically programmed through natural selection to be reactive in *specific* ways to *specific* environmental stimuli. *Phenotypic plasticity* is the most usual term for this genetically programmed capacity to vary responses to varying environmental cues: it occurs in organisms as simple as bacteria. Human language and the smile, for example, are such traits, worth pondering by students of human sexuality and gender. The speech apparatus and its neurological correlates are clearly under genetic control, as are, apparently, certain universal aspects of sound system and structure (grammar and syntax). Yet this universal sound-structure program is "filled" in each case by the specific rules of the language to which the individual is exposed. Human language is neither written on a *tabula rasa* nor predetermined: it is *both*. Likewise, the smile, present in newborns even if blind, maturationally develops sensitivity to specific visual and auditory stimuli, and then, under conscious and preconscious learning, becomes an automatic but controllable apparatus for social interaction, with widely differing usages from one society to another, within the universal general meaning-frame. Phenotypic plasticity of this sort is a critical notion for students of mammalian and certainly human behavior, including sexual behavior. (Weinrich, 1977, p. 162, notes a parallel between the process of child language acquisition and the easy acquisition of the "rules of sex-typed behavior" in a specific society, an idea that warrants further investigation.)

Genes and Homosexuality

While E. O. Wilson deals at length with phenotypic plasticity, or "behavioral scaling" (Wilson, 1975, pp. 19-21), his hypothesis regarding homosexuality quoted above does not employ this concept. Relying on questionable twin studies to claim genetic determination, he appeals to degree of "penetrance and expressivity" to explain variation, that is, other genes modifying individual expression, and the "influence" of the environment. While it is true that genes are "prior" in the sense that they are transmitted from previous generations, they are not "influenced" by the environment: rather, beginning with each new conception, *both environment and genes co-determine the phenotype*. One may also note Ruse's remark (1988, p. 131): "Obviously . . . we humans have to some extent escaped our biology." In fact we *have* both genotypes and phenotypes: *both* are biology and *both* are inescapable!

In Wilson's initial statement, it is clear that "genes favoring homosexuality" are conceived in terms of a relatively direct effect;

similar phrases occur in *On Human Nature* (Wilson, 1978, p. 141). Subsequent authors review genetic studies (Ruse, 1981, pp. 16-19; Ruse, 1988, pp. 84-129; Weinrich, 1977, pp. 124-130; Weinrich, 1987b, pp. 194-223). Ruse (1981, p. 19) distinguishes between fairly direct genetic control and significant environmental input: "there might be multiple causes of homosexuality. Some homosexuality could be fairly directly controlled by the genes, and some not so . . . [A]t least some homosexuality could have a genetic component in the sense explicated above, [but] it is highly improbable that the environment does not play an important role." This statement is, of course, a grudging recognition of the possible existence of multiple entities masquerading under a single term.

Weinrich, labelling himself an "interactionist," makes the greatest effort to discuss environment, but a curious contradiction emerges:

> There is more than one kind of homosexuality in the world. Most societies have most types and encourage them in different proportions. It is likely . . . that some of these types exist ultimately because of genetic factors that go at least as far back as our hunter-gatherer ancestors. . . . This means we need to gather data on genetic factors in order to explain *why we are what we are.* But it is also clear that each society has its own way of socially constructing and emphasizing these types— constructions that can change and that have enormously important influences on individual people's lives. These behaviors are constructed so drastically differently that people from one society trying to find themselves in another might just as well be looking for the Mad Hatter and the March Hare. (Weinrich, 1987b, pp. 106-107; author's italics)

Yet later Weinrich contradicts this (1987b, p. 357): "If modern homosexual men are the sociobiological inheritors of the berdache's emotions and strategies, then they should show some of the psychological characteristics of berdaches."

Peculiar indeed. If homosexual types are unrecognizable to their equivalents in other societies, then how are they identified by Weinrich and co-workers? Indeed, he asserts (1987b, p. 107) that "the effects of having particular genetic predispositions can be entirely different, depending on the social constructions of the society possessing those genes." But neither author tells us which types are genetic, which are not, nor does either provide hypotheses proposing how contrasting environments interact with these genetic types to produce contrasting outcomes.

Weinrich's interpretations reveal an "ethological" emphasis, a preference for rigid genetic control and fixed action patterns in spite of his reiterated commitment to interactionism, as witness his repeated references to "imprinting" (Weinrich, 1987b, pp. 122-127, 327-328, 340-341) as the means by which gender identity is formed. Popularized by Konrad Lorenz, imprinting is the innate response to specific stimuli presented during a limited period early in life, which then determines behaviors or object choice in adulthood. In the familiar example, a young bird's choice of mating object in adulthood may be determined by exposure to an adult, generally a parent, soon after hatching. The establishment of gender identity in humans by the age of three is appealingly analogous. This is the stuff of pop sociobiology. No evidence is offered, nor is counter-evidence reviewed. Indeed, child development specialists are increasingly skeptical of the applicability of imprinting in humans, except perhaps in regard to language acquisition. (The recent authoritative review by Kagan [1984], for example, never employs the concept.)

TEN PERCENT: ARE WE EVERYWHERE?

Kinsey's 1948 figures, and the mythic "ten percent" that they generated, have been widely critiqued since (Gonsiorek & Weinrich, 1991; Michaels, 1991; Ruse, 1988, pp. 3-6). They are derived from a single sample biassed by race and class, limited to a single moment in one society, and measure only sex acts. They provide no evidence for a persistent minority of celibate, homosexually oriented men throughout human history. Yet Wilson employs Kinsey's figures.

Subsequent authors offer other evidence of universality. The Greeks (presumably meaning Athenians) are mentioned, but as these authors know, but do not state, these were marrying, reproductive men (Ruse, 1988, passim; Weinrich, 1987b, pp. 88-93). A few other non-Western examples, briefly cited, are drawn mostly from Weinrich's 1976 thesis (Weinrich, 1977, pp. 166-175; Ruse, 1981, pp. 20-23; Ruse, 1988, p. 146). Yet Weinrich's own table (1977, pp. 203-205) clearly shows that not all of these cases involved homosexual activity.

Weinrich's more recent work devotes much space to the "berdache," another presumptively unitary phenomenon, relying primarily on Williams's *The Spirit and the Flesh* (1986), yet he never indicates how many of these cases of gender mixing in North America were in fact homosexual (Weinrich, 1987b, pp. 344-356). Lang (1990), in the most thorough review of the North American alternate gender literature, lists both marital and liaison partnerships and brief sexual contacts for male berdaches (Lang, 1990, pp. 222-226). While many maintained longstanding relations with other males, some established relations with women. Some had sexual relations with both sexes, while some were chaste, while married to or in partnerships with heterosexual men (Lang, 1990, pp. 220-221; see also Pilling, 1992). Which of these are "homosexuals" equivalent to those of Western societies? While early treatments such as Weinrich's 1976 thesis were valuable initial forays into the cross-cultural study of gender, the neglect of ethnographic data in the later works is striking. Only Carrier (1971, 1976) on Mexico, and Whitam's (1983; Whitam & Mathy 1986) quasi-cross-cultural studies of four societies, all of which were published in the *Archives of Sexual Behavior,* appear in the recent works by these authors. Nanda's (1984) preliminary report on the *hijras* of India is cited by Weinrich (1987b) but not by Ruse (1988); Blackwood's 1986 collection is cited by Ruse (1988) only; Callender and Kochems (1983) and Whitehead (1981) are cited by neither. This reveals an encysted, self-referential quality in the whole corpus of work on "sociobiology of homosexuality."

A similar situation obtains with regard to historical sources, which provide the same kind of cross-social information, through time rather than through space. Dover (1978) on the Athenians is cited, but Boswell (1980) is, not surprisingly, a favorite, as he argued strongly for an "essentialist" homosexuality throughout Western history. He is acknowledged in Wilson's *On Human Nature.* Yet those who follow gender research know that the essentialist-social constructionist debate was sparked by such early works as McIntosh (1968) and Foucault (1978). While Foucault finally appears in Ruse (1988), neither the historical work that he inspired nor the reconceptualizations of gender that have grown out of feminist scholarship are present. It is precisely these bodies of literature that question any simple assumption of a universal two or ten percent. In fairness, as noted above, constructionist scholarship has been appearing simultaneously with the development of "sociobiological" approaches. But that seems insufficient justification for the neglect of anthropological, historical, and theoretical gender and sexuality studies.

I offer one example of the importance of historical analyses in the conceptualization of homosexualities. In seventeenth-century England, the "fop" was an effeminate man who was obsessively heterosexual or at the most bisexual. His femininity of dress and manner was seen as a manifestation of his sexual obsession with all that was woman, even as a means to their seduction, or as a loss of virility due to too great exercise of the sexual pursuit of women. In the next century, this male effeminacy was seen as, and often was, a sign of sexual interest in other men. The heterosexual "fop" disappeared, to be replaced by the homosexual "sodomite" (Trumbach, 1989; Senelick, 1990). What genetical theory might explain this?

Terminology and public perception track, however crudely (just as they also influence) transformations in actual gender identities and behaviors. These historical shifts make a mockery of attempts to discriminate "transsexuals" and "cross-dressers" from "homosexuals" as eternally distinct human types. Did the English population undergo major genetic change in the eighteenth century, or dramatic changes in childhood gender socialization? Perhaps the forms of sexuality and gender are exquisitely responsive to social and demographic forces whose roles are as yet unidentified. The hypothesis specifying how genetic, endocrine, and early childhood factors interact with larger environmental forces to produce changing sexualities across time and space has yet to be proposed.

MEASURING FITNESS:
DOES BIRTH RATE = REPRODUCTIVE SUCCESS?

Hypotheses phrased within the framework of natural selection propose that traits have evolved because they offered greater survival value for the genes that helped produce them. The ultimate test of any such hypothesis is the demonstration of greater reproductive success for those possessing that trait, relative to those expressing it to a lesser degree or expressing alternative traits. When individuals invest time, resources, and energy in assisting the reproduction of their kin, then the measure must include the kin group or sibling set as a whole. The sibling or family group practicing inclusive fitness strategies ought to enjoy greater RS than similar families in similar circumstances without inclusive fitness behaviors. Such measures are lacking in the works reviewed here.

Worse, these authors equate birth rate with RS. Number of offspring is no guarantee either of their survival to adulthood or of their later successful reproduction (cf. Kirsch & Rodman, 1982, p. 186: "The criterion of evolutionary success is number of offspring [reproductive fitness]. . ."). Only in short-lived, fast-breeding organisms may numbers of offspring be used as a proxy for RS. In those with long pre-reproductive lives and long generation length, such as humans, counting the hatch may greatly mislead. The young reared to adulthood, or better, the completed family size of those young, is what matters. In humans, our capacity to invest in descendants "unto the tenth generation" additionally argues for an extended measure of RS.

Human RS varies by rank, status, class, and wealth, as well as by society, due to differences in mate access, mortality rates, and costs of childrearing. While fairly reliable data are often available for human females, men present difficulties due to uncertainty of paternity and high rates of promiscuity. As a further complication, the modern industrial world, that very environment in which public communities of preferentially homosexual men and women have emerged, has undergone a shift in birth rates, such that the upper and middle classes are at or below replacement levels. Thus the two sons of homosexual Oscar Wilde (one killed in World War I and the other a family progenitor) and the four daughters of homosexual

John Addington Symonds (three surviving to adulthood) were well within the mid-range of reproducing heterosexual men of their time, place, and class. Today's increase in non-breeding homosexuals may be no more than the consequence of less parental and familial concern for the reproduction of *all* offspring, given the sufficient replacements of some. None of these demographic considerations enters into the purportedly evolutionary analyses considered here.

DOES HOMOSEXUALITY = CELIBACY?

In presenting his inclusive fitness hypothesis, Wilson characterized homosexuals as "[f]reed from the special obligations of parental duties . . . ," that is, non-reproducing. This equation of childlessness with "homosexuality" is the central assumption underlying the inclusive fitness hypothesis, and the weakest. Its origins are transparent. It is no more than a middle-class heterosexist stereotype of homosexuals in West European societies. Like many other derogatory stereotypes with social control functions, it is self-fulfilling, the product of a majority consensus supporting the coercion of offspring into reproduction. The greatest hostility to celibate public homosexuality occurs in communities and classes with the most rigid gender roles, greatest concern to maintain and create the "nuclear" male-female family and greatest anxiety regarding the survival and economic security of their children. The normative equation of marriage with reproduction is so engrained that the term "celibate" (unmarried, from the French *celibataire)* is commonly misunderstood to mean "chaste" (i.e., heterosexually non-sexual). Similarly, the heterosexist equation of "sex" with "reproduction" provides no distinction between reproductive and non-reproductive sexuality.

Anyone already married who enters a sexual relation with a same-sex partner, in this society, must either deceive his or her spouse, or with the spouse's consent practice a highly stigmatized form of adultery. Such contacts, among men, are so stigmatized that they are often channelled into socially and legally dangerous public encounters in "tearooms" (Humphreys, 1970; Ross, 1983). Severing a marriage with children generally means loss of custody and contact. The possibility of parenting within a same-sex relationship was limited until recently not by lack of means but by the high costs of discovery and persecution. Still, this was more possible for some women than for men, since cooperative households of separated, divorced, or widowed women with children have long been tolerated in our society, so long as any sexual aspect of the relationship remains hidden.

For these reasons, during a brief period from, say, 1900 to 1970, identifiable public homosexuals in Western societies were almost all either non-reproductive or post-reproductive. For a time, coercion into marriage relaxed, while the equation of marriage with heterosexuality and reproduction remained. Those who moved into public gay life were, for one reason or another, able to refuse, or to terminate, coerced marital careers. Married men and women with bisexual or homosexual preferences were rarely captured in sociological samples, nor were the cooperative female households mentioned above. The much discussed "instability" of lesbian and gay relationships is surely related to the tendency for longterm and reproductive unions to be more private, less involved in the public gay community, having more to lose. It is of course true that some homosexuals, like some heterosexuals, prefer not to sire or bear children. But the lesbian "baby boom" of the 1980s and the establishment of a variety of public "alternative" gay families (Green & Bozett, 1991; Weston, 1991) demonstrate that many gays wish to parent and will risk doing so even with the most modest amelioration in social attitudes and legal disabilities. Thus the equation of "homosexuality" with heterosexual chaste celibacy in the lay mind is a self-fulfilling process of the "blaming the victim" sort: a society's own social and legal sanctions produce a visible population that generates a confirming stereotype. It is sad to see this mythic concept as a central assumption in the work of scientists. What is needed is an analysis of the semi-independent variables of marriage, reproduction, and homosexual relations of various sorts. (In a valuable and neglected work, Michael Ross, 1983, reviews many previous studies of married homosexual men and provides much evidence for social coercion.)

In his 1976 dissertation, Weinrich includes a section on "The Relationship Between Homosexuality and Non-Reproduction" (Weinrich 1977, pp. 141 ff), which proposes distinctions between transvestism, transsexualism, and homosexuality, reviews nonhuman and non-Western evidence, and claims the existence of "a continuum. At one end, we have homosexualities that interfere little or not at all with reproduction; at the other are homosexualities and transsexualities that interfere completely with reproduction." The subsequent section (1977, pp. 152ff) discusses possible reasons for the absence, in humans, of non-reproductive castes of individuals like those of the social insects. He then lists "six ways of being a homosexual" based on the presence or absence of marriage or children, and their timing in the life course. "Most of these cases," states Weinrich (1977, p. 160), "involve a cost to one's own reproductive success, and a benefit to one's own kin." However, these types are not related to the reproductive rates of similar individuals without homosexuality, nor are the kin benefits specified. Still, this is one passage in which an author recognizes marrying, reproducing "homosexuals" other than ancient Greeks (see also Weinrich, 1987a).

Weinrich then turns to non-Western "berdaches" and other cross-gendered roles accorded formal social status, to demonstrate that in hunter-gatherer societies (our presumed ancestors) "homosexuals" did have inclusive fitness functions (Weinrich, 1977, pp. 166ff). "Again and again, the investigator happens to mention [benefits] that accrue to *individuals or their kin* [my italics] as a result of non-reproduction" (Weinrich, 1977, p. 171). But the crucial distinction is lost. We may not assume without evidence that personal gains in wealth or status are invariably invested in kin. And, as noted above, the author fails to show a correlation between cross-gender identity, non-reproduction, and homosexual activity. For Weinrich, cross-gender identity is neatly concordant with homosexuality, shamanism, ritual performance, a capacity for theatricals, and higher than average I.Q., all supposedly characterizing modern Western "gays" as well (Weinrich, 1977, pp. 174-180; 1987b, pp. 344ff).

Weinrich notes that nonreproduction in women is status-graded, as Kinsey's positive correlation between education and lesbianism in the United States showed, and wonders whether this correlation is more widespread. He is apparently unaware of the literature on female celibacy, which clearly demonstrates status-grading, but without inevitable lesbianism (Boone, 1986; Chambers-Schiller, 1979, 1984; Dickemann, 1979a,b, 1981; Faderman, 1981; Vicinus, 1985). The cause-effect relationship between celibacy and nonreproduction is never examined. The essay leaves this reader with the impression that the author recognized, but sidestepped, the central flaws in his argument, so intent was he upon discussing homosexuality rather than celibacy. Nevertheless, this work comes closest, of those reviewed, to recognizing the need to disaggregate the two variables, and revise the inclusive fitness hypothesis accordingly.

In his 1987 work, Weinrich states, "sociobiological models take nonreproduction as the biological question at issue and assume that transsexuals are, like homosexuals, less likely than heterosexuals to reproduce" (1987b, p. 317). But in subsequent discussion, the question is implicit, except for a *footnote* (p. 321) which states, "whether homosexuality usually decreases RS is an empirical matter; it is certainly logical that homosexuals would have fewer children than heterosexuals, but it is not a logical necessity. In fact, the very few studies that did happen to collect data on RS [here again RS is confused with birthrate] in homosexuals show exactly what our hunches tell us: homosexuals do have fewer kids." Pillard and Weinrich's recent study *required* all subjects, homosexual and heterosexual, to be unmarried. They did find lower rates of reproduction in celibate gays than in celibate heterosexuals (Weinrich, 1987b, p. 321). This unfortunately sheds no light on the RS of the married homosexuals that Weinrich identified in his thesis.

In subsequent pages, Weinrich admits that in societies where "everyone marries" exclusive homosexuality is impossible, so a continuum from exclusive heterosexual to bisexual occurs. On the verge of a situational theory, with degree of homosexual activity being determined by intensity of marital coercion, he retreats, returning to "*non*reproductive and *non*heterosexual reproductive strategies (Weinrich, 1987b, p. 344), once more equating the two, with the "berdache" as his primary example. (The "everyone marries" situation produces an alternate hypothesis in Weinrich, 1987a.) A later section (1987b, p. 356) on the maiden aunt and bachelor uncle identifies them as spare parents in past times, but quickly shifts to the supposedly nonreproductive, homosexual berdache.

Michael Ruse (1981, pp. 10-11) deals with this matter more briefly. "Assuming that homosexual individuals have fewer offspring than heterosexual individuals, their apparent loss of reproductive fitness could be 'exonerated' in terms of the increased fitness of close relatives." "What information there is . . . suggests that adopting a homosexual life-style frequently *follows or is accompanied by* phenomena that would indeed lower the reproductive cost" (my italics; Ruse, 1981, p. 21). Ruse is more cautious and perhaps more precise than Weinrich: "no definitive case can be made for the [kin selection] hypothesis as yet. For instance, no proof has yet been offered showing that homosexual offspring really do increase the fitness of their relatives and thus, indirectly, increase their own inclusive fitness" (Ruse, 1981, p. 25). He correctly notes that an inclusive fitness strategy freely adopted by the individual may have different consequences than one imposed by "parental manipulation," but "because we have no quantified statistics on the benefits of having a homosexual sibling, there is presently no direct way to distinguish between kin selection and parental manipulation" (Ruse, 1981, p. 28). But his discussion of parental manipulation is as much about the production of chaste celibates as it is about homosexuals. Again an important point is relegated to a footnote (p. 32). Noting that Weinrich never mentions the Catholic clergy, Ruse asks, "Does having a priest in the family raise the family's status? Do priests actively aid their siblings and their nephews and nieces? Why do men become priests? . . . What connection, if any, is there between the priesthood and homosexuality?" Here again we see a dawning awareness of the conflation of the two independent but partially overlapping variables, homosexuality and celibacy, reduced to a passing comment.

Ruse's later book rests on the same equation, yet here again he is more concerned to specify the falsifiability of the hypotheses. "[T]he most obvious point of test arises over the presumption that homosexuals do in fact have fewer offspring . . . If this is true . . . then the sociobiological models are (at best) irrelevant, and (at most) false" (Ruse, 1988, p. 142). But this observation (again confusing birthrate with RS) does not lead, as it ought, to a consideration of celibacy.

What is happening here? Neither author proposes that one *must* be homosexual in order to be celibate, or in order to be nonreproductive. Neither proposes that one *must* be gay to aid kin. These questions, in their frank absurdity, reveal the fundamental unclarity of the authors. If there is *no necessity for homosexuality* in either case, then the inclusive fitness hypothesis is *a hypothesis about celibacy and nonreproduction.* Whether and when celibates are homosexual, whether celibate homosexuals differ from celibate heterosexuals, in their direct RS and their kin investments, are subsidiary questions. Because neither author operationalizes his hypothesis, neither confronts directly the fact that the inclusive fitness hypothesis has only secondary relevance to *some* homosexuals. The taxonomic confusion regarding whether "married reproducing homosexuals" are "homosexuals" or "bisexuals" or "heterosexuals" has come home to roost. By imposing (most of the time) celibacy as a criterion of homosexuality, a higher, though not perfect, correlation between "homosexuality" and nonreproduction is achieved by these authors, once more tautologically begging the question.

Celibacy, Homosexuality, and Investment

This is not the place to review the growing literature on celibacy. However, some summary remarks will suggest its relevance to the hypothesis. Throughout human history, much celibacy of both women and men has been the product of parental imposition. Male children have been emasculated to assume roles as servants, officials, or castrati, while daughters as well as sons have been allocated to celibate roles as religious, teachers, and servants. There is uneven but growing evidence that these parental strategies were often rewarded by tangible filial benefits. In patrilineal societies, where great effort is made to marry firstborns, who will normally inherit primary titles and estates, or, if female, be married to such an heir, it is usual to assign higher order births to chaste celibate roles, or to those with later marriage and lower reproduction, or (in the case of sons) to promiscuous celibacy. However, all roles and institutions attract members out of a variety of motives, so that none consist *only* of the products of parental allocation.

This observation relates to the authors' identification of "parental manipulation" as an alternative theory of homosexuality. To me, it seems rather to be an alternate *means* to celibacy, reduced reproduction, or homosexuality, but remains within the domain of inclusive fitness. I believe these authors contrast parental manipulation with inclusive fitness on the presumption that those entrained into celibacy/homosexuality by parents will contribute to the *parents'* gain, while those who "choose" homosexuality/celibacy themselves are more likely to aid their own siblings and siblings' offspring.

But the notion of choice is problematic. The inculcation of a *personality* that is dedicated to familial well-being throughout its lifetime may be a far more effective longterm parental strategy than merely delegating a child to a specific role or institution. Roles and circumstances come and go: personalities abide. On the other hand, individual offspring are more, or other, than simple congeries of parental wishes. An empirical investigation of behavioral differences between "delegated" and "chosen" life histories is needed. But the relation between celibate roles and homosexuality is not simple. Some castrati were preferentially homosexual, some bisexual, and some exclusively heterosexual; the same may be said of clergy, military, and educational personnel, and even of the temporary "celibates" of prisons. Recognizing the variations in form and frequency of imposed celibacy in human societies, we must ask whether all sexual choice is not to some degree situational, but at the same time acknowledge that situation is never the sole determinant.

After all, the increase in public homosexuality and the emergence of the homosexual identity in the modern West occurred during a period when both men and women were less coerced into marriage and reproduction by their parents and communities, and when women were more often able to support themselves independently of men. The significant numbers of women claiming a lesbian identity post-maritally during this period are surely in part situational. These women are no less "homosexual" than those who so identified in childhood. Either there are millions of "essential" homosexuals locked in heterosexual oppression around the world, whose identity depends not at all on opportunity and constraint, or something is wrong with our theory.

The other term of the proposed equation, namely inclusive fitness investment, is likewise oversimplified in these works. Humans do not generally invest in a single beneficiary, nor in relatives of a single class. Rather, they distribute benefits with an eye to the anticipated futures of those relatives. Often the investment is a matter of relative gain where two or more individuals are also participating in reciprocal aid. Further, not all investment results in RS gains: parents, for example, may exact care from their offspring long after their reproductive period, merely to prolong their own lives and well-being. (Weinrich, 1987b, p. 179, recognizes this distributive complexity in passing.)

Robert Trivers (1985, p. 198) makes two telling observations: "on the surface, the sexual and romantic side of homosexual relations would seem to interfere with kin-directed altruism: insofar as one is sexually attracted to another individual, one will naturally be inclined to invest some resources in intrasexual competition to gain this individual's favors. Should the relationship blossom into a love relationship, it will be natural to devote some of the same resources and energy that would go into a loving heterosexual relationship." And "[t]hat parents in our society often consciously fear the expression of a homosexual orientation in their children suggests that homosexuality is not normally a means for aiding the reproduction of kin; otherwise, they should be delighted, since they are more closely related to the recipients of this altruism than is the offspring." Further cautionary evidence is the heavy investment of time, money, and energy of many lesbians and gay man in organizations supporting the gay community and defending gay rights, and the enormous resources devoted to the fight against AIDS.

But again, it is not a question of one or the other. Perhaps some homosexuals are extremely "nonadaptive" nonreproductive, selfish investors in only their own survival and enjoyment. Others struggle to invest not only in their natal families or in their own offspring but in the creation of a safe environment for themselves, their loved ones, and their peers. But most are probably equilibrating, as most humans do, their contributions to self, sexual partners, loved ones, offspring, natal family, community, and human society as a whole. While the distribution of investments is difficult to measure, an initial test of the inclusive fitness hypothesis would be simple indeed. Births, completed family size, and the direction of major investments could all be determined most especially for publicly identified lesbians. But after fourteen years and much discussion, the inclusive fitness hypothesis still hangs, never operationalized, never tested, lacking even descriptive evidentiary data to support it.

NATURE : ESSENTIALISM :: NURTURE : SOCIAL CONSTRUCTIONISM

Dualistic reasoning has deep roots in Western thought, and is probably universally human. Most dialogues about human nature are still conceived in these terms. The nature-nurture debate was resolved in modern biology with the advent of neo-Darwinian theory, integrating modern genetics, ecology, and evolutionary theory in the 1940s and 1950s. Psychology and sociology have now produced parallel "interactionist" approaches, while the "multifactorial model" of physiological and psychological medicine is similar. Yet often those paying lip service to new integrative approaches are in fact locked into old dualistic modes of thought.

Nowhere is this fruitless opposition better exemplified than by the so-called "essentialist-social constructionist" debate in sex/gender scholarship. (Weinrich, 1987b, pp. 83-88, maintains that this debate differs from the nature-nurture debate, and prefers the term "realist" to "essentialist." In my view, his discussion belies him.) No one can seriously argue now for either extreme. Historical and anthropological work of the last decades, while by no means answering all of our questions about the existence of preferentially homosexual beings throughout history, has clearly demonstrated that those engaging in same-sex acts are not only defined by, but in part created by, the societies and families in which they grow and live, in identity, self-esteem, partner choice, and sexual style. At the same time, the very opportunities, contexts, and tolerances for such acts and beings are socially given. Yet, whatever behavior, emotion, or life-history is constructed must be built within the material body and brain, and these may be socially molded only within limits. Our acts of love and sex, our fantasies as our paraphernalia, are constructed in and from the shapes of our bodies and the wiring of our nervous systems.

Are there individual variations within our general human bioprogram that are relevant to the occurrence of homosexualities of one kind or another? Michael Ruse notes that sociobiological hypotheses may be *nongenetic,* that is, requiring no direct, one-to-one, invariant genetic cause. In 1979 (p. 69) he observed that the parental manipulation hypothesis requires only that there be genes "which will make one homosexual under certain environmental conditions, but . . . it is possible that everyone has these." In 1988 (p. 145) he acknowledges that both the kin selection and the parental manipulation hypotheses "do not necessarily posit special genes separating homosexuals from heterosexuals. At least in theory, everyone could be the same genetically (in this respect). It is potentially in us all, waiting to be triggered by the right environmental factors." But Ruse offers no testable environmental hypothesis, and supporting historical and cross-cultural evidence is absent. The author seems unaware that he has broken the essentialist-social constructionist sound barrier.

All the works reviewed here seem to define the environment, when it is acknowledged, solely in familial terms. The authors review psychological studies, Freudian and post-Freudian, with greater or lesser approval. While psychological development is certainly a crucial part of our understanding of gender variance, it is not enough. Studies of the changing definitions of gender and sexuality teach us that the expression of these dimensions of the psyche, so rigid and inflexible from some perspectives, is extremely malleable, undergoing major modifications in as little as a generation, at times with the speed and superficiality of a fad.

Yet responsible evolutionary ecology does have a contribution to make to the study of sex and gender, both in methodology and in theory. Sex/gender systems are caused; many of the causes are interactions of organisms with environmental variables already identified as relevant to the behavioral strategies of other organisms. A general theory of human sexuality, using the comparative method to analyze historical, anthropological, and sociological data, will make statistical predictions about the appearance of specific sexual practices and gender identities. But the inclusive fitness hypothesis, arising from several fundamental theoretical and substantive misconceptions, and lacking supporting data, contributes nothing to our understanding of "homosexuality."

In closing, I must comment on the moral and political functions of the hypothesis. Both Wilson's 1978 text and later treatments make clear that the hope of the authors is to demonstrate that "homosexuality" is evolved, therefore adaptive, natural, beneficial to heterosexual families, therefore good. Surprisingly for biologists, this argument imputes moral meaning to organic evolution, which has none. Evolution and natural selection are processes in the natural world. Humans impute values to these processes and their outcomes, for their own social purposes, but they do so erroneously. The processes of nature, whether comet showers, continental drift, glaciation, or natural selection, are intrinsically without moral value. In fact, the more we come to understand evolutionary processes, the more we recognize the massive amount of competition, coercion, pain, and death essential to them. Rape is natural, and widespread in the animal world: it is not thereby either inevitable or moral. Indeed, the "grandeur" that Darwin saw has just about leached out of our view of life, leaving only its paradoxical beauty of form and function. No human behavior should be justified in terms of this humanly lawless, though scientifically lawful, process. In fact, liberal attempts to justify sexual variance in evolutionary terms may conceal, at a deeper level, a desire to evaluate homosexuality by reference to heterosexist norms. If the behavior aids in the reproduction of heterosexuals, goes the argument in its crudest form, it can't be all bad. This kind of reasoning must be rejected out of hand.

The ecstasies of human love and sex, of whatever sort, do not stand or fall on the basis of their contributions to the competitive survival of familial genetic lines, or to the perpetuation of the planet's most dangerous species. To deny this is to evade the most fundamental paradox of humanity. We are at once products of, and members of, the natural world, and at the same time sentient observers, commentators, evaluators of ourselves and our home. No sloppy hypothecations can free us from this essential human dilemma.

REFERENCES

Alexander, R. D. (1974), The evolution of social behavior. *Annual Review of Ecology and Systematics, 5,* 325-383.

Alexander, R. D. (1987). *The biology of moral systems.* Hawthorne, NY: Aldine de Gruyter.

Alexander, R. D., & Borgia, G. (1978). Group selection, altruism, and the levels of organization of life. *Annual Review of Ecology and Systematics, 9,* 449-474.

Altman, D., et al. (1989). *Homosexuality, which homosexuality?* International Conference on Gay and Lesbian Studies. Amsterdam: Uitgeverij An Dekker; London: GMP.

Bell, A. P., & Weinberg, M. S. (1987). *Homosexualities: A study of diversity among men and women.* New York: Simon & Schuster.

Blackwood, E. (Ed.). (1986). *Anthropology and homosexual behavior.* New York: The Haworth Press, Inc. *(Journal of Homosexuality, 11*(3/4), Summer 1985).

Boone, J. L., III. (1986). Parental investment and elite family structure in pre-industrial states: A case study of late medieval-early modern Portuguese genealogies. *American Anthropologist, 88*(6), 859-878.

Boswell, J. (1980). *Christianity, social tolerance, and homosexuality: Gay people in Western Europe from the beginning of the Christian era to the fourteenth century.* Chicago: University of Chicago Press.

Bowlby, J. (1990). *Charles Darwin: A new life.* New York: W.W. Norton.

Callender, C., & Kochems, L. M. (1983). The North American berdache. *Current Anthropology, 24*(4), 443-456 (with comments and reply, 456-470).

Campbell, B. (Ed.). (1972). *Sexual selection and the descent of man; 1871-1971.* Chicago: Aldine.

Carrier, J. M. (1971). Participants in urban Mexican male homosexual encounters. *Archives of Sexual Behavior, 1*(4), 279-291.

Carrier, J. M. (1976). Cultural factors affecting urban Mexican male homosexual behavior. *Archives of Sexual Behavior, 5*(2), 103-124.

Chambers-Schiller, L. (1979). The cult of single blessedness: Attitudes toward singlehood in early nineteenth century America. *Bunting Institute Working Paper.* Cambridge, MA: The Mary Ingraham Bunting Institute of Radcliffe College.

Chambers-Schiller, L. (1984). *Liberty, a better husband: Single women in America: The generations of 1780-1940.* New Haven, CT: Yale University Press.

Daly, M., & Wilson, M. (1983). *Sex, evolution, and behavior* (2nd ed.). Boston, MA: Willard Grant.

Dawkins, R. (1976). *The selfish gene.* New York: Oxford University Press.

Dickemann, M. (1979a). Female infanticide, reproductive strategies and social stratification: A preliminary model. In N. A. Chagnon & W. Irons (Eds.), *Evolutionary biology and human social organization* (pp. 321-367). North Scituate, MA: Duxbury.

Dickemann, M. (1979b). The ecology of mating systems in hypergynous dowry societies. *Social Science Information, 18*(2), 163-195.

Dickemann, M. (1981). Paternal confidence and dowry competition: A biocultural analysis of purdah. In R. D. Alexander & D. W. Tinkle, (Eds.), *Natural selection and social behavior: Recent research and new theory* (pp. 417-438). New York: Chiron.

Dover, K. J. (1978). *Greek homosexuality.* Cambridge, MA: Harvard University Press.

Faderman, L. (1981). *Surpassing the love of man: Romantic friendship and love between women from the Renaissance to the present.* New York: Wm. Morrow.

Foucault, M. (1978). *The history of sexuality.* Vol. 1: *An introduction.* New York: Random House.

Fox, R. (Ed.). (1975). *Biosocial anthropology.* New York: Wiley.

Futuyma, D. J., & Risch, S. J. (1984). Sexual orientation, sociobiology and evolution. *Journal of Homosexuality, 9*(2/3), 157-168.

Ghiselin, M. T. (1969). *The triumph of the Darwinian method.* Berkeley, CA: University of California Press.

Gonsiorek, J. C., & Weinrich, J. D. (1991). The definition and scope of sexual orientation. In J. C. Gonsiorek & J. D. Weinrich (Eds.), *Homosexuality: Research implications for public policy* (pp. 1-12). Newbury Park, CA: Sage.

Green, G. D., & Bozett, F. W. (1991). Lesbian mothers and gay fathers. In J. C. Gonsiorek & J. D. Weinrich (Eds.), *Homosexuality: Research implications for public policy* (pp. 197-214). Newbury Park, CA: Sage.

Hamilton, W. D. (1964). The evolution of social behaviour, I, II. *Journal of Theoretical Biology, 7*(1), 1-52.

Hand, J. L. (1981). Sociobiological implications of unusual sexual behavior of gulls: The genotype/behavioral phenotype problem. *Ethology and Sociobiology, 2*(3), 135-145.

Humphreys, R. L. (1970). *Tearoom trade: Impersonal sex in public places.* Chicago: Aldine.

Hutchinson, G. E. (1959). A speculative consideration of certain possible forms of sexual selection in man. *American Naturalist, 93*(869), 81-91.

Kagan, J. (1984). *The nature of the child.* New York: Basic Books.

Kirsch, J. A., & Rodman, J. E. (1982). Selection and sexuality: The Darwinian view of homosexuality. In W. Paul, J. D. Weinrich, J. C. Gonsiorek, & M. E. Hotvedt (Eds.), *Homosexuality: Social, psychological, and biological issues* (pp. 183-195). Beverly Hills, CA: Sage.

Kirsch, J. A., & Weinrich, J. D. (1991). Homosexuality, nature, and biology: Is homosexuality natural? Does it matter? In J. C. Gonsiorek & J. D. Weinrich (Eds.), *Homosexuality: Research implications for public policy* (pp. 13-31). Newbury Park, CA: Sage.

Kitcher, P. (1985). *Vaulting ambition: Sociobiology and the quest for human nature.* Cambridge, MA: MIT Press.

Lang, S. (1990). *Männer als Frauen–Frauen als Männer: Geschlechtsrollenwechsel bei den Indianern Nordamerikas.* Hamburg: Wayasbah Verlag.

Levins, R. (1968). *Evolution in changing environments: Some theoretical explorations.* Princeton, NJ: Princeton University Press.

Maynard Smith, J. (1964). Group selection and kin selection. *Nature, 200,* 1145-1147.

McIntosh, M. (1968). The homosexual role. *Social Problems, 16,* 182-192.

Michaels, S. (1991, November). Problems in the sociological construction of homosexuality via survey research. Paper presented at the Fifth Annual Lesbian and Gay Studies Conference, Rutgers, NJ.

Nanda, S. (1984). The hijras of India: A preliminary report. *Medicine and Law, 3*, 59-75.

Pilling, A. (1992). Northwest California Indian gender classes: "Those who could not marry," "those men who have never been near a woman," "women who do men's things." *Society of Lesbian and Gay Anthropologists Newsletter 14*(2), 15-22.

Ross, M. (1983). *The married homosexual man: A psychological study.* London: Routledge & Kegan Paul.

Ruse, M. (1979). *Sociobiology: Sense or nonsense?* Dordrecht: D. Reidel.

Ruse, M. (1981). Are there gay genes? Sociobiology and homosexuality. *Journal of Homosexuality, 6*(4), 5-34.

Ruse, M. (1988). *Homosexuality.* Oxford: Basil Blackwell.

Senelick, L. (1990). Mollies or men of mode? Sodomy and the Eighteenth Century London stage. *Journal of the History of Sexuality, 1*(1), 33-67.

Stacey, P. B., & Koenig, W. D. (Eds.). (1990). *Cooperative breeding in birds: Longterm studies of ecology and behavior.* Cambridge: Cambridge University Press.

Trivers, R. (1974). Parent-offspring conflict. *American Zoologist, 14*(l), 249-264.

Trivers, R. (1985). *Social evolution.* Menlo Park, CA: Benjamin/Cummings.

Trumbach, R. (1989). Gender and the homosexual role in modern western culture: The 18th and 19th centuries compared. In D. Altman et al. (Eds.), *Homosexuality, which homosexuality?* (pp. 149-169). International Conference on Gay and Lesbian Studies. Amsterdam: Uitgeverij An Dekker; London: GMP.

Vicinus, M. (1985). *Independent woman: Work and community for single women, 1850-1920.* Chicago: University of Chicago Press.

Weinrich, J. D. (1977). Human reproductive strategy II. Homosexuality and non-reproduction: Some evolutionary models. In *Human reproductive strategy, I & II.* Ph.D. thesis, Harvard University, 1976. Ann Arbor, MI: University Microfilms International.

Weinrich, J. D. (1982). Is homosexuality biologically natural? In W. Paul et al. (Eds.). (1982). *Homosexuality: Social, psychological, and biological issues* (pp. 197-208). Beverly Hills, CA: Sage.

Weinrich, J. D. (1987a). A new sociobiological theory of homosexuality applicable to societies with universal marriage. *Ethology and Sociobiology, 8*(1), 37-47.

Weinrich, J. D. (1987b). *Sexual landscapes: Why we are what we are; why we love whom we love.* New York: Scribner's.

Weston, K. (1991). *Families we choose: Lesbians, gays, kinship.* New York: Columbia University Press.

Whitam, F. L. (1983). Culturally invariable properties of male homosexuality: Tentative conclusions from cross-cultural research. *Archives of Sexual Behavior, 12*(3), 207-226.

Whitam, F. L., & Mathy, R. M. (1986). *Male homosexuality in four societies: Brazil, Guatemala, the Philippines, and the United States.* New York: Praeger Scientific.

Whitehead, H. (1981). The bow and the burden strap: A new look at institutiona-lized homosexuality in native North America. In S. B. Ortner & H. Whitehead (Eds.), *Sexual meanings: The cultural construction of gender and sexuality* (pp. 80-115). Cambridge: Cambridge University Press.

Williams, W. L. (1986). *The spirit and the flesh: Sexual diversity in American Indian culture.* Boston: Beacon.

Wilson, E. O. (1971). *The insect societies.* Cambridge, MA: The Belknap Press of Harvard University Press.

Wilson, E. O. (1975). *Sociobiology: The new synthesis.* Cambridge, MA: The Belknap Press of Harvard University Press.

Wilson, E. O. (1978). *On human nature.* Cambridge, MA: Harvard University Press.

Sexual Preference and Altruism

Debra Salais, MA
Robert B. Fischer, PhD

Ball State University

SUMMARY. Several hypotheses have been offered to explain homosexuality. This study tests the prediction of the sociobiological model that male homosexuals should be more altruistic than heterosexuals. Subjects were dichotomized into homosexual (N = 76) and heterosexual (N = 51) groups on the basis of self-reported sexual feelings and behaviors. Both groups provided demographic information and completed Hogan's Empathy Scale. As predicted, the homosexuals were found to score significantly higher on the empathy assessment. Given the strong association between empathy and altruism, the sociobiological model was supported.

Evolutionary biologists interpret behaviors in an adaptive context. Such interpretations must not constitute conclusions but rather serve as working hypotheses. The latter, of course, are useful only

D. A. Salais is a graduate student in psychology and R. B. Fischer is Professor of Psychological Science, Ball State University.

The advice and assistance of Phillip Lee Kizer in many ways made this research possible. The help of S. Smith, C. Julian, P. Shaffer, and G. F. Meunier are greatly appreciated.

The kind permission granted by R. Hogan and the Psychological Corporation to use their materials is also appreciated.

Correspondence may be addressed to: Professor Robert B. Fischer, Department of Psychological Science, Ball State University, Muncie, IN 47306.

[Haworth co-indexing entry note]: "Sexual Preference and Altruism." Salais, Debra, and Robert B. Fischer. Co-published simultaneously in *Journal of Homosexuality* (The Haworth Press, Inc.) Vol. 28, No. 1/2, 1995, pp. 185-196; and: *Sex, Cells, and Same-Sex Desire: The Biology of Sexual Preference* (ed: John P. De Cecco, and David Allen Parker) The Haworth Press, Inc., 1995, pp. 185-196. Multiple copies of this article/chapter may be purchased from The Haworth Document Delivery Center [1-800-3-HAWORTH; 9:00 a.m. - 5:00 p.m. (EST)].

to the extent that they are congruent with the relevant data. It is therefore not surprising that sociobiologists have viewed otherwise maladaptive appearing behaviors as somehow promoting an individual's fitness. That is, behaviors are anticipated to enhance an individual's reproductive success. This must be the case unless there are compelling reasons to suspect that the phenotype (characteristic being assessed) in question is under negative selection pressures and, consequently, is declining in prevalence in the species (cf. Daly & Wilson, 1983; Wilson, 1975; Krebs & Davies, 1981; Trivers, 1985). It is hardly surprising that sociobiological hypotheses about human homosexuality have focused on the presumed benefits such activities would have for individuals or their kin. These hypotheses have taken several forms. At the very least, these interpretations attempt to show how inclusive fitness (Hamilton, 1964) would be only minimally affected. Employing the concept of inclusive fitness, the focus shifts from an examination of an individual to the reproductive success of a group of biologically related kin. Consequently, one interpretation is that exclusive homosexuality is a result of fitness promoting heterosexual tendencies (Symons, 1979).

Gallup and Suarez (1983) believe homosexuals are losers in heterosexual competition. Although some homosexuals may experience unsatisfying heterosexual contacts, it is difficult to determine whether this is a cause or an effect of sexual orientation. In such a context, homosexuality would not be adaptive in an evolutionary sense. It would also not be detrimental to the fitness efforts of the kin group (Hamilton, 1964). In essence, so long as the homosexual's activities did not drain the families resources or otherwise produce a negative impact on kin, the behavior could be viewed as evolutionarily benign. If the homosexual's behavior reduced competition with other kin group members (Trivers, 1974, 1985) for limited sexual resources, the behavior would be advantageous in times of limited availability of such resources.

Weinrich (1987) extends this line of reasoning by assuming that homosexuals may not suffer as great a loss of fitness as one might otherwise suppose. On one hand, homosexuals need not entirely forgo all procreative opportunities. Although they are less likely to reproduce (compared to heterosexuals), this does not mean that they cannot reproduce! It is not uncommon for homosexuals to enter into heterosexual relationships which may produce offspring (Bell & Weinberg, 1978). This might only slightly reduce the inclusive fitness costs to the homosexual's kin group. Moreover, the kin group could actually benefit from the presence of the homosexual to the extent that the homosexual's behavior reflected the influence of parental manipulation (Trivers, 1974, 1985) or produced direct benefits to be accrued via increased wealth or status associated with the homosexual him/herself (Weinrich, 1978, 1980; Churchill, 1967).

It is possible that the relatives of the homosexual might exhibit enhanced reproductive success due to behavioral and/or physiological characteristics. Those relatives who possess some of the genetic factors associated with homosexuality would, through an increase in reproductive success, more than compensate for any reduced fitness associated with the homosexual him/her self (Hutchinson, 1959; Wilson, 1975). Thus, it is possible, but not yet demonstrated, that the relatives of the homosexual might exhibit fitness-enhancing phenotypic traits due to the genes shared in common. Although homosexual behavior would not be fully expressed, other beneficial attributes might be well developed. It would be interesting if the apparent elevation in intelligence test performance evident in at least some homosexuals (Weinrich, 1980) was also apparent in their close relatives. Even if this were not the case, fitness benefits might be attainable if the kin could profit from the expected advantages of greater intellectual performance of their homosexual relative. Others report a lower than expected frequency of psychopathology in gays (Bell & Weinberg, 1978). This also might provide a substrate of benefits which might be available to kin.

Unquestionably, the most influential hypothesis concerning the presumed adaptive benefits of homosexuality is that formulated by Wilson (1975, 1978) and Trivers (1974). Homosexuals are seen as sacrificing their direct reproductive gains for the benefit of their kin. The mechanisms which permit this enhancement of inclusive fitness are apparent altruistic tendencies which are hypothesized to be unusually well developed in homosexuals. Altruism, in this sense, would assume behaviors which imposed some costs to the actor, with few, if any, attendant benefits. The recipient of the altruistic act would benefit at little cost to him/her self. Examples might include sharing the spoils of the benefit with others, giving curren- cy, goods, or services with no realistic expectation of repayment, volunteerism, etc. Wilson assumes the presence of evolutionary pressures to develop kin-directed altruism. Unfettered by the constraints of maintaining a reproductive union and investing one's resources in offspring, the homosexual should be able to accumu- late wealth and be free to provide services. Certainly in small, kin-delineated hunter-gatherer societies, any inclination to altruisti- cally bestow some accumulated benefits on kin would indirectly enhance one's inclusive fitness (Hughes, 1988; Irons, 1979; Hamil- ton, 1964). In this model, unlike that of Gallup and Suarez (1983), homosexuality is selected directly, not by default. Homosexuality is beneficial per se, and not due to having lost in heterosexual con- tests. Weinrich (1987) assumes the Wilson (1975, 1978) model to be essentially correct. This approach anticipates that the kin group will enjoy enhanced inclusive fitness due to phenotypic superiority of the homosexual and his/her relatives.

Apparently there have been no empirical tests of these hypothe- ses to date. One reason may be that it is difficult to specify, and certainly to manipulate, many of the benefits that kin might expect in Western society. *Post hoc* comparisons may certainly be influen- tial in supporting some theoretical alternatives (cf. Weinrich, 1980; Churchill, 1967). Others, such as the early development of homo- sexual orientation (Bell & Weinberg, 1978; Green, 1976), may miti- gate against competing models (Gallup & Suarez, 1983). Wilson's (1975, 1978) postulate of altruism as the driving force in the evolu- tion of homosexual behavior has two important attributes, however. One is that it is central to his model and that of Weinrich (1987). The other is that it is a testable construct. The study to be reported in this paper is a comparison of estimates of empathy/altruism in groups of homosexuals and heterosexuals. If the basic sociobiolog- ical model is correct, homosexuals are to be expected to be general- ly more empathetic and altruistic.

METHODS AND RESULTS

The study inferred altruism and sexual preference via a multiple choice questionnaire. Subject names were not recorded nor were most subjects directly contacted by the principal investigators. The instrument consisted of two sections: one assessing the subjects' sexual orientation and a variety of demographic variables, and the other an empathy scale (Hogan, 1969).

All subjects were current residents of Indiana and Ohio. The homosexuals were contacted primarily via a regional meeting of Dignity–an organization for gays. Although this organization has ties to the Catholic church it is open to all individuals. Attendees were told that a study concerning attitudes of homosexuals on a variety of topics was being conducted and they were asked to cooperate. They were told that the study did not attempt to measure psychopathology. Specifically, on the questionnaire the study was described as "part of our effort to examine several aspects of socially approved behaviors as to how they relate to demographic, social and sexual variables . . . we hope to uncover how beneficial social behaviors relate to one another." There was no mention of the true nature of the study (i.e., to assess altruism). Subjects were informed that their participation was voluntary; they were assured that their responses would remain anonymous and that only summaries of the data would be published. If they were interested, attendees were provided with questionnaires, computer scorable answer sheets, and metered envelopes for the return of the materials to the principal investigators. They were encouraged to take as many questionnaire packets as they thought they could use. They were to distribute the packets to friends or members of other gay organizations in the area. To accommodate the possibility that one subject might receive these materials from more than one source, they were requested to respond only once to the survey. Overall, there was a 40% return rate of materials. It is unknown what proportion of this number reflects packets which were taken by individuals and either not distributed or lost. Undoubtedly, some may have taken more packets than they could distribute to associates. A few other contacts were made independent of the Dignity conference. In all cases the procedures were the same.

The heterosexuals, and some additional homosexuals, were obtained from undergraduate and graduate students who volunteered to serve as subjects. These subjects were predominantly general studies majors (sophomores) taking introductory psychology. They were contacted via the course instructor and notices requesting volunteers for an attitude survey. No mention of sexual orientation was made during subject recruiting. These subjects completed the questionnaires in group settings and had their responses collected at that time. Anonymity was also stressed for this group, no identifiers were requested and answer sheets were shuffled as they were handed in.

The subject population was dichotomized on the basis of self-rankings of their sexual behaviors and feelings (Bell & Weinberg, 1978; McConaghy, 1987). These two questions requested that the subjects rate their current view of themselves along a seven-point scale (Bell & Weinberg, 1978; Kinsey, Pomeroy, & Martin, 1948). The scale was arranged as follows: 0 = exclusively heterosexual, 1 = mainly heterosexual with a small degree of homosexuality, 2 = mainly heterosexual with a substantial degree of homosexuality, 3 = equally heterosexual and homosexual. Questions 4, 5, and 6 were the same as 0, 1, and 2 except that the sexual preference terms were reversed. An individual was classified as being predominantly homosexual if the mean of the rankings on behaviors and feelings questions fell within the range of 4.5 and 6.0. Similarly, a predominantly heterosexual's average score would fall between 0.0 and 1.5.

Overall, only 7.4% of respondents were nonwhites and these data were not included in the analysis. Also, only 14% of the sample consisted of homosexual females. Although this percentage is high relative to expected frequencies in the population (cf. McConaghy, 1987), it was too small to permit effective matching on demographic variables. These females' data were excluded from the present analysis, although they will be retained for future work if a larger population of subjects can be obtained. The demographic data of the remaining subjects were analyzed in order to match the white homosexuals (N = 113) and heterosexuals (N = 79).

Multiple regression analysis indicated that three demographic factors produced the largest amounts of variance.[1] The remaining variables each explained less than 1% of the remaining variance. Demography indicated that the homosexuals tended to be sightly older and to come from larger, more urban areas.

Subjects were selected so that no significant differences between the groups on any of the demographic variables except for the two addressing sexual preference remained. After this procedure, 76 homosexuals and 51 heterosexuals remained in the study. Of these, approximately 80% in each group were 20-30 years of age.

The heterosexuals were predominately Protestant (52.9%) or Catholic (17.6%). There was an almost equal split among the homosexuals with respect to religious preference (Protestant, 44.7% and Catholic, 39.5%). This variable was of interest since many Dignity members were expected to be Catholic. The sample did not reflect an overwhelming predominance of Catholics. Other religions (non-specified) account for 11.8% of the heterosexual and 10.5% of the homosexual respondents. The remainder of the respondents expressed no religious affiliation. Approximately 70% of both groups came from urban areas although not from very large cities (generally under 500,000 people–heterosexuals 92.2%; homosexuals 86.8%).

Altruism was inferred via the subjects' responses to the 64 items which comprise Hogan's (1969) empathy scale. This instrument uses true-false responses to a series of questions drawn largely from the MMPI (Minnesota Multiphasic Personality Inventory) and CPI (California Personality Inventory) item pools. This type of scale provides reliable estimates of empathy (Hogan, 1969). In adult populations, there is a consistent relationship in the literature between estimates of empathy and altruism (cf. Eisenberg, 1986; Hoffman, 1981, 1982; Rosenhan, 1978). The Hogan scale is a valid and unobtrusive means to assess altruistic tendencies.

An empathy score was obtained for each subject and the data were analyzed treating sexual preference as the criterion variable. The homosexual males were found to score significantly higher on the empathy scale ($F 1, 125 = 3.89$, $p < 0.05$). On the 64 items of the Hogan Scale, the homosexuals had a mean score of $61.48 \pm SE$ 1.14 whereas the heterosexuals score was $57.78 \pm SE 1.46$. The 95% confidence interval for the homosexuals was from 59.13 to 63.65, indicating no substantial overlap with the mean score of the heterosexual males.

DISCUSSION

The overall significant effect indicating greater estimated empathy/altruism in homosexual males supports Wilson's hypothesis

(1975, 1978). Subsequent work needs to determine whether altruistic tendencies are associated with providing benefits to others. Homosexuals should nonrandomly dispense benefits according to genetic affinities with close relatives who have a high reproductive potential receiving more of the goods and services. Such an investigation needs to employ a non-Western sample; it is possible that our culture has persecuted and stigmatized homosexuals (Strommen, 1989) to the degree that altruistic tendencies may be suppressed even within the family. A fair test of the specific fitness benefits to kin would include gay subjects who are accepted and well integrated into family life. It is revealing that the Hogan scale demonstrated differences in empathy/altruism in spite of the context of what may have been a hostile social environment. A more invasive investigation of the actual behavior of homosexuals would be useful to determine if such attitudinal differences result in different degrees of altruistic behavior. To this end, it is perhaps not accidental that one of the few dimensions differentiating homosexual fathers from their heterosexual counterparts is that the former were more responsive to the needs of their offspring (Bigner & Jacobson, 1989). Such responsiveness is likely to be an outgrowth of empathetic tendencies.

One potential limitation of the generality of these findings concerns the use of Dignity, a religious-affiliated organization, to contact some of the homosexuals. If this sampling procedure yielded a greater degree of religious affiliation among the gays, and if empathy/altruism correlates positively with religion, the results of this study might reflect differences due to religion effects rather than sexual orientation. In both groups of subjects the vast majority professed affiliation with some form of organized religion. Moreover, more homosexuals (94.7%) claimed such ties than did heterosexuals (82.3%).

Ironically, the consequence of greater religious affiliation among the homosexuals actually strengthens the conclusions of the study. Research into the influence of religious beliefs on the likelihood that a person will exhibit empathy or prosocial behavior has found the relationship to be negative (Rokeach, 1969; Sorrentino, 1981). The more religiously devout a person was the less compassion, the less empathy, and the less desire to help another in need is evidenced. Sorrentino (1981) believes the lack of response may be due to the more religious subjects not attending to the situational determinants which indicate that someone is in need. The result is that empathy is markedly reduced in these individuals. Some (Rubin & Peplau, 1975) believe a more religious person is more likely to derogate a person in need, although others (Sorrentino, 1981) found that they were no more likely to do so than nonreligious persons. Although we simply obtained information about religious affiliation, not the intensity of religious beliefs, it would appear that the essential conclusion of our study could not be biased by a positive effect of religion on our measure of empathy/altruism. In fact, one might speculate that the homosexuals may have been more empathetic and altruistic in spite of an overall greater tendency to report a greater religious affiliation.

Although greater altruistic tendencies are required for the sociobiological model to have explanatory power, they are not sufficient. An additional requirement is that a genetic substrate exists to allow for the transmission of the trait through evolution over time. Since the time of Kallman's (1952) perhaps unrealistically high reported concordance rate in MZ (monozygotic) twin pairs, there has been a belief that there is a heritable component to sexual preferences. Subsequent work with twins (cf. Heston & Shields, 1968; Eckert, Bouchard, Bohlen, & Heston, 1986) has clearly indicated that the degree of genetic similarity plays a role in the expression of the trait. Pillard and Weinrich (1986) examined the incidence of homosexuality in non-twin siblings of index cases and support the hypothesis that the trait runs in families. The data focusing on twin and sibling incidences (Pillard, Poumadere, & Carretta, 1981) and the absence of specific identifiable environmental factors which would mitigate a genetic influence (Hubrec & Robinette, 1984) underscore the importance of the genome in the development of homosexuality.

An additional concern is the proximate physiological mechanisms which translate the genotypic influences into a neural substrate which could subserve a given class of behaviors. At present it seems that the prenatal brain is sensitive to changes in levels or the timing of the availability of endogenous hormones (Reinisch, 1974; Dörner, 1980). These hormonal influences are certainly influenced by genetic factors (Wolf, 1981; Gordon & Ruddle, 1981), perhaps through modifications of the timing of ontogenetic sequences (Marx, 1984). It seems that both prenatal (Money, 1987) and concurrent endocrine influences (Gladue, Green, & Hellman, 1984) may influence sexual orientation. Once again, the absence of useful nonbiological models (Bell, Weinberg, & Hammersmith, 1981) lends added support to the genetic-neuroendocrine influences in the etiology of homosexuality at least in males (Eckert et al., 1986; Pillard & Weinrich, 1986).

The sociobiological approach would seem to provide advantages in the attempt to better understand sexual orientation. One advantage is that it is truly scientific. It addresses the issue within the context of over a century of related research concerning evolutionary processes. It makes predictions at each level of analysis which are testable and therefore can objectively be refuted. Secondly, the sociobiological explanation is inherently positive. Unless the phenotype is declining in prevalence it is assumed that the trait is adaptive or at least benign. If so, one is then encouraged to delineate the proximate mechanisms which are involved. In the case of homosexuality, there are data supporting a model predicting that these individuals are likely to be altruistic and empathetic, that the phenotype is mediated by neuro-endocrine processes occurring during mid-gestation, and that these effects are mediated by genetic factors. In essence, a balanced polymorphism exists in our species with respect to sexual orientation because both heterosexuality and homosexuality can promote inclusive fitness. It would be useful to learn specifically to what degree and under which environmental circumstances fitness is enhanced.

NOTE

1. The three factors identified by multiple regression analysis were: population of locality of current resident ($F = 22.45$), $r^2 = 0.19$; age ($F = 9.18$), $r^2 = 0.24$; and classification of current residence as urban, suburban, or rural ($F = 5.38$), $r^2 = 0.27$.

REFERENCES

Bell, A. P., & Weinberg, M. S. (1978). *Homosexualities: A study of diversity among men and women.* New York: Simon and Schuster.

Bell, A. P., Weinberg, M. S., & Hammersmith, S. K. (1981). *Sexual preference: Its development in men and women.* Bloomington: Indiana University Press.

Bigner, J. J., & Jacobson, R. B. (1989). Parenting behaviors of homosexual and heterosexual fathers. *Journal of Homosexuality, 18*(1/2), 173-186.

Churchill, W. (1967). *Homosexual behavior among males: A cross-cultural and cross-species investigation.* New York: Horthorn Books, Inc.

Daly, M., & Wilson, M. (1983). *Sex, evolution, and behavior.* Boston: Willard Grant Press.

Dörner, G. (1980). Neuroendocrine aspects in the etiology of sexual deviations. In R. Forleo & W. Pasini (Eds.), *Medical sexology* (pp. 190-197), Littleton, MA: PSG Publishing Co.

Eckert, E. D., Bouchard, T. J., Bohlen, J., & Heston, L. L. (1986). Homosexuality in monozygotic twins reared apart. *British Journal of Psychiatry, 148,* 421-425.

Eisenberg, N. (1986). *Altruistic emotion, cognition, and behavior.* Hillsdale, NJ: Lawrence Erlbaum Associates.

Gallup, G. G., & Suarez, S. D. (1983). Homosexuality as a by-product of selection for optimal heterosexual strategies. *Perspectives in biology and medicine, 26,* 315-322.

Gladue, B. A., Green, R., & Hellman, R. E. (1984). Neuroendocrine response to estrogen and sexual orientation. *Science, 225,* 1496-1498.

Gordon, J. W., & Ruddle, F. H. (1981). Mammalian gonadal determination and gametogenesis. *Science, 211,* 1265-1271.

Green, R. (1976). One hundred ten feminine and masculine boys: Behavioral contrasts and demographic similarities. *Archives of Sexual Behavior, 5,* 425-446.

Hamilton, W. D. (1964). The genetical evolution of social behavior. *Journal of Theoretical Biology, 7,* 1-52.

Heston, L. L., & Shields, J. (1968). Homosexuality in twins. *Archives of General Psychiatry, 18,* 149-160.

Hoffman, M. L. (1981). The development of empathy. In J. P. Rushton & R. M. Sorrentino (Eds.), *Altruism and helping behavior: Social, personality and developmental perspective.* Hillsdale, NJ: Lawrence Erlbaum Associates.

Hoffman, M. L. (1982). Development of prosocial motivation: Empathy and guilt. In N. Eisenberg (Ed.), *The development of prosocial behavior.* New York: Academic Press.

Hogan, R. (1969). Development of an empathy scale. *Journal of Consulting and Clinical Psychology, 33,* 307-316.

Hubrec, Z., & Robinette, C. D. (1984). The study of human twins in medical research. *New England Journal of Medicine, 310,* 435-441.

Hughes, D. L. (1988). *Evolution and human kinship.* New York: Oxford University Press.

Hutchinson, G. E. (1959). A speculative consideration of certain possible forms of sexual selection in man. *American Naturalist, 48,* 81-91.

Irons, W. (1979). Investment and primary social dyads. In N. A. Chagnon & W. Irons (Eds.), *Evolutionary biology and human social behavior: An anthropological perspective* (pp. 181-212). North Scituate, MA: Duxbury Press.

Kallman, F. J. (1952). Twin and sibship study of overt male homosexuality. *American Journal of Human Genetics, 4*, 136-146.

Kinsey, A. C., Pomeroy, W. B., & Martin, C. E. (1948). *Sexual behavior in the human male*. Philadelphia: Saunders.

Krebs, J. R., & Davies, N. B. (1981). *An introduction to behavioral ecology*. Sunderland, MA: Sinauer Associates, Inc.

Marx, J. L. (1984). New clues to developmental timing. *Science, 226*, 425-427.

McConaghy, N. (1987). Heterosexuality/homosexuality: Dichotomy or continuum. *Archives of Sexual Behavior, 10*, 411-424.

Money, J. (1987). Sin, sickness, or status? *American Psychologist, 42*, 384-399.

Pillard, R. C., Poumadere, J., & Carretta, R. A. (1981). Is homosexuality familial? A review, some data, and a suggestion. *Archives of Sexual Behavior, 10*, 465-475.

Pillard, R. C., & Weinrich, J. D. (1986). Evidence of familial nature of male homosexuality. *Archives of General Psychiatry, 43*, 808-812.

Reinisch, J. M. (1974). Fetal hormones, the brain, and human sex differences: A heuristic, integrative review of the recent literature. *Archives of Sexual Behavior, 3*, 51-90.

Rokeach, M. (1969). Religious values and social compassion. *Review of Religious Research, 11*, 3-38.

Rosenhan, D. L. (1978). Toward resolving the altruism paradox: Affect, self-reinforcement, and cognition. In L. Wispe (Ed.), *Altruism, sympathy, and helping: Psychological and sociological perspectives*. New York: Academic Press.

Rubin, Z., & Peplau, L. A. (1975). Who believes in a just world? *Journal of Social Issues, 31*, 65-90.

Sorrentino, R. M. (1981). Derogation of an innocently suffering victim: So who's the "good guy"? In J. P. Rushton & R. M. Sorrentino (Eds.), *Altruism and helping behavior*. Hillsdale, NY: Lawrence Erlbaum Associates, Inc.

Strommen, E. F. (1989). "You're a what?": Family member reaction to the disclosure of homosexuality. *Journal of Homosexuality, 18*(1/2), 37-58.

Symons, D. (1979). *The evolution of human sexuality*. New York: Oxford University Press.

Trivers, R. L. (1974). Parent-offspring conflict. *American Zoologist, 14*, 249-264.

Trivers, R. L. (1985). *Social evolution*. Menlo Park, CA: Benjamin Cummings.

Weinrich. J. D. (1978). Nonreproduction, homosexuality, transsexualism, and intelligence: I. A systematic literature search. *Journal of Homosexuality, 3*, 275-289.

Weinrich, J. D. (1980). On a relationship between homosexuality and IQ test scores: A review and some hypotheses. In R. Forleo & W. Pasini (Eds.), *Medical sexology*. Littleton, MA: SPG Publishing Co., Inc.

Weinrich, J. D. (1987). A new sociobiological theory of homosexuality applicable to societies with universal marriage. *Ethology and Sociobiology, 8*, 37-47.

Wilson, E. O. (1975). *Sociobiology: The new synthesis*. Cambridge, MA: Harvard University Press.

Wilson, E. O. (1978). *On human nature*. Cambridge, MA: Harvard University Press.

Wolf, U. (1981). Genetic aspects of H-Y antigen. *Human Genetics, 58*, 25-28.

Biological Research on Sexual Orientation:
A Critique of the Critics

James D. Weinrich, PhD

University of California, San Diego

SUMMARY. Evolutionary biologists are tired of being accused of being too biologically deterministic, by critics who have little understanding of what biological or evolutionary theories actually imply. Misunderstandings came about because social-science disciplines often do not share evolutionary biology's tendency to build into their models multiple "normal" paths of development. Sociobiologists first explained homosexuality adaptively because they first try to explain *everything* adaptively. Most nonbiologists are unaware of this very strong evolutionary tradition.

It is now fashionable to discount scientific objectivity, but there are many examples of where such an attack is unwarranted. Kinsey produced a nontypological theory of sexual orientation in spite of his history as a taxonomist. Sociobiologists produced a nonpathological explanation of nonreproductive homosexuality in spite of the centrality of reproductive success in their models.

In judging whether a discipline is particularly likely to be misused in social debates, one must perform the appropriate intellectual "controls." One must examine appropriate uses as well as misuses, and one must examine other disciplines to see whether there are dif-

---

Dr. Weinrich is Assistant Adjunct Professor of Psychiatry at the University of California, San Diego, and is Principal Investigator of the Sexology Project at the HIV Neurobehavioral Research Center.

Correspondence may be addressed: 2760 Fifth Avenue #200, San Diego, CA 92103.

[Haworth co-indexing entry note]: "Biological Research on Sexual Orientation: A Critique of the Critics." Weinrich, James D. Co-published simultaneously in *Journal of Homosexuality* (The Haworth Press, Inc.) Vol. 28, No. 1/2, 1995, pp. 197-213; and: *Sex, Cells, and Same-Sex Desire: The Biology of Sexual Preference* (ed: John P. De Cecco, and David Allen Parker) The Haworth Press, Inc., 1995, pp. 197-213. Multiple copies of this article/chapter may be purchased from The Haworth Document Delivery Center [1-800-3-HAWORTH; 9:00 a.m. - 5:00 p.m. (EST)].

ferences in the *relative* likelihood of abuse. Indeed, many social-science theories have been even more clearly abused than biological ones.

Meurig Horton, of the High-risk Behavior Unit in the WHO's Global Program on AIDS, described his research into groups of men who engage in sex with men in developing countries, such as Indonesia and Brazil. "These countries have much wider notions of men who have sex with men than simply standard Western categories of gay," Horton said. One group in Indonesia represents a class of transvestites that has existed for a thousand years, with members in every village . . . Indonesian transvestites show that "just because something is socially constructed doesn't mean it can be changed," Horton said. "Sometimes it is easier to change biology than behavior."

–Check, 1993

Opponents of homosexuality . . . have been quick to cite such writings as those by Dr. [William] Byne . . . to bolster their claims that homosexuality is a sinful, chosen behavior . . . As the man caught in the middle, Dr. Byne says being quoted by antihomosexual groups irks him as much as the criticism he gets from gay-rights groups . . . He says he . . . has "taken a lot of heat from gay scientists doing biological research in this area. They say I have to take responsibility for the misuse of my work."

–Jefferson, 1993

On a popular talk show, a respected gay guest describes some biological research on sexual orientation as fascist (Rader, 1992). In New Orleans, a gay performance artist pulls a blue handkerchief out of a "male heterosexual brain," a pink handkerchief out of a "male homosexual brain," and opens up "Simon LeVay's brain" to reveal nothing (Schmaltz, 1992). These two cases of criticism, bordering on ridicule, exemplify misconceptions held by academics and activists about the nature of evolutionary or biological theories of sexual orientation. To put it bluntly, biologists are tired of being the whipping boys of such critics, who have little understanding of what biological or evolutionary points of view actually are or accurately imply.

I hope to clear up these misconceptions in two ways: first, by presenting many of the ideas of evolutionary biology with more attention to political consequences than has been given in the past, and second, by presenting some of the social context in which modern evolutionary theories of sexual orientation were developed. I will begin with the two major reasons why these misunderstandings came about.

Sociobiology and the evolutionary approach to behavior came to the attention of most academics in the mid-1970s, with the publication of Edward O. Wilson's book *Sociobiology: The New Synthesis* (Wilson, 1975), followed by *On Human Nature* (Wilson, 1978). These works were greeted by a controversy led by two prominent biologists in a committee of an organization called "Science for the People," headquartered in Cambridge, Massachusetts. This left-wing organization's politics meshed well with the politics of gay liberation of the time, so most gay activists avoided sociobiology and never took the time to investigate the possibilities that this theory offered for them. (A notable exception was the early republication of an excerpt from Wilson's 1978 book in the gay news-magazine, the *Advocate*, retitled "Gay As Normal"–Wilson, 1979.) It is important to note that this lack of interest on the part of gay activists was not mirrored by mainstream publications, which openly described the positive view of homosexuality put forth by sociobiology. Perhaps as a result, most specifically gay criticism of Wilson's book was muted (the most prominent exception being Futuyma & Risch, 1984, a paper which has faded into obscurity).

The second reason why evolutionary biology has not received the recognition it deserves in gay academia and politics is related to the low level of interest in technical and scientific topics in gay social and political circles, an interest which seems notable when compared to the interest held by society at large. For example, in the 1980s, several popular scientific publications were launched (viz., *Human Nature, Science 80, Discover,* etc.), because studies of newsstand sales of the major newsmagazines showed that cover stories dealing with scientific developments sold copies better than all other topics except three (those being sex, drugs, and rock and roll). But no parallel development occurred in gay publishing, where arts and literature continued to be the mainstream topics favored in gay publications even when they had no direct relevance to gay life. This bias persists today: no gay publication I am aware of has a regular column on scientific issues, other than the ubiquitous columns of updates about AIDS, nor has any gay publication ever published such a recurring column, no matter how irregularly.

These observations about the social and psychological status of science in the gay community are presented not as criticism, but as a description of the way things have been. If gay laypeople are uninterested in the latest theories in gay psychology, then so be it. But gay scholars should be held to a higher standard; their views should reflect genuine scholarship and not popular preferences.

Viewed with this history in mind, the popular response to the study by LeVay (1991) represented a sharp shift from previous patterns. LeVay found that a nucleus in the anterior hypothalamus was on average smaller in his sample of homosexual men than in his sample of heterosexual men. Within two weeks of the publication of this study, a trendy company was selling, at a gay rodeo in Los Angeles, t-shirts displaying a drawing of the human brain, with a pink triangle in the center and a legend underneath: "It's a brain thing." About a year later, the company promptly produced a t-shirt which referred to the even more recent finding concerning the anterior commissure ("New discovery!–34% larger!") by Allen and Gorski (1992). And within 36 hours of the announcement of the genetic-marker finding of Hamer's group (Hamer, Hu, Magnuson, Hu, & Pattatucci, 1993), the company was selling t-shirts based on the finding at the Gay Pride festival in San Diego ("Thanks, Mom–loved the genes").

This sudden explosion of gay-positive scientific imagery did not happen overnight. Groundwork for such a point of view had been laid for over 15 years by scientists of varying sexual orientations–some of which will be described below.

But far more important than the reaction of the gay community, and also more important than the purely scientific question of whether a trait "is" biological or environmental (forgive this imprecise and unscientific phrasing, but it is the phrasing which is common in popular culture) is the larger context into which the scientific finding is placed. There is absolutely no guarantee that this larger context will be gay-positive or evenhanded. Indeed, a student acquaintance recently told me that his Abnormal Psychology teacher has already begun to explain in her classes that homosexuality is a genetically-caused disorder, as opposed to an environmentally-caused one. Clearly, whether something has genetic as opposed to environmental causes or antecedents need not necessarily be related to a positive or a negative evaluation of the trait.

As I have stated repeatedly over the years, the only reason why biological explanations have the potential to be a sociopolitical advance for gay people is that the enemies of gay liberation have prematurely, and in my opinion stupidly, committed themselves to the position that homosexuality is an environmentally caused disorder. Now that the environmental part of this position is crumbling, this political group may become embarrassed, and the cause of gay liberation will be, for the moment, advanced. But we can predict that the next generation of right-wing theoreticians will reject these views and simply assert that homosexuality is a genetic pathology (or, if they're really smart, a multifactorial one). A few writers have already begun this process: Krauthammer (1993) wrote that since "only" half of the variance in sexual orientation is determined by genetics, the fact that the remaining half is "environmental, behavioral, pedagogical" means that society might exert "ever more stringent control of cultural influences and messages in the hope of 'saving' the genetically predisposed from homosexuality."

Notice that these politically conservative points of view gain considerable strength from a standard tenet of social psychology: that people will behave in accord with the ways in which they have been socialized. For if everyone, from birth to old age, is socialized to be heterosexual, then someone who turns out homosexual must be the very embodiment of pathology. Nowadays any social psychologist would be able to explain this "aberration" in non-pathological terms, and even be able to avoid use of a term like "aberration." But it has not been easy for social psychology to explain such contradictions to socialization theory. Moreover, the explanations typically lack predictive power, and such subtleties are lost in the grand battle of the oversimplifications of popular culture.

Worse, with the recent flood of biological studies of sexual orientation these *ex post facto* explanations can now be seen to have been premature, and they may turn out to be untrue.

In contrast, when I began my career as a graduate student in biology at Harvard, two years before the publication of Edward O. Wilson's *Sociobiology,* I heard heterosexual professors (some of them legendarily so) treat homosexuality not as a pathology to be explained as an example of what can go wrong with a fundamental evolutionary adaptation for heterosexuality (which had been the conventional medical and psychoanalytic view), but as an optional path of development whose evolutionary adaptedness was not obvious, and hence a puzzle worth investigating. Seeing it as a "puzzle" was not a put-down, nor an attempt to trivialize it or peripheralize it–quite the contrary. By asserting that its existence at very substantial rates in the population was a puzzle from the point of view of the general theory of evolution by natural selection, these professors were pointing it out as an intellectually important area to study, and raising the possibility that it might be of central importance in testing that theory. Accordingly, I took up the challenge of solving this puzzle, and have spent much of my academic career understanding the larger context of the theories by which variability in sexual orientation could be understood in humans.

The evolutionary biology I learned bore little resemblance to the caricature of sociobiology presented in the popular attacks. One cannot understand the true consequences of evolutionary biology on homosexuality and homosexuals without first clearing away these misconceptions. After I do so (in the next section), I will address the popular myth that most scientists are nothing more than blind apologists for their societies' social prejudices, and finally contrast the points of view of medicine and evolutionary biology. An account of the various evolutionary explanations of sexual orientation is available elsewhere (Weinrich, 1990).

THE EVOLUTIONARY APPROACH

Many of the misconceptions about evolutionary biology come from the poor education on this topic provided by the U.S. educational system. On the one hand, evolutionary biologists are familiar with such misinterpretation, and tolerate it because they know that people are rarely aware of their own biases and educational blind spots. Yet they also have some degree of contempt for it–just as most people do when they know that their critics are speaking from ignorance. This contempt is especially strong when it is directed at religious fundamentalists (and creationists)–an opposition group shared by gay liberationists and evolutionary biologists alike.

As I have watched the erroneous and sometimes silly attacks on biological theories over the years, it has struck me that many of the misconceptions may be projections on the part of social scientists based on their experience of their own disciplines. For example, neither sociology nor psychology has a strong tradition of theories which presuppose or deal with diversity in behavioral outcomes. Consider Erikson's theory of social development (Erikson, 1963), or Kohlberg's theory of moral development (Kohlberg, 1969, 1973)–arguably the two most influential developmental theories after that of Piaget (whose theory shares the same character). Each of these theories proposes that humans develop in a series of stages, which each theory names and elaborates. These theories are often taken to imply that one cannot progress to a higher stage until and unless one has mastered the tasks of the previous stage, and that the variability seen in social or moral development is appropriately modeled by placing the individual exhibiting a particular set of behaviors at a particular location on the hierarchy described by the theory. They claim that as people learn, grow, or mature, they pass from lower stages to higher stages, and that one cannot skip stages.

The Western ethnocentrism implicit in such theories should be obvious; these stages resemble the progression through grades in school. The patriarchal nature of this scheme has also been pointed out by feminist scholars (Gilligan, 1982, 1987). They have criticized Kohlberg's theory for describing masculine ways of viewing the world as higher, more developed stages, and thereby devaluing women's points of view, which they claim tend to reflect stages rated lower by the male originators of these theories.

Evolutionary biologists tend to be inherently suspicious of such theories, because we long ago abandoned any attempt to impose a single hierarchy onto the characteristics displayed by various species. There is no hierarchy of "lower" and "higher" organisms in modern evolutionary biology. There are no animals which are "smarter" or "dumber" than others in the sense that comparative psychologists once tried to establish. The reasons for this are worth examination.

It is often said that humans are the most intelligent animals on earth. That may be true in some sense of the phrase "most intelligent," but it is not true as a general statement. Even fruit flies are much more intelligent than humans in certain domains, and a similar statement is probably true for every other living organism. Horses are better than zebras at distinguishing different geometric patterns (squares from triangles from rounded shapes, etc.), but zebras are better at discriminating when the patterns are stripes of varying widths and orientations (Kalat, 1983). Rats do poorly when given a task in which they must distinguish different alternatives visually, but they do very well when the alternatives differ in smell (Kalat, 1983). Every organism which is still living in its evolutionarily natural environment is extremely well adapted to its niche, and it is fruitless to try to establish some grander kind of cross-species IQ test, or even criteria for being evolutionarily "advanced" or "primitive." Even the word "primitive" has a precise evolutionary meaning–"early" is a good approximation–but despite its contrasting lay usage, primitive does not mean simple. Evolutionary biologists are trained not to fall into the traps created by such usage conflicts–just as psychologists don't mistake schizophrenia for dual personality.

In fact, evolutionary biologists typically react in a specific way when they see variability in a given trait or phenomenon–and this reaction is different from that of many researchers from other disciplines. Their first impulse in explaining such variability is not to ask what went *wrong* with the process producing this variability but to ask what went *right*. An example will illustrate the thinking process.

One of the famous examples of variability, which evolutionary biologists call *polymorphism* (especially when it relates to physical features), is variation in the color of certain species of snails. Snails which taste good to visually-oriented predators (such as birds) "send" signals to those predators by their colors. When birds learn that snails of a certain color taste good, they will tend to seek out snails of that color to eat. Let us presume, to make the idea concrete, that it is green snails which are common in a population and which taste good to birds. This sets up a selection pressure: blue snails survive to reproduce relatively more often than green snails do, and any genes which produce a blue color will spread over the next several generations. Accordingly, the proportion of green snails will decrease and the proportion of blue snails will rise–and eventually birds will discover that the now common blue snails taste good. At this point, red snails will be favored by selection, as will the genes which produce that color. And so on, until the green snails are so uncommon that birds of that generation have failed to learn that they taste good. At that point, genes producing green snails will spread in the population–and the cycle will continue indefinitely. In fact, there is no single "best" color for a snail to be; it is best for a good-tasting snail to be a *different* color than the more common members of the same species.

This example may seem simple or even trite, but it is the basis for a huge industry within evolutionary biology: the understanding of variation. Not all variations are adaptive, and not all polymorphisms are maintained in this way (which is called *balancing selection*). But the tendency to look for the adaptation present in most examples of variation is trained into evolutionary biologists very early.

Of course, this tendency can be taken too far, by being turned into a dogma rather than a rule of thumb, or by being used uncritically rather than being continually subjected to empirical testing. Many authors (e.g., Gould, 1977) have warned against the danger of evolutionary explanations turning into "just-so stories," in which any fact could be fitted with *some* evolutionary explanation. But too many of the examples of just-so stories are themselves conjectural; evolutionary biologists are well aware of this possible fallacy in their theorizing and guard against it, with varying success.

More to the point, it is important to understand that this predisposition to pursue adaptive explanations of behavior is precisely the reason why homosexuality was first regarded not as a pathology but as yet another trait to be explained adaptively. The reason why sociobiologists first explained homosexuality adaptively is because they first try to explain *everything* adaptively. (And please note that I wrote "first," not "always.")

This predisposition was strong in evolutionary biology even before sociobiology was recognized as a subdiscipline. As I will explain below, sociobiology uses a theory called *kin selection* to explain how genes favoring or permitting the development of a homosexual orientation to spread. But even before the advent of kin selection, a prominent evolutionary biologist (Hutchinson, 1959) used the most adaptive theory he could think of (called, perhaps ironically, *heterozygote advantage*) to explain the high incidence of homosexual behavior discovered by Kinsey and his coworkers (Kinsey, Pomeroy, & Martin, 1948).

ETHICAL NEUTRALITY IN SCIENCE

It is commonly asserted that scientists used to be regarded as paragons of intellectual neutrality, discovering only objective truths and using the scientific method to avoid being biased toward any particular social view. The social revolution of the 1960s has produced such a change in this outlook that challenging the objectivity of scientists is nowadays rather fashionable. Interestingly enough, both the right wing and the left wing of the political spectrum seem to enjoy making such challenges. However, this revolution deserves a counterrevolution.

Although there have been many lamentable examples of the lack of scientific neutrality among scientists, we should not lose sight of the fact that the overwhelming majority of scientists, even those who do not believe that utter neutrality is actually attainable, still try to approach this goal as closely as they can. They frequently propose theories which contradict the assertion that scientists are inevitably and predictably blinded by their social position or the social constructs of the society or discipline in which they were raised. I will give two examples relevant here: Alfred Kinsey and modern sociobiological theories of homosexuality.

Kinsey, the famous sexologist, author of what came to be known as the "Kinsey Reports" (Kinsey et al., 1948; Kinsey, Pomeroy, Martin, & Gebhard, 1953), and founder of the research institute which now bears his name, began his career as an evolutionary biologist. His specialty before taking up sexology was the *taxonomy* (or evolutionary classification) of *gall wasps* (wasps which reproduce by causing plants to form galls, inside of which the wasps' eggs are laid). As I have discussed elsewhere (Weinrich, 1990), Kinsey's work in this area was directed at major evolutionary questions, such as the process by which one species splits into two.

But Kinsey is remembered primarily for his contributions to sex research. One of his major insights, for which he has been most often cited and applauded, was his homosexual/heterosexual rating scale, which reflected his finding that homosexual and heterosexual are not two different types of behavior, but two ends of a single continuum. One of Kinsey's fondest descriptions of this notion was that "Males do not represent two discrete populations, heterosexual and homosexual. The world is not to be divided into sheep and goats" (Kinsey et al., 1948, p. 639). Leaving aside the biblical reference (Matthew 25:31-33), which should not be overlooked, let me point out that in Kinsey's earlier specialty of taxonomy, *it was his job to tell the sheep from the goats* and his refusal to do so in the domain of what we now term sexual orientation is remarkable. He even stated that "the living world is a continuum in each and every one of its aspects" (Kinsey et al., 1948, p. 639), a statement which is not true when it comes to the reproductive barriers which separate species from each other. After all, what would be more natural than a taxonomist, trained at Harvard in evolutionary biology, riding into sexology on his high horse and proclaiming that he *did* know how to tell the sheep from the goats, the homosexual from the heterosexual? If one were to believe the skeptics, such a lapse of scientific neutrality would not only be common, it would be expected.

I do not believe that Kinsey was a perfectly neutral scientist; Robinson (1976) put an end to that notion once and for all. But he was not biased in the ways which one might expect, given his training, and he was not biased in the way that outsiders might naively expect evolutionary biologists to be biased. These facts, along with thousands more like them which can be drawn from the everyday lives of modern scientists, strongly challenge the skeptical view and the theories which purport to explain the scientific lapses which do, in fact, occur.

Another example, even more relevant to the topic of this paper, comes from the recent history of sociobiological explanations of sexual orientation. Activists and other people interested in preserving a tolerant or accepting view of homosexuals in society have every reason to be suspicious of a theory, such as modern sociobiology, which takes as a tenet the notion that humans (like all living things) evolved to maximize the number of copies of their genes in the next generation (Dawkins, 1976). Since most people would guess that homosexuals in modern populations have fewer children on average than heterosexuals do, activists would be more than justified in their worry at the application of such a relentlessly reproductionist view. After all, would it not seem obvious that this view would regard homosexuality as "biologically absurd and anatomically ridiculous" (Swanson, 1974)?

But sociobiology did not make such an assumption, and for the most part neither did pre-sociobiological evolutionary biologists. In fact, the Kinsey group's findings of an incidence of homosexuality orders of magnitude above what biologists term a *mutational equilibrium* level (Kinsey et al., 1948) specifically motivated one very prominent evolutionary biologist (Hutchinson, as explained above) to propose that homosexuality and bisexuality might *not* be evolutionarily maladaptive (Hutchinson, 1959).

It was the triumph of the sociobiological concept of kin selection, however, which provided the key to a whole new class of adaptive evolutionary explanations of variability in sexual orientation. It was these theories which were brand new at the time of my graduate training, and were first proposed by heterosexual scientists.

Kin selection proposes that natural selection causes individuals to act not to maximize the number of their children, but to maximize the number of copies of their genes in succeeding generations. When those genes physically come out of one's own body, they are called children (in lay terms) or *reproductive success* (in sociobiological jargon), but when they come out of the bodies of close relatives, they are figured into what is termed the total *inclusive fitness* of the index individual. Inclusive fitness is the sum of one's reproductive success (RS) and the RS of one's relatives, the latter devalued (i.e., multiplied) by one's *degree of relatedness* to those relatives. This degree of relatedness is the fraction of genes one shares with a relative by virtue of one's direct common descent; it ranges from 0 for two unrelated individuals to 1 for identical twins.

Full siblings have a degree of relatedness of 0.5, half siblings of 0.25, and so on.

The central dogma of sociobiology is that the overwhelming majority of human behavior can be explained as the result of its evolution by natural selection, and that accordingly, when one sees a behavior present in a human population at a frequency comfortably above a mutational equilibrium level (no more than one twentieth of one percent), it is probably in some way the result of adaptive evolution of behavior and not a pathological mutation or aberration. (This is not to imply that the behavior is *currently* adaptive in the environment in which it occurs, since environments have changed so strikingly from hunter-gatherer days.) This central dogma is usually confirmed, and occasionally disconfirmed, by sociobiological studies. This predisposition to seek adaptive rather than maladaptive explanations of behavior is so strong that my professors applied it to homosexuality without giving it a second thought, and never even used mildly homophobic phraseology when discussing sociobiological theories of homosexuality. For example, I never heard statements such as that made by Swanson (quoted above), who is not a sociobiologist, nor did I hear the statements one might otherwise have expected to hear, such as "Well, of course, 'adaptive' is a strange word to use in connection with homosexuality, but . . . "

BIOLOGY CONTRASTED WITH MEDICINE

As has been pointed out by Louis Gooren (this volume) and others, many of the lay misconceptions about biology result from confusing biology with medicine and the other healing professions. Most therapists, whether physiological or psychological, have a model of human nature and human behavior with which to diagnose and perhaps to cure human ailments. This model is used by therapists to define health and disease, two of their major preoccupations. Whereas evolutionary biologists have existed for only about a hundred years (that is, since Darwin), therapists have existed for millennia, and perhaps since prehistory. So it should not be a surprise (and it is not a criticism to point out) that most schools of therapy do not use the knowledge compiled by evolutionists in their work. For example, only recently have physicians formally investigated the possibility that a response such as fever might in many cases best be left to run its course, and not be manipulated by fever-reducing drugs, whereas one of the first hypotheses that an evolutionary biologist would investigate is that fever is an adaptive response of the body with which one might not want to interfere. Likewise, the application of evolutionary principles to psychotherapy has just begun (Glantz & Pearce, 1989).

Another difference between therapy and evolutionary biology also revolves around the issue of health and disease: therapists are paid money when they find disease and cure it, whereas diagnosis and cure are not important or structural concerns for evolutionary biologists. Accordingly, the theory of health and disease occupies a much more central position in therapy than it does in evolutionary biology. When we recall that evolutionary biologists tend to hypothesize adaptation rather than maladaptation, we can infer that there will be a striking difference between medicine and evolution in their respective tendencies to find pathology in any given category of behavior.

The problem of overpathologizing, then, lies not in evolutionary biology, but in the notion that there is only one normal or healthy pathway for human development, whether psychological or physiological. Because much medicine today has taken advantage of the last century's progress in physics, chemistry, biochemistry, and cellular biology, it is easy to confuse biology with medicine. But they are separate disciplines, with different traditions, and thus different approaches to many of the topics they can both address.

CONCLUSIONS

In his attack on psychiatric orthodoxy, Szasz (1970, chapter 13) used homosexuality as the classic example of psychiatry's creation of "the myth of mental illness." Although many of Szasz's other attacks missed the mark, his insights have been amply confirmed with respect to this DSM-II diagnosis. When medicine designated homosexuality per se as a mental illness, it indeed misused biology to create a pathology where none necessarily existed.

Interestingly enough–and supporting the points I have made in this paper–the remaining proponents of the psychiatric school pathologizing homosexuality once prominently featured biological justifications of their position. Socarides (1978), for example, states that homosexuality contradicts the fundamental nature of human beings as biologically male or female. Of course, this argument is evolutionarily simplistic; if biology provides adaptive explanations for a more subtle differentiation than uniformly heterosexual males and females, then such arguments collapse. Socarides' views are notably presociobiological. More recent proponents of the notion that homosexuality is a psychologically-caused pathology (e.g., Nicolosi, 1991) have taken a hard line against biological causes for sexual orientation variability (chap. 9) and cited pro-gay scholars such as Michael Ross and Thomas Forde Hoult in support of their position. Interestingly enough, Nicolosi (1991) did not cite contrary evidence (such as the paper by Pillard and Weinrich, 1986) in the main text or footnotes of the book, although he did happen to list that paper in his bibliography (p. 333)!

The fact that biological theories have been misused in the past to justify Nazism and other odious political ends reflects the nature of politics far more than the nature of biology. Any scientific theory regarded as true will face attempts at manipulation by both good and bad forces. As a scientist, I have been trained to study not only experimental groups but also control groups, and so let us conduct the appropriate intellectual "controls" here. Yes, biological arguments have been misused, but they have also been properly used by good people.

We must also control for academic discipline: have psychological theories (such as Skinner's behaviorism) been misused in a way that hurts gay people? Of course! Right now there is someone, somewhere, who is having his wits electrically shocked out of him or his meal vomited out of him in a behavioristic attempt to change his sexual orientation (or at least his sexual behavior). It is shocking in the intellectual sense that, when biology's ability to be misused is assessed, the appropriate control comparisons are rarely, if ever, made. Anyone who lived through the 1960s knows that when biological theories were misused, biology as a discipline was attacked, and biologists were aggressively told to take responsibility for the misuse of their theories. In spite of the documented misuses of behaviorism and other psychological theories *today* no one attacks psychology as a discipline, and few if any even attack behaviorism on these grounds. Rather, individual scientists and theories are criticized. And few have shown an interest in attacking the critics of biology whose theories are being misused today by the right wing.

I am not advocating a return to the excesses of the sixties, nor to the excesses of the fundamentalists. *All* of these oversimplifications are naive and poorly thought out, and as the introductory quotations to this paper demonstrate, what goes around comes around. It's time to get on with a truly insightful debate about the nature of all of the sciences and their relationships to human triumph and suffering.

REFERENCES

Allen, L. S., & Gorski, R. A. (1992). Sexual orientation and the size of the anterior commissure in the human brain. *Proceedings of the National Academy of Sciences (USA), 89*, 7199-7202.

Check, W. A. (1993, June 10). Let's talk about sex . . . Constraints hinder AIDS prevention efforts. *Conference News AIDS Berlin 1993* (daily newspaper at IX International AIDS Congress), p. 8.

Dawkins, R. (1976). *The selfish gene.* Oxford, UK: Oxford University Press.

Erikson, E. (1963). *Childhood and society* (2nd ed.). New York: Norton.

Futuyma, D. J., & Risch, S. J. (1984). Sexual orientation, sociobiology, and evolution. *Journal of Homosexuality, 9*(2/3), 157-168.

Gilligan, C. (1982). *In a different voice: Psychological theory and women's development.* Cambridge, MA: Harvard University Press.

Gilligan, C. (1987). Adolescent development reconsidered. In C. E. Erwin, Jr. (Ed.), *Adolescent social behavior and health.* San Francisco: Jossey-Bass.

Glantz, K., & Pearce, J. K. (1989). *Exiles from Eden: Psychotherapy from an evolutionary perspective.* New York: W. W. Norton.

Gould, S. J. (1977). *Ever since Darwin: Reflections in natural history.* New York: Norton.

Hamer, D. H., Hu, S., Magnuson, V. L., Hu, N., & Pattatucci, A. M. L. (1993). A linkage between DNA markers on the X chromosome and male sexual orientation. *Science, 261*, 321-327.

Hutchinson, G. E. (1959). A speculative consideration of certain possible forms of sexual selection in man. *American Naturalist, 93*, 81-91.

Jefferson, D. J. (1993, August 12). Science besieged: Studying the biology of sexual orientation has political fallout. *Wall Street Journal*, pp. A1, A4.

Kalat, J. W. (1983). Evolutionary thinking in the history of the comparative psychology of learning. *Neuroscience and Biobehavioral Reviews, 7*, 309-314.

Kinsey, A. C., Pomeroy, W. B., & Martin, C. E. (1948). *Sexual behavior in the human male.* Philadelphia: Saunders.

Kinsey, A. C., Pomeroy, W. B., Martin, C. E., & Gebhard, P. H. (1953). *Sexual behavior in the human female.* Philadelphia: Saunders.

Kohlberg, L. (1969). Stage and sequence: The cognitive-developmental approach to socialization. In D. A. Goslin (Ed.), *Handbook of socialization theory and research.* Chicago: Rand McNally.

Kohlberg, L. (1973). Implications of developmental psychology for education: Examples from moral development. *Educational Psychologist, 10*, 2-14.

LeVay, S. (1991). A difference in hypothalamic structure between heterosexual and homosexual men. *Science, 253*, 1034-1037.

Nicolosi, J. (1991). *Reparative therapy of male homosexuality: A new clinical approach.* Northvale, NJ: Jason Aronson.

Pillard, R. C., & Weinrich, J. D. (1986). Evidence of familial nature of male homosexuality. *Archives of General Psychiatry, 43*, 808-812.

Rader, D. (1992). Homosexuality and genetics: Born gay? *The Phil Donahue Show*, New York: Aired most markets January 3 or 4, 1992.

Robinson, P. (1976). *The modernization of sex: Havelock Ellis, Alfred Kinsey. William Masters and Virginia Johnson.* New York: Harper and Row.

Schmaltz, J. (1992, October 20). Have no fear–*Queer Pier*'s here. *Advocate*, pp. 66-67.

Socarides, C. W. (1978). *Homosexuality.* New York: Jason Aronson.

Swanson, H. D. (1974). *Human reproduction: Biology and social change.* New York: Oxford University Press.

Szasz, T. (1970). *The manufacture of madness: A comparative study of the Inquisition and the mental health movement.* New York: Harper and Row.

Weinrich, J. D. (1990). The Kinsey scale in biology, with a note on Kinsey as a biologist. In D. P. McWhirter, S. A. Sanders, & J. M. Reinisch (Eds.), *Homosexuality/heterosexuality: Concepts of sexual orientation* (pp. 115-137). New York: Oxford University Press.

Wilson, E. O. (1975). *Sociobiology: The new synthesis.* Cambridge, MA: Harvard University Press.

Wilson, E. O. (1978). *On human nature.* Cambridge, MA: Harvard University Press.

Wilson, E. O. (1979, May 3). Gay as normal: Homosexuality and human nature: A sociobiological view. *Advocate*, pp. 15, 18.

SECTION IV: IS SEXUAL PREFERENCE DETERMINED BY HORMONES?

Introduction

The *endocrine system* of the human body is a system of *glands* and organs that produce, receive, and manipulate many substances including *hormones* (see Figure 4, p. 280). Hormones are chemical substances produced in one organ of the body (e.g., the *pituitary gland* located above the back of the throat) and carried to another organ by the blood stream; they stimulate many processes in the body, including bone growth, muscle development, and the onset of *secondary sex characteristics*. Secondary sex characteristics (e.g., breast development and the widening of the hips in females, and the increased hairiness and lowered voice pitch in males) are the result of the heightened hormone levels that occur during puberty. These changes are stimulated specifically by two groups of hormones: *androgens* in males, and *estrogens* in females. There are several androgenic and estrogenic hormones; the strongest are primarily produced in the *gonads* (i.e., the testes in men and the ovaries in women) and are called *testosterone* and *estradiol*, respectively.

[Haworth co-indexing entry note]: "Introduction." Co-published simultaneously in *Journal of Homosexuality* (The Haworth Press, Inc.) Vol. 28, No. 3/4, 1995, p. 215; and: *Sex, Cells, and Same-Sex Desire: The Biology of Sexual Preference* (ed: John P. De Cecco, and David Allen Parker) The Haworth Press, Inc., 1995, p. 215. Multiple copies of this article/chapter may be purchased from The Haworth Document Delivery Center [1-800-3-HAWORTH; 9:00 a.m. - 5:00 p.m. (EST)].

Animal Models for the Development of Human Sexuality: A Critical Evaluation

Anne Fausto-Sterling, PhD

Brown University

SUMMARY. Biological explanations of human homosexuality build upon a theoretical framework developed from the study of animals, especially that of rodents. Researchers have constructed a physiological model to explain the origin and development of "masculine" and "feminine" behavior. According to this model hormones acting at critical stages in early development *organize* cells in key areas of the brain. After puberty these hormonally organized brain regions are purportedly capable of *activation* by post-pubertally produced circulating hormones. This model of sexual development, called the *organizational-activational (O/A)* model, has framed research on sexual behavior in animals and animal-based accounts of human behavior for more than 30 years. However, evidence from a variety of sources has slowly accumulated, requiring modification after modification of the original premise. Continuing to use the organizational-activational model now interferes with the acquisition of new knowledge. I sketch the outlines of an alternative bio-social program for research on the development of sexual behavior in animals.

Anne Fausto-Sterling is Professor of Medical Science at Brown University. Correspondence may be addressed: Brown University, Division of Biology and Medicine, Box G-160J, Providence, RI 02912.

[Haworth co-indexing entry note]: "Animal Models for the Development of Human Sexuality: A Critical Evaluation." Fausto-Sterling, Anne. Co-published simultaneously in *Journal of Homosexuality* (The Haworth Press, Inc.) Vol. 28, No. 3/4, 1995, pp. 217-236; and: *Sex, Cells, and Same-Sex Desire: The Biology of Sexual Preference* (ed: John P. De Cecco, and David Allen Parker) The Haworth Press, Inc., 1995, pp. 217-236. Multiple copies of this article/chapter may be purchased from The Haworth Document Delivery Center [1-800-3-HAWORTH; 9:00 a.m. - 5:00 p.m. (EST)].

In 1992 the publication of an article suggesting that there is a genetic basis for male homosexuality (Bailey & Pillard, 1991) followed closely on the heels of another claiming evidence that the microscopic architecture of the hypothalamus differs in male heterosexuals and homosexuals (LeVay, 1991). These two articles, in combination with media interest in the sexual preference of the authors themselves, unleashed a storm of controversy in which the principals have participated with great willingness (e.g., Gorman, 1991; Angier, 1991; Crabb, 1991).[1] Although media interest continues apace the press is unable to bring a critical focus to bear on the issues.

This article moves beyond these studies and examines instead the animal research that provides a backdrop for the current controversies. I contend that research on the biological bases of human sexuality employs an impoverished account of the development of animal behavior. A careful examination of the role of hormones in the development of sexual behaviors in animals suggests the need for a far more flexible and complex account of the interrelationships between hormones and behavior than these recently-publicized studies offer.

Carefully controlled, unambiguous studies on human subjects are virtually impossible. In a critical review of the literature on endocrine influences on human sexual behavior, McCauley and Urquiza (1988), for example, write that the research

> cannot be easily synthesized. The samples are extremely heterogeneous. Many of the individual studies have significant methodological problems; most apparent are the small sample populations, the lack of control or population norms, and problems of biased sampling. (p. 378)

Even if one is willing to set aside the methodological difficulties, problems of interpretation abound. How, for example, does one interpret human studies suggesting "that hormonal exposure plays a role in shaping sexual behavior profiles" (McCauley & Urquiza, 1988, p. 378)? Most people assume that such a statement means that hormones affect behavior by directly influencing the brain. Yet all of the relevant studies show that hormones more clearly affect the development of the genitalia or body type than the brain. In fact there is not a shred of anatomical evidence in humans that prenatal hormones alter brain development. Thus a "hormonal effect" could be quite indirect. For example, it is just as likely that an individual's experience is altered by the fact that hormonal disruptions of genital anatomy necessitated genital surgery or raised questions about the "real" sex of the person under study. Experimentally there is no way out of such an interpretative morass. Those who prefer to rely on the brain to explain behavior will choose one interpretation; those who lean towards experiential explanations will choose another. The best one seems able to do is to "conclude that something is going on" (Gladue, 1988, p. 402).

The usual recourse in defending a particular interpretation of research on human sexuality is to place it in the context of animal experimentation. The most common framework employed is the organization-activation (O/A) model that proposes that hormones present at a critical early point in development preset or organize the brain so that much later, at the time of puberty, the brain becomes susceptible to activation by circulating hormones. Since its first appearance (Phoenix et al., 1959), the O/A model has focused the research on hormones and behavior. I will argue, however, that it is a poor model for the development of animal behavior and provides few clues for the study of human behavior.

The work I will review focuses on the development of reproductive behaviors. There is a significant literature *purporting* to show the role of hormones in the development of animal sexual preference. But the vast majority of these studies never offer test animals a choice of sexual partners. The animals only have an opportunity for heterosexual coupling, one which they can take or leave. Furthermore, much of the animal literature confuses sexual preference with the concept of *heterotypical* behavior. The latter phrase refers to behavior that is typical of the opposite sex. For example male rodents mount other rodents more frequently than do females. Thus even though it is perfectly normal for females to mount another animal such behavior is often considered to be heterotypical. Many authors equate such heterotypical behavior with homosexuality although thoughtful investigators of animal behaviors think that these two concepts are distinct. Experiments show that animals exhibiting heterotypical behaviors also choose opposite sexed mates.[2] Adkins-

Regan (1988) cites a recent case in which authors attempting to develop a "neurohormonal theory of human homosexuality" cited 40 experiments from the animal literature. In fact only one of these measured sexual orientation.

In her review of the animal literature Adkins-Regan (1988) asks whether any of the species for which there exists experimental information can provide

> suitable models for understanding human sexual orientation? It may well be that for all of the non-primates the best answer is no; because of the profound cognitive and emotional components of the human phenomenon, sexual orientation in non-primates and humans is simply not homologous. (p. 345)

I argue that a complex array of factors–experiential, cognitive, and hormonal–profoundly affect the development of sexual behavior in non-primates and primates alike.

WHAT IS THE ORGANIZATIONAL-ACTIVATIONAL THEORY?

In 1959, Phoenix, Goy, Gerall, and Young published a study of the mating behavior of female guinea pigs which had received prenataltestosterone propionate (TP) injections. All subsequent work in this field is modeled on this study. Only a careful critique of its methodology can provide a basis for understanding the problems inherent in so much of the subsequent theorizing about hormones, the brain, and behavior. I will give a detailed account and critique of this key work.

Females received TP injections throughout much of their pregnancy.[3] The study compared 14 females from untreated mothers, 14 unmodified females, 9 hermaphrodites, and 8 males from untreated mothers. A small percentage of the female offspring were born without any visible damage to their external genitalia, but small changes in clitoral size might well have gone undetected. Although the internal organs of these females were affected by the injections, the authors described them as "unmodified." They compared these females with females born with completely masculinized genitalia, which were designated as "hermaphrodites." Controls included male siblings and animals from uninjected mothers. The authors offer no information about age of weaning or about the social situation in which the test animals grew up. Both of these bits of information, I will argue, are critical to a proper interpretation of their results.

In guinea pigs time to weaning varies from two weeks to a month, the time to sexual maturity varies from 1 to 3 months, and the average life span is 6-8 years. After rearing and weaning the guinea pigs the authors removed the animals' gonads at times ranging from 1.5 to 5 months after birth. The eight males in the study were castrated before their 21st day. Between the ages of 3 to 5 months all the animals were tested after an injection of estradiol benzoate (EB) and progesterone (P), or testosterone. As a measure of typical female behavior, the authors observed a neural reflex called lordosis, in which a female arches her back and raises her rump for mounting by another animal. This reflex action can occur in response to stimulation from another guinea pig or in response to human stroking. Rear-end mounting was viewed as typical male-like behavior.

Injections of EB and P served to bring the females into heat, the time during which the lordosis response is most visible. At the highest doses, 96% of the controls came into heat as compared with 77% of the unmodified and 22% of the hermaphroditic females. These latter two groups also took longer to respond to the EB/P injections and they stayed in heat for a shorter period of time. Although all of the tested animals exhibited lordosis, the average response time differed. Control females arched their backs for an average of 9.3 seconds, unmodified for an average of 6.0 seconds, and the hermaphrodites for an average of 2.0 seconds. Hermaphrodites did not differ from castrated males on any of these measures. The authors concluded that "the suppression of the capacity to display lordosis was proportional to the quantity of androgen injected prenatally" (Phoenix et al., 1959, p. 373).

The authors used mounting behavior as a measure of masculinity. Without adult hormone injections, neither control nor unmodified females showed any mounting behavior, but the hermaphrodites mounted about 1/3 as often as the castrated males.[4] All animals that received the EB/P regime which brought them into heat (control, unmodified, and hermaphrodite females and castrated males) mounted with equal frequency, although there were some differences in the time it took for an animal to initiate this behavior. Phoenix et al. concluded that male-like mounting was not suppressed by testosterone injection.

To examine the permanence of the effect from testosterone administered before birth, the authors tested animals at 6 to 9 and 11 to 12 months after birth. One test, using 3 hermaphrodites, showed that the percent responding to EB/P administration by coming into heat decreased from 33% (at 6 to 9 months) to 0 (at 11 to 12 months). At the same time, the mean number of mounts increased from 3 to 45.2. In contrast, 55% of the 7 unmodified females came into heat after EB/P injection at 6-9 months compared to 71% at 11-12 months. The mean number of mounts doubled in that time while the median maximum lordosis increased from 4.0 to 5.8 seconds. The authors write that these changes are not statistically significant, probably because the numbers used were so small. Yet they do conclude that the suppression of "the capacity for displaying the feminine component of the sexual behavior pattern . . . appears to have become permanent" (p. 377). They did not retest the animals after their first year of life.

Finally the authors examined the effects of TP on the behavior of hermaphrodites whose ovaries had been removed (*spayed* females). They compared five spayed untreated females with five spayed hermaphrodites and eight untreated males which had been castrated within the first three weeks of life. They obtained the following results: spayed, untreated females averaged 5.8 mounts, spayed hermaphrodites 15.4 mounts, and castrated males 20.5 mounts per test. They concluded that: prenatal TP treatment had an "organizing action" on "tissues mediating masculine behavior" (p. 378).

Phoenix et al. wrote that their results supported the hypothesis that "androgenic substances received prenatally have an organizing action on the tissues mediating mating behavior in the sense of altering permanently the responses females normally give as adults" (p. 379). To bolster this claim they used analogies involving the development of the internal and external genitalia, which respond to hormone exposure at particular embryonic stages.[5] More recently Feder (1981) has convincingly argued that such an analogy is unwarranted and muddies thinking about the development of sexual behaviors.

Phoenix et al. (1959) speculated that their theory could be extended to include "the masculinity and femininity of an animal's behavior" (p. 381). They further assumed that the hormone "acts on those central nervous system tissues in which patterns of behavior are organized" (p. 370). They also suggested that their studies would "direct attention to a possible origin of behavioral differences between the sexes which is ipso facto important for psychologic and psychiatric theory" (p. 370). Rather than being an innocent account of guinea pigs, the potential application of the work to humans was part of the vision from the very start.

The model they proposed contained the following key elements: (1) steroid hormones present at a critical early period organize parts of the brain responsible for sexual behaviors; (2) after puberty these brain regions may respond to activating hormones circulating through the body; and (3) organizational effects on the brain are permanent but activational effects are transitory. An explosion of research all modeled on the Phoenix et al. approach continued from the 1960s until the present. Let's examine in detail the three propositions of their organizational-activational model.

PROPOSITION 1:
DO HORMONES ORGANIZE THE PARTS
OF THE CENTRAL NERVOUS SYSTEM RESPONSIBLE
FOR SEXUAL BEHAVIOR?

This question can be divided into two sub-questions:

a. Can the experimental results be unequivocally attributed to changes in the brain?
b. Do known changes in the brain control sexual behavior?

Can the Experimental Results be Unequivocally Attributed to Changes in the Brain?

Figure 1 outlines Phoenix et al.'s experimental design. The details of subsequent work vary with the organism and the specific research question asked; nevertheless, the overall protocol depicted defines the model used to account for the development of sex differences in animal behavior. Briefly, experimenters treat test animals with hormones at a critical period of early development (the organizing treatment). The animal develops first in its birth litter and after weaning in a group of similarly treated animals. Shortly before puberty experimenters remove the treated animal's gonad in order to make sure that any data obtained from subsequent hormone injections (the activating treatment) can be attributed to the test procedures and not to animal's own hormone production. Finally, test animals receive injections of hormones and the experimenters record the effects on particular behaviors.

Figure 1 also shows two different ways of interpreting results from this experimental protocol. The first (upper panel) focuses on hormonal effects on the brain. Phoenix et al. and the many investigators who followed, for example, have argued that prenatal exposure to androgen permanently organized the brains of female hermaphrodites so that they became less able to come into heat and exhibit lordosis when challenged with an injection of activating hormone. The second interpretation (lower panel), however, suggests that the development of sexual behavior is far more complex. To begin with, prenatal hormone injections affect many different tissues. The most obvious changes are in the genitalia, which become heavily masculinized when exposed prenatally to testosterone. Even when hormone treatment doesn't completely masculinize the genitalia, less dramatic effects may be evident. In another of the classic, founding papers in this field, Harris and Levine (1965) report that hormone-treated females have smaller, rounder, and otherwise abnormal vaginal openings; de Jonge et al. (1988) found that all of the female rats exposed perinatally to androgen had closed vaginas and most (91%) had enlarged clitorises. Furthermore, testosterone-exposed females were larger than unexposed females (Harris & Levine, 1965).

Such physical differences could easily lead to different learning experiences. Larger females may learn to mount more often and those with enlarged genitalia may discover that certain forms of sexual activity are more pleasurable than others. De Jonge, for example, provides evidence that progesterone affects a female rat's

FIGURE 1. Shows the basic design of experiments leading to the organizational-activational hypothesis. "1" and "2" offer alternate frameworks in which to interpret experimental results.

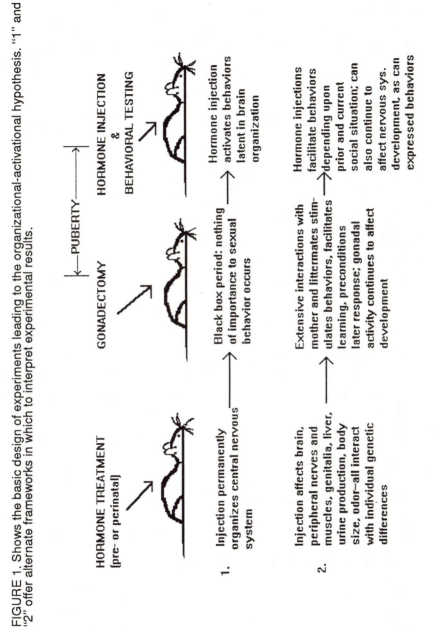

HORMONE TREATMENT
[pre- or perinatal]

GONADECTOMY

|←— PUBERTY —→|

HORMONE INJECTION
&
BEHAVIORAL TESTING

1. Injection permanently organizes central nervous system

Black box period: nothing of importance to sexual behavior occurs

Hormone injection activates behaviors latent in brain organization

2. Injection affects brain, peripheral nerves and muscles, genitalia, liver, urine production, body size, odor—all interact with individual genetic differences

Extensive interactions with mother and littermates stimulates behaviors, facilitates learning, preconditions later response; gonadal activity continues to affect development

Hormone injections facilitate behaviors depending upon prior and current social situation; can also continue to affect nervous sys. development, as can expressed behaviors mating interest only if a sexual reward is available. A closed vagina may make a female less receptive to mounting attempts and result in fewer juvenile learning experiences and lowered lordotic responses in adulthood. Feder (1981) reviewed the handful of papers which attempt to dissociate hormone effects on behavior and changes in genital development. In these examples carefully-timed chemical treatments can produce an animal with normal-looking external genitalia, but exhibiting altered behavior. Feder believes such changes in behavior may result from a combination of genital and central nervous system responses to hormone treatment.

Additional data also demonstrate a social component to the development of sexual behaviors. First, animals bred in isolation are sexually incompetent (Beach, 1968; Gerall et al.,1967; Valenstein & Young, 1955; Hard & Larsson, 1968; Thor, 1980). While isolation experiments don't tell us which components of social experience are required for normal sexual development, they do indicate a necessary experiential ingredient. Segal and Johnson (quoted in Harris & Levine, 1965) reported a near absence of mating when they placed female rats that did not ovulate with sexually experienced males. But after 3 months of continuous cohabitation 18 out of 60 of these females responded to male mounting. Other clues may be teased out of the original Phoenix et al. paper. When they tested hermaphrodites for mounting activity at 6-9 months of age they found a mean of 3 mounts, as compared to a mean of 45 when they retested at 11 to 12 months. Similarly, their unmodified females showed a higher percent response, an increase (probably not significant) of the median maximum lordosis, and a doubling of the mean number of mounts. They did not discuss these changes except to view them as evidence for a permanent effect of the early hormone treatments (see also Birke, 1989, and Moore, 1985).

Testosterone affects more than just the genitalia and the brain. For example male rat pups emit a different odor than do female pups. The odor production is testosterone dependent and induces dams (the mother rats) to lick their male offspring more frequently and vigorously than their female pups, especially in the anogenital region. The licking, in turn, affects adult male sexual behavior. Males raised by dams which had their nasal passages blocked (and thus licked them less) took longer to ejaculate and had a longer refractory period between ejaculations. Moore et al. (1992) also report that males raised by mothers which licked less had fewer spinal motor neurons in a region of the spinal cord associated with ejaculatory behavior. In other words, the development of a part of the central nervous system (a specific region of the spinal cord) is influenced by maternal behavior. The effect of testosterone is only indirect (on pup odor which stimulates licking).

Juvenile male rats also spend more time grooming their genitalia than do females and this additional stimulation affects the rapidity with which the males reach puberty. Licking behavior is also responsive to salt and water balance, pup leg extension, and urine release, each of which differs in male and female pups. Thus the emerging picture of the development of sexual behavior paints the brain as one among several elements affected by early hormone exposure. Some of these elements are anatomical, some physiological, some behavioral, and some social–and they all interact (Moore & Rogers, 1984; Moore, 1990).

Hormone treatment also affects muscle and nerve development outside of the brain. For example, male rats have a set of three muscles attached to the penis which are needed for erection and ejaculation. Nerve cells growing out of a particular region in the lower spinal cord connect to these muscles. The muscles and the nerves accumulate androgen which the muscles require for sexual function. In female rats one of these muscles degenerates shortly after birth unless they receive androgen during a particular period (Arnold & Breedlove, 1985). No one has determined whether testosterone-mediated changes in female mounting behavior might be related to the presence of this muscle which is normally lost during development. Finally, prenatal or perinatal testosterone treatment lowers thyroid function, affects the liver, and causes a wide variety of reproductive system abnormalities (Harris & Levine, 1965; and the work of Moore and colleagues and of de Jonge and colleagues).

Do Known Changes in the Brain Control Sexual Behavior?

The experiment that best demonstrates that the brain directly mediates hormonal effects on behavior is that of Christensen and Gorski (1978). They implanted testosterone pellets in female rats in specific regions of the hypothalamus at two or five days after birth.

As was the case in earlier experiments they left the ovaries intact during development. They found that the implants caused a more than threefold increase in mounting frequency when injected into one particular part of the brain (the preoptic area of the hypothalamus). Otherwise the implants did not significantly alter lordotic behavior as could have been predicted from the results of Phoenix et al.

This single study (which to my knowledge has not been replicated) demonstrates a specific behavioral effect of perinatal hormones on the brain, but fails to show that the brain mediates the suppressing effect of testosterone on lordosis.[6] Indeed a number of studies provide evidence that steroids can influence nerve growth. Most of these link nerve development and hormones without establishing a specific connection to a particular sex-related behavior. Christensen and Gorski's paper is the sole exception.[7] Even if there were more evidence directly linking the brain to a sexual behavior, a key question would remain: can the organizational-activational model adequately explain how sexual and/or sex-related behaviors develop? Does it account for the diverse sets of information we currently have about experience, genetic background, general physiology, peer and maternal interaction, etc., etc.?

With the second interpretation of the data presented in Figure 1 (lower panel), it becomes apparent that the diverse effects of early hormone treatment must be considered. Rarely mentioned, for example, is the fact that different genetic strains of animals exhibit different patterns of sexual activity. Södersten (1976) describes a strain of rats in which intact males exhibit significant levels of lordosis, often considered to be an exclusively female behavior. Van de Poll et al. (1981) describes a strain which shows no hormonally induced alterations in aggressive behavior. Luttge and Hall (1973) and McGill and Haynes (1973) report strain differences in how mice respond to testosterone treatment.

Any adequate model of sexual behavior must begin with individual genetic differences and incorporate the effects of an extensive period of maternal interaction and experience gained from littermate, cagemate, and partner interaction. To date only the studies of de Jonge and her colleagues and of Moore have attempted to analyze hormonal effects on behavior in this more complex framework.

Moore proposes two perspectives. In one (1990), she represents the effects of early testosterone treatment as a cascade. The number of affected organs grows as hormones influence the scent glands and the brain early in the process and subsequently alter liver physiology, genital anatomy, and muscle development. Finally maternal licking, overall body size, play, exploration, and self-grooming behaviors all interact with hormonal effects. There are no linear connections in Moore's model. Instead, behavior results from the intersection of a web which links physiology, anatomy, and behavior. Moore demonstrates, for example, how maternal licking causes and is caused by the interrelationships between pup odor, pup urine production and retention, pup leg extension behavior, maternal water and salt balance related to lactation, and attraction to pup odor. The relationships are complex and decentralized. Hormones become part of a web that includes–among other things–experience, the brain, peripheral muscles, and physiology.

PROPOSITION 2:
AFTER PUBERTY THE ORGANIZED BRAIN REGIONS RESPOND TO ACTIVATING HORMONES CIRCULATING THROUGH THE BODY

The organizational/activational model assumes that a critical period of hormone susceptibility occurs either prenatally or perinatally. This period could reflect a period of high hormone synthesis and/or a period in which key developing tissues exhibit special sensitivity to the presence of hormones. Whatever the mechanism of the sensitive period, proponents of the O/A model generally ignore the possibility that there are pre-pubertal hormone effects. These could occur during the period I have designated in Figure 1 as a Black Box. Phoenix et al. (1959), for example, didn't bother to remove the ovaries from their masculinized female rats until just before or just after puberty. Then they did so in order to be certain that "activational" effects they wished to measure came from their injected sources and not from an intact gonad. Their lack of concern about the continued presence of intact ovaries during development stemmed in part from the belief that estrogens played no active role in female development; that is, that females just passively happened. This contrasted with their view of male development as an active process (see Fausto-Sterling, 1987, 1989; Gilbert, 1988).

Evidence suggests, however, that ovarian hormones affect the development of sex-related behaviors more or less continuously until the time of puberty. For example, Gerall et al. (1973) found that measures of female mating behavior were higher in both female and castrated male rats which had ovaries implanted at various times prior to puberty. Implanted animals also had smaller body weights at puberty, a result proportional to the length of time the ovary had been implanted. They concluded that "physiological amounts of ovarian hormones, while not necessary for development of female potentiality, permanently influences it . . ." (p. 449). Södersten (1976) also presented evidence that ovarian secretions during post-natal development can alter the response of adult female rats to estrogen. Furthermore, perinatal hormone treatments may themselves alter the activity of the intact ovary. For example, 20-day-old intact androgenized female rats have blood concentrations of estradiol 15 times higher than untreated females of the same age (Cheng & Johnson, 1973/4). By ignoring the weeks between birth and puberty, experimenters miss possible effects on behavior of ongoing hormonal activity, including possible effects of behavior on hormone activity in communally raised animals, and possible effects of the initial hormone treatment on subsequent hormone production.

Although many mammals do have an initial discrete period of sensitivity to testosterone treatment, at least some do not. For example, the sensitive period in the pig runs more or less from birth until puberty and the effects of injected hormones on behavior are progressive over time. For these animals the possibility that experience might interact with hormone production is especially clear. Juvenile pigs frequently engage in sexual play in both male-male and male-female combinations (Adkins-Regan et al., 1989). In rats, de Jonge et al. (1988) reported that both masculine copulatory responses and an increased orientation towards other females could result either from specific sexual experience during adulthood or from hormonal treatments during puberty or early adolescence. Their results are consistent with the report of Gerall et al. (1973) that an ovary present around puberty in either male or female rats facilitated the appearance of female behavior when the animals were examined as adults. Finally, Tobet and Fox (1992) cite evidence that at least some hormonal effects on brain anatomy in the rat result from an accumulation of prenatal and perinatal hormones. Pointing out that varying levels of specific hormones circulate during the course of an individual's life span, they call for "a life-span approach" to understanding the role of hormones in the development of sex differences in neural structure.

PROPOSITION 3:
ORGANIZATIONAL EFFECTS ON THE BRAIN ARE PERMANENT BUT ACTIVATIONAL EFFECTS ARE TRANSITORY

In an article on the sexual differentiation of the nervous system, Toran-Allerand (1984) writes: "It is generally believed that testicular androgens exert an inductive, or organizational, influence in the developing CNS [central nervous system] during restricted (critical), late fetal or early postnatal periods of neural differentiation, at which time the tissue is sufficiently plastic to respond permanently and irreversibly to these hormones." What evidence is there to support the notion of permanence and the idea that adult nerve tissue cannot respond in more than a temporary (activational) manner to hormone exposure?

Phoenix et al. concluded their experiments after testing treated guinea pigs twice, once at 6 to 9 months and again at one year of age. Guinea pigs, however, can live as long as eight years. No studies that I know of have tested them throughout their lifetime. This is true as well for virtually all of the other mammals studied in similar fashion, although the claim of permanence may be more accurate for animals such as mice which normally live to be only 1 to 2 years old.

Effects such as those measured by Phoenix et al. and others may simply be ones which show up in the months immediately following puberty; these may in fact change with subsequent life experience. For instance, perinatally androgenized female rats, under certain circumstances, will show a lowered frequency or intensity of lordosis. Extensive testing, however, can overcome such changes

(Brown-Grant, 1974). Similarly, testosterone can typically activate mounting in developmentally normal rats (Beach, 1971). As one reviewer states, "the essential 'wiring' for these behaviors persists . . . In this sense Beach was correct in questioning the idea that perinatal steroids change the essential structure of the nervous system" (Feder, 1981, p. 143).

Other difficulties arise when invoking the notion of permanence. Activating effects are supposed to be transitory, lasting from a few hours to a few days. In contrast permanent organization events are supposed to last a lifetime. In practice this has meant several months to about a year. How then does one classify as temporary or permanent hormonal effects on the brain which last for weeks rather than days or months? Arnold and Breedlove (1985) cite a variety of such cases from both songbirds and mammals. In many of these animals particular brain structures respond to hormone exposure by growth or to hormone reduction by shrinkage. If the brain can respond to hormonal stimuli with anatomical changes which can endure for weeks or even months, then the door opens wide for theories in which experience can play a significant role (see Thor & Holloway, 1984, for a review of studies on social play in young rats). Hormonal systems, after all, are exquisitely responsive to experience, be it in the form of nutrition, stress, or sexual activity (to name but a few possibilities). Thus, not only does the distinction between organizational and activational effects blur, so too does the dividing line between so-called biologically and socially shaped behaviors.

CONCLUSION

We humans pride ourselves on our capacity to learn. We have developed complex theories of the psyche and the subconscious and are arguably the most mentally complex of all animals. Yet even animals without backbones have the capacity to learn by observation. A fascinating recent study demonstrated that untrained octopi can learn by watching trained ones (Fiorito & Scotto, 1992). It seems ironic, therefore, that our most touted accounts of the development of sexual behaviors in advanced mammals omit learning and experience altogether. Because the control of hormone synthesis differs between primates and other species (Baum, 1979), a strong case can be made that the studies on the hormonal basis of sexual behaviors in non-primates tell us little, if anything, about primates, including humans (Adkins-Regan, 1988; Feder, 1981). In this paper, however, I have made a broader claim–that the theories we have derived from rodent experimentation are completely inadequate even for rodents.

It is time for the community of researchers interested in the role of hormones in the development of animal behavior to look at all the data. The older work of Frank Beach and the newer writings of scientists such as Birke, Moore, Arnold and Breedlove, and Tobet and Fox provide ready-made models which can be used to build complex and interesting theories of sexual development. Despite differences in hormone physiology, more complex accounts which view the body as a flexible part of the explanatory system might provide better models for understanding human behavior. We should stop depicting animals as organisms impervious to their surroundings. Instead we should strive to understand how animal physiology–including the brain–develops in relationship to experience, how experience changes the body, and how the body alters experience. It will be more difficult to design experiments appropriate to such an approach. But the studies will certainly be interesting, informative, and of greater human relevance than past animal research.

NOTES

1. I do not say this critically, and it is no secret that I have also publicly stated my views on the particular studies in question. See Anne Fausto-Sterling, *Myths of Gender: Biological Theories about Women and Men* (New York: Basic Books, 1992).

2. Feminist scholars have conceptualized gender as a set of socially constructed attributes which different cultures attach to particular sexes. Different cultures differently define gender. In the United States, for example, a woman auto mechanic violates gender norms; using her mechanical skills to earn a living would be an example of heterotypical behavior. One could NOT conclude from this, however, that she was a lesbian. Violating gender norms, which differ from culture to culture, should not be confused with sexual preference.

3. Later researchers refined the timing of the injections.

4. The specific observation situation, i.e., what mounting partners were offered is not described.

5. In a longer version of this paper I plan to discuss the force of this analogy, relying in part on an analysis by Cynthia Seiwert, "The brain as reproductive organ: An analysis of the organizational theory of hormone action" (unpublished manuscript, 1988).

6. Christensen and Gorski also show a direct effect on the regulation of gonadotropins by implantation of testosterone into the brain. I have not dwelled on the physiology of hormone regulation in this review, hence have not mentioned this aspect of their work in the text.

7. Breedlove (1992) notes that "the primary site of steroid action for the masculinization of the SDN-POA (sexually dimorphic nucleus of the preoptic area) remains unknown. Neither is the behavior function of the SDN-POA clearly established."("Sexual dimorphism in the Vertebrate Nervous System," *Journal of Neuroscience, 12*, 4133-4142. Quote is on p. 4136.)

REFERENCES

Adkins-Regan, E. (1988). Sex hormones and sexual orientation in animals. *Psychobiology, 16*, 335-347.

Adkins-Regan, E., Orgeur, P., & Signoret, J. P. (1989). Sexual differentiation of reproductive behavior in pigs: Defeminizing effects of prepubertal estradiol. *Hormones and Behavior, 23*, 290-303.

Angier, N. (1991, August 30). Zone of brain linked to men's sexual orientation. *The New York Times*, p. E1.

Arnold, A. P., & Breedlove, A. P. (1985). Organizational and activational effects of sex steroids on brain and behavior: A reanalysis. *Hormones and Behavior, 19*, 469-498.

Bailey, J. M., & Pillard, R. C. (1991). A genetic study of male sexual orientation. *Archives of General Psychiatry, 48*, 1089-1096.

Baum, M. J. (1979). Differentiation of Coital Behavior in Mammals: A comparative analysis. *Neuroscience and Biobehavioral Reviews, 3*, 265-284.

Beach, F. A. (1971). Hormonal factors controlling the differentiation, development and display of copulatory behavior in the ramstergig and related species. In Tobach, E., Aronson, L. R., & Shaw, E. (Eds.), *The biopsychology of development* (New York).

Birke, L. I. A. (1989). How do gender differences in behavior develop? A reanalysis of the role of early experience. *Perspectives in Ethology, 8*, 215-242.

Brown-Grant, K. (1974). On 'critical periods' during the post-natal development of the rat in *Endocrinologie sexuelle de la période Périnatale*, Forest & Bertrand, J. (Eds.), pp. 357-375. Paris: INSERM.

Cheng, H. C., & Johnson, D. C. (1973/4). Serum estrogens and gonadotropins in developing androgenized and normal female rats. *Neuroendocrinology, 13*, 357-365.

Christensen, L. W., & Gorski, R. A. (1978). Independent masculinization of neuroendocrine systems by intracerebral implants of testosterone or estradiol in the neonatal female rat. *Brain Research, 146*, 325-340.

Crabb, C. (1991, September 9). Are some men born to be homosexual? *Newsweek*, p. 58.

De Jonge, F. (1986). *Sexual and Aggressive Behavior in female rats: Psychological and endocrine factors.* Nederlands Instituut voor Hersenonderzoek, Amsterdam.

De Jonge, F. H., Muntjewerff, J.-W., Louwerse, A. L., & Van de Poll, N. E. (1988). Sexual behavior and sexual orientation of the female rat after hormonal treatment during various stages of development. *Hormones and Behavior, 22*, 100-115.

Fausto-Sterling, A. (1987). Society writes biology; Biology constructs gender. *Daedalus, 116*, 61-76.

Fausto-Sterling, A. (1989). Life in the XY Corral. *Women's Studies International Forum, 12*, 319-331.

Feder, H. H. (1981). Perinatal hormones and their role in the development of sexually dimorphic behaviors. In N. T. Adler, ed., *Neuroendocrinology of Reproduction* (pp. 127-158). New York: Plenum.

Fiorito, G., & Scotto, P. (1992). Observational learning in Octopus vulgaris. *Science, 256*, 545-546.

Gerall, H. D., Ward, & Gerall, A. A. (1967). Disruption of the male rat's sexual behavior induced by social isolation. *Animal Behavior, 15*, 54-58.

Gerall, A. A., Dunlap, J. L., & Hendricks, S. E. (1973). Effect of ovarian secretions on female behavioral potentiality in the rat. *Journal of Comparative and Physiological Psychology, 82*, 449-465.

Gilbert, S. (1988). *Developmental Biology,* 2nd Edition. Sunderland, MA: Sinauer Associates.

Gladue, B. (1988). Hormones in relationship to homosexual/bisexual/ heterosexual gender orientation. In J. M. A. Sitzen (Ed.), *Handbook of Sexology: Vol. 6: The pharmacology and endocrinology of sexual function* (pp. 388-409). Amsterdam: Elsevier.

Gorman, C. (1991, September 9). "Are Gay Men Born that Way?" *Time*, pp. 60-61.

Hard, E., & Larsson, K. (1968). Dependence of mating behavior in male rats on the presence of littermates in infancy. *Brain Behavio. Evol., 1*, 405-419.

Harris, G. W., & Levine, S. (1965). Sexual differentiation of the brain and its experimental control. *Journal of Physiology, 181*, 379-400.

LeVay, S. (1991). A difference in hypothalamic structure between heterosexual and homosexual men. *Science, 253*, 1034-1037.

Luttge, W. G., & Hall, N. R. (1973). Differential effectiveness of testosterone and its metabolites in the induction of male sexual behavior in two strains of albino mice. *Hormones and Behavior, 4*, 31.

McCauley, E., & Urquiza, A. J. (1988). Endocrine influences on human sexual behavior. In J. M. A. Sitzen (Ed.), *Handbook of Sexology Vol 6: The Pharmacology and Endocrinology of Sexual Function* (pp. 352-377), quote on p. 378. Amsterdam: Elsevier.

McGill, T. E., & Haynes, C. M. (1973). Heterozygosity and retention of ejaculatory reflex after castration in male mice. *Journal of Comparative Physiology and Psychology, 84*, 423.

Moore, C. (1985). Another psychobiological view of sexual differentiation. *Developmental Review, 5*, 18-55.

Moore, C. L. (1990). Comparative development of vertebrate sexual behavior; levels, cascades and webs. In D. A. Dewsbury (Ed.), *Issues in Comparative Psychology* (pp. 278-299) New York: Sinauer.

Moore, C. L., & Rogers, S. (1984). Contributions of self-grooming to onset of puberty in male rats. *Developmental Psychobiology, 17*, 243-253.

Moore, C. L., Dou, H., & Juraska, J. M. (1992). Maternal stimulation affects the number of motor neurons in a sexually dimorphic nucleus of the lumbar spinal cord. *Brain Research, 572*, 52-56.

Phoenix, C. H., Goy, R. W., Gerall, A. A., & Young, W. C. (1959). Organizing action of prenatally administered testosterone propionate on the tissues mediating mating behavior in the female guinea pig.

Södersten, P. (1976). Lordosis behavior in male, female and androgenized female rats. *Journal of Endocrinology, 70*, 409-420.

Thor, D. H. (1980). Isolation and copulatory behavior of the male laboratory rat. *Physiology and Behavior, 25*, 63-67.

Thor, D. H., & Holloway, W. R. (1984). Social play in juvenile rats: A decade of methodological and experimental research. *Neuroscience and Biobehavioral Reviews, 8*, 455-464.

Tobet, S. A., & Fox, T. O. (1992). Sex differences in neuronal morphology influenced hormonally throughout life. In A. A. Gerall, H. Moltz, & I. I. Ward, (Eds.), *Handbook of Neurobiology*, Vol II (pp. 41-82). New York: Plenum.

Toran-Allerand, C. D. (1984). On the genesis of sexual differentiation of the central nervous system: Morphogenetic consequences of steroidal exposure and possible role of α-fetoprotein. In G. J. de Vries et al. (Eds.), *Progress in Brain Research 61* (pp. 63-97). Amsterdam: Elsevier.

Valenstein, E. S., & Young, W. C. (1955). An experiential factor influencing the effectiveness of testosterone propionate in eliciting sexual behavior in male guinea pigs. *Endocrinology, 56*, 173-177.

van de Poll, N. E., de Jonge, F. H., van Oyen, H. G., van Pelt, J., & de Bruin, J. P. C. (1981). Failure to find sex differences in testosterone activated aggressive behavior in two strains of rats. *Hormones and Behavior, 15*, 94-105.

Biomedical Concepts of Homosexuality: Folk Belief in a White Coat

Louis J. G. Gooren, MD, PhD

Free University Hospital, Amsterdam, The Netherlands

SUMMARY. Biological and medical tradition teaches that sexuality exists for the sole purpose of reproduction. Within this tradition homosexuality has no biological significance. It is conceived as a pathological condition wherein a homosexual has the internal or external characteristics of the opposite sex. The initial search for such cross-sex physical characteristics in homosexuals (e.g., wide hips in males, wide shoulders in females) failed. The search then focussed on so-called sex hormones. It was hypothesized that homosexuals had an excess of hormones of the opposite sex. The researchers are now hypothesizing that homosexuals have a cross-sex brain organization. To date, no evidence for such cross-sex differentiation has been credibly demonstrated. This paper describes the results of unsuccessful attempts to replicate studies which are based on the assumption that homosexuals have a cross-sexed brain organization due to perinatal hormonal factors.

Biomedicine has a tradition of teleology, the belief that natural processes are shaped by a purpose and are directed towards an end

Louis J. G. Gooren is Professor of Transsexology at the Free University Hospital of Amsterdam.

Correspondence may be addressed: Department of Andrology/Endocrinology, AZVU, P.O. Box 7057, 1007 MB Amsterdam, The Netherlands.

[Haworth co-indexing entry note]: "Biomedical Concepts of Homosexuality." Gooren, Louis J. G. Co-published simultaneously in *Journal of Homosexuality* (The Haworth Press, Inc.) Vol. 28, No. 3/4, 1995, pp. 237-246; and: *Sex, Cells, and Same-Sex Desire: The Biology of Sexual Preference* (ed: John P. De Cecco, and David Allen Parker) The Haworth Press, Inc., 1995, pp. 237-246. Multiple copies of this article/chapter may be purchased from The Haworth Document Delivery Center [1-800-3-HAWORTH; 9:00 a.m. - 5:00 p.m. (EST)].

by some driving force. Thus hunger is the force that instigates one to ingest food and thereby to preserve one's biological existence. Similarly, eroticism and sexuality are thought to be instruments subserving procreation and therewith the preservation of the species.

This belief system has particularly taken root in the medical sciences. The pure biologist describes processes as they are encountered in the world of living creatures without much of a value judgement. By contrast, medicine delineates biological processes as normal versus abnormal, healthy versus diseased. In short, it is a science with normative values. The delineation and definition of pathological versus healthy functioning has emerged for the greater part from the study of bodily diseases themselves. It has, in general, led to a set of values and norms for health and disease in clinical medicine. For instance, cardiology has been able to formulate how many heart beats per minute are required for a normal circulation of blood. A too low or too high frequency is not compatible with life.

The understanding of biomedical processes has been advanced enormously by animal experimentation. It is assumed that with certain limitations the nature of biological processes in animals provides reliable models for our human biological existence. It permits investigation, experimentation, and definition of what is healthy or normal versus what is not.

BIOMEDICINE AND HOMOSEXUALITY

In the biomedical tradition, human sexual activity that holds a promise of the fusion of an egg with a sperm cell is seen as natural. Sexual activity that precludes that goal by its nature is considered unnatural. Confronted with same-sex sexual encounters, biomedicine has tried to explain this phenomenon as a deviation from a natural process. The desire to engage in sexual acts with a man was viewed as a natural female trait. Consequently, a man with the desire to have sex with another man was conceptualized as a female; conversely, a woman with the desire to have sex with another woman was conceptualized as a male.

EARLY BIOLOGICAL RESEARCH

Physical Comparisons

One of the earliest investigations into the possibility of cross-sexed physical characteristics was conducted by Magnus Hirschfeld and his contemporaries. They conceptualized male homosexuals as men with such cross-sexed physical characteristics (e.g., wider hips, reduced sexual hairiness, and small-sized genitalia) (Hirschfeld, 1918). This research was based on the presupposition that homosexuals were a third sex, intermediate between male and female. Although they failed to find such cross-sexed characteristics, the concept of the female element in the male body was not relinquished by the biomedical community. On the contrary, when differences could not be found in external physical characteristics researchers turned to internal domains.

Hormonal Comparisons

The study of sex hormones took a very exciting turn in the early 1920s when maleness and femaleness were believed to be clearly differentiated hormonal states. Hormones originating from the gonads were called sex hormones. The source of male sex hormones was the secretion of the testis; that of the female sex hormones was ovarian secretion. With the introduction of the concept of sex hormones, scientists suggested that they had found the key to understanding what makes a man a man and a woman a woman.

In the first textbook of sexual endocrinology, *Sex and Secretions*, the French Canadian zoologist, Frank R. Lillie (1939), stated: "there are two sets of sex characters, so there are two sex hormones, the male hormone controlling the 'dependent' male characters, and the female determining the 'dependent' female characters." Sex hormones were believed to be the chemical substance of masculinity and femininity, which were strictly dichotomous states.

As reviewed by Meyer-Bahlburg (1984), many studies have addressed sex hormone levels in homosexual men and homosexual women. In these studies male homosexuals had testosterone levels within the normal range of male reference values. Gross deficiencies of testosterone were conspicuously rare. Other studies found no differences, while two studies showed elevated levels of testosterone in homosexual men. No correlation could be demonstrated between the amount of circulating testosterone and the preferred role in sexual activity or the degree of effeminacy in non-sexual gender role behavior. Some researchers found elevated estrogen levels in homosexual men, but their findings failed to be confirmed by other studies. Some studies of testosterone levels in homosexual women found evidence of elevated levels, but others did not. Investigations of the estrogen levels of homosexual women showed no deviation from the norm.

Since the 1970s, measurements of hormonal levels in blood or urine are reliable, but there are a number of confounding variables: (1) Hormones are produced in bursts of secretion and, as a consequence, fluctuate within certain margins. (2) Another fluctuation, called the circadian rhythm, occurs naturally throughout the day. Hormonal levels in the morning are approximately 25% higher than in the late afternoon. (3) Aging has a profound effect on testosterone production; with advancing age testosterone levels decline and estrogen levels rise in men. Such hormonal fluctuations have not been appropriately considered in these studies and their results are therefore questionable.

Probably the most important and fundamental objection to these types of research is the conceptualization of testosterone as the male hormone and estrogen as the female hormone. As early as 1939, the American physiologist Evans stated: "It would appear that maleness or femaleness cannot be looked upon as implying the presence of one hormone and the absence of another, but that differences in the absolute and especially relative amounts of these two kinds of substances may be expected to characterize each sex and, though much has been learned, it is only fair to state that these differences are still incompletely known" (Evans, 1939, pp. 21-22). Science now has advanced sufficiently to relinquish the concept of male and female hormones (i.e., male and female in the sense that they determine or contribute to our status of being men or women). We know that both testosterone and estrogen have multiple actions in men and women (Whalen, 1984).

THE BRAIN AND HOMOSEXUALITY

After many years of research it has become clear that sexual differentiation into male and female is a multi-step process in mammals. Each step is characterized by the potential to develop into a male or a female. Each step has a critical period which, once passed, constitutes a point of no return. The genetic coding on the sex chromosomes carries the information for the undifferentiated gonad to become either an ovary or a testis, or, in extremely rare cases, ovotestis, a combination of both (as found in hermaphrodites). Subsequent steps are dependent on the hormonal products of the testis. Testicular hormones steer the organism toward male development.

In the beginning of this century, it became apparent in guinea pigs that not only do their internal and external genitalia undergo a sexual differentiation, but so does their nervous system (Steinach, 1926). Mating patterns are imprinted in the brain following these steps. Female is the basic pattern of development, while male development only takes place in the presence of sufficient amounts of testosterone or its derivative hormones during the critical period of development in which the brain is sexually differentiated.

This sexual differentiation was easy to observe in lower mammals like the guinea pig, but has never been proven to occur in higher mammals like the monkey and man. Experiments generally have consisted of observations of male rats who had their testes removed at the critical period of brain sexual differentiation while interacting with noncastrated male rats. Observers reported that the castrated rats showed a stereotyped female coital pattern (called "lordosis") and that they were subsequently "mounted" (the male coital pattern) by noncastrated male rats. This so-called cross-sex behavior was believed to be analogous with homosexuality in humans (Dörner, 1980). Amazingly enough these experimenters failed to study the sexual interaction of two castrated rats which would have been more faithful to their concept of the interaction of two homosexual men. (For review see Gooren, 1990; Gooren, Fliers, & Courtney, 1990.)

The process of brain sexual differentiation takes place in most mammals around birth. In lower animals (such as rats) it is composed of two elements: (1) a perinatal implanting of female or male stereotyped behavior; and (2) the differentiation of what is called the estrogen feedback effect (EFE) (Baum, 1983). A positive EFE occurs when the luteinizing hormone (LH) levels increase in response to an estrogen stimulus. (This LH increase is the mechanism that induces the release of an ovum in the middle of the menstrual cycle.) A negative EFE occurs when LH levels decrease in response to an estrogen stimulus. In lower animals an implanting of male coital patterns (mounting) is associated with a negative EFE, and of female patterns (lordosing) with a positive EFE.

Some investigators (Dörner, 1980; Gladue, Green, & Hellman, 1984) have tested the EFE in homosexual men. They reported finding a type of EFE that was intermediate between that of heterosexual men and women. This result was the basis for their claim that homosexual men had brain structures like those of females.

I have attempted extensive replication of the work of Dörner and Gladue et al. with transsexuals (Gooren, 1986a). I tested the EFE in male-to-female and female-to-male transsexuals before and after they had received any hormonal or surgical treatments. According to Dörner and Gladue, sexual response is implanted on the brain around birth. If true, the response of transsexuals would remain unchanged by any hormone treatment or by surgery. In fact, the transsexuals in my studies showed exactly the same EFE as their biological counterparts; that is, a normal female response in females who were to become males, and a normal male response in males who were to become females. After hormonal treatment and surgery their EFEs were again determined. The male-to-female transsexuals now showed a female type of EFE and the female-to-male transsexuals showed a male type. This finding failed to support the theory that EFE in humans becomes sexually differentiated before birth. Rather, it suggests that the pattern of response is not immutably implanted.

This conclusion is supported by the work of Norman and Spies (1986), who transplanted ovaries into male monkeys. In these monkeys a positive EFE could be observed. This leads us to conclude that the EFE in higher mammals like the monkey and man is not the result of a prenatal sexual differentiation of the brain. Men and women can show either type of response provided that the appropriate endocrine milieu is created. Therefore, the EFE cannot serve as an indicator of the brain differentiation in higher mammals.

I have also attempted to replicate Dörner (1980) and Gladue et al.'s (1984) investigations of homosexual men using larger samples of homosexual and heterosexual men. I was unable to find any differences in their EFE (Gooren, 1986b). Regardless of sexual orientation, some men showed a response similar to that reported only in homosexual men by Dörner and Gladue. Rejecting the theory that subsequent LH increase was an expression of a positive EFE (as claimed by Dörner and Gladue), I postulated that the differences between the men who showed a more female-like LH response and those who showed a more male-like response were due to testicular functions. In fact, when the testes were stimulated with a powerful endocrine stimulus (human chorionic gonadotropin [hCG]), it could indeed be shown that those men who had the highest (female-like) LH responses to estrogen also had the weakest production of testosterone, following hCG administration.

A number of factors affect testicular production of testosterone, such as aging, drug use, and viral infections. The description of the subjects in the studies of Dörner (1980) and Gladue et al. (1984) are not detailed enough to exclude the possibility that their results were influenced by such factors. In my study which failed to find differences between homosexual and heterosexual men, these two groups had been carefully matched on the basis of these factors.

There is another serious defect in the research of Dörner and Gladue et al. which led them to conclude that homosexual men show an LH response to estrogen that is intermediate between that of heterosexual men and women. Rather than testing LH responses to estrogen, they should have studied it in response to the administration of the synthetic hypothalamic hormone luteinizing hormone-releasing hormone (LHRH). LHRH is the physiological releasing hormone of pituitary LH secretion. If their homosexual subjects had a positive EFE, they would have found that the LH response to LHRH would have been greater following estrogen exposure (Young & Jaffe, 1976). Since they omitted the latter test, there is technically no reason to accept their claim that they encountered a positive EFE in homosexual men.

In my replication study I have administered the latter endocrine test and in all cases, including men who had LH responses to estrogen, the LH responses to LHRH decreased following estrogen exposure. Therefore the responses of LH to estrogen found by Dörner and Gladue et al. in homosexual men can be viewed as a response of LH to falling testosterone levels and not as an expression of a positive EFE.

CONCLUSIONS

After reviewing the preceding literature on the relationship between homosexuality and biological factors from an endocrine viewpoint, it is difficult to be impressed with its quality. Sexology likes to view itself as an interdisciplinary science. In reality, few sexologists have had a thorough professional training in more than one scientific discipline. Workers in the so-called "soft" sciences like psychology and sociology are often overly impressed with the so-called "hard" data of the natural sciences.

Indeed, it is now possible to obtain laboratory results that are reliable. However reliable the measures, they only have significance if they can be interpreted as part of a particular biological system. Sexologists outside the biomedical field have often put too much faith on the significance of "hard" laboratory data. And they are seldom in a position to assess the appropriateness of the theoretical background from which these "hard" data are drawn. Biomedical scientists outside of sexology are in a position to scrutinize the scientific rigor of such studies, but seldom do so because they believe that it is not serious science.

Most endocrinologists do not have much respect for endocrine studies done by sexologists outside their field. Even more disheartening is that many sexologists from the social sciences and humanities are alienated from the biomedical research in sexology. Too often biology is treated as deterministic–fixed and unresponsive to obvious environmental variations (Money, 1988). The broader view is that the molecular biology of our body is an indispensable requirement for our human existence. The latter is characterized by differing levels of organization and integration, physiology and sociology. Due to their complexity, the various levels of the human experience must be dissociated and studied in isolation. However, the interpretation of the data collected in this fashion must be applied to only that level of our existence and cannot explain our full human existence.

If I were asked whether there is a biology of homosexuality, my answer would be yes. It is, however, a biology that allows multifarious expressions of sexuality. It is not true that biology causes people to have certain sexual encounters. It is more likely that other levels of human existence shape sexual expression.

REFERENCES

Baum, M. J. (1983). Hormonal modulation of sexuality in primates. *Bioscience, 35*, 578-593.

Dörner, G. (1980). Sexual differentiation of the brain. *Vitamins and Hormones, 38*, 325-381.

Evans, H. M. (1939). Endocrine glands: Gonads, pituitary, and adrenal. *Annual Review of Physiology.* The Hague: Martinus Nijhoff.

Gladue, B. A., Green, R., & Helman, R. E. (1984). Neuroendocrine response to estrogen and sexual orientation. *Science, 225*, 1496-1499.

Gooren, L. J. G. (1986a). The neuroendocrine response of luteinizing hormone to estrogen administration in the human is not sex-specific but dependent on the hormonal environment. *Journal of Clinical Endocrinology and Metabolism, 63*(3), 588-593.

Gooren, L. J. G. (1986b). The neuroendocrine response of luteinizing hormone to estrogen administration in heterosexual, homosexual, and transsexual subjects. *Journal of Clinical Endocrinology and Metabolism, 63*(3), 583-588.

Gooren, L. J. G. (1990). The endocrinology of transsexualism: A review and a commentary. *Psychoneuroendocrinology, 15*, 3-14.

Gooren, L. J. G., Fliers, E., & Courtney, K. (1990). Biological determinants of sexual orientation. *Annual Review of Sex Research, 1*, 175-196.

Hirschfeld, M. (1918). Ist die Homosexualität körperlich oder seelisch bedingt? [Is homosexuality biologically or psychologically determined?] *Münchner medizinische Wochenschrift, 11*, 295-300.

Lillie, F. R. (1939). Biological introduction. In E. Allen (Ed.), *Sex and internal secretions* (2nd ed.). Baltimore: Williams & Wilkins.

Meyer-Bahlburg, H. F. L. (1984). Psychoendocrine research on sexual orientation: Current status, future options. *Progress in Brain Research, 61*, 375-399.

Money, J. (1988). *Gay, straight, and in-between.* New York: Oxford University Press.

Norman, R. L., & Spies, H. G. (1986). Cyclic ovarian function in a male macaque: Additional evidence for a lack of sexual differentiation in the physiological mechanisms that regulate the cyclic release of gonadotropins in primates. *Endocrinology, 118*, 2608-2610.

Steinach, E. (1926). Antagonistische Wirkungen der Keimdrüsenhormone. *Biologia Generalis, 2,* 815-834.

Whalen, R. E. (1984). Multiple actions of steroids and their antagonists. *Archives of Sexual Behavior, 13,* 497-502.

Young, J. R., & Jaffe, R. B. (1976). Strength duration characteristics of estrogen effects on gonadotropin releasing hormone in women. Part II: Effects of varying concentrations of estradiol. *Journal of Endocrinology and Metabolism, 42,* 432-442.

Hormones and Sexual Orientation: A Questionable Link

Amy Banks, MD

Harvard Medical School

Nanette K. Gartrell, MD

University of California, San Francisco

SUMMARY. This paper critically reviews the studies which explore a possible causal relationship between sex hormones and the development of sexual orientation. Early studies focused on hormone measurements in adult men and women. While definitive interpretations are hindered by methodological problems, the studies as a whole do not support a causal relationship between postnatal hormone levels and sexual orientation. More recently, a theory that prenatal hormone levels produce varying degrees of brain androgenization and subsequent dimorphic sex role behavior has consistently been supported by studies in lower mammals. Attempts to generalize the causes of sexual orientation from animals to humans have been controversial. Efforts to measure the estrogen feedback as an indication of brain androgenization have produced inconsistent results. Studies of men and women who experienced prenatal defects in hor-

Amy Banks is Clinical Instructor in Psychiatry at the Harvard Medical School and McLean Hospital.

Nanette K. Gartrell is Associate Clinical Professor of Psychiatry, University of California, San Francisco.

Correspondence may be addressed to: Amy Banks, McLean Hospital, 115 Mill Street, Bowditch Hall, Belmont, MA 02178.

[Haworth co-indexing entry note]: "Hormones and Sexual Orientation: A Questionable Link." Banks, Amy, and Nanette K. Gartrell. Co-published simultaneously in *Journal of Homosexuality* (The Haworth Press, Inc.) Vol. 28, No. 3/4, 1995, pp. 247-268; and: *Sex, Cells, and Same-Sex Desire: The Biology of Sexual Preference* (ed: John P. De Cecco, and David Allen Parker) The Haworth Press, Inc., 1995, pp. 247-268. Multiple copies of this article/chapter may be purchased from The Haworth Document Delivery Center [1-800-3-HAWORTH; 9:00 a.m. - 5:00 p.m. (EST)].

247

mone metabolism (i.e., CAH and testicular feminization) have not found a concurrent increase in homosexual behavior. Overall, the data do not support a causal connection between hormones and human sexual orientation.

In the past decade the AIDS epidemic has made the issue of sexual orientation explosively controversial not only in political and religious spheres, but also in the medical community. In the face of this debate, it is important to remember that scientists possess political and religious beliefs as well as medical knowledge. As laboratory tests and brain imaging techniques become more sophisticated and precise, assuming causal associations between biological factors and human thought and behavior will be more and more tempting. It is imperative that improved research techniques and methodology be combined with the growing body of information regarding human sexuality.

Over the past two decades, increasingly sophisticated measurements of sex hormones in blood and the development of neuroendocrinology have kept alive the investigation of the possible relationship between sex hormones and sexual orientation. Current work in this area can be divided into two categories: (1) measurements of absolute sex hormone and gonadotropin levels in the blood of gay men and lesbians; and (2) studies of prenatal hormone levels (either inferred through longitudinal reports of congenital syndromes known to alter production or receptivity of hormones in utero, or by measured neuroendocrine responses, i.e., positive estrogen feedback), which may vary according to biological sex. The results of all these studies do not suggest a clear connection between sex hormones and homosexuality. With results that are so inconsistent, perhaps it is time to step back from the research and to think not only about the answers to the questions, but also the questions themselves. Is the search for a biological explanation for homosexuality a scientific attempt to understand a noted difference in human behavior, or is it a political attempt to find a cause in the hope that it can be eradicated? Many of these studies have fundamental flaws in their designs.

SEX HORMONE MEASUREMENTS IN ADULTS

Testosterone

The presumed connection between hormones and homosexuality dates back to the mid 1930s when clinicians, observing effeminate behavior in some homosexual men, attempted to "masculinize" them with treatments of testosterone and other androgens (Glass & Johnson, 1944; Meyer-Bahlburg, 1977). Ironically, these treatments increased the homosexual behavior and had no effect on the patient's sexual orientation. Other researchers were unable to substantiate an increase in homosexual behavior in castrated or hypogonadal males who were presumed to have lowered testosterone levels (Meyer-Bahlburg, 1977; Bancroft et al., 1974; Bremer, 1958; Money, 1970; Murray et al., 1975; Tauber, 1940).

Improved techniques allowed testosterone to be measured more accurately in blood than in urine (Lipsett & Korenam, 1964; Lipsett et al., 1968; Southern et al., 1965). Kolodny et al. (1971) reported that plasma testosterone levels in homosexual men (with a Kinsey scale rating of 5-6) were significantly lower than in exclusively heterosexual men (Kinsey scale = 0). Some homosexual men with low levels of testosterone also showed an increase in luteinizing hormone (LH) levels, the pituitary hormone which stimulates testosterone secretion from the testicular Leydig cells, and an increase in follicular stimulating hormone (FSH) levels, the pituitary hormone which stimulates spermatazoa production in the seminiferous tubles. These same men also had a reduced sperm count (Kolodny et al. 1972). Meyer-Bahlburg (1977) concluded that the more exclusively homosexual a man was, the lower his testosterone level was likely to be. The results of such studies are difficult to interpret. Research has shown that a number of factors affect the amount of testosterone secreted, including psychological stress, depression, sexual activity, exercise, drug use, and viral infections (Yesavage et al., 1985; Kolodny et al., 1974; Fox et al., 1972; Kreuz et al., 1972). These factors were not controlled for in Kolodny's studies. Many of Kolodny's homosexual subjects were marijuana users and would thus be expected to have lower testosterone levels (Gartrell, 1982). In addition, four gay subjects had no spermatozoa in their semen, which suggests the possibility of primary testicular disease.

Although testicular disease is not encountered more often in homosexual than heterosexual males (Meyer-Bahlburg, 1977), any male with this condition would be expected to have decreased testosterone levels. Since the publication of Kolodny's study in 1971, fourteen studies have evaluated testosterone levels in the blood of homosexual males. These data are summarized in Table 1.

The following conclusions can be drawn from the data.

1. Most homosexual men have testosterone measurements that are within the normal range for healthy males.
2. The negative correlation between homosexuality and testosterone level shown by Kolodny has not been substantiated by other researchers.
3. These studies generally show equal testosterone levels in homosexual and heterosexual men. Nine researchers showed no difference in mean testosterone levels between homosexuals and heterosexuals (Doerr et al., 1973; Tourney & Hatfield, 1973; Barlow et al., 1974; Pillard et al., 1974; Parks et al., 1974; Dörner et al., 1975; Stahl et al., 1976; Livingstone et al., 1978; Jaffee et al., 1980). Two studies found that mean testosterone was significantly higher in homosexual men than heterosexuals (Birk et al., 1973; Brodie et al., 1974), and two studies found significantly lower testosterone in homosexuals (Kolodny et al., 1971; Starka et al., 1975).
4. Measurements of testosterone unbound to transporting proteins in the plasma (free testosterone) in men were inconclusive. Doerr et al. (1976) reported that homosexual men had elevated free testosterone, Stahl et al. (1976) reported that homosexual men had reduced free testosterone, and Friedman et al. (1977) reported that they showed no differences when compared to heterosexual male controls.

Some researchers have investigated the association between testosterone levels and lesbianism. Gartrell et al. (1977) studied forty women (21 lesbians with a Kinsey rating of 6 and nineteen heterosexual women with a Kinsey rating of 0). All women were found to have testosterone levels within the normal range for healthy females; however, the lesbian subjects had testosterone levels in the higher end of the range than the heterosexual subjects. Downey et al.

(1987) repeated Gartrell et al.'s study with subjects more closely matched for factors known to affect testosterone levels (e.g., stress and physical activity in women). Although the sample size was small (14 subjects), there was no significant difference in testosterone levels between lesbians and heterosexual women. Dancey (1990), evaluated hormone measurements in four groups of females differentiated by degree of lesbian experience. This study did not show a significant difference in testosterone levels among the four groups of women. Overall, it is important to note that hormone measurements in women are even more complicated than for men because of the variation in hormone levels throughout the menstrual cycle. Fitness can also affect testosterone levels in women. For example, intense physical training and body leanness has been associated with lower testosterone levels in menstruating runners but higher levels in amenorrheic runners (Ronkainen et al., 1985).

Gay men and lesbians have long been identified as, respectively, effeminate and masculine. The theory that testosterone levels reflect excesses or deficiencies of masculinity within this population is arguably flawed because it does not consider the majority of gay men and lesbian women who do not fit these stereotypes. Despite many methodological difficulties, particularly within the studies of homosexual men, the available data do not support the theory that a testosterone excess or deficiency produces homosexual behavior.

Gonadotropins and Other Hormones

Other hormones, particularly the gonadotropins LH and FSH, have also been studied in attempts to correlate hormonal variations and homosexual behavior–with conflicting results. Kolodny et al. (1971, 1972) measured LH and FSH in homosexual and heterosexual men. Although they found no significant difference in FSH levels of fifteen subjects with a Kinsey scale rating of 5 or 6, four of these men had no spermatozoa in their semen (azoospermia) and thus would predictably have an increase in LH level (Gartrell, 1982). When the measurements of the four subjects with azoospermia are excluded, the remaining homosexuals had LH levels within a normal to low range. Since Kolodny's study, there have been seven others comparing gonadotropin levels in homosexuals and heterosexual men (see Table 2). Five studies have reported no LH level

TABLE 1. Male Homosexuality: Testosterone Measurements (Blood).

		Subject Characteristics		Results	
Author	N	Sexual Orientation	Age Range	Mean Total Testosterone	Significance (HvsC)
Kolodney et al. (1971)	4	Kinsey 2		775ng/100ml	No difference
	6	K3		681ng/100ml	No difference
	5	K4 H	18-24	569ng/100ml	No difference
	7	K5		372ng/100ml	H<C**
	8	K6		264ng/100ml	H<C**
Birk et al. (1973)	50	Heterosexual C	17-24	689ng/100ml	
	19	Homosexual H (K0-6)	22-40	1024ng/100ml	
		Kolodney (1971) C		689ng/100ml	H>C**
Doerr et al. (1973)	32	K3-6 H	20-63	537ng/100ml (median)	
	46	Not Assessed C	20-33	536 (median)	No difference
Tourney and Hatfield (1973)	13	K5-6 H	18-32	920ng/100ml	
Barlow et al. (1974)	11	Heterosexual C	18-32	650ng/100ml	No difference
	15	K5-6 H	15-35	Range 330-1183ng/100ml	No difference
	Kolodney 1971 C				
Brodie et al. (1974)	19	K6 H	Mean 26.0	800ng/100ml	
	20	Heterosexual C	Mean 23.4	604ng/100ml	H>C**
Pillard et al. (1974)	28	K5-6 H	19-34	695ng/100ml	
	36	Heterosexual C		787ng/100ml	No difference
Parks et al. (1974)	6	K4-6 H	15-19	Range 383-979ng/100ml	
	6	K0-2 C	16-19	Range 483-936ng/100ml	No difference

Author	N	Sexual Orientation	Age Range	Mean Total Testosterone	Significance (HvsC)
Dörner et al. (1975)	11	Homosexual H		595ng/100ml	No difference
	20	Heterosexual C	17-62	585ng/100ml	
Starka et al. (1975)	18	Homosexual(a) H	16-74	498ng/100ml	H<C**
	3	Homosexual(b)		449ng/100ml	H<C**
	79	Not assessed C	16-60	739ng/100ml	
Stahl et al. (1976)	35	Homosexual H	19-40	590ng/100ml	
	38	Heterosexual C	20-40	562ng/100ml	No difference
Livingstone et al. (1977)	9	Homosexual H	19-33	471.3ng/100ml	
		Heterosexual C		455ng/100ml	No difference
Jaffee et al. (1980)	77	Hetero only		739.5+/−28.0	
	8	hetero remote homo		809.5+/−19.3	
	53	both hetero & homo	mean range 24.5 - 26.8	759.3+/−37.2	No difference
	28	homo remote hetero		770.1+/−49.2	
	24	homo only		710.5+/−50.6	
				Mean Free testosterone	
Doerr et al. (1976)	26	K3-6 H	20-33	10.7% (median)	H>C*
	26	Not assessed C		9.7% (median)	
Stahl et al. (1976)	35	Homosexual H	19-40	10.7ng/100ml	H<C**
	38	Heterosexual C	20-40	13.3ng/100ml	
Friedman et al. (1977)	20	K6 H	Mean 32	7.46ng/100ml	No difference
	18	K0 C	Mean 28	6.50ng/100ml	

*Adapted from Meyer-Bahburg (1977) and Gartrell (1982)

Abbreviations: N = Number   (a) Effeminate   (b) Masculine
           C = Control Subjects   * = P< 0.05   ** = p < 0.01
           H = Homosexual Subjects
           K = Kinsey Scale Number   *** = p < 0.001

difference between the groups (Parks et al., 1974; Dörner et al., 1975; Friedman et al., 1977; Tourney et al., 1975; and Jaffee et al., 1980). Two studies have shown LH levels higher in homosexual than in heterosexual men (Doerr et al., 1976; Rohde et al., 1977).

The results of FSH measurements have been equally inconsistent. Parks et al. (1974), Tourney et al. (1975), and Jaffee et al. (1980) reported no significant difference between FSH levels in homosexual and heterosexual subjects. Rohde et al. (1977) reported FSH elevations in their homosexual subjects. Livingstone et al. (1978) found that pituitary output of LH and FSH stimulation by luteinizing hormone-releasing hormone (LHRH) was comparable in both homosexual and heterosexual subjects.

In women, FSH stimulates the growth of granulosa cells in the ovarian follicle and controls estrogen formation within these cells, while LH stimulates androgen production in the ovarian theca cells. The androgen diffuses to the granulosa cells where it is converted to estrogen. FSH and LH levels in lesbians have been the subject of only one investigation. Loraine et al. (1970) found urine FSH to be lower in 25% of their lesbian subjects and LH output to be significantly higher in 75% of their lesbian as compared with heterosexual women. This study is particularly difficult to interpret because of glaring methodological flaws, including: (1) unreliability of hormone measurements in urine; (2) the small number of subjects; (3) incomplete sexual histories; (4) poor matching of subjects; and (5) the fact that 75% of the subjects reported menstrual irregularities. Clearly, further research is needed before offering even tentative conclusions on FSH and LH levels in lesbians.

Other hormone levels have been less extensively documented. Estrogen was found elevated in a group of homosexual men (Doerr et al., 1973, 1976) and normal in another group (Friedman et al., 1977). Three studies reported normal prolactin levels (a pituitary hormone essential for lactation in humans and controlled by the hypothalamus) in homosexual men (Kolodny et al., 1972; Friedman & Frantz, 1977; Jaffee et al., 1980). Other studies have also shown elevations in dihydrotestosterone (an androgen derived from testosterone which acts on peripheral tissues producing external virilization and sexual maturity at puberty) (Doerr et al., 1976), androstenedione (an adrenal androgen and precursor to testosterone), and cortisol (an adrenal glucocorticoid) (Friedman et al., 1977). Downey et al. (1987) and Dancey (1990) both reported no significant differences in androstenedione levels in lesbians as compared to heterosexual women. Downey et al. (1987) also reported no significant difference in cortisol levels, while Dancey (1990) reported no significant differences in progesterone and oestradiol levels.

Although this body of literature appears confusing in its disparity, the results are understandable if one considers various methodological limitations. Meyer-Bahlburg et al. (1977), Gartrell (1982), Feder (1984), Birk (1981), and Ricketts (1984) have discussed problems in study design and theoretical formulation. One central problem concerns the identification of homosexual subjects. While most authors used the Kinsey scale to assess the degree of homosexual behavior (see McGuire, this volume), the rating considered to be definitive for homosexuality ranged from 4 to 6. Subjects were considered heterosexual if they were assigned a rating of 0 to 2. This range in the ratings of sexual orientation illustrates some of the difficulty of seeking a biological connection. Is it the sexual act that defines a person as homosexual, or is it the feelings and associated behaviors involved in same-gender relationships? Until there is a consensus on this theoretical question and thus a more uniform approach to studying sexual orientation, the literature will remain inconclusive.

Another theoretical problem arises because of the assumption that differences in hormone levels are due to differences in sexual orientation. Gartrell (1982) has noted a wide range of demographic variations in subjects. Homosexual subjects have been obtained from prisons, psychiatric hospitals, VD clinics, colleges, and gay/lesbian organizations. Heterosexual subjects included research lab staff, military recruits (who were assumed to be heterosexual), and students. These markedly different groups of subjects could be expected to show different psychological profiles and even hormone levels (Meyer-Bahlburg, 1977) on the basis of differing backgrounds. Without close matching of demographic variables, it is irresponsible to conclude that sexual orientation caused any of the hormonal variation.

The studies also varied widely in their consideration of factors which are believed to affect hormone levels. Controlling for such

TABLE 2. Male Homosexuality: Gonadotropin Measures.

Subjects Characteristics

Author	N	Sexual Orientation	Age Range	LH	Significance (H vs. C)	FSH	Significance (H. vs. C)
Kolodney et al. (1971,1972)	4	K2 H	18-24	8.5mu/ml	No difference		
	6	K3		8.8mu/ml	No difference		
	5	K4		6.8mu/ml	No difference		
	7	K5		27.8mu/ml	H>C**	12.3mu/ml	No difference
	8	K6		46.5mu/ml	H>C**	24.9mu/ml	
	50	Heterosexual C	17-24	8.3mu/ml		Range 4-25mu/ml	
Parks et al. (1974)	6	K4-6 H	15-19	Range 10.2-13.5 mu/ml	No difference	Range 6.3-9.3mu/ml	No difference
	6	K0-2 C	16-19	Range 10.0-12.0mu/ml	No difference	Range 5.1-9.6mu/ml	No difference
Dörner et al. (1975)	21	Homosexual H	20-59	13.5mu/ml	No difference		
	20	Heterosexual C	17-62	14.7mu/ml	No difference		
Tourney et al. (1975)	14	K5-6 H	18-32	3.26ng/100ml		17.5ng/100ml	
	11	Heterosexual C		3.46ng/100ml	No difference	11.6ng/100ml	No difference
Doerr et al. (1976)	26	K3-6 H	20-33	35.1ng MRC (median) 69/104ml			
	26	Not assessed C		24.9/ml (median)	H>C**		

Author	N	Sexual Orientation	Age Range	LH	Significance (H vs. C)	FSH	Significance (H. vs. C)
Friedman et al. (1977)	20	K6 H	Mean 32	54ng LER 907/ml			
	18	K0 C	Mean 28	64.2/ml	No difference		
Rohde et al. (1977)	50	K5-6 H	20-49	28.2mu/ml	H>C**	6.89mu/ml	
	40	C					
	24	Heterosexual	20-45	12.6mu/ml		4.17mu/ml	H>C**
Jaffee et al. (1980)	77	Heterosexual		13.4		10.1	
	8	Hetero with remote homo		13.7		10.9	
	53	Hetero and homo	mean range 24.5-26.8	14.3	No difference	11.6	No difference
	28	Homo with remote hetero		11.9		12.0	
	24	Homosexual		13.2		12.1	
Livingstone et al. (1978)	9	Homosexual H	19-33	Mean LH and FSH response to LH releasing hormone (LRH) not significantly different.			
		Heterosexual C					

Abbreviations: See Table 1
LH = Luteinizing Hormone
FSH = Follicle Stimulating Hormone

factors is becoming increasingly difficult as neuroendocrinology develops and we learn more about the interdependencies between the central nervous and hormone systems. Finally, hormone measurements have been obtained through many different laboratory techniques (e.g., RIA, complete protein binding, gas-liquid chromatography, and thin-layer chromatography). While such techniques have improved, comparison across studies using different techniques is unreliable.

PRENATAL HORMONE THEORIES

Positive Estrogen Feedback

In the late 1960s, a German researcher, G. Dörner, developed a theory about hormonal influence on the development of sexual orientation. Utilizing a rat model, he proposed that hormones prenatally affect brain development, resulting in a sexually dimorphic brain and consequently dimorphic gender role behavior (see Fausto-Sterling and Gooren, this volume). Female rats have a specific hypothalamic-pituitary organization which, when they are exposed to estrogen at a particular point in their menstrual cycle, will respond with an initial decline in LH secretion followed by an increase. Dörner hypothesized that this LH surge was due to a sexually dimorphic brain organization. He isolated a gender specific period of brain differentiation in rats which was dependent on androgen levels (Dörner et al., 1975). He has attempted to generalize his work with rats to human gender role development, theorizing that homosexual men, with a relative deficiency in androgens at this critical prenatal period, abolish the positive estrogen feedback mechanism within their brains (Dörner et al., 1987). (See Figure 1.)

Dörner (1975) tested this theory of brain androgenization on 3 groups of men–21 homosexual, 5 bisexual, and 20 heterosexual–by injecting estrogen and then measuring LH levels over a period of four days. He reported that 13 out of 21 homosexuals had a LH response which was significantly elevated above the baseline after an initial decline of LH from the estrogen injection. In comparison, a similar increase in LH above the baseline level was seen in only 2

FIGURE 1. From Gold and Josimovich (1980).

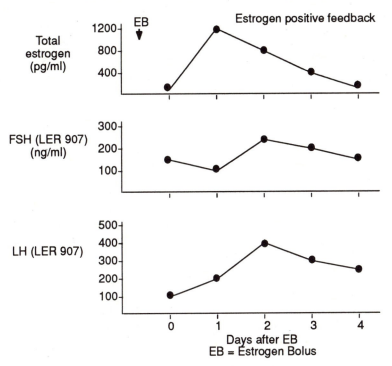

out of 25 heterosexual men and in none of the bisexuals. Although the rise in LH in the homosexual men was weaker and more delayed than that found in heterosexual women in the control group, Dörner argues that the increase is the result of a more feminized brain for homosexual men. Subsequently, Gladue (1984) in a similar study compared the degree of positive estrogen feedback in heterosexual women, gay men, and heterosexual men. His results are similar to Dörner's, with 9 out of 14 gay men, 0 out of 17 heterosexual men, and 11 out of 12 heterosexual women having a statistically significant positive estrogen feedback at 72 and 96 hours after administration of estrogen.

Two researchers have reported no association between positive estrogen feedback and male homosexuality. Gooren (1986a and this volume) studied LH response to estrogen in a mixed group of volunteers (6 transsexual women, 6 transsexual men, 6 lesbians, 6 heterosexual women, 23 homosexual men, and 15 heterosexual men). He reported no significant differences in the three groups of genetic females, but did show variations in estrogen responsiveness in the male groups. He found a positive estrogen feedback on the fourth day after estrogen administration in 5 out of 15 heterosexuals, 11 out of 23 homosexuals, and none of the transsexual men. Gooren also noted that LH response to estrogen injections was highest in men whose blood testosterone response to estrogen was most depressed, regardless of their sexual orientation. In a second study by Gooren (1986b), LH responsiveness to estrogen injection was measured in transsexual men before and after hormonal treatment for gender reassignment. He was able to demonstrate that the LH response to estrogen was absent in the transsexual men prior to sex-change surgery and estrogen injections. After these treatments, the same group of men was reported to have developed an estrogen feedback, thus raising the possibility that LH response to estrogen is not prenatally imprinted on the brain but rather could be affected by postnatal hormonal environment. Hendricks et al. (1989), in a study of 16 homosexual and 39 heterosexual men, supported Gooren's finding of a positive estrogen feedback in both groups. His group was unable to produce a correlation between increased LH levels after estrogen injections and decreased testosterone levels reported by either Gladue et al. (1984) or Gooren (1986a).

Inconsistencies in study conclusions can in part be caused by methodological problems such as poorly matched subjects, insufficient control of factors influencing hormone levels, assignment of sexual orientation ratings, and variable laboratory techniques. For example, Dörner's 1975 study was conducted on a group of homosexual men in treatment for venereal disease, which raises the possibility of testicular disease affecting hormone levels. Hendricks et al. (1989) suggest that some of Gladue's (1984) subjects may have been HIV+, which would undoubtedly affect the testosterone response to increased LH, as well as the estrogen feedback response.

In women, the corresponding theory would predict that lesbians are prenatally exposed to an excess of androgen, producing a more masculinized brain and a diminished positive estrogen feedback response or none at all. However, Gooren (1986a) found no differences in positive estrogen feedback among his heterosexual, homosexual, and transsexual women.

As a whole, positive estrogen feedback as a marker for prenatal hormone abnormalities in homosexuals is unclear. Gooren (1986b) has suggested that positive estrogen feedback does not differentiate a masculine from a feminine endocrine system. He argues that an elevated LH response to LHRH after estrogen administration would be a better marker, although no studies have attempted to verify this.

Gooren's (1986b) work, which suggests that LH response to estrogen can be manipulated, underscores our need to explore different explanations for results, rather than accepting a single, and perhaps biased, conclusion. Baum et al. (1985) report that the positive estrogen feedback in non-human primates is not determined prenatally and can be manipulated by estrogen administered after birth. He theorizes that the inability of estrogen to increase LH secretion in males with intact testicles may be secondary to a testicular hormone which inhibits the neuroendocrine response to estrogen. Further research is needed before concluding that brain differences are prenatally determined or that a positive estrogen feedback can be considered a marker for homosexuality in men.

In Utero Hormone Abnormalities

Another way to investigate the possible correlation between prenatal hormones and sexual orientation is to conduct longitudinal studies of subjects who are known to have had in utero hormonal abnormalities. In chromosomal males (46, XY), a partial androgen insensitivity syndrome results from a chemical deficiency that makes it impossible to respond to normal levels of testosterone. Because the condition is prenatal, these infants are often born with incompletely-differentiated genitalia and may appear more female than male. The androgen insensitivity extends into adulthood, resulting in varying degrees of feminization, including breast growth at puberty. Money and Ogunro (1974) reported on ten cases of such subjects (eight raised as boys and two raised as girls). Each subject had a heterosexual orientation based not on their chromosomal gender but on their gender of rearing.

In cases of complete androgen insensitivity (testicular feminization syndrome) [TFS], the child is routinely considered to be a girl despite the male (46, XY) chromosomal pattern. Masica et al. (1971) reported on 10 TFS subjects raised as females; none became lesbian. Money et al. (1984) compared androgen-insensitive (AI) subjects with congenital adrenal hyperplasia (CAH) subjects who are chromosomally female (46, XX) with a metabolic variation caused by an enzymatic defect in the biosynthesis of cortisol. In CAH, masculinization occurs as the adrenal gland increases the production of androgens (a precursor to cortisol) in an effort to generate more cortisol. Only two out of fifteen AI subjects reported bisexual activity and none were identified as exclusively lesbian.

Because TFS newborns look like girls, there has been no group of them reared as boys. However, if the prenatal hormone theory holds true, it may be possible to look at other evidence of feminization in the brain of these children. Anono et al. (1978) compared the ability to generate a positive estrogen feedback in five TFS patients to ten normal control women. None of the TFS women were able to generate an LH response to estrogen injection, which contrasted sharply with the non-TFS women who generated a significant response. Although no information was gathered regarding the sexual orientation of the subjects in this study, the results raise questions about the role of androgens in the sexual differentiation of the brain in TFS women, and raises suspicions about the assumption that TFS women have a more feminized brain.

In chromosomal females (46, XX) with CAH, the increased androgen results in a masculinization of the female genitalia at birth and, if untreated, in a masculine physical appearance, including a deepening of the voice and a lack of breast development at puberty. As in AIS, there can be varying degrees of this condition and therefore varying degrees of masculinization. Money et al., in a 1984 study comparing thirty early-treated CAH subjects to 27 control subjects with either AIS or Mayer-Rokitansky-Kuster syndrome (MRKS), a congenital syndrome in which a 46, XX female has atresia of the vagina and vestigial mullerian structures. Individuals with MRKS cannot be distinguished behaviorally or erotosexually from those with AIS (Lewis & Money, 1983). He reported a significantly increased incidence of homosexual experiences in the CAH group. In late-treated CAH, Ehrhardt et al. (1967) reported

18% of the subjects engaged in homosexual behavior, although none were exclusively lesbian. Lev-Ran (1974) reported no lesbian behavior or erotic imagery in 18 subjects in the Soviet Union. Lev-Ran suspects that the total lack of homosexual fantasy and behavior may have been due to stricter social mores against homosexuality. It is important to note that he provided no information regarding the incidence of lesbian experiences in the general Soviet population. Finally, Money and Dalery (1976) described 7 CAH patients with extreme fetal adrenogenital syndrome. Four were raised as girls, and three as boys. Follow-up was limited to the subjects raised as boys, and all four turned out to be heterosexual.

A separate group of women with potential prenatal androgen excesses came from mothers exposed to progestin during their pregnancies which had been administered to prevent miscarriages. Despite original reports (Ehrhardt et. al., 1967) suggesting an increase in "masculine" behaviors, the follow-up (Money & Mathews, 1982) on the females as adults showed no evidence of homosexual experience or imagery.

The results of these longitudinal studies do not support a connection between prenatal hormone levels and sexual orientation. In cases of either partial or complete androgen insufficiency, although gender assignment has varied, sexual orientation has not. Each subject reported a heterosexual orientation in accordance with the gender in which they were raised. A small though inconsistent increase in lesbian activities among the CAH subjects has been reported–18% vs. 13% reported by Kinsey et al. (1953). Details of gender rearing are absent.

CONCLUSION

At this time the literature does not support a causal connection between hormones and homosexuality. Studies of testosterone levels have not shown a deficiency in male homosexuals nor an excess in lesbians. Other postnatal hormone levels, including gonadotropins, have not been studied adequately in lesbians. In homosexual men the results have been inconsistent and inconclusive. Prenatal hormones cannot be measured directly and thus any alteration in levels must be inferred. Results from measurements of the positive estrogen feedback in homosexual men are inconsistent, though there is a growing body of work which suggests this may not be a prenatally fixed neuroendocrine response. Studies of known prenatal defects suggest that sexual orientation is associated with the gender of rearing of the child.

Some of the contradictions within this body of research may be understandable. Neuroendocrinology is expanding rapidly and it may be impossible at this time to identify and control for the growing number of factors which affect hormone levels. We must respect our relative ignorance in this area to avoid simplistic, linear theories which fail to incorporate the wide range of human sexual expression, thought, and behavior (Doell & Longino, 1988). Methodological and theoretical pitfalls may be avoided in future research if scientists not only search for differences in human sexuality but also try to understand them.

REFERENCES

Anono, T., Miyake, A., Kinugasa, T., Kurachi, K., & Matsumoto, K. (1978). Absence of positive estrogen feedback of estrogen on LH release in patients with testicular feminization syndrome. *Acta Endocrinologia, 87,* 259-267.

Bancroft, J., Tennet, G., Loucas, D., & Cass, J. (1974). The control of deviant sexual behavior by drugs. 1. Behavioral changes following estrogens and anti-androgens. *British Journal of Psychiatry, 135,* 310-315.

Barlow, L. H., Abel, G. G., Blanchard, E. B., & Mevissakalian, M. (1974). Plasma testosterone levels and male homosexuality: A failure to replicate. *Archives of Sexual Behavior, 3*(6), 571-575.

Baum, M. J., Carroll, R. S., Erskine, M. S., & Tobet, S. A. (1985). Neuroendocrine response to estrogen and sexual orientation. [letter], *Science, 230*(4728), 960-961.

Birk, L., Williams, G. H., Chasin, M., & Rose, L. I. (1973). Serum testosterone levels in homosexual men. *New England Journal of Medicine, 289*(23), 1236-1238.

Birk, L. A. (1981). Is homosexuality hormonally determined. *Journal of Homosexuality, 6*(4), 35-49.

Braunwald, E. et al. (Eds). (1987). Harrison's principles of internal medicine. Eleventh Edition. New York: McGraw-Hill, 1694-1853.

Bremer, J. (1958). Asexualization: A follow-up study of 244 cases. Oslo: Oslo University Press.

Brodie, H. K. H., Gartrell, N., Doering, C., & Rhue, T. (1974). Plasma testosterone levels in heterosexual and homosexual men. *American Journal of Psychiatry, 131*(1), 82-83.

Dancey, C. P. (1990). Sexual orientation in women: An investigation of hormonal and personality variables. *Biological Psychiatry, 30,* 251-264.

Doell, R., & Longino, H. (1988). Sex hormones and human behavior: A critique of the linear model. *Journal of Homosexuality, 15*(3/4), 55-78.

Doerr, P., Kockett, G., Bogt, H. H., Pirke, K. M., & Dittmar, F. (1973). Plasma testosterone, estradiol, and semen analysis in male homosexuals. *Archives of General Psychiatry, 29*(6), 829-833.

Doerr, P., Pirke, K. M., Kockett, G., & Dittmar, F. (1976). Further studies on sex hormones in male homosexuals. *Archives of General Psychiatry, 33,* 611-614.

Dörner, G., Docke, F., Gotz, F., Rohde, W., Stahl, F., & Tonjes, R. (1987). Sexual differentiation of gonadotrophin secretion, sexual orientation and gender role behavior. *Journal of Steroid Biochemistry, 27*(4-6), 1081-1087.

Dörner, G., Rohde, W., Stahl, F., Krell, L., & Masius, W. G. (1975). A neuroendocrine predisposition for homosexuality in men. *Archives of Sexual Behavior, 4*(1), 1-8.

Downey, J., Ehrhardt, A. A., Schiffman, M., Dyrenfurth, I., & Becker, J. (1987). Sex hormones in lesbian and heterosexual women. *Hormones and Behavior, 21*(3), 347-357.

Ehrhardt, A., Evers, K., & Money, J. (1967). Influence of androgen and some aspects of sexually dimorphic behavior in women with the late treated andrenogenital syndrome. *Johns Hopkins Medical Journal, 123*(3), 115-122.

Feder, H. H. (1984). Hormones and sexual behavior. *Annual Review of Psychology, 35,* 165-200.

Fox, C. A., Ismail, A. A. A., Love, D. N., Kirkham, K. E., & Loraine, J. A. (1972). Studies on the relationship between plasma testosterone levels and human sexual activity. *Journal of Endocrinology, 52,* 51-58.

Friedman, R. C., & Frantz, A. G. (1977). Plasma prolactin levels in male homosexuals. *Hormones and Behavior, 9,* 19-22.

Friedman, R. C., Drenfurth, I., Linkie, D., Tendler, R., & Fleiss, J. L. (1977). Hormones and sexual orientation in men. *American Journal of Psychiatry, 134*(5), 571-572.

Gartrell, N. K., Loriaux, D. L., & Chase, T. N. (1977). Plasma testosterone in homosexual and heterosexual women. *American Journal of Psychiatry, 134*(10), 1117-1119.

Gartrell, N. K. (1982). (review article) Hormones and homosexuality. In W. Paul, J. D. Weinrich, J. C. Gonsiorek, and M. E. Hotredt (Eds.), *Homosexuality: Social, psychological and biological issues.* Beverly Hills: Sage Publications, 169-182.

Gladue, B. A. (1984). Neuroendocrine response to estrogen and sexual orientation. *Science, 225* (4669), 1496-9.

Glass, S. J., & Johnson, R. W. (1944). Limitations and complications of organotherapy in male homosexuality. *Journal of Clinical Endocrinology, 4,* 550-554.

Gold, J., & Josimovich, J. (1980). *J. Gynecological Endocrinology.* Hagerstown, MA: Harper & Row Inc., 300.

Gooren, L. (1986a). The neuroendocrine response of LH to estrogen administration in heterosexual, homosexual and transsexual subjects. *Journal of Clinical Endocrinology and Metabolism, 63*(3), 583-586.

Gooren, L. (1986b). The neuroendocrine response of LH to estrogen administration in the human is not sex specific but dependent on the hormonal environment. *Journal of Clinical Endocrinology and Metabolism, 63*(3), 589-93.

Hendricks, S. E., Graber, B., Rodriquez-Sierra, J. (1989). Neuroendocrine responses to exogenous estrogen: No difference between heterosexual and homosexual men. *Psychoneuroendrocrinology, 14*(3), 177-185.

Jaffee, W. L., McCormack, W. M., & Vaitukaitis, J. L. (1980). Plasma hormones and the sexual preference of men. *Psychoneuroendocrinology, 5*, 33-38.

Kinsey, A. C., Pomeroy, W. B., Martin, C. E., & Gebhard, P. H. (1953). *Sexual behavior in the human female.* Philadelphia: W. B. Saunders.

Kolodny, R. C., Jacobs, L. S., Masters, W. H., Toro, G., & Daughaday, W. H. (1972). Plasma gonadotrophins and prolactins in male homosexuals. *Lancet, 2*(776), 18-20.

Kolodny, R. C., Masters, W. H., Hendryx, J., & Toro, G. (1971). Plasma testosterone and semen analysis in male homosexuals. *New England Journal of Medicine, 285*(21), 1170-1174.

Kolodny, R. C., Masters, W. H., Kolodner, R. M., & Toro, G. (1974). Depression of plasma testosterone after chronic intensive marijuana use. *New England Journal of Medicine, 290*(16), 872-874.

Kreuz, L. E., Rose, R. M., & Jennings, J. R. (1972). Suppression of plasma testosterone levels and psychological stress: A longitudinal study of young men in officer candidate school. *Archives of General Psychiatry, 26*, 479-483.

Lewis, V. G., & Money, J. (1983). Gender-identity/role: G-I/R Part A: XY (androgen-insensitivity) syndrome and XX (Rokitansky) syndrome of vaginal atresia compared. In L. Dennerstein & G. Burrows (Eds.), *Handbook of psychosomatic obstetrics and gynaecology.* Amsterdam: Elsevier Biomedical Press, 51-60.

Lev-Ran, A. (1974). Sexuality and educational levels of women with the late treated adrenogenital syndrome. *Archives of Sexual Behavior, 3*(1), 27-32.

Lipsett, M. B., Migeon, C. J., Kirschner, M. A., & Barden, C. W. (1968). Physiologic basis of disorders of androgen metabolism. *Annals of Internal Medicine, 68*(6), 1327-1344.

Lipsett, M. B., & Korenman, S. G. (1964). Androgen metabolism. *Journal of the American Medical Association, 190*(8), 147-152.

Livingstone, I. R., Sagel, J., Distiller, L. A., Morley, E., & Katz, M. (1978). The effect of luteinizing releasing hormone (LHRH) on pituitary gonadotrophins in male homosexuals. *Hormone Metabolism Research, 10*(3), 248-249.

Loraine, J. A., Ismael, A. A. A., Adamopoulous, D. A., & Dove, G. A. (1970). Endocrine functions in male and female homosexuals. *British Medical Journal, 4*, 406-408.

Masica, D., Money, J., & Ehrhardt, A. (1971). Fetal feminization and female gender identity in the testicual feminization syndrome of androgen insensitivity. *Archives of Sexual Behavior, 1*(2), 131-142.

Meyer-Bahlburg, H. F. L. (1977). Sex hormones and male homosexuality: A comparative perspective. *Archives of Sexual Behavior, 6*(4), 297-325.

Money, J. (1970). Use of an androgen-depleting hormone in the treatment of male sex offenders. *Journal of Sex Research,* 165-172.

Money, J., & Ogunro, C. (1974). Behavioral sexology: Ten cases of genetic male intersexuality with impaired prenatal and pubertal androgenization. *Archives of Sexual Behavior, 3*(3), 181-205.

Money, J., & Dalery, J. (1976). Iatrogenic homosexuality: Gender identity in seven 46, XX chromosomal females with hyperadrenocortical hermaphroditism born with a penis. Three reared as boys, four reared as girls. *Journal of Homosexuality, 1*(4), 357-371.

Money, J., & Mathews, D. (1982). Prenatal exposure to virilizing progestins: An adult follow-up study of twelve women. *Archives of Sexual Behavior, 11*(1), 73-83.

Money, J., Schwartz, M., & Lewis, V. (1984). Adult erotosexual status and fetal hormonal masculinization and demasculinization 46, congenital virilizing adrenal hyperplasia and 46 XY androgen-insensitivity syndrome compared. *Psychoneuroendocrinology, 9*(4), 405-414.

Murray, M. A., Bancroft, J. H., Anderson, D. C., Tennent, T. G., & Carr, P. J. (1975). Endocrine changes in male sex deviants after treatment with anti-androgens, estrogens or tranquilizers. *Journal of Endocrinology, 67,* 179-188.

Parks, G. A., Korth-Schutz, S., Penny, R., Hilding, R. F., Dumars, K. W., Farasier, S. D., & New, M. I. (1974). Variation in pituitary-gonadal function in adolescent male homosexuals and heterosexuals. *Journal of Clinical Endocrine Metabolism, 39*(4), 796-801.

Pillard, R. C., Rose, R. M., & Sherwood, M. (1974). Plasma testosterone levels in homosexual men. *Archives of Sexual Behavior, 3*(5), 453-458.

Ricketts, W. (1984). Biological research on homosexuality, Ansell's Cow or Occam's Razor? *Journal of Homosexuality, 9*(4), 65-93.

Ronkainen, H., Pakarinin, A., Kirkinen, P., & Kauppila, A. (1985). Physical exercise induced changes and seasonal-associated differences in the pituitary-ovarian function of runners and joggers. *Journal of Clinical Endocrine Metabolism, 60,* 416-422.

Rohde, W., Stahl, F., & Dörner, G. (1977). Plasma basal levels of FSH, LH, and testosterone in homosexual men. *Endokrinologie, 70*(3), 241-248.

Southern, A. L., Tochimoti, S., Cramondy, N. C., & Isurugh, K. (1965). Plasma production rates of testosterone in normal adult men and women and in patients with the syndrome of feminizing testes. *Journal of Clinical Endocrinology, 25,* 1441-1450.

Stahl, F., Dörner, G., Ahrens, L., & Graudenz, W. (1976). Significantly decreased apparently free testosterone levels in plasma of male homosexuals. *Endokrinologie, 68*(1), 115-117.

Starka, I., Sipova, I., & Hynie, J. (1975). Plasma testosterone in male transsexuals and homosexuals. *Journal of Sex Research, 11,* 134-138.

Tauber, E. S. (1940). Effects of castration upon the sexuality of the adult male. *Psychosomatic Medicine, 2,* 74-87.

Tourney, G., Petrilli, A. J., & Hatfield, L. M. (1975). Hormonal relationships in homosexual men. *American Journal of Psychiatry, 132*(3), 288-290.

Tourney, G., & Hatfield, L. M. (1973). Androgen metabolism in schizophrenics, homosexuals, and normal controls. *Biological Psychiatry, 6*(1), 23-26.

Yesavage, J. A., Davidson, J., Widrow, L., & Berger, P. A. (1985). Plasma testosterone levels, depression, sexuality and age. *Biological Psychiatry, 20,* 199-228.

Does Peace Prevent Homosexuality?

Gunter Schmidt, PhD
Ulrich Clement, PhD

SUMMARY. This study attempted to replicate a series of investigations by Gunter Dörner and his associates that concluded that more homosexual men are born in wartime than in times of peace. That conclusion is based on Dörner's belief that war induces stress in pregnant women and that stress causes a drop in fetal androgen levels which in turn leads to the development of a homosexual "orientation." The replication not only failed to support the Dörner conclusion but also found that even those cities that suffered the most severe bombing during World War II showed no evidence of increased numbers of homosexuals. The authors conclude that homosexual men can go on loving peace and getting involved in the peace movement.

Dörner and co-workers (1980, 1983, 1987) asserted that in wartime more homosexual men are born than in times of peace. A high

Gunter Schmidt is a professor in the Department of Sexual Research of the University of Hamburg, Germany. Correspondence may be addressed: Abteilung für Sexualforschung der Universität Hamburg, Martinistrasse 52, D-2000 Hamburg 20, Germany.

Ulrich Clement is a professor in the Psychosomatic Clinic of the University of Heidelberg, Germany. Correspondence may be addressed: Psychosomatische Klinik der Universität Heidelberg, Thibautstrasse 2, D-6900 Heidelberg 1, Germany..

This article is a reprint of a Letter to the Editor that first appeared in the *Archives of Sexual Behavior* (Vol. 19, No. 2, 1990). Reprinted by permission of the Office of Rights/Permissions, Plenum Publishing Corporation.

[Haworth co-indexing entry note]: "Does Peace Prevent Homosexuality?" Schmidt, Gunter, and Ulrich Clement. Co-published simultaneously in *Journal of Homosexuality* (The Haworth Press, Inc.) Vol. 28, No. 3/4, 1995, pp. 269-275; and: *Sex, Cells, and Same-Sex Desire: The Biology of Sexual Preference* (ed: John P. De Cecco, and David Allen Parker) The Haworth Press, Inc., 1995, pp. 269-275.

proportion of the 865 homosexual men treated for venereal diseases in six regions of the German Democratic Republic (GDR) were born between 1941 and 1947 (related to the annual total births in the German Reich, Soviet Occupation Zone, GDR). Dörner *et al.* (1987) drew on evidence from experiments on rats, which showed that prenatal stress leads to a "significant decrease in plasma testosterone levels of male rat fetuses and newborns . . . followed by bisexual or even predominatly heterotypical (homosexual) behavior in adulthood" (p. 18). They suggested that the findings on men born in wartime can be explained in psychoendocrinological terms: war means stress, stress induces a lack of androgens in male fetuses, a lack of androgens encourages the development of a homosexual orientation. To quote Dörner *et al.'s* (1983) conclusion: "These findings indicate that prevention of war . . . may render a partial prevention of the development of sexual deviation" (p. 87).

There are two clear objections to Dörner's approach (cf. Schmidt, 1984):

The Data. It is unlikely that such a highly selected sample (venereal disease, six districts, limited period of investigation) could provide valid estimates for the incidence of homosexuality in different generations. One also wonders why the patients would or should tell the doctor that they are homosexual. Dörner *et al.* gave no details about the ages of the patients, and omitted a check on a possible age effect. This is necessary when investigating different generations. The variation described in the relative incidence of homosexuality could be due to age variations because homosexuals of different ages may suffer more or less frequently from venereal diseases, depending on how active they are sexually. Thus WWII-period aged persons with many partners could be more likely to appear at such clinics.

Their Interpretation. Even if homosexuals are born more often during wartime, it seems rash to offer a purely endocrinological explanation. In Dörner *et al.'s* view, the immense upheaval that war entails, its profoundly threatening and destructive effects on society at large, the family, and the individual, can be reduced, at least as far as any links with homosexuality are concerned, to a hormonal disturbance. This reveals an ignorance about psychic and social factors. In wartime children tend to grow up more often without a father or to be separated from other members of the family.[1] If homosexuality really occurs more frequently during wartime, it would be just as reasonable to take this as "proof" of certain psychodynamic theories of homosexuality, e.g., the lack of a father, a particularly close bond between mother and son.

We reinvestigated Dörner *et al.'s* empirical findings, i.e., the statistical connection between homosexual behavior in men and their date of birth (before, during, and after the Second World War), drawing on two studies of West German students carried out by the Department of Sex Research, University of Hamburg, in 1966 and 1981 (Giese and Schmidt, 1968; Clement, 1986; Clement *et al.,* 1984).

Table I summarizes the main features of both studies. We combined both samples and divided them into four cohorts or generations according to the year of birth: one pre-war (1936-1940), one wartime (1941-1945), and two post-war (1951-1955, 1956-1960) (Table II). Six variables of homosexual behavior during adolescence and adulthood (prior 12 months) were analyzed: accumulative incidence before age 20; incidence at ages 15 and 18, and during the prior 12 months; incidence of 2 or more partners at ages 12-18, and during the prior 12 months.

As Table III shows, there are almost no differences between the generations for homosexual activity during adolescence (apart from the fact that those born between 1951 and 1955 had more homosexual experiences before their 20th birthday). During adulthood,

TABLE I. Sexual Behavior in West German Students: 1966 and 1981: Overview

1966	1981
Postmailed questionnaire	Postmailed questionnaire
Random sample	Random sample
12 German universities	13 German universities
Refusal rate 40.2%	Refusal rate 63.4%
$N = 3666$	$N = 1922$
$N\male = 2835$	$N\male = 1106$
$N\female = 831$	$N\female = 816$
92% 21-30 years old at interview (born 1936-1945)	81% 21-30 years old at interview (born 1951-1960)

TABLE II. Generations Studied

Generation	Born	Age at study	N♂	N♀
G1 (prewar)	1936-1940	26-30	657[a]	98[b]
G2 (war)	1941-1945	21-25	2000	620
	1946-1950[c]	–	–	–
G3 (postwar)	1951-1955	26-30	329	180
G4 (postwar)	1956-1960	21-25	600	456

[a]8% (of 657) born in 1940.
[b]7% (of 98) born in 1940.
[c]Data missing.

TABLE III. Incidence of Homosexual Behavior in Men, By Generation (%)

	Prewar	War	Postwar	
	G1	G2	G3	G4
	(n = 657)	(n = 2000)	(n = 329)	(n = 600)
Accumulative incidence before age 20	19	18	25	18
Incidence, age 15	10	9	10	7
Incidence, age 18	6	5	5	4
Incidence, 2 or more partners, age 12-18	8	9	9	8
Incidence, last 12 months	3.7	3.9	7.0	5.3
Incidence, 2 or more partners, last 12 months	2.9	1.6	3.9	3.5

homosexual activity is more frequent in the two postwar generations than in the prewar or wartime groups (the latter group shows the lowest values). This difference may be explained by the fact that between Generations 1 and 2 on the one hand and Generations 3 and 4 on the other attitudes towards sexuality became more liberal (Clement *et al.*, 1984). The increased rate of homosexual activity in these groups, which can also be observed in women,[2] permits one to conclude that in a less sexually repressive society the willingness to get involved, at least temporarily, in homosexual relationships rises slightly.

But to return to Dörner *et al.'s* hypothesis about homosexual behavior and war: The civilian population suffered most in the big cities (over 100,000 inhabitants) and towards the end of the war (1943-1945). Tables IV and V show the data for students who were born under especially difficult circumstances during the worst stages of the war compared with control groups. There is no evidence that they were more homosexual, not even in the "extreme" group born in big cities between 1943 and 1945. Where there are differences, there are more signs of homosexual behavior in the groups of low stress.

TABLE IV. Incidence of Homosexual Behavior in Men, Growing up in Large Cities (> 100,000), By Generation (%)

	Prewar	War	Postwar	
	G1	G2	G3	G4
	($n = 303$)	($n = 843$)	($n = 139$)	($n = 225$)
Accumulative incidence before age 20	21	19	23	20
Incidence, age 15	10	10	8	8
Incidence, age 18	6	5	4	4
Incidence, 2 or more partners, age 12-18	8	9	9	7
Incidence, last 12 months	4.0	3.8	7.2	4.0
Incidence, 2 or more partners, last 12 months	2.3	1.8	3.5	1.7

TABLE V. Incidences of Homosexual Behavior in Men, Breakdown of Generation 2 (%)

	Total		Large cities[a]	
	Born 1941-1942 ($n = 883$)	Born 1943-1945 ($n = 1117$)	Born 1941-1942 ($n = 363$)	Born 1943-1945 ($n = 480$)
Accumulative incidence before age 20	18	18	20	18
Incidence, age 15	9	9	12	9
Incidence, age 18	5	5	5	5
Incidence, 2 or more partners, age 12-18	10	9	11	8
Incidence, last 12 months	4.1	2.9	5.0	2.9
Incidence, 2 or more partners, last 12 months	2.3	1.3	2.2	1.4

[a] > 100,000 population.

To sum up: Our data do not reveal the slightest evidence that wartime stress during the prenatal period increases the incidence of homosexual behavior. There are two conclusions to be drawn:

1. Homosexual men can go on loving peace and getting involved in the peace movement.
2. This paper is a good example of how research often involves nothing more than dealing with our self-produced problems. As soon as someone's idea attains a certain status by being printed in a serious journal, dozens of researchers seize on the idea and try to confirm, disprove, or modify it.

We cram figures into computers and wade through mountains of data in paying our respects to each other's flights of fancy. Any attempt to change this state of affairs would be like jousting with windmills. Nevertheless, we propose to make a beginning with the necessary Don Quixotry and state: On the question of homosexuality and war, no further research is needed.

NOTES

1. In our study, 17 and 18% of boys born 1936-1940, 1941-1945 grew up without father compared to 6 and 4% born 1951-1955, 1956-1960, respectively.
2. In this study the incidence of homosexual behavior in the prior 12 months in female students was 1.0% (G1, $n = 98$); 1.1% (G2, $n = 620$); 4.4% (G3, $n = 180$); 3.3% (G4, $n = 456$).

REFERENCES

Clement, U. (1986). *Sexualität im sozialen Wandel*, Enke, Stuttgart.

Clement, U., Schmidt, G., and Kruse, M. (1984). Changes in sex differences in sexual behavior. A replication of a study on West German students. *Arch. Sex. Behav.* 13: 99-120.

Dörner, G., Schenk, B., Schmiedel, B., and Ahrens, L. (1983). Stressful events in prenatal life H. (1980). Prenatal stress as a possible aetiogenic factor homosexuality in human males. *Endokrinologie* 7ⁿ: 365-368.

Dörner, G., Schenk, B., Schmiedel, B., and Ahrens, L. (1983). Stressful events in prenatal life of bi- and homosexual men. *Exp. Clin. Endocrinol.* 81: 88-90.

Dörner, G., Götz, F., Ohkawa, T., Rohde, W., Stahl, F., and Tönjes, R. (1987). Prenatal stress and sexual brain differentiation in animal and human beings. Abstracts, International Academy of Sex Research, 13th Annual Meeting, June 21-25, in Tutzing.

Giese, H., and Schmidt, G. (1968). *Studenden-Sexualität. Verhalten und Einstellung*, Rowohlt, Reinbek.

Schmidt, G. (1984). Allies and persecutors. Science and medicine in the homosexuality issue. *J. Homosex.*, 10: 127-140.

SECTION V: IS SEXUAL PREFERENCE DETERMINED BY THE BRAIN?

Introduction

The brain is the least understood organ in the human body. Its complex neurological arrangement operates through electrochemical means not yet fully explainable by our sciences. A full explanation of what we do know about the brain would require far too involved a discussion for the purposes of introducing our next section. We will therefore confine our discussion to the structures of the brain discussed in the following papers and primarily focus on identifying these structures (see Figures 1-4).

The brain contains a number of cell types, but for our purposes we are most interested in the *neurons* or nerve cells. These cells are comprised of a central cell body, branched treelike structures called *dendrites* that receive information from other neurons, and a single fiber called the *axon* that transmits information away from the cell body to other neurons. The brain is often referred to as consisting of gray and white matter. The gray areas are occupied largely by neurons and other cells, while the white areas are comprised chiefly of axons en route from one region of the brain to another.

[Haworth co-indexing entry note]: "Introduction." Co-published simultaneously in *Journal of Homosexuality* (The Haworth Press, Inc.) Vol. 28, No. 3/4, 1995, pp. 277-282; and: *Sex, Cells, and Same-Sex Desire: The Biology of Sexual Preference* (ed: John P. De Cecco, and David Allen Parker) The Haworth Press, Inc., 1995, pp. 277-282. Multiple copies of this article/chapter may be purchased from The Haworth Document Delivery Center [1-800-3-HAWORTH; 9:00 a.m. - 5:00 p.m. (EST)].

FIGURE 1. MRI of the human brain.

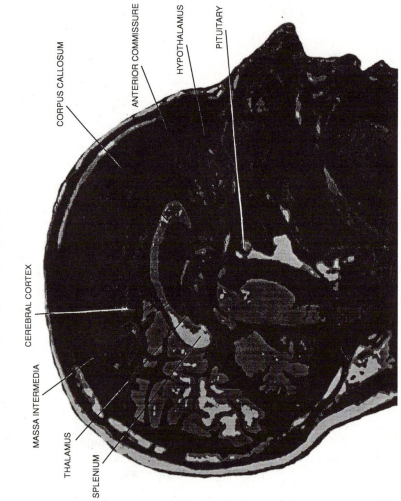

CORPUS CALLOSUM

ANTERIOR COMMISSURE

HYPOTHALAMUS

PITUITARY

CEREBRAL CORTEX

MASSA INTERMEDIA

THALAMUS

SPLENIUM

FIGURE 2. Lobes of the human brain.

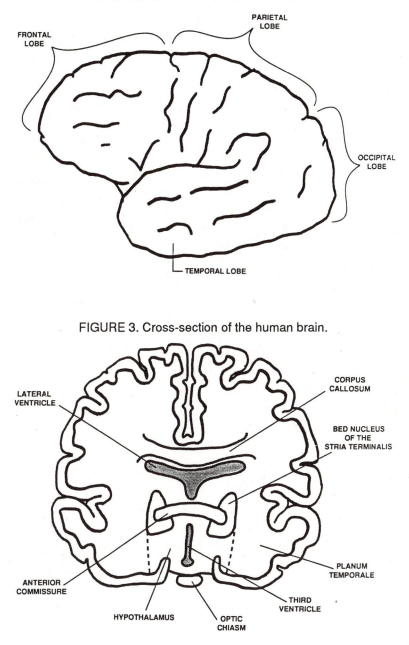

FIGURE 3. Cross-section of the human brain.

FIGURE 4. The hypothalamus, pituitary, and hypothalamic-pituitary hormones. (Note: This is a hypothetical cross-section of the hypothalamus used to illustrate the approximate locations and relative sizes of the structures indicated; not all these structures would appear in the same plane.)

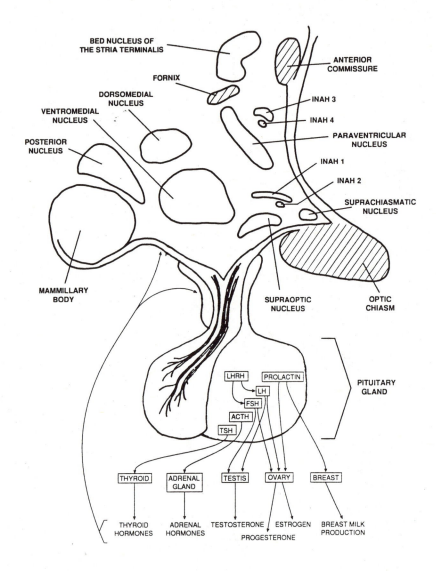

The outer layer of the brain is the convoluted *cerebral cortex* which is thought to be responsible for higher brain functioning. The cerebral cortex and related structures exist nearly symmetrically in two halves of the brain which are called the left and right hemispheres. The *planum temporale* is a portion of the *temporal lobe* that is believed to be involved in language functions and in most individuals is larger on the left side of the brain than on the right.

The left and right hemispheres are connected by and communicate with one another through a number of commissures which are bundles of axons. The largest of these *commissures* is called the *corpus callosum*. The hind part of the corpus callosum is called the *splenium*. The splenium is not clearly demarcated from the rest of the corpus callosum, so for the purposes of research the callosum has often been divided from front to back into five equally spaced segments. The hind segment is then considered to be the splenium. The *anterior commissure* is much smaller than the corpus callosum and connects portions of both the temporal and *frontal lobes* from each hemisphere. The anterior commissure courses across the upper portion of the *hypothalamus*.

The *thalamus* is a large ovoid mass of gray matter which, like the cortex, exists in two symmetric halves. The two halves of the thalamus are interconnected in most individuals by a small gray structure called the *massa intermedia*. The thalamus is reciprocally connected with many different parts of the brain and functions as a relay station for neuronal communications.

The hypothalamus is the portion of the brain situated just below the thalamus. The hypothalamus is reciprocally connected with other brain regions and with the pituitary gland. Through these connections it serves as a critical link in the neural systems that coordinate diverse visceral, endocrine, and behavioral functions. Its left and right halves are separated by a fluid-filled structure called the *third ventricle*. The hypothalamus may be divided into a medial cell-dense region and a less dense cellular lateral region. From front to back the hypothalamus is divided into four areas: preoptic, anterior, tuberal, and posterior. There are no clear boundaries between adjacent areas. Rather, the areas are merely named according to the topographic region of the hypothalamus in which they lie. The areas of the hypothalamus can be considered together to constitute a continuous matrix of loosely arranged cells within which lie the hypothalamic nuclei, which are clusters of more densely packed cells. Unfortunately, researchers are often careless in their designation of hypothalamic cell groups: some groups are called different names by different authors, and often the same name is used by different authors to refer to different nuclei. Many authors fail to make the crucial distinction between the hypothalamic areas and nuclei. Hence the term medial preoptic nucleus is frequently used to refer to the entire medial preoptic area. These inconsistencies in nomenclature have introduced major problems of interpretation when dealing with the functions of specific parts of the hypothalamus.

Brain Research, Gender, and Sexual Orientation

D. F. Swaab, MD, PhD

Netherlands Institute for Brain Research
and University of Amsterdam

L. J. G. Gooren, MD, PhD

Free University of Amsterdam

M. A. Hofman, PhD

Netherlands Institute for Brain Research

SUMMARY. Recent brain research has revealed structural differences in the hypothalamus in relation to biological sex and sexual orientation. Differences in size and cell number of various nuclei in the hypothalamus for homosexual versus heterosexual men have recently been reported in two studies. We have found that a cluster of cells in the preoptic area of the human hypothalamus contains about twice as many cells in young adult men as in women. We have called

Dick Swaab is Professor of Neurobiology at the University of Amsterdam and Director of the Netherlands Institute for Brain Research.

Louis Gooren is Professor of Transsexuality at the Free University, Amsterdam.

Michel Hofman is a staff member of the Netherlands Institute for Brain Research.

Correspondence may be addressed to Professor Swaab, Netherlands Institute for Brain Research, Meibergdreef 33, 1105 AZ Amsterdam, The Netherlands.

[Haworth co-indexing entry note]: "Brain Research, Gender, and Sexual Orientation." Swaab, D. F., L. J. G. Gooren, and M. A. Hofman. Co-published simultaneously in *Journal of Homosexuality* (The Haworth Press, Inc.) Vol. 28, No. 3/4, 1995, pp. 283-301; and: *Sex, Cells, and Same-Sex Desire: The Biology of Sexual Preference* (ed: John P. De Cecco, and David Allen Parker) The Haworth Press, Inc., 1995, pp. 283-301. Multiple copies of this article/chapter may be purchased from The Haworth Document Delivery Center [1-800-3-HAWORTH; 9:00 a.m. - 5:00 p.m. (EST)].

this cluster the sexually dimorphic nucleus (SDN). The magnitude of the difference in the SDN depends on age. In other human research, two other hypothalamic nuclei (interstitial nuclei of the anterior hypothalamus [INAH] 2 and 3) and part of the bed nucleus of the stria terminalis (BST) have been reported to be sexually dimorphic in the human.

Sexual differentiation of the human brain takes place much later than originally claimed. At birth the SDN contains only some 20% of the cells found at 2 to 4 years of age. The cell number rapidly increases in boys and girls at the same rate until 2 to 4 years of age. After that age period, a decrease in cell number takes place in girls, but not in boys. This causes the sexual differentiation of the SDN. This postnatal period of hypothalamic differentiation indicates that, in addition to genetic factors, a multitude of environmental and psychosocial factors may have profound influence on the sexual differentiation of the brain.

No difference in SDN cell number was observed between homosexual and heterosexual men. This finding refutes Dörner's hypothesis that homosexual males have a "female" hypothalamus. However, in a sample of brains of homosexual men we did find that an area of the hypothalamus called the suprachiasmatic nucleus (SCN) contains twice as many cells as the SCN of a heterosexual group. A recent report by LeVay claims that another nucleus, INAH-3, is more than twice as large in heterosexual as in homosexual men, whereas Allen and Gorski found that the anterior commissure was larger in homosexual men than in heterosexual men or women. Preliminary research on male-to-female transsexuals is also discussed.

The functional implications of these findings in determining adult sexual orientation are as yet far from clear.

FEMALE/MALE DIFFERENTIATION OF THE HUMAN HYPOTHALAMUS

Based on observations of non-human mammalian species, many researchers believe that the human brain undergoes a female/male differentiation during its prenatal stage of development, caused by genetic information (Pillard et al., 1981; Bailey & Pillard, 1991) and the organizing effects of sex hormones. However, the stage of development in which sex hormones determine sexual differentiation of the human brain and the exact influences of hormonal actions on gender and sexual orientation are, in fact, unknown.

There are three peak periods of gonadal hormone levels which could be of importance for female/male differentiation: (1) the first half of gestation when the genitalia are formed (Reyes et al., 1974); (2) in the perinatal period; and (3) during puberty (Winter, 1978). The brain area that has been assumed to be the primary area of female/male differences in reproduction, gender identity, and sexual orientation is the hypothalamus (Dörner, 1979, 1988; Gladue et al., 1984). The supposition of Dörner and Staudt (1972) is that a structural female/male differentiation of the human hypothalamus takes place between 4 and 7 months of pregnancy. Dörner's supposition is based on two observations: (1) that during this period various hypothalamic cell groups, the supraoptic, ventromedial, and paraventricular nucleus, can be distinguished structurally; and (2) on the observation that the matrix layer around the third ventricle, in which the cells are formed, has disappeared by 7 months of gestation. Only much later did it become clear that cell death, not cell division may be the most important mechanism in female/male differentiation of the brain (Nordeen et al., 1985; Swaab & Hofman, 1988).

Sexually Dimorphic Nucleus (SDN)

The sexually dimorphic nucleus (SDN) of the preoptic area of the hypothalamus was first described in rats by Gorski et al. (1978). It is still the most conspicuous anatomical female/male difference in the mammalian brain. This cell group, which is 3 to 8 times larger in male than in female rats, is so clearly differentiated that it can even be noted with the naked eye. Lesions of the SDN affect masculine sexual behavior, i.e., mounting behavior, in the rat (Anderson et al., 1986; Turkenburg et al., 1988; De Jonge et al., 1989). However, the extent of the changes in rat sexual behavior following SDN lesions is so modest that the major function of the SDN has probably not yet been discovered.

Human SDN

We have found an SDN in the preoptic area of the human hypothalamus that is–judged by its locale and cellular structure–probably homologous to that in the rat (Swaab & Fliers, 1985). However, proof for such a homology is lacking at this moment. Measurements of the human SDN have revealed that the volume is more than twice as large and contains about twice as many cells in adult men as in women.

The human SDN corresponds to the intermediate nucleus as described by Braak and Braak (1987) and to the intermediate lateral hypothalamic area in early descriptions by Brockhaus (1942) and Feremutsch (1955). The sex difference which we observed in the SDN was not present in other hypothalamic nuclei. The magnitude of the sex difference was found not to remain constant throughout adulthood, but to depend on age (Figure 1). In men, a major reduction in SDN cell number was observed between the ages of 50 and 60 years, so that the female/male difference became smaller. In women over 70 years of age cell death was found to be more rapid than in men, the cell number dropping to only 10 to 15% of that found in early childhood. It appears that the sex difference in the SDN increases again in older people (Hofman & Swaab, 1989).

This effect of aging and the fact that sexual differentiation in the human SDN only occurs after the 4th year of age (Swaab & Hofman, 1988) might explain why Allen et al. (1989), who had a

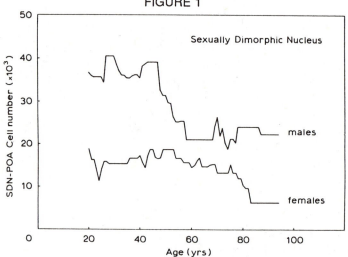

FIGURE 1

sample of human adults biased for age, did not find a significant sex difference in the size of the SDN, which they called interstitial nucleus of the anterior hypothalamus 1 (INAH-1). In the study of Allen et al., 40% of the adult subjects came from the age group in which the SDN sex difference is minimal, compared to 29% in our study (Hofman & Swaab, 1989). Moreover, subjects over 70 years of age were underrepresented in Allen's study: 20% compared to the 37.5% in case of a proportional distribution of all ages. In our study, 32% of the subjects belonged to this old age group. So it seems likely that Allen et al. were unable to establish a significant sex difference in the INAH-1 (= SDN) because they used a biased sample. If we had studied only subjects within the age distribution of Allen's study, the sex difference in SDN volume would have been reduced from 2 (Hofman & Swaab, 1989) to only 1.4 times, and this difference would not have been statistically significant. The age distribution, however, does not explain why LeVay (1991) could not find a sex difference in the volume of INAH-1 either. However, only the size of the nucleus, but not its cell numbers, have been determined by this author.

Other Human Sexually Dimorphic Nuclei

Allen et al. (1989) described two other cell groups (INAH 2 and 3) in the preoptic-anterior hypothalamic area that were larger in the male than in the female human brain. LeVay (1991) could not confirm the sex difference in INAH-2, but did find such a difference in INAH-3. Since immunocytochemical characterization of the neurons was not performed, it is not clear whether the nuclei have to be considered as islands of the bed nucleus of the stria terminalis (BST), the paraventricular nucleus (PVN), of some other structure, or as separate anatomical entities. In addition, counts of the number of cells of the INAHs in the two sexes are lacking.

A clear sex difference was described by Allen and Gorski (1990) in what they called the "darkly staining posteromedial component of the bed nucleus of the stria terminalis (BNST-dspm). They found that the volume of this area was 2.5 times larger in males than in females. However, cell counts were not performed in this study either.

Another area, the suprachiasmatic nucleus (SCN) was found to have a female/male difference in shape (Swaab et al., 1985). Though the shape of the SCN was more elongated in women and more spherical in men, no significant female/male difference was observed in volume nor total cell number of the SCN. It is not known whether this difference in shape correlates with sex differences in SCN afferent or efferent connections.

Since only few human brain structures in the two sexes have been investigated and a sex difference in relative human brain size exists (Swaab & Hofman, 1984), we expect that many more female/male differences in the human brain will be found.

Development of the Human SDN

As early as mid-pregnancy the origins of the SDN can be observed in the human fetal brain (Swaab & Hofman, 1988; Polzovic et al., 1988). Yet the SDN cell number (Figure 2) and volume at

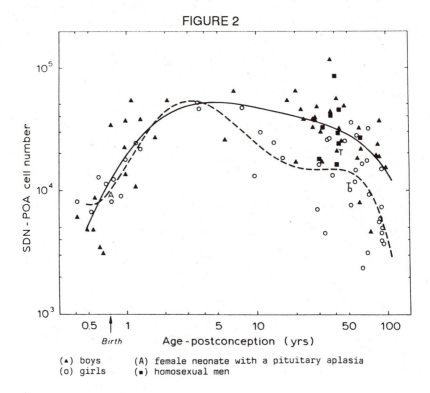

FIGURE 2

(▲) boys   (A) female neonate with a pituitary aplasia
(o) girls   (■) homosexual men

birth are only 22% and 18%, respectively, of the values found between 2 and 4 years of age. In the second half of pregnancy and during the first postnatal years there is no significant female/male difference in the size of the SDN. During the first postnatal years the SDN cell number rapidly increases in both boys and girls up to the age of 2 to 4 years. Only after this period does the human SDN differentiate according to sex. In women there is a decrease in both SDN volume and cell number, whereas in men, these remain unaltered up to the age of about 50 (Swaab & Hofman, 1988).

Our results do not support the proposition that gonadal hormones stimulate the formation of cells of the SCN during the fetal or perinatal period. In mid and later pregnancy, the levels of sex hormones are much higher in boys than in girls (Reyes et al., 1974; Winter, 1978). Yet, the SDN size and cell number have the same magnitude in boys and girls up to the age of 2 to 4 years. The discovery of the late postnatal female/male differentiation of the human hypothalamus is consistent with the observation that neither estrogen, androgen, nor progestin receptors are found in the human fetal brain at mid-pregnancy (Abramovich et al., 1987). The sex difference in the volume of the BNST-dspm seems to occur only in adulthood, although there is reason for caution in accepting these conclusions. The sample size of subjects between 10 and 20 years of age was small in the study of Allen and Gorski (1990); and it may be that the sexual dimorphism of the BST is already present in adolescents.

In general, these data support the notion that female/male differentiation of the human hypothalamus takes place after birth and before adulthood, rather than during mid-pregnancy. The observation that sexual differentiation of the human SDN does not take place earlier than 4 years after birth, calls for a reevaluation of the possible relationship between the sex dimorphism of the SDN and the perinatal testosterone peak in boys, which lasts only some 90 days (Forest & Cathiard, 1975). It is possible that this testosterone peak prevents SDN cell death which normally occurs in females. A similar mechanism is supposed to take place in the spinal cords of rats (Nordeen et al., 1985).

In addition, one may speculate that not only hormones, but also other factors (such as stress) might be involved in sexual differentiation of the brain in early childhood (cf. Swaab & Hofman, 1988; Gooren et al., 1990). A case in point is the history of a 20½-year-old man who had suffered a complete loss of testes at birth, but showed the conventional gender identity, gender role, and sexual functioning (Gooren & Cohen-Kettenis, 1988). This case may support the idea that factors other than hormones may be involved in sexual differentiation of the brain, or, conversely, that the hormonal factors in development of gender and sexual orientation exert their effects before birth.

THE HUMAN HYPOTHALAMUS, SEXUAL ORIENTATION, AND GENDER IDENTITY

We had the opportunity to study the structure of the anterior hypothalamus in relation to sexual orientation. We investigated 34 subjects; eighteen males from 22 to 74 years of age, the sexual orientation of whom was generally not known, served as a comparison group. The homosexual male group consisted of 10 non-demented AIDS subjects aged 25 to 43. Six non-demented heterosexuals, 4 males, 2 females, aged 21 to 73 years, who had also died of AIDS, served as a control group. Two areas of the hypothalamus were studied; the SDN (see before) and the suprachiasmatic nucleus (SCN). The main results were as follows: cell numbers in the SDN of the reference group, the male homosexuals, and the heterosexual subjects did not differ. However, the SCN volume in homosexual men was 1.7 times as large as that of the reference group of male subjects and contained 2.1 times as many cells (Figure 3).

The SCN is considered to be the principal component of the biological clock generating and coordinating hormonal, physiological, and behavioral circadian rhythms (i.e., day-night rhythms with a period length of nearly 24 hours) (Moore, 1978; Rusak & Zucker, 1979; Moore-Ede et al., 1982). In addition, the SCN is thought to be involved in reproduction, at least in laboratory animals (Södersten et al., 1981; Swaab et al., 1987).

A prominent theory on the causes of human sexual orientation is that it develops as a result of an interaction between the prenatal brain and sex hormones (Gladue et al., 1984; Erhardt et al. 1985; Dörner, 1988; McCormick et al. 1990). A multitude of factors,

FIGURE 3

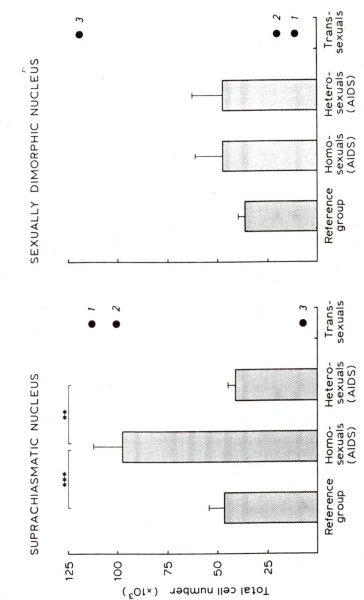

SEXUALLY DIMORPHIC NUCLEUS

SUPRACHIASMATIC NUCLEUS

Total cell number (×10³)

including genetic information (Pillard et al., 1981; Bailey & Pillard, 1991), maternal stress (Dörner et al., 1980; Anderson et al., 1986; Ellis et al., 1988), and chemicals (Swaab & Mirmiran, 1986) are thought to influence the process of female/male differentiation of the brain and sexual orientation. Recent *in vitro* observations suggest that sexual differentiation of some neuronal systems may even take place in the absence of sex hormones (Reisert & Pilgrim, 1991).

According to Dörner's hypothesis, male homosexuals would have a female differentiation of the hypothalamus. Dörner's hypothesis concerning sexual orientation became testable immediately after we had found that the SDN of the preoptic area of the human hypothalamus contains twice as many cells in men as in women (Swaab & Fliers, 1985; Swaab & Hofman, 1988; Hofman & Swaab, 1989). In contrast to this hypothesis, neither the SDN volume nor the cell number in the hypothalamus of homosexual men (who died of AIDS), however, differed from that of the male reference group in the same age range (Figure 2; Swaab & Hofman, 1988). More recent data (Figure 3) confirmed and extended this observation with a heterosexual control group of subjects also suffering from AIDS (Swaab & Hofman, 1990). The fact that no difference in SDN cell number was observed between homo- and heterosexual men who died of AIDS refutes Dörner's hypothesis that male homosexuals have a "female" hypothalamus.

The SCN and Sexual Orientation

Swaab and Hofman (1990) observed that the SCN in homosexual men contains 2.1 times as many cells as the SCN of the reference group (Figure 3). This finding cannot be attributed to differences in technical errors such as shrinkage of hypothalamic tissue during the experimental procedure. The difference in SCN cell number in relation to sexual orientation cannot, however, be directly related to female/male differentiation of the brain since no differences in SCN volume or cell number were found between males and females (Swaab et al., 1985; Hofman et al., 1988).

The larger SCN (and, in particular, an increase in the number of neurons) in homosexual men raises a number of questions about the way this difference may have developed. It appears very unlikely that homosexual behavior as such would increase the neuronal number in any brain structure. Yet the development of SCN cell numbers (Swaab et al., 1990) suggests that the explanation for the larger SCN in homosexual men most likely may be found in early brain development. At birth, the SCN contains only 13-20% of the adult number of cells, but in the postnatal period development is rapid. Cell counts reach a peak around 13-16 months after birth (Swaab et al., 1990). The SCN cell numbers found in adult homosexual men were in the same order of magnitude as found around 13-16 months after birth. The normal pattern is that the cell numbers decline to the adult value of about 35% of the peak values. In homosexual men, therefore, this postnatal cell death in the SCN seems to have been curtailed.

The possibility that sex hormones play some role in SCN development is also reinforced by an observation of Södersten et al. (1981). They showed that the amplitude of the circadian rhythm in sexual behavior, of which the SCN is the basis, is enhanced in male rats which were treated neonatally with anti-estrogens. This observation makes it more likely that a larger SCN, as reported here for homosexual men, may relate to a difference in the interaction with sex hormones during development. This possibility should be tested in animal experiments and further explored in human subjects.

One might argue that the present finding of an enlarged SCN in male homosexuals who died of AIDS only holds for a particular subset of homosexual men (i.e., those likely to acquire AIDS through contact with a high number of frequently changing sexual partners with whom receptive anal intercourse was performed [Curran et al., 1985; Van Griensven et al., 1987]). The possibility that an enlarged SCN may be related to the level of sexual activity rather than to sexual preference certainly warrants further study. Experiments in rats, however, have shown a close correlation between sexual activity and SDN size (Anderson et al., 1986). Our observation that the size of the SDN in homosexual men did not differ from that of the male reference group nor from that of the heterosexual men that died of AIDS, does not support this possibility.

An alternative explanation for the enlarged SCN found in homosexual men who died of AIDS is that it might be related to the disturbed function of the gonads in adulthood that has been found in AIDS patients (Croxson et al., 1989). Our observation that the SCN in heterosexual male AIDS patients is not enlarged seems to exclude this possible explanation. Certainly homosexual men who had not died of AIDS should be studied in the future. In this respect, it is interesting that we observed an enlarged SCN in two (primary) male-to-female transsexuals who did not suffer from AIDS (Swaab et al., 1987; Figure 3).

The functional association between sexual orientation in men and SCN size is not clear at this moment. Various observations in animals suggest that the SCN, apart from being the biological clock, may be involved in reproductive processes (Södersten et al., 1981; Swaab et al., 1987). Judged from its nucleolar size, the SCN is also activated around puberty in rats (Anderson, 1981). In addition, lesions of the SCN area in the female rat reduced the positive feedback response of gonadotropic hormones to estrogens (Gray et al., 1978; Wiegand et al., 1980). However, recently it was observed that lesions in the adult male rat SCN did not alter sexual orientation (F. H. De Jonge, F. Kruyver, & W. van de Broek, unpubl. results). This observation argues in favour of the possibility that sexual orientation and the size of the SCN are not causally related but may be subject to the same influences in development.

The relationship between a large SCN and homosexuality is unexpected and, for the time being, difficult to interpret. The relationship need not be causal in the sense that it is a necessary and sufficient condition for developing a homosexual orientation. It is imperative to study more material before definitive conclusions can be drawn. We have no information on the size of the SCN in female homosexuals, for instance, or in bisexuals. Until more data have been collected our finding is open to various interpretations. It is particularly pertinent to study the SDN and SCN in subjects whose prenatal/postnatal history has been atypical (an excess of androgens in females/a deficiency or insensitivity to androgens in males) as has been done in earlier work on sexual orientation (e.g., Money et al., 1984). Also the finding of LeVay (1991) of a larger INAH-3 and that of Allen and Gorski (1992) of a larger anterior commissure in homosexual men, can at present not be interpreted in functional terms.

Gender Identity and Transsexuality

It has been proposed that one's self-identification as a man or as a woman, like sexual orientation, develops as a result of an interaction between the developing brain and sex hormones. Transsexuality is considered to be the result of a disturbance of this interaction (Gladue et al., 1984; Dörner, 1988). In view of the similarity between the hypotheses on the development of gender identity and sexual orientation, it is of interest that 60% of the male-to-female transsexuals are androphile and that some 10% are biphile. In no less than 95% of the cases, female-to-male transsexuals are gynaecophilic (Coleman, Bockting, & Gooren, 1992). These data indicate that indeed similar (but as yet unknown) mechanisms may play a role in the development of both gender identity and sexual orientation.

Finally, we were given the opportunity to study the hypothalami of 3 male-to-female transsexuals (Figure 4). Two of them appeared to have a large SCN with high cell numbers and a small SDN with low cell numbers. The third transsexual subject, however, had a small SCN and a large SDN. These two different patterns could not be related to sexual orientation of these three subjects in any simple way. These findings suggest, however, that a relationship might exist between (1) a large SCN and small SDN and primary transsexuality (i.e., awareness of gender problems from early childhood onwards) on the one hand, and (2) a small SCN and large SDN and secondary transsexuality (i.e., awareness of transsexuality later in life) on the other. It is obvious that more data are necessary in order to establish whether such a relationship indeed exists.

CONCLUSIONS

In keeping with observations in many mammalian species the human hypothalamus has been hypothesized to undergo sexual differentiation during development due to an organizing effect of sex hormones. We have found a sexually dimorphic nucleus (SDN) in the preoptic area of the human hypothalamus that contains about twice as many cells in young adult men as in women. The magnitude of the sex difference in the SDN depends on age. In the litera-

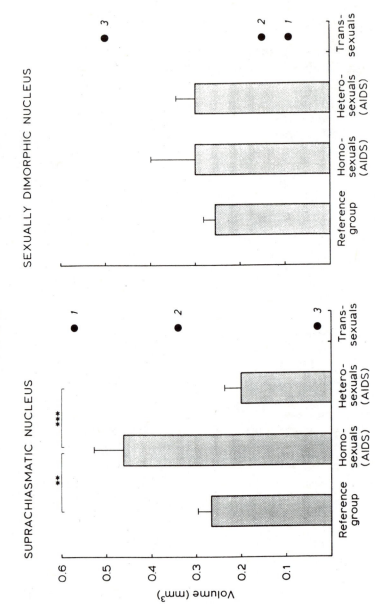

FIGURE 4

296

ture two other hypothalamic nuclei (INAH 2 and 3) and a part of the bed nucleus of the stria terminalis (BST) have been reported to be sexually dimorphic in humans.

At birth, the SDN contains only some 20% of the cell number found at 2 to 4 years of age. The cell number rapidly increases in boys and girls at the same rate until 2 to 4 years of age, after which the SDN differentiates according to sex due to a decrease in cell numbers in girls. This period of sexual differentiation of the human hypothalamus is much later than formerly presumed. This offers the possibility that, in addition to genetic information, a multitude of postnatal factors may interact with the process of sexual differentiation of the brain, e.g., hormones, other chemical compounds, and psycho-social factors.

No difference in SDN cell number was observed between homosexual and heterosexual men. This refutes the most global formulation of Dörner's hypothesis that male homosexuals would have a "female" hypothalamus. However, in a sample of brains of homosexual men we found that the suprachiasmatic nucleus (SCN) contained twice as many cells as in the brains of the reference group. The observation that a similarly enlarged SCN was present in a woman with Prader-Willi syndrome suggests that (sex) hormones and SCN development might be interrelated. Recent reports claimed INAH-3 to be more than twice as large in heterosexual men as in homosexual men (LeVay, 1991) and the anterior commissure to be larger in homosexual men (Allen & Gorski, 1992). Preliminary data suggest that the SCN is large and the SDN small in primary male-to-female transsexuals and that the SCN is small and the SDN large in secondary male-to-female transsexuals.

In conclusion: differences in size and cell number have been reported in a number of hypothalamic nuclei in relation to sexual orientation and gender identity. However, the functional implications of these findings are far from clear.

AUTHOR NOTE

Brain material was obtained from the Netherlands Brain Bank (coordinator Dr. R. Ravid) and from Dr. L. J. G. Gooren (Dept. of Endocrinology, Free University, Amsterdam, The Netherlands), Dr. R. S. Williams (Neuropathology Laboratory, Shriver Center, Walton, USA), Dr. L. Mrzljak and Dr. I. Kostovic (Dept. of

Anatomy, Univ. of Zagreb, Yugoslavia), Dr. P. G. Barth (Dept. of Pediatrics and Neurology, AMC, Univ. of Amsterdam, The Netherlands), and Dr. H. P. H. Kremer (Dept. Neurology, Univ. of Leyden, The Netherlands). General pathology and neuropathology were performed either at the Free University of Amsterdam (Dr. W. Kamphorst) or at the AMC, Univ. of Amsterdam (Dr. D. Troost). We want to thank Mr. B. Fisser for his technical assistance and Ms. W. T. P. Verweij for her secretarial help.

REFERENCES

Abramovich, D. R., Davidson, I. A., Longstaff, A., & Pearson, C. K. (1987). Sexual differentiation of the human midtrimester brain. *European Journal of Obstetrics, Gynecology and Reproductive Biology, 25*, 7-14.

Allen, L. S., Hines, M., Shryne, J. E., & Gorski, R. A. (1989). Two sexually dimorphic cell groups in the human brain. *Journal of Neuroscience, 9*, 497-506.

Allen, L. S., & Gorski, R. A. (1990). Sex difference in the bed nucleus of the stria terminalis of the human brain. *J. Comp. Neurol., 302*, 697-706.

Allen, L. S., & Gorski, R. A. (1992). Sexual orientation and the size of the anterior commissure in the human brain. *Proc. Natl. Acad. Sci. USA, 89*, 7199-7202.

Anderson, C. H. (1981). Nucleolus: Changes at puberty in neurons of the suprachiasmatic nucleus and the preoptic area. *Exp. Neurol., 74*, 780-786.

Anderson, R. H., Fleming, D. E., Rhees, R. W., & Kinghorn, E. (1986). Relationship between sexual activity, plasma testosterone and the volume of the sexually dimorphic nucleus of the preoptic area in prenatally stressed and non-stressed rats. *Brain Res., 370*, 1-10.

Bailey, J. M., & Pillard, R. C. (1991). A genetic study of male sexual orientation. *Arch. Gen. Psychiatry, 48*, 1089-1096.

Bailey, J. M., Willerman, L., & Parks, C. (1991). A test of the maternal stress theory of human male homosexuality. *Arch. Sex. Behav., 20*, 277-293.

Braak, H., & Braak, E. (1987). The hypothalamus of the human adult: Chiasmatic region. *Anat. Embryol., 176*, 315-330.

Brockhaus, H. (1942). Beitrag zur normalen Anatomie des Hypothalamus und der Zona incerta bei Menschen. *J. Psychol. Neurol., 51*, 96-196.

Coleman, E., Bockting, W. O., & Gooren, L. J. G. (1993). Homosexual and bisexual identity in sex-reassigned female-to-male transsexuals. *Arch. Sex. Behav., 22*, 37-50.

Croxson, T. S., Chapman, W. E., Miller, L. K., Levit, C. D., Senie, R., & Zumoff, B. (1989). Changes in the hypothalamic-pituitary-gonadal axis in human immunodeficiency virus-infected homosexual men. *J. Clin. Endocrinol. Metab., 68*, 317-321.

Curran, J. W., Meade Morgan, W., Hardy, A. M., Joffe, H. W., Darrow, W. W., & Dowdle, W. R. (1985). The epidemiology of AIDS: Current status and future prospects. *Science, 229*, 1352-1357.

De Jonge, F. H., Louwerse, A. L., Ooms, M. P., Evers, P., & Van de Poll, N. E.

(1989). Lesions of the SDN-POA inhibit sexual behavior of male Wistar rats. *Brain Res. Bull., 23*, 483-492.

Dörner, G. (1979). Psychoneuroendocrine aspects of brain development and reproduction: In L. Zichella & P. Pancheri (Eds.), *Psychoneuroendocrinology in reproduction: An interdisciplinary approach* (pp. 239-252). Amsterdam: Elsevier.

Dörner, G. (1988). Neuroendocrine response to estrogen and brain differentiation in heterosexuals, homosexuals, and transsexuals. *Arch. Sexual Behav., 17*, 57-75.

Dörner, G., Geiser, T., Ahrens, L., Krell, L., Munz, G., Sieler, H., Kittner, E., & Muller, H. (1980). Prenatal stress and possible aetiogenetic factor homosexuality in human males. *Endokrinologie, 75*, 365-368.

Dörner, G., & Staudt, J. (1972). Vergleichende morphologische Untersuchungen der Hypothalamusdifferenzierung bei Ratte und Mensch. *Endokrinologie, 59*, 152-155.

Ehrhardt, A. A., Meyer-Bahlburg, H. F. L., Rosen, L. R., Feldman, J. F., Veridiano, N. P., Zimmerman, I., & McEwen, B. S. (1985). Sexual orientation after prenatal exposure to exogenous estrogen. *Arch. Sex. Behav., 14*, 57-75.

Ellis, L., Ames, M. A., Peckham, W., & Burk, D. (1988). Sexual orientation of human offspring may be altered by severe maternal stress during pregnancy. *J. Sex. Res., 25*, 152-157.

Feremutsch, K. (1955). Strukturanalyse des menschlichen Hypothalamus. *Monatschr. Psychiatr. Neurol., 121*, 87-113.

Forest, M., & Cathiard, A. M. (1975). Patterns of plasma testosterone and Δ-4-androstenedione in normal newborns: Evidence for testicular activity at birth. *J. Clin. Endocrinol. Metab., 41*, 977-981.

Gladue, B. A., Green, R., & Helleman, R. E. (1984). Neuroendocrine response to estrogen and sexual orientation. *Science, 225*, 1496-1499.

Gooren, L. J. G., & Cohen-Kettenis, P. (1988). Erotosexuality in a man lacking physiological postnatal androgen exposure. *J. Psychol. Hum. Sexuality, 1*, 129-135.

Gooren, L. J. G., Fliers, E., & Courtney, K. (1990). Biological determinants of sexual orientation. *Ann. Rev. Sex. Res., 1*, 175-196.

Gorski, R. A., Gordon, J. H., Shryne, J. E., & Southam, A. M. (1978). Evidence for a morphological sex difference within the medial preoptic area of the rat brain. *Brain Res., 148*, 333-346.

Gray, G. D., Södersten, P., Tallentrie, D., & Davidson, J. M. (1978). Effects of lesions in various structures of the suprachiasmatic-preoptic region on LH regulation and sexual behavior in female rats. *Neuroendocrinology, 25*, 174-191.

Hofman, M. A., Fliers, E., Goudsmit, E., & Swaab, D. F. (1988). Morphometric analysis of the suprachiasmatic and paraventricular nuclei in the human brain. *J. Anat., 160*, 127-143.

Hofman, M. A., & Swaab, D. F. (1989). The sexually dimorphic nucleus of the preoptic area in the human brain: A comparative morphometric study. *J. Anat., 164*, 55-72.

LeVay, S. (1991). A difference in hypothalamic structure between heterosexual and homosexual men. *Science, 253*, 1034-1037.

McCormick, C. M., Witelson, S. F., & Kingstone, E. (1990). Left-handedness in homosexual men and women: Neuroendocrine implications. *Psychoneuroendocrinology, 15*, 69-76.

Money, J., Schwartz, M., & Lewis, V. G. (1984). Adult erotosexual status and fetal hormonal masculinization: 46,XX congenital virilizing adrenal hyperplasia and 46,XY androgen-insensitivity syndrome compared. *Psychoneuroendocrinology, 9*, 405-414.

Moore, R. Y. (1978). Central neural control of circadian rhythms. In W. F. Ganong & L. Martini (Eds.), *Frontiers in neuroendocrinology* (pp. 185-206), Vol. 5. New York: Raven Press.

Moore-Ede, M. C., Sulzman, F. M., & Fuller, C. A. (1982). *The clocks that time us: Physiology of the circadian timing system.* Cambridge, MA: Harvard University Press.

Nordeen, E. J., Nordeen, K. W., Sengelaub, P. R., & Arnold, A. P. (1985). Androgens prevent normally occurring cell death in a sexually dimorphic spinal nucleus. *Science, 229*, 671-673.

Pillard, R. C., Poumadere, J., & Carretta, R. A. (1981). Is homosexuality familial? A review, some data, and a suggestion. *Arch. Sex. Behavior, 10*, 465-475.

Polzovic, A., Marinkovic, R., Gudovic, R., Mihic, N., & Grkovic, D. (1988). Vascularization of the preoptic area in the human fetus. In M. Bajic (Ed.), *Advances in the biosciences* (pp. 143-146), Vol. 70. Neuron, Brain and Behaviour. Oxford: Pergamon Press.

Reisert, I., & Pilgrim, C. (1991). Sexual differentiation of monoaminergic neurons–genetic or epigenetic? *TINS, 14*, 468-473.

Reyes, F. I., Boroditsky, R. S., Winter, J. S. D., & Faiman, C. (1974). Studies on human sexual development. II. Fetal and maternal serum gonadotropin and sex steroid concentrations. *J. Clin. Endocrinol. Metab., 38*, 612-617.

Rusak, B., & Zucker, I. (1979). Neural regulation of circadian rhythms. *Physiol. Rev., 59*, 449-526.

Södersten, P., Hansen, S., & Srebro, B. (1981). Suprachiasmatic lesions disrupt the daily rhythmicity in the sexual behaviour of normal male rats and of male rats treated neonatally with anti-estrogen. *J. Endocrinol., 88*, 125-130.

Swaab, D. F., & Fliers, E. (1985). A sexually dimorphic nucleus in the human brain. *Science, 228*, 1112-1115.

Swaab, D. F., & Hofman, M. A. (1984). Sexual differentiation of the human brain. A historical perspective. In G. J. De Vries, J. P. C. De Bruin, H. B. M. Uylings, & M. A. Corner (Eds.), *Sex differences in the brain. Progress in brain research* (pp. 361-374), Vol. 61. Amsterdam: Elsevier.

Swaab, D. F., & Hofman, M. A. (1988). Sexual differentiation of the human hypothalamus: Ontogeny of the sexually dimorphic nucleus of the preoptic area. *Dev. Brain Res., 44*, 314-318.

Swaab, D. F., & Hofman, M. A. (1990). An enlarged suprachiasmatic nucleus in homosexual men. *Brain Res., 537*, 141-148.

Swaab, D. F., & Mirmiran, M. (1986). Functional teratogenic effects of chemicals on the developing brain. In M. M. Cohen (Ed.), *Monographs in Neural Sciences* (pp. 45-57), Vol. 12. Basel: S. Karger.

Swaab, D. F., Fliers, E., & Partiman, T. S. (1985). The suprachiasmatic nucleus of the human brain in relation to sex, age and senile dementia. *Brain Res., 342*, 37-44.

Swaab, D. F., Roozendaal, B., Ravid, R., Velis, D. N., Gooren, L. J. G., & Williams, R. S. (1987). Suprachiasmatic nucleus in aging, Alzheimer's disease, transsexuality and Prader-Willi syndrome. In E. R. de Kloet, V. M. Wiegant, & D. De Wied (Eds.), *Neuropeptides and brain function. Progress in brain research* (pp. 301-311), Vol. 72. Amsterdam: Elsevier.

Swaab, D. F., Hofman, M. A., & Honnebier, M. B. O. M. (1990). Development of vasopressin neurons in the human suprachiasmatic nucleus in relation to birth. *Devel. Brain Res., 52*, 289-293.

Turkenburg, J. L., Swaab, D. F., Endert, E., Louwerse, A. L., & Van de Poll, N. E. (1988). Effects of lesions of the sexually dimorphic nucleus on sexual behavior of testosterone-treated female Wistar rats. *Brain Res. Bull., 22*, 215-224.

Van Griensven, G. J. P., Tielman, R. A. P., Goudsmit, J., V. d. Noordaa, J., De Wolf, F., De Vroome, E. M. M., & Coutinho, R. A. (1987). Risk factors and prevalence of HIV antibodies in homosexual men in The Netherlands. *Am. J. Epidem., 125*, 1048-1057.

Wiegand, S. J., Terasawa, E., Bridson, W. E., & Gray, R. W. (1980). Effects of discrete lesions of preoptic and suprachiasmatic structures in the female rat: Alterations in the feedback regulation of gonadotropin secretion. *Neuroendocrinology, 31*, 147-157.

Winter, J. S. D. (1978). Prepubertal and pubertal endocrinology. In F. Falkner & J. M. Tanner (Eds.), *Human Growth. I. Principles and Prenatal Growth* (pp. 183-213), Vol. 2. London: Baillière Tindall.

Science and Belief:
Psychobiological Research
on Sexual Orientation

William Byne, MD, PhD

Mount Sinai School of Medicine

SUMMARY. The dominant paradigm that generates support for biological theories of sexual orientation has profound conceptual flaws. Not only does it equate the motor patterns of copulation in rodents with sexual orientation in humans, it assumes that the brain regions that regulate these behaviors in rodents participate in governing sexual orientation in humans. Reports of sex differences in the rodent brain generate speculation concerning the existence of differences in the human brain associated not only with sex but also with sexual orientation. Thus, recent years have witnessed numerous attempts to demonstrate that the brains of homosexuals exhibit characteristics that are typical of the opposite sex. In some cases, these attempts have come decades after persuasive evidence suggested that the brain characteristic in question does not differ between the sexes in humans. If a particular feature of the human brain does not differ between men and women, the phrase "typical of the opposite sex" is meaningless. It is, then, illogical to argue–even from the perspective of the biologically deterministic paradigm–that the feature should be typical of the oppo-

William Byne is Director of the Laboratory of Neuroanatomy in the Department of Psychiatry at Mt. Sinai School of Medicine, New York City, and a psychiatrist in private practice.

Correspondence may be addressed: 590 West End Ave., Suite 1D, New York, NY 10024.

[Haworth co-indexing entry note]: "Science and Belief: Psychobiological Research on Sexual Orientation." Byne, William. Co-published simultaneously in *Journal of Homosexuality* (The Haworth Press, Inc.) Vol. 28, No. 3/4, 1995, pp. 303-344; and: *Sex, Cells, and Same-Sex Desire: The Biology of Sexual Preference* (ed: John P. De Cecco, and David Allen Parker) The Haworth Press, Inc., 1995, pp. 303-344. Multiple copies of this article/chapter may be purchased from The Haworth Document Delivery Center [1-800-3-HAWORTH; 9:00 a.m. - 5:00 p.m. (EST)].

site sex in homosexuals. This paper analyzes the assumptions and evidence that support biologically deterministic theories of sexual orientation. It is concluded that support for these theories derives as much from their appeal to prevailing cultural ideology as from their scientific merit. This appeal may explain why seriously flawed studies pass readily through the peer review process and become incorporated rapidly into the biologically deterministic canon where they remain viable even when replication attempts repeatedly fail.

As long as there are entrenched social and political distinctions between sexes, races or classes, there will be forms of science whose main function is to rationalize and legitimize these distinctions.

Elizabeth Fee, 1979, p. 433

Western medicine's interest in homosexuality is a relatively recent development. Prior to the late eighteenth century homosexual behavior was viewed either as a sin, within the domain of the church, or as a crime, and hence within the jurisdiction of governments (Katz, 1992). Homosexuality came within the domain of medicine only after eighteenth-century reconceptualizations of gender established the concept of sexual orientation (Trumbach, 1989) and led, in the nineteenth century, to the view of homosexuality as a disorder of sexual desire. Interest in the etiology of this "disorder" has waxed and waned over the past century and a half, with most authorities arguing for the primacy of biological, psychological, or social factors.

During the 1970s the biological theories gained in popularity as some social science scholars abandoned psychosocial for biological theories (Bell, Weinburg, & Hammersmith, 1981) and as tremendous progress was made in our understanding of the manner in which sexual behaviors in laboratory animals are regulated by the endocrine and nervous systems (Goy & McEwen, 1980). During the 1980s convincing evidence demonstrated that learning and environment influence not only behaviors but the structure and chemistry of the brain itself (Bhide & Bedi, 1984; Kraemer et al., 1984; Turner & Greenough, 1985). As a result, the nature/nurture debate entered a dormant period and a semblance of an interactionist approach emerged, but little attention was paid to the ways in which biology and experience might actually interact to shape sexual orientation. Instead, advocates for the primacy of either nature or nurture concluded that there must be some role for the other, if only to the extent that their own theories lacked total explanatory power. It became fashionable, even for psychoanalysts to uncritically endorse the evidence favoring a direct role for biological factors in shaping sexual orientation (e.g., genes for homosexuality and critical periods for hormones to shape particular aspects of sexual identity and sexual partner selection). Others often failed to appreciate the distinction between the biological substrate that necessarily underlies all behaviors of biological beings and the specific biological constraints on the potentialities of sexuality advocated by the strict biological determinists.

During the past three years, as yet uncorroborated studies have reported that the size of three brain structures varies with sexual orientation in men (Swaab & Hofman, 1990; LeVay, 1991; Allen & Gorski, 1992). During this same period genetic studies have suggested that sexual orientation is moderately heritable in men (Bailey & Pillard, 1991) and women (Bailey et al., 1993), and that genes predisposing to homosexuality in men may reside in the tip of the X chromosome (Hamer et al., 1993). These studies have revived the nature/nurture debate as, taken at face value, they seem to shift the weight of evidence heavily toward the primacy of biological influences. For example, writing in the *New York Times,* Bailey and Pillard (December 17, 1991, p. 19) asserted, "Science is rapidly converging on the conclusion that sexual orientation is *innate*" (emphasis added).

This paper has two broad goals: (1) to examine the assumptions and evidence that support the notion that sexual orientation is appreciably and *directly* influenced by biological factors; and (2) to show how ideology at the level of the peer review process encourages the publication of flawed studies that promote the dominant ideology at the expense of scientific progress.

BASIC ASSUMPTIONS

The social, cultural, and historical contexts within which scientists work impose more than methodological constraints on their studies. They also impose conceptual constraints–influencing the research questions that scientists find salient as well as the hypotheses that they generate and find worthy of consideration or dismiss. These conceptual constraints also act as blinders that prevent plausible alternative hypotheses from even being formulated, much less tested.

Two broad assumptions are readily apparent within the psychobiological literature that addresses itself to the issue of sexual orientation. According to the first assumption, hereafter referred to as the "intersex assumption," homosexuals manifest a state of sexual differentiation that in some ways is intermediate between heterosexual men and heterosexual women. According to the second assumption, hereafter referred to as the "defect assumption," this intermediate state of differentiation results from some developmental anomaly–either biological or psychosocial. As discussed below each of these assumptions is questionable and premised on a number of equally questionable presuppositions.

The intersex assumption is evident in the pervasive conceptualization of homosexuality as "central nervous system hermaphroditism" (see Meyer-Bahlburg, 1984). This concept has led to the search in male homosexuals for female-typical brain structures, cognitive profiles, and hormonal measures and responses (LeVay, 1991; Allen & Gorski, 1992; Gladue et al., 1984; Dörner et al., 1975, McCormack & Witelson, 1991). For this assumption to be valid, the brains of heterosexual men and women must differ with regard to the observed parameters, though the required sex differences have not been conclusively demonstrated. This assumption also equates the androphilia (attraction to men) of homosexual men with the androphilia of heterosexual women, and, conversely, the gynephilia (attraction to women) of homosexual women with that of heterosexual men. However, to this author's knowledge, no research has even addressed, let alone validated, these equations.

The validity of the assumption that homosexual men are in some ways physically or psychologically similar to women is, perhaps, buttressed by the observation that some gay men exhibit characteristics that are stereotypically associated with women. However the assumption that desire for sexual relations with a man is necessarily feminine is a limited and culture-bound concept. It is perhaps a more common belief in societies in which the social stigmatization of homosexuality and the illegality of homosexual behaviors prevents many, if not most, homosexuals from publicly identifying themselves as such. Such an assumption was not present in societies that celebrated the homosexual exploits of archetipically masculine heroes such as Hercules, Achilles, and Julius Caesar (Boswell, 1980). Nor does it apply to cultures in which receptive fellatio is believed to be a prerequisite for attaining manhood (Herdt, 1984).

The "defect" assumption is evident in the recent biological literature, even in the writings of authors who consider themselves to be gay affirmative. It is responsible for their descriptions of homosexuality as an "affliction" (Renshaw, 1988), a "genetic disarrangement" (Kaplan & Sadock, 1985, p. 19), or a hormonal "defect," "deficiency," "abnormality," or "aberration" (Goy & McEwen, 1980, p. 72; Meyer-Bahlburg, 1977, p. 317; West, 1983, p. 223). This assumption is rooted in the tradition of teleology, which as described by Gooren (this volume) is the belief that natural processes are shaped by a pre-established purpose. Homosexual behavior is thus thought to be abnormal if it is perceived to defeat the presumed purpose of eroticism and sexuality, namely reproduction and preservation of the species. But sexual behavior may serve a variety of social functions other than reproduction (de Waal, 1987). Homosexual behavior may also be seen as abnormal if it is perceived to be "unnatural." However, homosexual behaviors occur in almost every mammalian species studied (Churchill, 1967, p. 60). Rather than being at cross purposes with evolutionary success, in at least some species, such as dolphins (Richard Connor, personal communication) and bonobo chimpanzees (de Waal, 1987), homosexual behaviors may even promote social cohesion.

Moreover, some human societies have required homosexual relations of all males. Ford and Beach (1951) suggested that the prevalence of homosexual behavior in such cultures argues against the notion that it only arises within a pathological context. However, among animals, sexual behavior directed exclusively toward members of the same sex is exceedingly rare outside the neuroendocrine laboratory. Exclusive homosexuality in adulthood is also exceedingly rare or unheard of in human cultures that require homosexual relations of all males (Money & Ehrhardt, 1972).

According to Gadpaille (1980), on the basis of cross-species and cross-cultural observations, "To be within the purview of biological normalcy, homosexuality cannot be preferential or intrapsychically obligatory in adulthood." That is, by relegating intrapsychic processes to the biological domain, he implies that exclusively homosexual behavior cannot occur in biologically normal individuals. However, application of the same cross-species criteria could raise questions concerning the "biological normalcy" of behavior that is exclusively heterosexual.

BIOLOGY: THEORIES AND EVIDENCE

Genetic Evidence

Most biological speculation concerning the development of sexual orientation involves the disciplines of genetics and endocrinology. The genetic research has been reviewed recently by Byne and Parsons (1993) and by McGuire (this volume). In summary, there is little agreement concerning the degree to which sexual orientation is heritable (Bailey & Pillard, 1991; King & McDonald, 1992; Bailey et al., 1993). While some authors have speculated about the existence of "genes for homosexuality," genes in themselves cannot directly specify any behavior or cognitive schema. Instead, genes direct a particular pattern of RNA synthesis which in turn specifies the production of a particular protein. There are necessarily many intervening pathways between a gene and a specific behavior and even more intervening variables between a gene and a pattern that involves both thinking and behaving. The term "homosexual gene" is, therefore, without meaning, unless one proposes that a particular gene, perhaps through a hormonal mechanism, organizes the brain specifically to support a homosexual orientation.

Such "homosexual genes" are not required for homosexuality to appear heritable. For example, if a hypothetical gene influenced a particular temperamental trait in a manner that would influence how individuals react with their environment as their sexuality develops, that gene might, in certain environments, predispose a person to the development of a homosexual orientation (see Byne & Parsons, 1993, for further discussion). In such a scenario, experiential factors would be the proximate cause of sexual orientation. Nevertheless, homosexuality would appear to be heritable. This is because heritability estimates merely indicate the degree to which a given outcome is associated with genetic factors. They tell us nothing about the nature of those genetic factors, nor about the manner by which they influence a given outcome.

Since the review by Byne and Parsons (1993), Dean Hamer's group at the National Institutes of Health has published a study suggesting that genes influencing sexual orientation may reside on the X chromosome (Hamer et al., 1993). Owing to its conceptual complexity, that study is perhaps the most misunderstood of the recent biological studies pertaining to sexual orientation. A popular misconception is illustrated by the following quote from *Clinical Psychiatry News* (Schuster, 1993): "*Science* last month published a study that shows a particular genetic sequence on the tip of the long arm of the X chromosome. That sequence is the same in 33 of 40 pairs of gay brothers." That statement is misleading because it suggests that the 66 men from the 33 concordant pairs were shown to share a common sequence. However, the study merely showed that in 33 of the 40 pairs, both brothers shared a common sequence. By analogy, each pair of brothers would be expected to share a common last name. Because the study included 40 pairs, one would expect there to be approximately 40 different last names. The logic of the quote from *Clinical Psychiatry News,* however, would imply that all 80 men in the study had the same last name. The study of Hamer et al. is discussed in detail by McGuire elsewhere in this volume.

Hormonal Evidence

Historically, maleness has been equated with the testicular hormone, testosterone. On the basis of the intersex assumption much attention has focused on the speculation that homosexuality in men results from low testosterone levels in adults. Similarly, there has been speculation that homosexuality in women is the result of elevated testosterone levels. As reviewed by Byne and Parsons (1993) and by Gooren (this volume) this speculation remained influential for three decades despite the absence of convincing data and despite the failure of hormonal treatments to alter sexual orientation in adult homosexuals. The current consensus opinion is that no causal relationship exists between adult hormonal status and sexual orientation (Meyer-Bahlburg, 1984).

The Prenatal Hormonal Hypothesis

Currently, the major impetus for speculation and research concerning an endocrinological basis for sexual orientation derives from animal studies. These studies show that one can elicit a female-typical mating behavior, lordosis, from male rats that were experimentally deprived of testosterone during a critical phase of early development (see Meyer-Bahlburg, 1984). Conversely, mounting, which is often accepted as a male-typical sexual behavior (although it is exhibited readily by normal females of some species, especially when they are in heat), is displayed with increased frequency in female rats that were exposed to testosterone in early development. Such studies have established the prenatal hormonal hypothesis for sexual differentiation of the rodent brain. Based on the intersex assumption researchers have applied this hypothesis to sexual orientation in humans (see Byne & Parsons, 1993, for further discussion). According to this hypothesis heterosexuality in men and homosexuality in women result from prenatal exposure to high levels of androgens (i.e., so-called "male sex hormones," one of which is testosterone), while homosexuality in men and heterosexuality in women result when fetal androgen levels are low enough to allow the brain to retain its intrinsically female pattern of organization (see Torand-Allerand, 1993, for a criticism of the view that the brain is intrinsically female).

The problems inherent in using studies of mating behaviors in rodents such as mounting and lordosis to formulate a theory of sexual orientation in humans are immense. Nevertheless, much of the literature regards procedures that increase lordosis in male rodents as appropriate models for elucidating the origins of homosexuality in men. Those that increase mounting behavior in female rodents are often viewed as models for understanding the origins of homosexuality in women.

Some of the same hormones that participate in masculinization of the rodent brain also participate in masculinization of the external genitalia. Thus, one might question how the prenatal hormonal theory could account for exclusive homosexuality in individuals with normal genitalia for their genetic sex. The concept of the "critical period" is often invoked to account for this discrepancy.

Sexual differentiation of the brain in rodents is not a singular process but a chain of events occurring in an overlapping temporal sequence. Various events in this sequence are largely independent of one another and may involve different hormones and different regions of the brain (see Goy & McEwen, 1980; Olsen, 1983). Each event is thought to be maximally sensitive to the organizing actions of testosterone during a specific period of development, often referred to as its "critical period" (Goy & McEwen, 1980). To account for exclusively homosexual behavior in men with normal male genitalia, one needs only to propose that the critical period for genital differentiation occurs before, after, or in between the periods in which sexual orientation is determined. In rodents, however, the developmental period for behavioral masculinization of the brain, marked by increasing mounting behavior, overlaps with the period of external genital differentiation. To this author's knowledge, developmental testosterone exposure that results in any degree of genital masculinization in laboratory animals of either sex is invariably associated with some degree of mounting. For example, male rats castrated shortly after birth will exhibit both lordosis and mounting. Thus, the prenatal hormonal hypothesis *as derived from animal studies* cannot account for *exclusively* homosexual behavior in men with normal male genitalia.

In the neuroendocrine laboratory, the neonatally castrated male rat displaying lordosis when mounted by another male is considered the homosexual. It is crucial to note that the display of lordosis is little more than a reflex that can be reliably elicited not only by the appropriate sexual stimulus but also by a nonsexual stimulus such as the touch of the researcher's hand (Pfaff, 1980). Thus, perhaps the only sexually motivated and male-oriented animal in this laboratory situation is the mounter. Ironically, this male is considered to be the model for heterosexuality in men and, therefore, escapes scientific scrutiny and labeling. Similarly the female rat that displays lordosis when mounted by another female rat provides the model for heterosexuality in women. If we apply such reasoning to humans, then we would be forced to conclude that only one partner is homosexual when two same-sex individuals engage in sexual intercourse and that the homosexual is obvious from the positions taken. The paradigm for rats thus focuses on copulatory behavior and ignores partner selection, whereas in humans it is the latter that distinguishes homosexuals from heterosexuals.

HOMOSEXUALITY AND THE BRAIN

Premised on the intersex assumption, numerous studies have attempted to demonstrate that homosexuals have brains that are in some ways characteristic of the opposite sex. This approach is valid only to the extent that relevant sex differences can be clearly identified in the human brain. If the parameter in question is not sexually dimorphic to begin with, the argument that it should be characteristic of the opposite sex in homosexuals is illogical.

Is the Human Brain Sexually Dimorphic?

Given the facts that there are sex differences in virtually every other organ system, that various regions of the brain contain receptors for gonadal steroids ("sex hormones"), and that men and women have different levels of these hormones in their circulations, it would perhaps be surprising if no sex differences existed in the brain. However, the simple facts are: (1) No presumed sexually dimorphic cognitive or behavioral brain function has been shown to be independent of learning and experience. (2) Even though reports of structural sex differences abound, the only structural sex difference in the human brain that has proven to be consistently replicable is the dimorphism in its overall size, which is larger in men; the extent to which this difference is simply in proportion to the sex difference in body size is controversial (Schluter, 1992). (3) Even if structural sex differences were to be clearly established, present knowledge of brain function would not permit us to draw any definitive conclusions regarding their neurophysiological significance, let alone their psychological or social consequences. (4) Historically, claims for sex differences in the human brain have been interpreted, without sound scientific rationale, in a manner that legitimizes sexual stereotypes and discrimination.

DO HOMOSEXUALS HAVE INTERSEX BRAINS?

Neurohormonal Studies

Many reviews of the literature pertaining to brain sex differences include a discussion of the brain's involvement in regulating the secretion of gonadotropic hormones (pituitary hormones that among other things participate in regulating the menstrual cycle). For example, on the basis of rodent research it is concluded that, "the cyclic release of gonadotropic hormones from the pituitary in females is known to reflect a sex difference in the brain rather than [in] the pituitary" (Kelly, 1987). Such reviews then explain that this sex difference develops in response to sex differences in early testosterone exposure (Gorski, 1978; Kelly, 1987). The failure of the authors of such reviews to include relevant human and nonhuman primate data invites readers (including scientists not schooled in the intricacies of comparative endocrinology) who know that women but not men have menstrual cycles to assume that brain-pituitary relationships are sexually dimorphic and developmentally influenced by testosterone in humans as in rats. The assumption that this neuroendocrine sex difference resides in the human brain as well as in the rat brain lends undue credence to the notion that other sex differences in the rat brain also exist in the human.

Belief that a brain sex difference is involved in regulating the menstrual cycle in women has been so strong that, until recently, it was taken as an established truth rather than as a hypothesis in need of experimental verification. Thus, without first demonstrating that human brains are sexually dimorphic in this regard, two laboratories assessed hormonal correlates of the brain's ability to support cyclic ovarian function in attempts to demonstrate that male homosexuals have female-typical brains (Dörner et al., 1975; Gladue et al., 1984; for details and discussion, see Byne & Parsons, 1993; Gooren, this volume; Banks & Gartrell, this volume). These reports came decades after reports in the clinical and primate literature suggested that the brain's potential to regulate the ovarian cycle is not sexually dimorphic in monkeys nor in humans (Bartter et al., 1951; Goy & Resko, 1972; Hodges & Hearn, 1978; Karsch et al., 1973; Speroff, 1965; Wilkins et al., 1952). Subsequently, when the hypothesized sex difference was researched directly in humans (see Gooren, this volume) and nonhuman primates (Norman & Spies, 1986) it could not be confirmed. More recent studies have failed to demonstrate that hormonal responses discriminate among men on the basis of sexual orientation (Gooren, 1986a,b; Hendricks et al., 1989; see also Gooren, this volume; Banks & Gartrell, this volume).

A corollary of the hypothesis that the brain mechanism that regulates the menstrual cycle is sexually dimorphic and female-typical in homosexual men is that it should be male-typical in homosexual women. If this were true one would predict that lesbians would not have menstrual cycles and would consequently be infertile. The growing number of lesbian mothers attests to the fallacy of that notion.

Sex Differences in Cognition and Brain Lateralization?

In recent years there has been considerable interest in delineating possible biological substrates of presumed sex differences in cognitive abilities such as male superiority in visuospatial ability. The evidence for such cognitive sex differences is inconclusive because the relevant literature is fraught with conflicting results and inconsistencies in defining and measuring the abilities in question (Carroll & Maxwell, 1979; Kagan, 1982; Kinsborne, 1980). Furthermore, sex differences for some laboratory tasks can be eliminated by a single practice session, and researchers have been unable to find these sex differences in some cultures (Kagan, 1982). Moreover, sex differences account for only 1%-5% of the total variation in visuospatial abilities seen in the population (Hyde, 1981). Because the range of abilities within each sex is far greater than the minute statistical differences between them, sex is a poor predictor of aptitude for the so-called "sexually dimorphic" cognitive abilities. In other words, group statistics do not suggest that Dick has visuospatial skills superior to Jane's. To address that issue, one needs to look at Dick's and Jane's individual test scores–not their sex. Such statistical results are not promising bases for constructing biologically deterministic theories of cognitive sex differences. A popular theory that attempts to account for the observed male advantage in tasks requiring visuospatial ability is that males process visuospatial information predominantly with the right side of the brain, while females use both sides of the brain more equally (which is called symmetrical functioning). However, extensive reviews of the literature have shown that most studies fail to demonstrate sex differences in cerebral lateralization of cognitive functions. Those that report sex differences do not all agree on the direction of the difference (McGlone, 1980; McKeever, 1981). Furthermore, it is not clear why favoring one hemisphere should be superior for visuospatial processing to using both. Indeed, some authors have made contradictory claims: that females are more lateralized than males, and that bilateral representation of visuospatial functions is conducive to greater ability (see Spreen et al., 1984, p. 67). Whatever the claim, the assumptions that males are superior at visuospatial tasks and that this superiority has a biological basis are not adequately questioned. Whatever sex difference in lateralization is found is then assumed to be causally related to the presumed sex difference in ability. Similarly, the fact that women tend to score higher than men on particular verbal tasks, together with inconclusive evidence that language is represented more symmetrically between the hemispheres in women has generated speculation that women are superior at these tasks *because* their hemispheres function more symmetrically than those of men (see Bleier, 1984). Just as there is no reason to assume that symmetric hemispheric function is detrimental to visuospatial ability, there is no reason to assume that it enhances language skills.

Sexual Orientation Differences in Cognition and Brain Lateralization?

Despite the controversy concerning the existence and extent of sex differences in hemispheric lateralization and specific cognitive abilities, some researchers have claimed to demonstrate that, as compared with heterosexual men, homosexual men exhibit feminized cognitive profiles, specifically decreased visuospatial ability and increased verbal ability (McCormack & Witelson, 1991; Willmott & Brierley, 1984). Based on the assumption that the presumed sex differences have a biological basis, McCormack and Witelson (1991) suggest that the cognitive profiles of homosexual men primarily reflect a prenatal hormonal status (McCormack & Witelson, 1991). This interpretation ignores the possibility that statistically significant experiential differences may exist between homosexual men as a group and heterosexual men as a group (e.g., different degrees of participation in sports or reading). Such differences could influence cognitive interests, and these could, in turn, influence measured abilities.

The issue of right- or left-handedness is sometimes assumed to be relevant to sexual orientation because of the presumed sex difference in cerebral lateralization and because each hand is controlled predominately by the opposite side of the brain. Recently, McCormack et al. (1990) reported an increase in the incidence of "left-hand preference" in both gay men and lesbian women. It is important to note that these researchers did not assess handedness in a control group of heterosexual men and women but instead compared their assessments of handedness in Canadian gays and lesbians with a previous assessment of 1692 adults (men and women combined) in Britain. Moreover, they defined "left-hand preference" as "nonconsistent right-hand preference," and the increased left-hand preference in gay men was not statistically significant. A subsequent study reported a significant elevation of left-handedness in gay men, but again the comparison was made to normative population data rather than to a matched control group (Becker et al., 1992). One study that compared homosexual and heterosexual men presenting to a venereal disease clinic failed to detect an increase in left-handedness in gay men but reported "a shift toward non-right-handedness" (Lindesay, 1987). Other studies have found no association between homosexuality and handedness (Willmott & Brierley, 1984; Marchant-Haycox et al., 1991; Satz et al., 1991). Illustrating how capricious such data can be, the Marchant-Haycox group (1991) found no association of sexual orientation with handedness, although they found increased left-handedness among men who had been tested for HIV infection irrespective of whether the test was negative or positive.

On the basis of a statistical correlation between high visuospatial abilities and left-handedness, Geshwind and Behan (1982) suggested that left-handedness results from elevated prenatal testosterone levels. While the association between prenatally elevated testosterone levels and subsequent left-handedness would be consistent with the prenatal hormonal hypothesis and the observation of increased left-handedness in lesbians, contradictions arise if one attempts to account for the reports of increased left-handedness in gay men in terms of the prenatal hormonal hypothesis. Specifically, we have an association between left-handedness and high testosterone levels on the one hand, and an association between left-handedness and male homosexuality on the other. Furthermore, men tend to show greater left-hand preference than women (Chapman & Chapman, 1987). Should we now amend the prenatal hormonal hypothesis of sexual orientation to allow for an association between high prenatal testosterone levels and subsequent homosexuality in men?

Geshwind came close to proposing such an amendment when he speculated in an interview (Fettner & Check, 1984, p. 58) that high prenatal testosterone levels predispose to immunological disorders and that homosexuals are susceptible to AIDS because they have "a special immune configuration based on the sex hormone status during pregnancy which probably has parallel effects, i.e., both in altering the sexual orientation and also affecting the immune system." Geshwind's choice of words allowed him to skirt the logical contradiction that would result from the insertion of either "increased" or "decreased" testosterone levels in the place of "hormone status."

Sex Differences in Brain Structure?

The search for anatomical sex differences in the brain has a long history of producing results that were consistent with the researchers' biases but were ultimately discredited by their inability to be replicated (see Gould, 1981; Bleier, 1984; Fausto-Sterling, 1992; Herrn, this volume). Reputable scientists during the nineteenth century believed that one's social status reflected the development of one's brain and that this could be ascertained by gross anatomical measurements of various brain regions. For example, it was believed that women were less intelligent than men and, therefore, had less developed brains.

Some actually produced evidence that buttressed this claim. More specifically, whichever part of the brain was presumed to be the seat of intellect was found to be smaller in women than in men. Thus, toward the middle of the nineteenth century, women were found to have less developed frontal lobes than men, but toward the end of the century, compared to men, women were found to have greater frontal lobes and relatively less developed parietal lobes compared to men (Bleier, 1984, p. 50). I do not wish to suggest that scientists, past or present, were fraudulent in their work. Instead, it is more likely that they simply stopped measuring brains at the point that the data seemed to confirm their hypotheses. Unfortunately, scientists tend to question their methods and data more rigorously when the data fail to conform to their expectations. When their expectations are met, they tend to assume that their methods are valid and their results correct.

Reviewing the neuroanatomical sex differences literature in 1909, Mall concluded: "Each claim for specific [sex] differences fails when carefully tested, and the general claim that the brain type of woman is foetal [fetal] or simian [ape] type is largely an opinion without any scientific foundation. Until anatomists can point out specific differences which can be weighed or measured, or until they can assort a mixed collection of [male and female] brains, their assertions regarding male and female types are of no scientific value" (Mall, 1909). In 1984, Swaab and Hofman suggested that "That time may have come." The basis of their statement was two reports, one of which described a sex difference involving the left/right asymmetry of a cerebral structure called the planum temporale (Wada et al., 1975); the other described a sex difference in the size of a portion of the corpus callosum, the major bundle of connections between the left and right cerebral hemispheres (de Lacoste-Utamsing & Holloway, 1982). Although neither study has been corroborated, both continue to be cited widely as evidence for anatomical sex differences in the human brain (Kelly, 1986; Allen & Gorski, 1990, 1992; Allen et al., 1989, 1991; LeVay, 1991; Kimura, 1992; Swaab & Hofman, 1984). Because of the influence these studies continue to exert on thinking about sexual differentiation of the human brain, and because they are widely misunderstood and mis-cited, I will examine them in detail.

Planum Temporale

In 1968 Geshwind and Levitsky reported that this segment of the temporal lobe in most individuals is larger on the left than the right side of the brain. This anatomical asymmetry is widely believed to have functional significance because the planum temporale is involved in language functions that, in most individuals, are carried out predominately by the left side of the brain. In 1975 Wada et al. published a study which replicated the earlier report of Geschwind and Levitsky. It also investigated the development of the anatomical asymmetry and reported a difference in the proportion of men and women with a reversed pattern of asymmetry (i.e., larger planum on the right than on the left). That study has been widely mis-cited as demonstrating a variety of sex differences (Allen & Gorski, 1990, 1992; Allen et al., 1991; Swaab & Hofman, 1984).

In the abstract of their study the Wada group states that the planum was larger on the left than on the right in most subjects but in 10% a reversed asymmetry was found and that "females dominated ($p < 0.05$) in the latter group." One is surprised to find no mention of the number of male and female brains examined and no mention of what statistical methods were used. One can, however, derive the number of male and female brains by reading percentages from graphs and using these percentages along with bits of information in the text to set up and algebraically solve simultaneous equations. It appears that Wada et al. examined 36 adult female brains and 42 adult male brains. Of these 78 brains, 70 had a larger planum on the left than on the right. The remaining 8 brains showed a reversed pattern of asymmetry. Six of these were from women and 2 were from men. Wada et al. conclude "the distribution of the right/left ratio for male and female shows a predominance of females in the adult series for a reversal of asymmetry ($p < 0.05$)." While they do not state which statistical test they used to arrive at this significance level, the appropriate test of statistical significance would be chi-square analysis. This procedure shows that the male/female difference is not statistically significant ($p = 0.07$). But even if this difference were significant, it would not demonstrate the sex differences that have been attributed to it: e.g., "greater morphological brain asymmetry in the temporal planum" in men (Allen et al., 1991) and "a trend for the temporal planum to be larger in adult males than in females" (Swaab & Hofman, 1984).

The Corpus Callosum Controversy

Using brains obtained at autopsy, de Lacoste-Utamsing and Holloway (1982) reported that in the midsagittal plane, the cross-sectional area of the splenium of the corpus callosum is "larger" in females than in males. *Science* magazine published this study despite the weak statistical significance of its finding (p = .08), the small sample size (9 males, 5 females), and the unstated method of sample selection. These shortcomings did not dissuade the authors from claiming to have found evidence for an anatomical basis for sex differences in hemispheric lateralization. Specifically, they proposed that the "larger" splenium in females suggests more fibers interconnecting the hemispheres, and thus more symmetry in the functioning of the hemispheres. This report was rapidly incorporated into the scientific literature, including authoritative textbooks where it has been presented as "a clear-cut sex difference in the human brain" (Kelly, 1986). Moreover, the report has remained influential (Allen et al., 1989; LeVay, *New York Times* (letter), October 7, 1991; Gibbons, 1991; Kimura, 1992) for over a decade despite the fact that it has failed to be supported by nearly two dozen studies, many of which employed living subjects and advanced imaging techniques (see Table 1).

Paradoxically, Witelson (1991) found that these studies, taken together, suggest a trend for the splenium to be larger in men than in women–a conclusion opposite to the report of de LaCoste-Utamsing and Holloway. Had there been any scientific rationale for linking the size of the splenium with visuospatial ability to begin with, we now might propose that women should have superior visuospatial skills compared to men. Ironically, work in laboratory animals suggests that the relationship between the size of the splenium and the degree to which the two sides of the brain work together may be the reverse of that hypothesized by de Lacoste-Utamsing and Holloway (see Demeter et al., 1988). Specifically, cortical asymmetries are inversely related to callosal size in rodents that were selectively bred for variation in callosal size (Cassells et al., 1990) and are

TABLE 1. Summary of Studies on Splenium of Human Corpus Callosum

---

STUDIES REPORTING SPLENIUM LARGER IN WOMEN

1. de Lacoste-Utamsing & Holloway (1982)

- -

STUDIES REPORTING SPLENIUM LARGER IN MEN

1. Bean (1906)

2. Mall (1909)

- -

STUDIES REPORTING NO SEX DIFFERENCE IN SPLENIAL SIZE

*1. Allen et al. (1991)	*11. Oppenheim et al. (1987)
2. Bell & Variend (1985)	*12. O'Kusky et al. (1988)
*3. Byne et al. (1988)	*13. Reinarz et al. (1988)
*4. Clarke et al. (1988)	*14. Steinmetz et al. (1992)
5. Demeter et al. (1988)	*15. Swayze et al. (1989)
*6. Emory et al. (1991)	16. Weber & Weiss (1986)
*7. Habib et al. (1991)	*17. Weis et al. (1989)
8. Holloway & de Lacoste (1986)	18. Witelson (1985)
*9. Kertez et al. (1987)	19. Witelson (1989)
*10. Nasrallah et al. (1986)	*20. Yoshii et al. (1986)

* Studies using magnetic resonance imaging and living subjects.

absent in rodents born without a corpus callosum (Schmidt & Caparelli-Daquer, 1989).

One reason for the confusion in the literature on the callosum is that in addition to reporting a sex difference in the size of the splenium, de LaCoste-Utamsing and Holloway (1982) also reported that the splenium is more bulbous and has a larger maximal width in women than in men. Many authors have failed to distinguish between measures of the splenium's shape or maximal width and measures of its size (i.e., cross-sectional area). This distinction is crucial to de Lacoste-Utamsing and Holloway's assertion that "the *larger* splenium in the female could imply that more fibers connect the posterior cerebral cortex" in females than in males. In this context the word "larger" must be taken to mean cross-sectional area and not simply shape or maximal width. For example, the same number of electrical wires of equal caliber could be passed through a passageway that measures 2 cm wide and 2cm long as through one that measures 4 cm wide and 1 cm long since both would have a cross-sectional area of 4 ccm^2. Furthermore, the same number of fibers could be passed through a passageway with a cross-sectional area of 4 ccm^2 regardless of its shape. While a few studies have found the splenium to be either more bulbous or to have a greater maximal width in women (de Lacoste-Utamsing & Holloway, 1982; de Lacoste et al., 1986; Clarke et al., 1989; Allen et al., 1991), the majority have not (Bell & Variend, 1985; Witelson, 1985; Weber & Weis, 1986; Kertez et al., 1987; Oppenheim et al, 1987; Byne et al., 1988; O'Kusky et al., 1988; Demeter et al., 1988; Witelson, 1989, 1991; Habib et al., 1991). Some studies have even found the splenium to be wider or more bulbous in males (Clarke et al., 1989 [infants only]; Habib et al., 1991).

Even if there were to be a statistical trend for the splenium to be more bulbous in women as a group than in men as a group, it is clear that the shape of the splenium is poorly correlated with sex. Although Gorski's group reported a "*dramatic* sex difference in the shape of the corpus callosum" (emphasis added), on the basis of callosal shape, they could not sort a collection of male and female brains by sex any better than could be done by chance alone (Allen et al., 1991).

Even if a sex difference were conclusively demonstrated in either the shape or maximal width of the splenium, we would have no basis for interpreting its implications. There is certainly no reason to propose that a sex difference in the shape or maximal width of the splenium has any relationship to the number of interhemispheric connections that pass through it. Nevertheless, some authors (Allen et al., 1991; Holloway & de Lacoste, 1986) seem to attribute the same meaning to reports of such sex differences that de Lacoste-Utamsing and Holloway, in their original uncorroborated study (1982), attributed to their report of a larger cross-sectional area in females. Others have failed to differentiate between measures of maximal splenial width and splenial cross-sectional area and have erroneously suggested that Holloway and de Lacoste (1986) and Gorski's group (Allen et al., 1991) successfully replicated the 1982 finding of de Lacoste-Utamsing and Holloway in its entirety (LeVay, Oct. 7, 1991, letters, *New York Times*; Kimura, 1992; Holloway & de Lacoste, 1986). The report of Reinarz et al. (1988) has also been mis-cited as confirming the conclusions of de Lacoste-Utamsing and Holloway (1982) (Hines et al., 1992). Reinarz et al., however, found no sex difference in the posterior fifth of the callosum which de Lacoste-Utamsing and Holloway had defined as the splenium. Instead, they found a sex difference in the posterior fourth of the callosum, which the original authors also measured but did not find sexually dimorphic. Furthermore, the sex difference reported by the Reinarz group was not in the absolute size of the posterior fourth but in the quotient obtained by dividing the cross-sectional area of the posterior fourth by the total cross-sectional area of the callosum. This quotient was significantly greater in women than in men.

Some authors have suggested that failures to confirm de Lacoste-Utamsing's and Holloway's finding are in part a result of subsequent researchers' failures to exactly replicate their methods (Allen et al., 1991). However, even de Lacoste-Utamsing and Holloway (1986) have apparently been unable to confirm their own finding of a larger splenium in females. In their study titled "Sex Differences in the Corpus Callosum: A Replication and Extension Study," they failed to report measures of splenial cross sectional area although they stated in their abstract that they had confirmed their previous report that the splenium is "larger" in women. Since the sex difference in splenial size (i.e., cross-sectional area) was the only finding in their original study to which they attributed any functional significance, it seems most unlikely that they failed to measure it in their replication study. Surely they would have included these measurements had they been consistent with their initial report. Five years after the initial report, Holloway confessed to a reporter at the *San Francisco Examiner* that he was terribly embarrassed that he had rushed to publish the 1982 study (February 22, 1987).

Other Interhemispheric Connections

According to Gorski's group (Allen et al., 1991), another possible reason for the poor replicability of de LaCoste-Utamsing and Holloway's original report of sex differences in the splenium lies in difficulties in partitioning the splenium from the rest of the callosum. Ignoring the animal research suggesting a reverse relationship between functional symmetry and the size of connecting structures, they measured two additional connecting structures to test the hypothesis that the presumed increased hemispheric functional symmetry in women results from increased interhemispheric connections in general. These structures, the anterior commissure (AC) and the massa intermedia (MI) offer the advantages of being better defined than the splenium and they are smaller, and presumably less heterogeneous, than the corpus callosum. The AC is a bundle of neuronal fibers that interconnects portions of the temporal and frontal lobes on each side of the brain. The MI is a group of cells that connects the right and left halves of the brain. The function of the MI is unknown. It may, in fact, be only a vestigial structure since it is absent in 32% of adult men and 22% of adult women (Allen et al., 1991).

Allen and her collaborators (Allen et al., 1991), like de Lacoste-Utamsing and Holloway (1982) before them, hypothesized that women should have larger connections between the two sides of the brain. Consistent with their hypothesis they reported that both the AC and MI are significantly larger in women. To determine if this difference was statistically significant, they used a test that requires matching each male brain with a female brain of a comparable age and then observing the pattern of male-female differences for each pair. Such a matching procedure would be necessary if there was evidence that the size of either structure varies with age in one or both sexes. However, they reported that the size of neither structure varied with age in adults. It is, therefore, arguable whether such matching was warranted in their study. Unfortunately, their report does not indicate whether the sex differences were statistically significant without matching.

Neither of these reported sex differences has been confirmed by other laboratories. In fact, the only other study of possible sex differences in the AC found it to be larger in men ($p < 0.05$) (Demeter et al., 1988). These authors suggested that their finding may have been a statistical artifact and made no interpretation of its functional significance. Unfortunately, Allen and Gorski cite the study of Demeter et al. but fail to mention the discrepant results.

With respect to possible functional implications, no more is known about the functions of the MI and AC than about the corpus callosum. It would be particularly difficult to ascribe a significant role to the MI in any brain function, including sexually dimorphic functions, because it is absent in more than 20% of men and women. For example, assuming that Allen and Gorski are correct and the MI tends to be smaller in men, would one expect women with no MI to be more masculine in some regard than men with a small one?

Do Homosexuals Have Opposite-Sex Commissures?

Again, there is no convincing evidence that the requisite sex differences exist. Despite the lack of evidence for a sex difference in the corpus callosum, LeVay (*New York Times,* letter, October 7, 1991) suggests that male homosexuals may be found to have female-typical callosa. He erroneously asserts that the 1982 study of de Lacoste-Utamsing and Holloway has been replicated in its entirety and that the sex difference they reported is like that reported in laboratory animals. As shown above, however, the 1982 study (de Lacoste-Utamsing & Holloway) stands alone in finding women to have a larger splenium and is contradicted by nearly two dozen studies. Furthermore, when a sex difference in the corpus callosum has been reported in laboratory animals, it has been larger in males (Berrebi et al., 1988).

A recent report by Allen and Gorski (1992) confirms their previous report that the AC is larger in women than in men and extends the previous study by showing that the AC is also larger in homosexual men than in heterosexual men. This study is clearly in need of replication as the reported sex difference is contradicted by the study of the Demeter group (Demeter et al., 1988). Even if the findings of Allen and Gorski prove to be replicable, the size of the AC alone would tell us nothing about an individual's sexual orientation because the overlap of AC sizes between homosexual and heterosexual men was tremendous–the size of the AC of 27 out of 30 homosexual men fell within the range established by 30 heterosexual men.

Hypothalamic Sex Differences?

Over the past 16 years, various types of structural sex differences have been demonstrated in the hypothalamus of laboratory rodents. These findings are thought to be significant because the region displaying the sex differences in rodents contributes to regulating sexually dimorphic behavioral and endocrinological reproductive functions. The best studied structural sex difference in the rodent hypothalamus was described by Roger Gorski at UCLA in 1978 and involves a cell group–or nucleus–that is approximately 8 times larger in male than in female rats (Gorski et al., 1978). Gorski called this nucleus the sexually dimorphic nucleus of the preoptic area (SDN-POA).

Shortly after the initial description of the SDN-POA, the Bleier group (1982) examined the hypothalamus of several rodent species and discovered that the SDN-POA is merely one of several sexually dimorphic nuclei in the medial preoptic and anterior hypothalamic areas. Some of the sex differences described by the Bleier group were subsequently demonstrated in other laboratories and extended to other species (Hines et al., 1985; Byne and Bleier, 1987a; Simerly et al., 1988; Shapiro et al., 1991). Because several preoptic nuclei are sexually dimorphic, the name "SDN-POA" is a misnomer. Nevertheless, the term "SDN-POA" as used here refers specifically to the cell group described in the rat by Gorski et al. or to its presumed counterpart in other species.

A decade and a half after its discovery, we still have no idea what the rat's SDN-POA does. Its size is positively correlated with the frequency with which rats engage in mounting behavior, and this correlation has generated considerable interest among some researchers interested in sexual orientation. It is crucial to note, however, that the SDN-POA can be destroyed on both sides of the brain in male rats without influencing their sexual behavior. Interestingly, while an SDN-POA has been found in all other rodents examined, anatomists have been unable to identify a comparable cell group in mice (Bleier et al., 1982; Young, 1982). That brings up an interesting question: If we cannot generalize the existence of the SDN-POA from rats to mice, why should we expect to do so in humans?

In 1985 a group of researchers in the Netherlands looked in human brains for the counterpart of the rat's SDN-POA, and reported in *Science* that they had found it (Swaab & Fliers, 1985). The nucleus they studied had been previously identified and designated the *intermediate nucleus* (Brockhaus, 1942). Swaab and Fliers reported evidence that this nucleus is larger in men than in women, and on the basis of its purported sexual dimorphism and location, it was thought to be the counterpart of the SDN-POA in the rat. These researchers, therefore, renamed the intermediate nucleus the "sexually dimorphic nucleus" or SDN. Subsequently they provided evidence that the putative sex difference in the human SDN develops postnatally and that size of the human SDN does not vary with sexual orientation (Swaab & Hofman, 1988).

Two subsequent studies done in other laboratories failed to detect a sex difference in the human SDN (Allen et al., 1989; LeVay, 1991). The first of these (Allen et al., 1989) described sex differences in two other nuclei which were designated as the second and third interstitial nuclei of the anterior hypothalamus (INAH2 and INAH3) (Table 2). These authors renamed the former intermediate nucleus (which Swaab and Fliers had designated as the human SDN) the first interstitial nucleus (INAH1).

The Hypothalamus and Sexual Orientation

Recently, Simon LeVay extended the study by Allen et al. (1989) to include homosexual men (LeVay, 1991) in addition to presumably heterosexual men and women. While he found no sex difference in INAH1 or INAH2, he corroborated the report that INAH3 is larger in heterosexual men than in women. He also reported that the size of INAH3 varies with sexual orientation, being similar in size in homosexual men and presumed heterosexual women (Table 2).

In his report published in *Science,* LeVay suggested that INAH3 is comparable to the SDN-POA in rats and that it may play a role in

TABLE 2. Summary of Studies of Hypothalamic Interstitial Nuclei

	INAH1	INAH2	INAH3	INAH4
Swaab & Fliers, 1985	Larger in men	Not studied	Not studied	Not studied
Allen et al., 1989	No sex difference	Larger in men	Larger in men	No sex difference
LeVay, 1991	No sex difference	No sex difference	Larger in heterosexual men than in women or gay men	No sex difference

the "generation of male-typical sexual behavior." To support the latter conjecture, he cited work showing that size of the SDN-POA correlates positively with the frequency of mounting behavior displayed by male rats, and that lesions in the region of the SDN-POA disrupt mounting behavior in rats and primates. Critically, however, he failed to point out that lesions restricted to the SDN-POA do not impair mounting behavior in male rats (Arendash & Gorski, 1983).

In rats, the effective lesion site for disrupting mounting behavior lies above, not within the SDN-POA (Arendash & Gorski, 1983). Thus, the SDN-POA does not play a critical role in mounting behavior in male rats and the correlation between its size and mounting frequencies clearly does not reflect a causal relationship. While any role of the INAH3 in sexual orientation in humans is ultimately a question independent of its similarity to the SDN-POA in rats, evidence derived from studies of the SDN-POA does not support the notion that the INAH3 is crucial to the "generation of male-typical sexual behavior" in humans.

Similarly, in the primate studies referenced by LeVay, the region of the hypothalamus implicated in the regulation of male sex behavior was found to be above and behind the region where one would expect to find a nucleus comparable to the rat's SDN-POA or the human's INAH3 (Slimp et al., 1978; Perachio et al., 1979). LeVay suggested that "lesions in this region in male monkeys impair heterosexual behavior without eliminating sexual drive." Thus his statement that this region is "a likely biological substrate for sexual orientation," invites the reader to conclude that the lesions converted the monkey's sexual motivation from heterosexual to homosexual. Importantly, he failed to note that "the lesioned males' performances actually improved" with regard to the frequency of pressing a lever for access to females (Slimp et al., 1978, p. 114). Thus, one cannot conclude that the lesions decreased heterosexual motivation. Nor can one infer that the lesions increased homosexual motivation because the males were not given an opportunity to interact with other males following the lesions.

In addition to its theoretical shortcomings, LeVay's study can be faulted for a number of technical reasons (Byne & Parsons, 1993), including sketchy sexual and medical histories, heavy reliance on the brains of men who had died from AIDS, and small sample–19 homosexual males, all of whom died of AIDS; 16 presumed heterosexual males of unknown sexual history, 6 of whom died of AIDS; 6 women presumed to have been heterosexual.

The reliance on the brains of AIDS victims poses a serious interpretive difficulty because decreased testosterone levels are common in their cases (Croxson et al., 1989). In some mammalian species, the size of sexually dimorphic hypothalamic nuclei varies with the amount of testosterone circulating in the blood stream (Commins & Yahr, 1984). Furthermore, some of the drugs used to treat opportunistic infections associated with AIDS are also known to lower testosterone levels (Croxson et al., 1989). Some AIDS patients receive steroids that could further reduce testosterone, and still others have liver abnormalities that could increase estrogen levels. Because the major risk for HIV infection in heterosexual men is intravenous drug use, and, compared with the majority of homosexual men, intravenous drug users may have restricted access to medical care and often fail to comply with medical regimens, it is conceivable that the size of INAH3 in the men in LeVay's study reflected endocrine status at the time of death or some other aspect of AIDS or its treatment rather than sexual orientation. Unfortunately, the medical histories published in the LeVay study are inadequate to test this hypothesis.

According to Swaab and Hofman (1990) another hypothalamic nucleus, the suprachiasmatic nucleus (SCN), is larger in homosexual than heterosexual men. This finding, which also has yet to be corroborated, does not support the prenatal hormonal hypothesis because in humans the size of the SCN does not vary with sex (Swaab & Hofman, 1990). Moreover, existing evidence does not suggest a primary role for the SCN in the regulation of sexual behaviors. The SCN does, however, participate in regulating the temporal patterns of hormonal secretion, which in turn, modulate the expression of particular reproductive behaviors in laboratory rodents (Bleier & Byne, 1985).

THE PEER REVIEW PROCESS AND THE PRESS

Reviewing the sexological research on homosexuality from an endocrinological point of view, Gooren (this volume) concludes that it is "hard to be impressed." The same holds true for the anatomical literature, including the studies themselves and the review articles that, for the most part, uncritically catalogue their conflicting, often contradictory, results as well as their often unsubstantiated claims. One has to wonder what accounts for this sad state of affairs. In addition to the problems discussed elsewhere in this volume, part of the difficulty lies with the peer review process that allows seriously flawed studies to be published in prominent interdisciplinary journals if and when they support the biologically deterministic paradigm. On the contrary, studies that challenge this paradigm, even if methodologically superior, may not receive a ready welcome. They may either be relegated to relative obscurity in specialty journals or fail to be published at all. The difficulties that Ruth Bleier and I encountered in publishing a study that failed to find sex differences in the splenium of the corpus callosum are illustrative.

Following the publication in 1982 of the study by de LaCoste-Utamsing and Holloway that claimed to have found a larger and more bulbous splenium of the corpus callosum in women than in men, we felt it would be important to follow it up using a larger sample of brains (Byne et al., 1988).

Our study was based on magnetic resonance imaging (MRI)

brain scans of living subjects. After eliminating scans from brains with known pathology, we repeated the measurements of de La-Coste-Utamsing and Holloway on all of the remaining scans available from the MRI unit that had recently been established at our research facility. Although we failed to find a sex difference in the splenium, we did detect a statistically significant sex difference in another part of the callosum as well as an effect of age on the length of the callosum in men but not women. We suggested that these differences might be statistical artifacts and would need replication prior to speculation about their possible meaning. We submitted our paper to *Science,* which sent it to two reviewers. One reviewer recommended publication as a valuable addition to the literature. The other reviewer concluded that although "the paper has merit" it should not be published in *Science.* A number of worrisome points led the latter reviewer to this conclusion: (1) "We have no idea what size of the corpus callosum means." True, but neither did de La-Coste-Utamsing and Holloway, despite their conjectures; (2) "These authors have not addressed the issue of handedness." True, but neither did de LaCoste-Utamsing and Holloway; (3) "Some of the cases apparently had brain pathology." Our manuscript clearly stated that we had eliminated all brains with known pathology; (4) "While the study criticizes the previous work for small numbers, they have 9/bin average [i.e., an average of 9 subjects per group] compared with 7/bin and this is not too different." True, de LaCoste-Utamsing and Holloway had 9 males and 5 females or an average of 7 per bin (i.e., group), but we had 17 men and 22 women or an average of 19 subjects of each sex.

While *Science* found the study of de LaCoste-Utamsing and Holloway important and rigorous enough to publish despite its several flaws, the editors decided that our study did not meet their standards. *Science* refused to allow us to appeal their decision despite the fact that it was based at least in part on the comments of a reviewer who had either carelessly or maliciously misrepresented our study.

We then submitted the paper to another interdisciplinary journal. Again one reviewer recommended publication and the other rejection. In this case the comments of the negative reviewer are particularly informative. The review begins, "While the findings of this study are essentially negative, *they provide fairly conclusive evidence that there are no general sex-related differences* in the size of the human corpus callosum. . . . It is perhaps important that erroneous conclusions published in the literature be refuted by more substantial data. But since the earlier work was poorly conceived and poorly executed, it is difficult to rate a paper that calls its findings in question in the top of its field" (emphasis added). This reviewer suggested that our study would be more appropriate for a specialty journal.

We next submitted the paper to a specialty journal. Again the paper received one positive and one negative review. The negative review in this instance seems to have been written by the negative reviewer above as evidenced by the following comments: "The present paper uses magnetic resonance imaging to show that there is no significant [sex] difference in the size of the corpus callosum. We can assume that the earlier paper is wrong and misleading, and therefore correcting this error has some value to the scientific community. On the other hand, *it is hard to argue that a negative finding contradicting a poor paper constitutes an advance in science.* . . . My conclusion is that this paper is not appropriate for publication in the *Journal*" (emphasis added). In other words, published studies making unsubstantiated claims–even claims of potential social import–can go unchallenged because of the very fact that they were "poorly conceived and poorly executed." Such an attitude impedes the self-correcting process of the scientific method and thus undermines science at its foundation. Fortunately, this time the editor sided with the positive reviewer and published our study–three years after its completion.

A further problem with the peer review process in science is that reviewers know the identity of the authors whose work they critique. In contrast to some other disciplines that acknowledge the possibility of personal and professional bias on the part of reviewers, in science the assumption is that knowledge of the investigator and his or her affiliations is essential to the process of judging the merit of any study. As discussed by Bleier in an address to the American Association for the Advancement of Science (Chicago, February 17, 1987) the possible consequences of this system are obvious: One is that it makes for a potentially closed system that perpetuates and protects the dominant paradigm against methodological or theoretical challenges. Another is that unacceptably flawed studies are published and then uncritically welcomed into the canon primarily because of the name and prestige of the senior author. Meanwhile, the work of those who challenge dominant paradigms is discounted and goes unpublished and, thus, constitutes a suppressed body of negative evidence. This apparent absence is then viewed as support for the dominant paradigm.

Such closed systems are particularly prone to develop in fields such as sex research that are small enough to be dominated by relatively few individuals. Rogers (1982) argues this point in describing the fate of a critical review co-authored with Walsh. To their dismay "every one of the dozen or so medical journals held in [their] university's library which publishes this sort of material has on its editorial board either John Money or one of his collaborators." They were "thus unable to express a contrary view in the journals in which Money publishes so prolifically, but were forced to go to sociological journals, not even housed in [their] medical school library."

The scope of such bias is impossible to ascertain. Even if we can entertain contrary views, human nature dictates that we will be more skeptical of studies that fail to conform to our own belief systems. Thus, we will, perhaps unwittingly but nevertheless surely, hold to a higher standard of review studies that contradict our personal views. When a field is dominated by a few individuals with similar belief systems regarding the phenomena under study, the outcome may be to protect ideology at the expense of science.

Science *and Journalistic Responsibility*

Several weeks after *Science* published LeVay's report of a hypothalamic correlate of sexual orientation, it published an editorial concerning journalistic responsibility (Koshland, 1991). Regarding the tendency of the news media to hype sensational and poorly researched reports, he writes: "an individual publications's (or broadcast group's) willingness to cry 'wolf' uncritically may be destroying the press's own credibility and its ability to provide legitimacy" to responsible scientists. He continues, "the press has been too willing to publicize . . . cries . . . which so far have been consistently wrong." Dr. Koshland would do well to heed his own words. Indeed, as its editor, he must assume final responsibility for *Science*'s decision to publish, and to hype through press releases, poorly documented pronouncements of "sex differences!" and "homosexual differences!" which so far seem to have been consistently wrong. These include the reports discussed in the present paper that the splenium is larger in women than in men (de Lacoste-Utamsing & Holloway, 1982), that a hormonal test can determine sexual orientation in men (Gladue et al., 1984), and that *the* "sexually dimorphic nucleus" in humans is sexually dimorphic (Swaab & Fliers, 1985).

LeVay's study was initially rejected by the in-house reviewers at *Science* (LeVay, personal communication). Although *Science* rarely allows resubmission of manuscripts, an exception was made in this case. Because *Science* refuses to comment on this exceptional treatment, one can only speculate as to why their initial decision had been to reject the manuscript even before sending it out for peer review. Perhaps the reason for this is that the paper did not meet the minimal standards to which even animal research in this area is held. This paper had a single author who did all of the tissue processing as well as all of the anatomical measurements and statistical tests. Even in animal work, the standard has been that all measurements are made not only blindly but also by more than one investigator. Certainly, the editors at *Science* should have been more cautious and required that a co-investigator repeat and verify LeVay's measurements prior to publication of a study that was sure to be of great interest to the general public as well as to the scientific community. While LeVay has stated that there was no suitable co-investigator in his laboratory at the time he conducted this study (quoted in Marshall, 1992), there is no lack of qualified anatomists who would have been (and still would be) more than willing to check his measurements.

Dr. Koshland's editorial continues: "The press cannot be expected to have in-house scientists for every occasion." Certainly an in-house scientist would have been helpful in reviewing the "News and Comment" that *Science* published to accompany LeVay's article (Barinaga, 1991; Gibbons, 1991). Indeed, the level of scientific scholarship in covering this story was higher in *Mademoiselle* (Harrison, January, 1992, pp. 48-49). The "News and Comment" piece naively assumes homosexuals to be neurological intersexes and, in an attempt to provide LeVay's thesis scientific ground, it uncritically catalogues numerous contradictory reports of brain sex differences as if they corroborate one another. Along the way a number of amusing, but embarrassingly misinformed, blunders are made.

First, the piece complains about the "nagging possibility" that some factor other than sexual orientation accounts for LeVay's findings. Then, it asserts that the suprachiasmatic nucleus is not part of the hypothalamus, when it is one of the better defined and most widely studied portions of the hypothalamus. Swaab is stated to have "scooped Gorski" in describing *the* sexually dimorphic nucleus in the human brain, when in fact the two groups described different nuclei and Gorski's group could find no sex difference in the nucleus described by Swaab. Given the disarray in the literature on the corpus callosum it is remarkable that the piece asserted that, "although it is clear that there are differences between males and females in the corpus callosum, researchers don't always agree on what those differences are." If researchers can't agree what the sex differences are, how can it be clear that any exist?

Even though *Science* found room in its pages to print this misleading and inaccurate example of hyperbolic tabloid-quality journalism, a 500-word "Technical Comments" piece analyzing the conceptualization and methodology of the LeVay study was rejected because according to one of *Science*'s editors (Christine Gilbert) they had "already devoted considerable space to a discussion of LeVay's report." Nevertheless, they returned to LeVay's report a year later and again devoted considerable space to it in a "Special News Report" (Marshall, 1992) that repeated many of the same factual and conceptual errors as their initial "News and Comment."

The author of the latter article had received, upon his request, a copy of my correspondence with LeVay in which I suggested that he share his material with other anatomists. Compliance with my request would have generated a consensus opinion among anatomists concerning the replicability of LeVay's measurements. *Science*'s lack of objectivity is illustrated by their mischaracterization of my request as a "demand," by their failure to emphasize that my request would have allowed other anatomists of LeVay's choosing to examine his material, and by the suggestion that results obtained in compliance with my request would have been biased by my "intellectual conflict." Because only LeVay would have had access to information concerning the sex and sexual orientation of the subjects from which the material was obtained, it is clear that results obtained in compliance with my request would have been insulated from my biases.

According to the stated editorial policy of *Science*: "When a paper is accepted for publication in *Science*, it is understood that any materials and methods necessary to verify the conclusion of the experiments reported will be made available to other investigators under appropriate conditions." If *Science* stood by that policy, one would have expected it to encourage LeVay to comply with my request rather than to publish an article in which the nature and scope of that request were distorted. On November 12, 1992 (after the publication of the "Special News Report), I wrote to *Science* asking what the "appropriate conditions" would be for others to have access to LeVay's material but to date there has been no response.

CONCLUSION

Recent studies have renewed interest in the nature of biological contributions to sexual orientation. If current studies are to lead to a new era of understanding, we must keep in mind the errors of the past. Attempts to prove that gay men have feminized gonadotropin responses were made decades after strong evidence suggested that the brain mechanism regulating the response does not differ between men and women. It required 25 studies to convince some that testosterone levels in adulthood do not reveal sexual orientation (Meyer-Bahlburg, 1984). Twenty-two contradictory studies have yet to lay to rest the one single study that found women to have a larger splenium than men. When will we know the truth concerning the latest wave of studies reporting biological correlates of sexual orientation? If the studies of gonadotropin responses, testosterone levels, and the corpus callosum serve as examples, it may be well over a decade from now. These examples, then, should serve as a warning against hasty interpretations of findings based on limited sample sizes, shaky methodologies, and extremely limited knowledge about the functions of particular brain structures and even less knowledge about the biological substrates of the mind.

REFERENCES

Allen, L. S., & Gorski, R. A. (1990). Sex differences in the bed nucleus of the stria terminalis of the human brain. *Journal of Comparative Neurology, 302,* 697-706.

Allen, L. S., & Gorski, R. A. (1992). Sexual orientation and the size of the anterior commissure in the human brain. *Proceedings of the National Academy of Sciences, USA, 89,* 7199-7202.

Allen, L. S., Hines M., Shryne, J. E., & Gorski R. A. (1989). Two sexually dimorphic cell groups in the human brain. *Journal of Neuroscience, 9,* 497-506.

Allen, L. S., Richey, M. F., Chai, Y. M., & Gorski, R. A. (1991). Sex differences in the corpus callosum of the living human being. *Journal of Neuroscience, 11,* 933-942.

Arendash, G. W., & Gorski, R. A. (1983). Effects of discrete lesions of the sexually dimorphic nucleus of the preoptic area or other medial preoptic regions on the sexual behavior of male rats. *Brain Research Bulletin, 10,* 147-154.

Bailey, J. M., & Pillard, R. C. (1991). A genetic study of male sexual orientation. *Archives of General Psychiatry, 48,* 1089-1096.

Bailey, J. M., Pillard, R. C., Neale, M. C., & Agyei, Y. (1993). Heritable factors influence sexual orientation in women. *Archives of General Psychiatry, 50,* 217-223.

Barinaga, M. (1991). Is homosexuality biological? *Science, 253,* 956-957.

Bartter, F. C, Albright, F., Forbes, A. P., Leaf, A., Dempsey, E., & Carroll, E. (1951). The effects of adrenocorticotropic hormone and cortisone in the adrenogenital syndrome associated with congenital adrenal hyperplasia: An attempt to explain and correct its disordered hormonal pattern. *Journal of Clinical Investigation, 30,* 237-251.

Bean, R. B. (1906). Some racial peculiarities of the negro brain. *American Journal of Anatomy, 5,* 353-432.

Becker, J. T., Bass, S. M., Dew, M. A., Kingsley, L., Selnes, O. A., & Sheridan, K. (1992). Hand preference, immune system disorder and cognitive function among gay/bisexual men: The multicenter AIDS Cohort Study (MACS). *Neuropsychologia, 30,* 229-235.

Bell, A. D., & Variend S. (1985). Failure to demonstrate sexual dimorphism of the corpus callosum in childhood. *Journal of Anatomy, 143,* 143-147.

Bell, A. P., Weinberg, M. S., & Hammersmith, S. K. (1981). *Sexual preference: Its development in men and women.* Bloomington, IN: Indiana University Press.

Berrebi, A. S., Fitch, R. H., Ralphe, D. L., Denenburg, J. O., Friedrich, V. L., Jr.,

& Denenberg, V. H. (1988). Corpus callosum: Region-specific effects of sex, early experience, and age. *Brain Research, 438*, 216-224.

Bhide, P. G., & Bedi, K. S. (1984). The effects of a lengthy period of environmental diversity on well-fed undernourished rats. II. Synapse to neuron ratios. *Journal of Comparative Neurology, 227*, 305-310.

Bleier, R. (1984). *Science and gender: A critique of biology and its theories on women.* New York: Pergamon Press.

Bleier, R., & Byne, W. (1985). Septum and hypothalamus. In G. Paxinos (Ed.), *The rat nervous system* (pp. 87-118). New York: Academic Press.

Bleier, R., Byne, W., & Siggelkow, I. (1982). Cytoarchitectonic sexual dimorphisms of the medial preoptic and anterior hypothalamic areas in guinea pig, rat, hamster and mouse. *Journal of Comparative Neurology, 212*, 118-130.

Boswell, J. (1980). *Christianity, social tolerance, and homosexuality.* Chicago, IL: University of Chicago Press.

Brockhaus, H. (1942). Beitrag zur normalen Anatomie des Hypothalamus und der Zona incerta beim Menschen. Versuch einer architektonischen Gliederung. *Journal of Psychology and Neurology, 51*, 96-196.

Byne, W., & Bleier R. (1987a). Medial preoptic sexual dimorphisms in the guinea pig. I. An investigation of their hormonal dependence. *Journal of Neuroscience, 7*, 2688-2696.

Byne, W., & Bleier, R. (1987b). How different are male and female brains? *Trends in Neurosciences, 10*, 198-199.

Byne, W., Bleier, R., & Houston, L. (1988). Variations in human corpus callosum do not predict gender: A study using magnetic resonance imaging. *Behavioral Neuroscience, 102*, 222-227.

Byne, W., & Parsons, B. (1993) Sexual orientation: The biological theories reappraised. *Archives of General Psychiatry, 50*, 228-239.

Carroll, J. B., & Maxwell, S. E. (1979). Individual differences in cognitive abilities. *Annual Review of Psychology, 83*, 1026-52.

Cassells, B., Collins, R. L., & Wahlsten, D. (1990). Path analysis of sex difference, forebrain commissure area and brain size in relation to degree of laterality in selectively bred mice. *Brain Research, 529*, 50-56.

Chapman, L. J. & Chapman, J. P. (1987). The measurement of handedness. *Brain and Cognition, 6*, 175-183.

Churchill, W. (1967). *Homosexuality among males: A cross-cultural and cross-species investigation.* New York: Hawthorne Books.

Clarke, S., Kraftsik, R., Van Der Loos, H., & Innocenti, G. M. (1989). Forms and measures of adult and developing human corpus callosum: Is there sexual dimorphism? *Journal of Comparative Neurology, 280*, 213-230.

Commins, D., & Yahr, P. (1984). Adult testosterone levels influence the morphology of a sexually dimorphic area in the Mongolian gerbil brain. *Journal of Comparative Neurology, 224*, 132-140.

Croxson, T. S., Chapman, W. E., Miller, L. K., Levit, C. D., Senie, R., & Zumoff, B. (1989). Changes in the hypothalamic-pituitary-gonadal axis in human immunodeficiency virus-infected men. *Journal of Clinical Endocrinology and Metabolism, 89,* 317-321.

de Lacoste, M. C., Holloway, R. L., & Woodward, D. J. (1986). Sex differences in the fetal human corpus callosum. *Human Neurobiology* 5, 93-96.

de Lacoste-Utamsing, M. C., & Holloway, R. L. (1982). Sexual dimorphism in the human corpus callosum. *Science, 216,* 1431-1432.

Demeter, S., Ringo, J. L., & Doty, R. W. (1988). Morphometric analysis of the human corpus callosum and anterior commissure. *Human Neurobiology, 6,* 219-226.

de Waal, F. (1987). Peace making among primates: Tension regulation and nonreproductive functions of sex among captive bonobos. *National Geographic Research, 3,* 318-335.

Dörner, G., Rohde, W., Stahl, F., Krell, L., & Masius, W. G. (1975). A neuroendocrine predisposition for homosexuality in men. *Archives of Sexual Behavior, 4,* 1-8.

Emory, L. E., Williams, D. H., Cole, C. M., Amparo, E. G., & Meyer, W. J. (1991). Anatomic variation of the male corpus callosum in persons with gender dysphoria. *Archives of Sexual Behavior, 20,* 409-421.

Fausto-Sterling, A. (1992). *Myths of gender: Biological theories about women and men.* New York: Basic Books, Inc.

Fee, E. (1979). Nineteenth century craniology: The study of the female skull. *Bulletin of the History of Medicine, 33,* 415-433.

Fettner, A. G., & Check, W. A. (1984). *The truth about AIDS: Evolution of an epidemic.* New York: Holt, Rinehardt and Winston.

Ford, C. S., & Beach, F. A. (1951). *Patterns of sexual behavior.* New York: Harper and Bros.

Gadpaille, W. (1980). Cross-species and cross-cultural contributions to understanding homosexual activity. *Archives of General Psychiatry, 37,* 349-356.

Geshwind, N., & Behan, P. (1982). Left-handedness: Association with immune disease, migraine, and developmental learning disorder. *Proceedings of the National Academy of Science USA, 79,* 5097-5100.

Geschwind, N., & Levitsky, W. (1968). Left/right asymmetries in temporal speech region. *Science, 161,* 186-187.

Gibbons, A. (1991). The brain as sexual organ. *Science, 253,* 957-959.

Gladue, B. A., Green, R., & Hellman, R. E. (1984). Neuroendocrine response to estrogen and sexual orientation. *Science, 225,* 1496-1499.

Gooren, L. (1986a). The neuroendocrine response of luteinizing hormone to estrogen administration in heterosexual, homosexual and transsexual subjects. *Journal of Clinical Endocrinology and Metabolism, 63,* 583-588.

Gooren L. (1986b). The neuroendocrine response of luteinizing hormone to estrogen administration in the human is not sex specific but dependent on the hormonal environment. *Journal of Clinical Endocrinology and Metabolism, 63,* 589-93.

Gorski, R. A. (1978). Sexual differentiation of the brain. *Hospital Practice,* October, 55-62.

Gorski, R. A., Gordon, J. H., Shryne, J. E., & Southam, A. M. (1978). Evidence for a morphological sex difference in the medial preoptic area of the rat brain. *Brain Research, 148*, 333-346.

Gould, S. J. (1981). *The mismeasure of man.* New York: W. W. Norton & Company.

Goy, R. W., & McEwen, B. S. (1980). *Sexual differentiation of the brain.* Cambridge, MA: MIT Press.

Goy, R. W., & Resko, J. A. (1972). Gonadal hormones and behavior of normal and pseudohermaphroditic nonhuman female primates. *Recent Progress in Hormone Research, 28*, 707-733.

Habib, M., Gayraud, D., Oliva, A., Salamon, G., & Khalil R. (1991). Effects of handedness and sex on the morphology of the corpus callosum: A study with brain magnetic resonance imaging. *Brain and Cognition, 16*, 41-61.

Hamer, D. H., Hu, S., Magnuson, V. L., Hu, N., & Pattatucci, A. M. L. (1993). A linkage between DNA markers on the X chromosome and male sexual orientation. *Science, 261*, 321-327.

Hendricks, S. E., Graber, B., & Rodriguez-Sierra, J. F. (1989). Neuroendocrine responses to exogenous estrogen. No differences between heterosexual and homosexual men. *Psychoneuroendocrinology, 14*, 177-185.

Herdt, G. H. (1984). Semen transactions in Sambia culture. In G. H. Herdt (Ed.), *Ritualized homosexuality in Melanesia* (pp. 167-210). Berkeley, CA: University of California Press.

Hines, M., Chiu, L., McAdams, L. A., Bentler, P. M., & Lipcamon, J. (1992). Cognition and the corpus callosum: Verbal fluency, visuospatial ability, and language lateralization related to midsagittal surface areas of callosal subregions. *Behavioral Neuroscience, 106*, 3-14.

Hines, M., Davis, F. C., Coquelin, A., Goy, R. A., & Gorski, R. A. (1985). Sexually dimorphic regions in the medial preoptic area and the bed nucleus of the stria terminalis of the guinea pig brain: A description and an investigation of their relationship to gonadal steroids in adulthood. *Journal of Neuroscience, 5*, 40-47.

Hodges, J. K., & Hearn, J. P. (1978). A positive feedback effect of oestradiol on LH release in the male marmoset monkey, *Callithrix jaccus. Journal of Reproduction and Fertility, 52*, 83-86.

Holloway, R. L., & de Lacoste, M. C. (1986). Sexual dimorphism in the human corpus callosum: An extension and replication study. *Human Neurobiology, 5*, 87-91.

Hubbard, R. (1993) The search for sexual identity. *New York Times*, August 2, p. A15.

Hyde, J. (1981). How large are cognitive gender differences? *American Psychologist, 36*, 982-901.

Kagan, J. (1982). The idea of visuospatial ability. *New England Journal of Medicine, 306*, 1225-1227.

Kaplan, H. I., & Sadock, B. J. (1985). *Study guide and self examination: Review for modern synopsis of comprehensive textbook of psychiatry*, Volume 4. Baltimore, MD: Williams and Wilkins.

Karsch, F. J., Dierschle, D. E., & Knobil, E. (1973). Sexual differentiation of pituitary function: Apparent difference between primates and rodents. *Science, 179,* 484-486.

Katz, J. N. (1992). *Gay American history: Lesbians and gay men in the U.S.A.* New York, NY: Penguin Books.

Kelly, D. (1987). Sexual differentiation of the brain. *Trends in Neurosciences, 9,* 499-502.

Kelly, D. D. (1986). Sexual differentiation of the nervous system. In E. R. Kandel & J. H. Schwartz (Eds.), *Principles of neural science* (pp. 771-783). New York: Elsevier.

Kertez, A., Polk, M., Howell, J., & Black, S. E. (1987). Cerebral dominance, sex, and callosal in MRI. *Neurology, 37,* 1385-1388.

Kimura, D. (1992). Sex differences in the brain. *Scientific American,* September, 119-125.

King, M., & McDonald, E. (1992). Homosexuals who are twins: A study of 46 probands. *British Journal of Psychiatry, 160,* 407-409.

Kinsborne, M. (1980). If sex differences in brain lateralization exist they have yet to be discovered. *Behavioral and Brain Sciences, 3,* 241-242.

Koshland, D. (1991). Credibility in science and the press. *Science, 254,* 629.

Kraemer, G. W., Ebert, M. H., Raymond, L., & McKinney, W. T. (1984). Hyper-sensitivity to d-amphetamine several years after early social deprivation in rhesus monkeys. *Psychopharmacology, 82,* 266-271.

LeVay, S. (1991). A difference in hypothalamic structure between heterosexual and homosexual men. *Science, 253,* 1034-1037.

Lindesay, J. (1987). Laterality shift in homosexual men. *Neuropsychologia, 25,* 965-969.

Mall, F. P. (1909). On several anatomical characters of the human brain said to vary according to race and sex, with special reference to the frontal lobes. *American Journal of Anatomy, 9,* 1-32.

Marchant-Haycox, S. E., McManus, I. C., & Wilson, G. D. (1991). Left-handed-ness, homosexuality, HIV infection and AIDS. *Cortex, 27,* 49-56.

Marshall, E. (1992). Sex on the brain. *Science, 257,* 620-621.

McCormack, C. M., & Witelson, S. F. (1991). A cognitive profile of homosexual men compared to heterosexual men and women. *Psychoneuroendocrinology, 16,* 458-473.

McCormack, C. M., Witelson, S. F., & Kingstone, E. (1990). Left-handedness in homosexual men and women: Neuroendocrine implications. *Psychoneuroen-docrinology, 15,* 69-76.

McGlone, J. (1980). Sex differences in human brain asymmetry: A critical survey. *The Behavioral and Brain Sciences, 3,* 215-263.

McKeever, W. F. (1981). Sex and cerebral organization: Is it really that simple? In A. Ansara, N. Geschwind, A. Galaburta, M. Albert, & N. Gartrell (Eds.), *Sex differences in dyslexia* (pp. 97-108). Towson, MD: The Orton Dyslexia Society.

Meyer-Bahlburg, H. F. L. (1977). Sex hormones and male homosexuality in comparative perspective. *Archives of Sexual Behavior, 6,* 297-325.

Meyer-Bahlburg, H. F. L. (1984). Psychoendocrine research on sexual orientation: Current status and future options. *Progress in Brain Research, 71,* 375-397.

Money, J., & Ehrhardt, A. A. (1972). *Man and woman, boy and girl.* Baltimore, MD: Johns Hopkins University Press.

Nasrallah, H. A., Andreasen, N. C., Coffman, J. A., Olson, S. C., Dunn, V. D., Ehrhardt, J. C., & Chapman, S. M. (1986). A controlled magnetic resonance imaging study of corpus callosum thickness in schizophrenia. *Biological Psychiatry, 21,* 274-282.

Norman, R. L., & Spies, H. G. (1986). Cyclic ovarian function in a male macaque: Additional evidence for a lack of sexual differentiation in the physiological mechanisms that regulate the cyclic release of gonadotropins in primates. *Endocrinology, 118,* 2608-2610.

O'Kusky, J., Strauss, E., Kosaka, B., Wada, J., Li, D., Druhan, M., & Petrie J. (1988). The corpus callosum is larger with right-hemisphere cerebral speech dominance. *Annals of Neurology, 24,* 379-383.

Olsen, K. L. (1983). Genetic determinants of sexual differentiation. In J. Balthazart, E. Prove, & R. Gilles (Eds.), *Hormones and behavior in higher vertebrates.* Berlin/Heidelberg: Springer-Verlag.

Oppenheim, J. S., Lee, C. P., Nass, R., & Gazzaniga, M. S. (1987). No sex-related differences in human corpus callosum based on magnetic resonance imagery. *Annals of Neurology, 21,* 604-606.

Perachio, A., Marr, L. D., & Alexander, M. (1979) Sexual behavior in male rhesus monkeys elicited by electrical stimulation of preoptic and hypothalamic areas. *Brain Research, 177,* 127-144.

Pfaff, D. W. (1980). *Estrogens and brain function.* New York: Springer-Verlag.

Reinarz, S. J., Coffman, C. E., Smoker, W. R., & Godersky, J. C. (1988). MR imaging of the corpus callosum: Normal and pathologic findings and correlation with CT. *American Journal of Roentgenology, 151,* 791-798.

Renshaw, D. (1988). Bisexuality (book review). *Journal of the American Medical Association, 259,* 3057.

Rogers, L. (1982). The ideology of medicine. In S. Rose (Ed.), *Against biological determinism* (pp. 79-83). London: Allison and Busby Limited.

Satz, P., Miller, E. N., Selnes, O., Van-Gorp, W., D'Elia, L. F., & Visscher, B. (1991). Hand preference in homosexual men. *Cortex, 27,* 295-306.

Schluter, D. (1992). Brain differences (letter). *Nature, 359,* 181.

Schmidt, S. L., & Caparelli-Daquer, E. M. (1989). The effects of total and partial callosal agenesis on the development of morphological brain asymmetries in the BALB/cCF mouse. *Experimental Neurology, 104,* 172-180.

Schuster, L. (1993). Growing evidence suggests homosexuality is at least partly determined by genetics. *Clinical Psychiatry News,* August, p. 2.

Shapiro, L. E., Leonard, C. M., Sessions, C. E., Dewsbury, D. A., & Insel, T. A. (1991). Comparative neuroanatomy of the sexually dimorphic hypothalamus in monogamous and polygamous voles. *Brain Research, 541,* 232-240.

Simerly, R. B., McCall, L. D., & Watson, S. J. (1988). Distribution of opioid peptides in the preoptic region: Immunohistochemical evidence for a steroid-sensitive enkephalin sexual dimorphism. *Journal of Comparative Neurology, 276*, 442-259.

Slimp, J. C., Hart, B. L., & Goy, R. W. (1978) Heterosexual, autosexual and social behavior of adult male rhesus monkeys with medial preoptic-anterio hypothalamic lesions. *Brain Research, 142*, 105-122.

Speroff, L. (1965). The adrenogenital syndrome and its obstetrical aspects. *Obstetrics and Gynecology Survey, 20*, 185-214.

Spreen, O., Tupper, D., Risser, A., Tuokko, H., & Edgell, D. (1984). Human developmental neuropsychology. New York: Oxford University Press.

Steinmetz, H., Jancke, L., Kleinschmidt, A., Schlaug, G., Volkmann, J., & Huang, Y. (1992). Sex but no hand difference in the isthmus of the corpus callosum. *Neurology, 42*, 749-752.

Swaab, D. F., & Fliers, E. (1985). A sexually dimorphic nucleus in the human brain. *Science, 228*, 1112-1114.

Swaab, D. F., & Hofman, M. A. (1988). Sexual differentiation of the human hypothalamus: Ontogeny of the sexually dimorphic nucleus of the preoptic area. *Developmental Brain Research, 44*, 314-318.

Swaab, D. F., & Hofman, M. A. (1984). Sexual differentiation of the human brain: A historical perspective. *Progress in Brain Research, 61*, 361-383.

Swaab, D. F., & Hofman, M. A. (1990). An enlarged suprachiasmatic nucleus in homosexual men. *Brain Research, 537*, 141-148.

Swayze, V., Andreasen, N., Shun, J., & Alliger, R. (1989). The corpus callosum in schizophrenia and mania: A controlled MRI study. *Schizophrenia Research, 2*, 130.

Torand-Allerand, C. D. (1993). Sex on the brain (letter). *Scientific American*, January, 12.

Trumbach, R. (1989). Gender and the homosexual role in modern western culture: The 18th and 19th centuries compared. In D. Altman, C. Vance, M. Vicinus, & J. Weeks (Eds.), *Homosexuality, which homosexuality?* (pp. 149-169). London: GMP Publishers.

Turner, A. M., & Greenough, W. T. (1985). Differential rearing effects on rat visual cortex synapses. I. Synaptic and neuronal density and synapses per neuron. *Brain Research, 329*, 195-203.

Wada, J. A., Clarke, R., & Hamm, A. (1975). Cerebral hemispheric asymmetry in humans. *Archives of Neurology, 32*, 239-246.

Weber, G., & Weis, S. (1986). Morphometric analysis of the human corpus callosum fails to reveal sex-related differences. *Journal für Hirnforschung, 2*, 237-240.

Weis, S., Weber, G., Wegner, E., & Kimbacher, M. (1989). The controversy about a sexual dimorphism of the human corpus callosum. *International Journal of Neuroscience, 47*, 169-73.

West, D. J. (1983). Homosexuality and lesbianism. *British Journal of Psychiatry, 43*, 221-226.

Wilkins, L., Crigler, J. F., Silverman, S. H., Gardner, L. I., & Migeon, C. J. (1952).

Further studies on the treatment of congenital adrenal hyperplasia with corti- sone. II. The effects of cortisone on sexual and somatic development with an hypothesis concerning the mechanism of feminization. *Journal of Clinical Endocrinology and Metabolism, 12*, 277-295.

Willmott, M., & Brierley, H. (1984). Cognitive characteristics and homosexuality. *Archives of Sexual Behavior, 13*, 311-319.

Witelson, S. F. (1985). The brain connection: The corpus callosum is larger in left-handers. *Science, 229*, 665-668.

Witelson, S. F. (1989). Hand and sex differences in the isthmus and genu of the human corpus callosum. *Brain, 112*, 799-835.

Witelson, S. F. (1991). Neural sexual mosaicism: Sexual differentiation of the human tempero-parietal region for functional asymmetry. *Psychoneuroendo- crinology, 16*, 131-153.

Yoshii, F., Barker, W., Apicella, A., Chang, J., Sheldon, J., & Duara, R. (1986). Measurements of the corpus callosum on magnetic resonance scans: Effects of age, sex, handedness and disease. *Neurology, 36* (Suppl. 1), 133.

Young, J. K. (1982). A comparison of the hypothalami of rats and mice: Lack of a gross sexual dimorphism in the mouse. *Brain Research, 239*, 233-239.

Sexuality in the Brain

Ruth G. Doell, PhD

San Francisco State University

SUMMARY. Research on the biological "causes" of homosexuality focuses primarily upon the hypothesis that hormonal influences during fetal life "organize" certain parts of the brain which thus become centers for sexual orientation and behavior later in life. This paper briefly summarizes criticisms of this research that demonstrate little evidence for the operation of such centers and emphasizes alternative scenarios for the development of sexual orientation and behavior which have been slighted by the biological and medical communities. Finally, I suggest that commitment to a belief in a biological mechanism which supports the hierarchy of power by those who benefit from that power maintains the viability of the hypothesis in the face of negative evidence.

The idea of homosexuality (and heterosexuality) as a condition of persons is of relatively recent origin (D'Emilio & Freedman, 1988), arising with the conceptual separation of homosexual acts from homosexual attraction in the nineteenth century (Weeks, 1986). Along with this redefining of human sexuality, sexual orientation became reified as an essential component of self-identity. It is this notion of an essential difference dividing people that

Ruth G. Doell is Professor Emerita of Biology at San Francisco State University. Correspondence may be addressed: Department of Biology, San Francisco State University, 1600 Holloway, San Francisco, CA 94132.

[Haworth co-indexing entry note]: "Sexuality in the Brain." Doell, Ruth G. Co-published simultaneously in *Journal of Homosexuality* (The Haworth Press, Inc.) Vol. 28, No. 3/4, 1995, pp. 345-354; and: *Sex, Cells, and Same-Sex Desire: The Biology of Sexual Preference* (ed: John P. De Cecco, and David Allen Parker) The Haworth Press, Inc., 1995, pp. 345-354. Multiple copies of this article/chapter may be purchased from The Haworth Document Delivery Center [1-800-3-HAWORTH; 9:00 a.m. - 5:00 p.m. (EST)].

allowed the development and flourishing of a biological theory of homosexuality in this century. Theories about the origins of homosexuality appeared earlier of course, at least with the medicalization of same-sex acts in the nineteenth century (Greenberg, 1988), but it is only in the twentieth century that serious attention has been paid by biologists to its development in humans.

Early theories focused upon hormonal variations that might possibly be associated with such a "condition" but the complete lack of supporting evidence for this idea has discouraged scientists from pursuing it. Instead, building upon evidence obtained in animal studies they turned to developing a theory of sexualization of the brain as an explanation for homosexuality in humans. The choice of the brain as an organ of sexuality was crucial. Because our understanding of the function of the brain, unlike hormonal status which can be accurately ascertained, is still so limited, almost anything can be attributed to it. Not too long ago a theory of brain size differences, smaller brains in women, was postulated to explain the alleged intellectual inferiority of women (Gould, 1981). When it was recognized that brain size is correlated with body size, this notion fell into disrepute, and a new hypothesis of greater or lesser lateralization of brain function was developed in order to account for various cognitive differences between men and women (Fausto-Sterling, 1985). For example, the alleged superior spatial abilities of men were attributed to their greater lateralization of brain function. Women's alleged inferior spatial abilities would then be attributed to interference with neural processing involved in spatial problem solving by their more connected hemispheres. As preliminary evidence failed to confirm these hypotheses, they have faded from prominence. However, new studies appear from time to time, such as the recent one concerning superiority in math ability in boys as compared with girls (Benbow & Stanley, 1980).

The attribution of homosexuality to some difference in the anatomy and physiology of the brain stems from studies in rodents and monkeys that demonstrate developmental effects on mating behaviors by hormones reaching the brain before or soon after birth. These effects are fairly clear-cut in several, although not all, species of rodents and sub-human primates (Goy & McEwen, 1980). In such species "masculinization" of the female's behavior by androgen treatment and "feminization" of the male's behavior by lack of androgen has been most clearly demonstrated although most of these reflex-like behaviors are capable of modification by environmental (social) factors (Goldfoot & Neff, 1985). The accompaniment of the behavioral alterations seen after hormonal treatment by anatomical changes in particular brain regions (Goy & McEwen, 1980) has seemed to clinch the argument in favor of brain control over sexual behaviors, at least in some species of animals. And it is via an evolutionary connectedness between humans and other species that the hypothesis is extended to humans. It is therefore postulated that humans have critical periods of prenatal or early postnatal development during which over- or under-exposure to androgens either masculinizes or feminizes the brain. In this way gendered or sexual behaviors that are manifested at a later stage are appropriate or inappropriate to the particular anatomical sex. Studies on humans with various endocrinological histories purport to show inappropriate gender role behavior (Ehrhardt & Meyer-Bahlberg, 1981), but these studies have been criticized on both methodological and ideological grounds (Longino & Doell, 1983; Lewontin et al., 1984) as well as for their failure to be replicated in later work (Slijper, 1984).

More pertinent to the subject of this volume is the research undertaken to show a relationship between sexual orientation and the so-called luteinizing hormone (LH) surge. A sharp increase in LH release from the pituitary gland is the normal response to increasing estrogen production by the ovaries during the early phase of the menstrual cycle. This LH surge is followed by ovulation. In heterosexual men the response to an injection of estrogen (mimicking the natural rise that occurs in women) is markedly lower than the response to such an injection seen in women. A number of studies, primarily by Dörner and his colleagues (Dörner et al., 1975), have reported that the LH response of homosexual men lies between that of "normal" men and women, i.e., their LH surge is, in his word, "feminized." Further studies of transsexuals by the Dörner group (Dörner et al., 1976) seemed to support the idea of a relationship between sexual orientation and the LH response to injected estrogen, and, by extension from the animal model described above, an effect of prenatal hormone exposure on the brain was postulated as the mechanism causing the "abnormal" sexual orientation, in spite of the fact that there is no animal equivalent of human homosexual behavior and despite the marked differences in brain structure and organization between animals and humans. The "natural," causal relationship between anatomical sex and both gender and sexual orientation is thus inferred to be altered by abnormal hormonal exposure *in utero*. Lesbians are masculinized women and gay men are feminized males. The resort to such outdated stereotypes is indicative of the contrived nature of the hypotheses involved. Indeed, these LH surge studies have more recently been shown to be flawed. Work by Gooren (1986, also this volume) has provided evidence that the critical factor governing the extent of the LH surge is the level of circulating estrogen in the subjects at the time of the experiment and that this surge is not related to sexual orientation.

Another research project, one related to and following upon the gender role behavior studies mentioned earlier, tentatively identifies prenatal exposure to the synthetic estrogen diethylstilbestrol (DES) as predisposing the female offspring of such treated pregnancies to the development of lesbianism (Ehrhardt et al., 1985). The subject group was small, there were only thirty participants, and the effects were marginal. The authors make no strong claims regarding a causal role of the hormone treatment; they only state that it could have been a contributing factor.

Evidence for a genetic basis for homosexuality has recently been published by Hamer et al. (1993), who claim to have found a locus on the X chromosome which is associated with homosexuality in men. Given the controversial nature of these findings and the criticism directed at studies of human behavioral genetics in general (Hogan, 1993), especially the lack of strict criteria as to what would constitute meaningful data, this evidence must be treated with considerable skepticism.

Another recent addition to the research on biological correlates of homosexuality alleges the existence of anatomical differences in the size of particular parts of the brains of homosexual men as compared with heterosexual men. These differences are then postulated to be causally related to the sexual orientation of the subjects in the research, even though no function of this particular brain region with respect to sexual behavior has been demonstrated (LeVay, 1991). The brain region in question is a small cluster of neurons in the hypothalamus that is alleged to be slightly larger in heterosexual men than in homosexual men. Again it is only by analogy with the anatomy of the brain of the rat, where neural connections associated with the facilitation of lordosis (the arching of the back typical of the female mating posture in this species) have been demonstrated (Harlen et al., 1984) and where such behavior is dependent upon the previous (perinatal) appropriate hormonal environment, that some connection between the brain differences in humans can be referred to sexual behavioral differences. But of course the insurmountable problem with this analogy is that the mating behaviors of rats and the sexual behaviors of humans are not homologous. The former are reflex-like and the latter are complex, intentional behaviors mediated by higher (cortical) brain mechanisms rather than by the reflex centers of the lower brain. In addition there is almost no evidence of same-sex sexual behaviors amongst animals in their natural environments. In fact we have some difficulty in understanding what homosexuality actually is in humans—an erotic preference (orientation) or a behavior (same-sex genital contact) (Richardson, 1983-84). Most humans have affectionate relationships with persons of both sexes throughout their lives and by virtue of social and personal norms only some of these are permitted to advance to sexual interaction. There is nothing reflex-like about our sex partner choices, nor about our copulatory behaviors once those choices have been made. Of course we are dependent, as are other animals, upon an intact neuromuscular system for our ability to interact sexually with others and to reproduce. Because this latter ability dictates differences in anatomy and physiology between the sexes, we should not be surprised to find differences between the brains of men and women related to the control of reproductive functions (ovulation, etc.). But the details of the mechanism by which more complex behaviors in humans are brought about are completely unknown at present and likely to remain so for some time.

What then are we to make of this recent demonstration of differences in the size of one hypothalamic nucleus between homosexual and heterosexual men? Surely the answer is: Not much. The study is a small one, involving only 19 homosexual and 16 heterosexual subjects, and with such a degree of variation among both groups as to suggest immediately the need for many more subjects before a real size difference could be demonstrated. This, coupled with some uncertainty as to the sexual preference of some of the subjects in the study, leaves me rather surprised both that it was published at all, at so premature a stage of the research, and that it has been so widely accepted by some of the scientific community. These studies leave out of consideration entirely cross-cultural studies of homosexuality that demonstrate variability and change in sexual orientation. Such findings cannot be reconciled with a hormonal, causal mechanism.

It is not surprising that LeVay, who has come out as gay, finds a biological explanation for same-sex attraction appealing. Many gays admit that seeing their sexuality as inherent and unchangeable is easier to live with than the alternative—the social constructionist view in which some degree of choice is involved and where the possibility of change is raised. The simplicity of the biological position has appeal as well for the broader community of citizens in that it fits into preconceived notions of what is—the status quo. But why would the scientific community accept these contrived explanations with so little questioning of the quality of the observations or of the lack of consideration of quite well known alternative (social constructionist, interactionist) explanations?

I think we have to look rather more deeply into the structure of our societal institutions for an understanding of the enthusiasm with which biologists greet each new biological explanation of the status quo. Biologists, as natural scientists, are most comfortable with explanatory models that are simple, linear, and mechanistic (Doell & Longino, 1988). They are accepting of complexity and interaction of sorts, the kind that can be added to or subtracted from an underlying "main cause," which could on occasion overwhelm that cause completely. However, they are not attuned to notions of agency, of the self-influencing of outcomes that has to be a consideration in the development of social constructionist models of human behavior. Thus it may be difficult for biologists to understand the degree of complexity of truly interactionist theories of human behavior. Instead, their training as biologists may lead them to cling to a mechanical explanation. This adherence can be discerned in H. F. L. Meyer-Bahlburg's (1984) plea for continuing to investigate the psychoendocrine model of sexual orientation in spite of "so many serious problems" with it. He goes on to offer the timeworn argument of the continuity of anatomy and physiology throughout the mammalian class, and of the role of sex hormones in their development and function, ignoring his own cautionary note a few paragraphs earlier in this same article regarding differences between primates and lower mammals in brain mechanisms of hormonal regulation. And of course he fails to mention the striking differences in control of complex behaviors which evolved in social primates and especially in humans. He is quite right to emphasize anatomical and physiological similarities in reproductive processes throughout the mammalian class because the evidence here is uncontroversial. We should not be surprised at the finding of anatomical differences in or near the hypothalamus in men and women (Swaab & Fliers, 1985), since these regions may well be involved in the physiological processes regulating the menstrual cycle in women and the noncyclic release of sex-related hormones in men. Our understanding of the neural circuitry regulating these functions in humans, as with our understanding of brain function in general, is minimal at this stage in our research endeavors and we cannot make useful comparisons with anatomical or behavioral evidence in rodents. Meyer-Bahlburg's yen for a mechanical explanation seems to reveal a lack of understanding of social interactionist theory which is further substantiated by his reference to social learning theory as being no more compelling than is the psychoendocrine theory (Meyer-Bahlburg, 1984). This dismissal of social learning theory reflects an ignorance of the enormous literature available attesting to the complexity and variability in the developmental histories of homosexual individuals. In addition it ignores the interesting and compelling cross-cultural studies demonstrating the wide range of gender and sexual behaviors in other cultures (Blackwood, 1984; Herdt, 1981). Even the reading of our own historical record tells of changing perceptions of the meaning of homosexual behavior in Western society.

All scientific theory undergoes modification and change as it matures and so will our theories of sexuality continue to be modified as we bring the experiences of different cultures and different individuals in our own culture into our understanding of the process of sexual identity development. The signature of real scientists lies in the openness with which they greet new findings that bring into question their pet theories.

But there is much more than just the ego involvement of the scientists lurking in the background that has to do with why theories of sexual orientation are controversial and strongly held. That more has to do with norms that are deeply embedded in our social structure. I want to extend my discussion beyond social and biological theorizing about sexual orientation to the significance of sexuality itself and its role in self-identity in our culture.

Sexuality plays a central role in self and social identity in the United States. It is the primary organizing modality that structures our lives. Whether or not we come out, live alone or with someone, are married, or rear children are important decisions that will have major, long-lasting effects on our lives and behaviors. There is a positive ambiance that is associated culturally with marriage and a stigma that is attached to homosexual lifestyles. No matter how liberal we are, the society in which we are reared condemns homosexual practices.

The acceptance of an innate essential difference, biologically derived, does not alter the stigma. It permits tolerance but by no means guarantees it, much less can it remove the stigma. Only a recognition of the bisexual capacities of humans along with a recognition of the way in which societies construct sexual categories for purposes of controlling groups and distributing power, coupled with a determination to change the status quo, will permit the development of egalitarianism in our culture. By bisexual capacities of humans I mean that we all probably develop, from infancy, the capacity to have heterosexual, homosexual, or bisexual relationships. Which adjective describes our relationships as adults will depend upon our culture and our experience within it, including our experiences as pre-adolescents and adolescents when sexual feelings develop along with the maturation of reproductive functions. The emotional experiences associated with interpersonal relationships during these critical years of our development may seem so natural to us and so little of our "choosing" that this formative period may take on the appearance of revealing an already present identity rather than the forming of one. On the other hand the presence in our culture of the negative associations attached to homosexuality means that at least to some degree the acceptance of homosexual relationships is likely, sooner or later, to be a conscious decision on the part of an individual. This decision could lead to the adoption of a gay identity and a gay lifestyle along with all their ramifications (DuBay, 1987).

The source of the stigma is the fear of loss of power by dominant groups within our society (Foucault, 1978). Power hierarchies are maintained in myriad ways but most important among these is the ranking of individuals on the basis of alleged inherent differences. Thus women and minorities have both been rated inferior on the basis of purported cognitive deficiencies. The ranking of homosexuality as inferior to heterosexuality is seen as necessary in order to maintain the superior status of male heterosexuals which would be threatened by the recognition that categories such as gender, race, and sexual orientation are socially constructed.

REFERENCES

Benbow, C., & Stanley, J. (1980). Sex differences in mathematical ability: Fact or artifact? *Science, 210*, 1262-1264.

Blackwood, E. (1984). Sexuality and gender in certain native American tribes: The case of cross-gender females. *Signs, 10*(1), 27-42.

D'Emilio, J. D., & Freedman, E. B. (1988). *Intimate matters: A history of sexuality in America.* New York: Harper and Row.

Doell, R. G., & Longino, H. E. (1988). Sex hormones and human behavior: A critique of the linear model. *Journal of Homosexuality, 15*(3/4), 55-78.

Dörner, G., Rohde, W., Stahl, F., Krell, L., & Masius, W. G. (1975). A neuroendocrine predisposition for homosexuality in men. *Archives of Sexual Behavior, 4*, 1-8.

Dörner, G., Rohde, W., Seidel, K., Haas, W., & Schott, G. (1976). On the evocability of a positive oestrogen feedback action on LH secretion in transsexual men and women. *Endokrinologie, 67*, 20-25.

DuBay, W. H. (1987). *Gay identity.* Jefferson, NC: McFarland.

Ehrhardt, A. A., & Meyer-Bahlburg, H. F. L. (1981). Effects of prenatal sex hormones on gender related behavior. *Science, 211*, 1312-1318.

Ehrhardt, A. A., Meyer-Bahlburg, H. F. L., Rosen, L. R., Feldman, J. F., Veridiano, N. P., Zimmerman, I., & McEwen, B. S. (1985). Sexual orientation after prenatal exposure to exogenous estrogen. *Archives of Sexual Behavior, 14*(1), 57-77.

Fausto-Sterling, A. (1985). *Myths of gender.* New York: Basic Books.

Foucault, M. (1978). *The history of sexuality. Vol.1, An introduction.* Translated by R. Hurley. New York: Pantheon.

Goldfoot, D. A., & Neff, D. A. (1985). On measuring behavioral sex differences in social contexts. In N. Adler, D. Pfaff, & R. W. Goy (Eds.), *Handbook of behavioral neurobiology,* Vol. 7, "Reproduction" (pp. 767-783). New York: Plenum.

Gooren, L. (1986). The neuroendocrine response of luteinizing hormone to estrogen administration in the human is not sex specific but depends on the hormonal environment. *Journal of Clinical Endocrinology and Metabolism, 63*(3), 589-593.

Gould, S. J. (1981). *The mismeasure of man.* New York: W. W. Norton.

Goy, R. W., & McEwen, B. S. (1980). *Sexual differentiation of the brain.* Cambridge, MA: MIT Press.

Greenberg, D. E. (1988). *The construction of homosexuality.* Chicago: University of Chicago Press.

Hamer, D. H., Hu, S., Magnuson, V. L., Hu, N., & Pattatucci, A. M. L. (1993). A linkage between DNA markers on the X chromosome and male sexual orientation. *Science, 261*, 321-327.

Harlen, R. E., Shivers, B. D., & Pfaff, D. W. (1984). In G. J. DeVries, J. P. C. DeBruin, H. B. M. Uylings, & M. A. Corner (Eds.), *Sex differences in the brain* (pp. 239-255). Amsterdam: Elsevier.

Herdt, G. (1981). *Guardians of the flutes.* New York: McGraw-Hill.

Horgan, J. (1993). Eugenics revisited. *Scientific American, 268*(6), 120-131.

LeVay, S. (1991). A difference in hypothalamic structure between heterosexual and homosexual men. *Science, 253*, 1034-1037.

Lewontin, R. C., Rose, S., & Kamin, L. J. (1984). *Not in our genes.* New York: Pantheon Books.

Longino, H., & Doell, R. (1983). Body, bias and behavior: A comparative analysis of reasoning in two areas of biological science. *Signs, 9*(2), 206-227.

Meyer-Bahlburg, H. F. L. (1984). Psychoendocrine research on sexual orientation. Current status and future options. In G. J. DeVries, J. P. C. DeBruin, H. B. M. Uylings, & M. A. Corner (Eds.). *Sex Differences in the brain* (pp. 375-398). Amsterdam: Elsevier.

Richardson, D. (1983/84). The dilemma of essentiality in homosexual theory. *Journal of Homosexuality, 9*(2/3), 79-90.

Slijper, F. M. E. (1984). Androgens and gender role behavior in girls with congenital adrenal hyperplasis (CAH). In G. J. DeVries, J. P. C. DeBruin, H. B. M. Uylings, & M. S. Corner (Eds.), *Sex differences in the brain* (pp. 417-422). Amsterdam: Elsevier.

Swaab, D. F., & Fliers, E. (1985). A sexually dimorphic nucleus in the human brain. *Science, 228*, 1112-1115.

Weeks, J. (1986). *Sexuality.* New York: Tavistock Publications.

SECTION VI: MISLABELING, SOCIAL STIGMA, SCIENCE, AND MEDICINE

Introduction

In our last section, two papers reveal what can happen when science and medicine attempt to "correct" behaviors which are socially stigmatized. Scientific and medical researchers have often intervened in attempts to control or eradicate such behaviors by manipulating the physical processes that are assumed to be the underlying causes of that behavior. Our first paper discusses how biomedical researchers conflate bisexuality with either homosexuality or heterosexuality. People who lay claim to a bisexual identity are stigmatized as fencesitters, immature, indecisive, or closet homosexuals and heterosexuals. The second paper discusses the stigma of left-handedness and traces the origins and demise of society's taboo against it, and the subsequent abandonment of "treatments" originally prescribed by the sciences. Our final paper discusses the use of a drug, depo-provera, to subdue certain sexual behaviors. It paints the spectacle of medicine compromising the Hippocratic oath in a desperate attempt to suppress sexual behavior, the antecedents

[Haworth co-indexing entry note]: "Introduction." Co-published simultaneously in *Journal of Homosexuality* (The Haworth Press, Inc.) Vol. 28, No. 3/4, 1995, pp. 355-356; and: *Sex, Cells, and Same-Sex Desire: The Biology of Sexual Preference* (ed: John P. De Cecco, and David Allen Parker) The Haworth Press, Inc., 1995, pp. 355-356. Multiple copies of this article/chapter may be purchased from The Haworth Document Delivery Center [1-800-3-HAWORTH; 9:00 a.m. - 5:00 p.m. (EST)].

355

of which have yet to be proven to be biological. Both these papers speak to the motivation behind attempts to find biological markers of sexual preference and the potential dangers of pursuing such research.

Biology of Bisexuality: Critique and Observations

Paul H. Van Wyk, PhD

Auburn University

Chrisann S. Geist, PhD

University of Illinois

SUMMARY. Differentiation of human sexual orientation, particularly bisexuality, has been little studied. Most studies have lumped bisexuals with homosexuals. Those examining bisexuals separately have uniformly observed that bisexuals are often unlike either heterosexuals or homosexuals. Some authors have overgeneralized the results of animal studies as applying to humans. While animal models can provide useful hypotheses, human sexual orientation is unique. Therefore, conclusions about human sexuality based on animal research are suspect. Human sexual orientation is influenced by biological, cognitive, cultural, and subcultural variables in interaction, leading to multiple types of heterosexuals, bisexuals, and homosexuals. Understanding of human sexual orientation will improve only if these factors are accounted for in research and theory. Several

---

Paul H. Van Wyk is Adjunct Associate Professor, Department of Psychology, Auburn University.

Chrisann S. Geist is Professor and Director of Graduate Studies, Division of Rehabilitation Education Services, University of Illinois.

Correspondence may be addressed to Dr. Van Wyk, Rt. 3, Box 13, Union Springs, AL 36089, or to Dr. Geist, DRES, University of Illinois at Urbana-Champaign, 1207 S. Oak, Champaign, IL 61820.

[Haworth co-indexing entry note]: "Biology of Bisexuality: Critique and Observations." Van Wyk, Paul H., and Chrisann S. Geist. Co-published simultaneously in *Journal of Homosexuality* (The Haworth Press, Inc.) Vol. 28, No. 3/4, 1995, pp. 357-373; and: *Sex, Cells, and Same-Sex Desire: The Biology of Sexual Preference* (ed: John P. De Cecco, and David Allen Parker) The Haworth Press, Inc., 1995, pp. 357-373. Multiple copies of this article/chapter may be purchased from The Haworth Document Delivery Center [1-800-3-HAWORTH; 9:00 a.m. - 5:00 p.m. (EST)].

357

studies seem to indicate that some bisexuals have a predominantly heterosexual or homosexual orientation, but high erotic responsiveness and more "masculine" characteristics, leading to versatility in sexual behavior. Early exposure to masculinizing hormones seems to predispose human females toward bisexuality rather than exclusive homosexuality.

Interest in biological bases of sexual behavior has been sufficient to generate thousands of studies of hormonal and other biological influences on animal sexual behavior (see reviews by Adkinsregan, 1988; Feder, 1984; Goy & McEwen, 1980; Meyer-Bahlburg, 1977, 1979; Plapinger & McEwen, 1978; Reinisch, 1974). There have been many fewer studies in humans. Of studies in humans, most have examined either current or retrospective differences between adult "heterosexuals" and "homosexuals," often not carefully defining the sexual orientation of their subjects. Bisexual and predominantly homosexual subjects have often been treated together as a presumably homogeneous group, contrasted with comparison groups of presumably heterosexual subjects, whose sexual orientation may not have actually been ascertained.

Twenty-eight percent of the "homosexual" sample of Bieber, Dain, Dince, Drellich, Grand, Gundlach, Kremer, Rifkin, Wilbur, and Bieber (1962), for example, was known to be bisexual rather than exclusively homosexual. The bisexuals and homosexuals were lumped together and compared with heterosexuals; bisexuals were never compared with homosexuals. Hatterer's (1970) study followed a similar procedure. Fifty-three percent of Saghir and Robbins's (1973) sample of "homosexual" men reported having had one or more stable heterosexual relationships. Many of Weinberg and Williams's (1974) "homosexual" subjects were married, and 49% of them were bisexual to some degree. Of Masters and Johnson's (1979) "homosexual" sample, 83% actually fell in the bisexual range (Kinsey 2-4). Bailey and Pillard (1991) also presumed the homogeneity of homosexuals and bisexuals, contrasting them with heterosexuals.

Those studies which have separately examined heterosexuals, bisexuals, and homosexuals have consistently found that bisexuals differ from both heterosexuals and homosexuals. Bisexual individuals are not necessarily like homosexuals, as implied by those studies which lump homosexual and bisexual subjects together. Nor are bisexuals necessarily halfway between heterosexuals and homosexuals, as those studies which differentiate between the three, but do not examine the data for curvilinearity of relationships, tacitly assume.

ANIMAL MODELS

In animals, behavior tends to be controlled more or less by known biological variables, including hormones. There is ample evidence from hundreds of studies that hormones, either prenatally, perinatally, or in adulthood, can influence the sexual behavior of mammals (Feder, 1984). These hormones include estrogens, androgens, progestins, and their antagonists. Most such studies have been done on rodents such as mice, rats, guinea pigs, and hamsters, although many other species, including ferrets, sheep, dogs, monkeys, and apes have also been studied.

In the normal course of development, if the mammalian fetus has a Y (male) chromosome, testes develop, produce a substance which prevents development of a uterus and fallopian tubes, and secrete testosterone (androgen), which masculinizes and defeminizes both the external genitals and the brain. These events occur either before or shortly after birth, depending on the species. At puberty, circulating levels of sex hormones rise and are' capable of activating or deactivating masculine or feminine sexual and reproductive behaviors. The exact sequence, timing, and details of these events vary significantly from species to species and even from strain to strain of the same species. If the fetus does not have a Y chromosome, development follows the female pattern (Money, 1988).

Experimental manipulations, including administration of hormones and castration, are capable of masculinizing and defeminizing genetic females or feminizing and demasculinizing genetic males of many species to the extent that both the appearance and the behavior of the adult animal are nearly indistinguishable from those of the opposite genetic sex. In some species, such as sheep, where the critical time period for masculinization of the genitals does not overlap the critical time period for masculinization of the brain, it is possible to create by treatment with androgens ewes whose bodies appear female, but whose sexual behavior is indistinguishable from that of rams in terms of mounting other ewes in heat (Clarke, 1977). Insertive intercourse is of course impossible, since there is no penis.

On the basis of these data several authors including Dörner, Rohde, Stahl, Krell, and Masius (1975), Dörner, Doecke, Goetz, Rohde, Stahl, and Toenjes (1987), Ellis and Ames (1987), and Imperato-McGinley, Peterson, Gautier, and Sturla (1979) have concluded either implicitly or explicitly that human sexual orientation must be similarly controlled.

Dörner and colleagues (1975, 1987) are among the chief proponents of the theory that androgenization of the brain (normally by testosterone produced in the fetal or neonatal testes) before or shortly after birth causes brain masculinization, which in turn causes sexual activity with females, and that lack of androgenization results in brain feminization, which in turn results in sexual behavior with males. In rodents and some other mammals this is largely true, though somewhat oversimplified. Implicit in Dörner's theory is the concept that sexual orientation is fixed in adulthood. This appears to be true for many individuals, particularly those with exclusive sexual orientations. However for bisexuals this seems to be less often true. In fact, in sequential bisexuality, proportions of sexual behavior engaged in with females and males vary over time by definition. Any theory which does not allow for changes in sexual orientation over time during adulthood cannot account for these data.

HUMAN UNIQUENESS

Direct generalizations from animal research to humans are often unsupportable and seriously misleading for a number of reasons, including the absence of exclusive homosexuality in other species, lack of correspondence between specific animal sexual behaviors and human sexual orientation, human cross-cultural variations, and contradictions between the predictions of simplistic biological reductionist theories and observed data.

Human sexual orientation has no analogue in other species. Many species, including primates, engage in sexual behavior with members of their own sex (Kinsey, Pomeroy, Martin, & Gebhard,

1953). However, except in humans, exclusive life-long homosexuality has only been observed in experimental settings (Erwin & Maple, 1976; Ford & Beach, 1951; West, 1977). Therefore, other species offer at most analogues for bisexuality and heterosexuality in humans, not an analogue for exclusive homosexuality, as most biological reductionists imply.

The sexual behaviors which are most frequently used as indicators of "homosexuality" in animal studies are strongly sex-typed in most other species, but either have no direct analogues in human behavior, or are engaged in by men and women, heterosexual, bisexual, and homosexual people.

Specific Behaviors

In animal studies, lordosis, a reflex concave arching of the back that facilitates insertive intercourse, and which in the absence of experimental manipulation is more frequently observed in rodent females than in rodent males, is the most frequently used measure of "homosexual" orientation in experimentally manipulated male rodents. Hormonally feminized or demasculinized male rodents display lordosis significantly more frequently than do untreated control males. However, if a control male mounts a lordosing treated male, only the treated male is presumed to be displaying "homosexual" behavior. There is no human analogy to lordosis. Human coitus most often occurs face-to-face, and although both women and men can present in a manner mimicking lordosis, this is not a species-specific reflex response, nor a characteristic that distinguishes heterosexual from homosexual relationships. In fact, the position is rather more common in heterosexual than in lesbian relationships, and most male homosexuals engage in other sexual behaviors considerably more often than they engage in "lordosis."

Mounting and thrusting are the most frequently used measures of "homosexual" behavior in experimentally manipulated female rodents. If a hormonally treated female animal mounts an untreated lordosing estrous control, simplistic biological reductionism treats only the mountor, not the mountee, as "homosexual." Mounting and thrusting are found in all human sexual behavior regardless of its sexual orientation. Female heterosexuals and bisexuals often mount and thrust with supine heterosexual or bisexual men. Some individuals of each sexual orientation also engage in other activities more frequently than in mounting and thrusting.

Ricketts (1984, pp. 84-85) brilliantly skewers simplistic biological reductionism, stating:

> Males could find themselves mounting and thrusting with admirable vigor, but with males instead of females. Alternatively, females might find themselves with a desire for male partners but with an irritating tendency to insist upon mounting them. Bisexuals could be those who mount, thrust, and lordose, but only with partners of the opposite sex; they could be those who pursue objects of both sexes but who, once they get them, rigidly insist on either mounting and thrusting or on lordosing, but not both; they could be individuals who mount, thrust, and lordose, and who do so with reckless disregard for the biological sex of their partners.

Since the basis for ascribing human sexual orientation depends primarily on the gender of persons to whom one is sexually attracted, rather than on the specific motor behaviors one engages in with them during sexual interaction, perhaps a better animal analogy would be the courtship behaviors of other mammals. Although these have been much less studied than lordosis and mounting and thrusting, such behaviors have been found to be susceptible to hormonal manipulations in animals. For example, Fadem and Barfield (1981) found that the perinatal hormonal environment influenced hopping, darting, ear-quivering, and affiliative behavior in female rats. We are not suggesting, however, that if women were to be observed hopping, darting, and wiggling their ears more in the presence of males than of females, or affiliating more with males than with females, that this would prove either that the women were heterosexual or that these behaviors were influenced by the presence or absence of prenatal or perinatal hormones.

Cultural Variation

In contrast with the rigidly stereotyped sexual behavior of most other species, human sexual behavior is highly variable both cross-culturally and within individual cultures. The incidence of male adolescent or adult homosexual behavior varies from essentially zero in Mangaia (Marshall, 1971) to apparently universal among the Sambia of New Guinea and other similar Melanesian cultures (Baldwin & Baldwin, 1989; Herdt, 1981, 1984, 1990).

Sequential bisexuality is the norm among Sambian males. Preadolescent boys are required to fellate older males and swallow the semen because it is believed that without this "male milk" they will fail to mature properly. Upon initiation into adulthood, Sambian men marry and engage in heterosexual behavior, first requiring their young brides to fellate them and later to have intercourse. Homosexual behavior between adult males is rare among the Sambia.

Subcultural variation also exists. Most large cities have a gay community, and subcultures within the gay community. Bisexual subcultures are less common, but the American swinging community has a norm which encourages female bisexual participation (O'Neill & O'Neill, 1970). Some segments of the women's movement encourage bisexuality (Blumstein & Schwartz, 1976). McCaghy and Skipper (1969) describe bisexuality in the striptease subculture. Humphreys (1970) describes married male bisexuals who participate in the "tearoom" subculture, while Reiss (1961) describes the subculture of bisexual teenage male prostitutes. Breslow, Evans, and Langley (1986) compare heterosexual, bisexual, and homosexual male sadomasochists. Each of these subcultures has very different norms and customs.

Human cultures and subcultures vary not only in incidence, frequency, and enjoyment of heterosexual, homosexual, and bisexual behavior, but in assignment of gender-role behaviors. In Tchambuli society, for example, women do most of the heavy work, while men occupy themselves mostly in artistic pursuits and other tasks that most other societies traditionally assign to women (Mead, 1950). Hoult (1984, p. 147) asks, "Would a Tchambuli woman who was "masculinized" *in utero* turn out to be a fluttery Southern belle?" The above examples are only a few of the many cross-cultural variations. Anyone familiar with the anthropological literature can find dozens if not hundreds more, including assignment of individuals, usually males, to a third gender role, that of *berdache*, or man-woman (Herdt, 1990; Marshall, 1971).

The entire concept of gender role is cultural and uniquely human, with no parallel in any other species. Since heterosexuality, bisexuality, homosexuality, transvestism, and transsexualism are partly dependent on sex of assignment and rearing and subsequent gender role conformity or non-conformity (Bell, Weinberg, & Hammersmith, 1981; Green, 1985; Green, Roberts, Williams, Goodman, & Mixon, 1987; Money, 1986; Money & Ehrhardt, 1972; Money & Ogunro, 1974; Van Wyk & Geist, 1984), any reductionist animal model fails to account for much of the data.

BISEXUALS

Diversity

There are many different types of bisexuals in the world, just as not all heterosexuals or homosexuals are the same. The anthropological literature chronicles many of the different styles of sexual adjustments humans can make. Bell and Weinberg (1978) devote an entire book to describing differences among homosexuals, including bisexuals. Saghir and Robbins (1973) also found much diversity among their male and female "homosexuals," not surprising since their methodology generally failed to differentiate between bisexuals and homosexuals.

Blumstein and Schwartz (1976) emphasize the diversity found among bisexual women, including those involved in group marriage, prostitution, the women's movement, libertarian ideology, incarceration, group sex, and close friendships or emotional relationships which became sexual. Sometimes these bisexual behaviors are adopted in adulthood after development with an exclusively heterosexual or homosexual orientation, resulting in sequential as opposed to lifelong bisexuality. Brownfain (1985) describes similar sexual orientation changes in men after reaching adulthood. Mexican male bisexuals manage to maintain a heterosexual identity as long as they play the inserter role in contact with other males (Carrier, 1985). In this they differ from many United States bisexuals, but not from the teenage male prostitutes described by Reiss (1961). Brownfain (1985), Coleman (1985), Matteson (1985), and Wolf (1985) each describe differences among married bisexual men, who in turn differ from Dixon's (1985) bisexual swinging husbands. Attempts to clarify the origins of sexual orientation must take these complexities into account.

Eroticism

Several studies comparing bisexuals with heterosexuals or homosexuals find the bisexuals to have higher rates of sexual activity or fantasy, or greater levels of erotic interest than do the others. Van Wyk and Geist (1984) found that male and female behavioral bisexuals (those scoring between 2.0 and 4.0 on the Kinsey scale on the basis of overt behavior) had more heterosexual fantasy than did either behaviorally exclusive heterosexuals or predominant or exclusive behavioral homosexuals. Dixon's (1985) bisexual men had significantly more orgasms per week from both vaginal and oral sexual activities with females than did his heterosexuals. They also masturbated more, but the heterosexuals had happier marriages. Bressler and Lavender's (1986) female bisexuals had more total orgasms per week, and described them as stronger, than did heterosexuals or homosexuals. Goode and Haber (1977) found their bisexual women to be more heterosexually precocious than those who were exclusively heterosexual. The bisexuals were more experienced in several types of heterosexual contact. Their masturbation frequencies were higher, and they enjoyed masturbation more. Goode and Haber characterized them as sexual "adventurers."

Masculinity

Ehrhardt, Evers, and Money (1968) studied 23 women with late-treated adrenogenital syndrome, in which the adrenal glands secrete an excess of androgenic masculinizing hormones due to a defect in steroid metabolism, who had been raised as girls since infancy. Twenty-two women reported on their sexual behavior with partners. Of these, 6 women reported none, 12 were exclusively heterosexual, and 4 were bisexual. None was exclusively or predominantly homosexual. Twenty-one women reported on sexual dreams and fantasies. Of these, 2 women reported none, 9 were exclusively heterosexual, and 10 were bisexual. None was exclusively homosexual. Lev-Ran (1974) studied 18 late-treated women with adreno-genital syndrome, none of whom apparently was bisexual or homo-sexual.

Money (1985) studied 30 young women with early-treated adre-nogenital syndrome, of whom 23 provided information about their sexual orientation. By history of behavior and fantasy, 12 were heterosexual, 11 bisexual, and none homosexual. By self-rating of current orientation, 12 were exclusively heterosexual, 6 bisexual, and 5 predominantly or exclusively homosexual.

Ehrhardt, Meyer-Bahlburg, Rosen, Feldman, Veridiano, Zimmer-man, and McEwen (1985) studied 30 young women who were exposed to diethylstilbestrol (DES) before birth. Although formally classified as an estrogen, DES masculinizes and defeminizes brain tissues. Of the 30 women, 29 provided data on lifelong sexual orientation. Of these, 24 were exclusively or predominantly hetero-sexual, 4 were bisexual, and 1 was exclusively homosexual in overt behavior; while 22 were predominantly or exclusively heterosexual, 6 were bisexual, and 1 was predominantly homosexual in sexual responsiveness.

What is remarkable here is the high incidence of bisexuality observed by Ehrhardt et al. (1968, 1985) and Money (1985) in women exposed to masculinizing hormones, and the relative dearth of predominant or exclusive homosexuality seen in all four studies. Simplistic biological reductionism predicts homosexuality rather than bisexuality or heterosexuality as a result of masculization/defem-inization.

Van Wyk and Geist (1984) found that of 3,392 adult American white women obtained from sources without known homosexual bias, only 0.7% were behaviorally bisexual while 1.8% were pre-dominantly or exclusively homosexual. That is, only 0.7% had between 1/3 and 2/3 of their overt sexual experience with other females, while 1.8% had more than 2/3 of their overt sexual experi-ence with other females. Of 3,849 men, 1.2% were behaviorally bisexual, while 4.7% were predominantly or exclusively homo-sexual. High correlations between fantasies and overt behavior were observed. Ellis, Burke, and Ames (1987) likewise found more predominant or exclusive homosexuals than bisexuals both behav-iorally and in fantasy among both males and females. Therefore the high number of bisexuals relative to homosexuals among women with adrenogenital syndrome or DES exposure appears unusual and noteworthy.

A meta-analysis was performed comparing sexual orientation data on women from Van Wyk and Geist (1984) with the combined behavioral data from Ehrhardt et al. (1968, 1985), Lev-Ran (1974), and Money (1985). The results of Chi-square analysis were significant well beyond the .001 level. Lest anyone become concerned about low expected frequencies in the Chi-square table, statistician Dr. Gary Morris (1980) states on the basis of Montecarlo studies that the Chi-square test becomes conservative when expected cell frequencies are low. Table 1 shows the high proportion of bisexual women among those with early exposure to masculinizing hormones as compared with women obtained from sources with no known sexual bias. Therefore, early exposure of human females to masculinizing hormones appears to predispose toward bisexuality rather than toward exclusive homosexuality.

In women, LaTorre and Wendenburg (1983) found differing personality characteristics for bisexuals, heterosexuals, and lesbians. Bisexuals were consistently more masculine and less feminine than either heterosexual or lesbian subjects.

Some evidence exists to support the concept of specific biological precursors of bisexual orientation in genetic males (Money, 1988). For example 47,XYY syndrome, marked by an extra male Y chromosome, seems to predispose toward bisexuality, paraphilia, and impulsiveness, but not toward heterosexuality.

LeVay (1991) examined at autopsy the brains of 18 homosexual men, 1 bisexual man, 16 presumably heterosexual men, and 6 pres-

TABLE 1. Sexual Behavior of Women Exposed to Masculinizing Hormones vs. Women from Sources with No Known Sexual Bias.*

Number of women:	Heterosexual	Bisexual	Homosexual
Masculinizing hormones	66	19	1
Unbiased sources	3,309	23	60

* Chi-square (2) = 322.4, $p \ll .001$

umably heterosexual women, finding differences in size of the INAH 3 nucleus of the anterior hypothalamus between heterosexual men and homosexual men. LeVay concluded that INAH 3 is dimorphic with sexual orientation in men. However, the 1 known bisexual subject in LeVay's study matches the INAH 3 size of the heterosexual men rather than that of most of the homosexuals with which he was grouped.

Van Wyk (1984), in critiquing the research of Dörner et al. (1975), pointed out that the luteinizing hormone (LH) response of bisexual men experimentally injected with estrogen by Dörner et al. was more "masculine" than that of their heterosexual men. Therefore, by the logic of Dörner et al. the bisexual men appear to have hypermasculinized brains, which do not, however, compel them to have sex only with females. Dörner's own data contradict the predictions of his theory.

DISCUSSION

The search for biological bases of sexual orientation has generated thousands of research studies, mostly on animals. However, human sexual orientation has no counterpart in animals, so caution is warranted regarding attempts to generalize from animals to humans.

There is enormous variation across cultures in the expression or inhibition of almost all types of sexual activity, including bisexuality, which ranges from near absence in Mangaia to near universality among males in parts of Melanesia. Any attempt to define biological bases for human sexual orientation must take this variation into account. Since expression of bisexuality, heterosexuality, and homosexuality are culture-dependent, biological differences among bisexuals, celibates, heterosexuals, and homosexuals might well turn out to be minimal.

We have not progressed very far in defining biological bases of sexual orientation in the nearly eighty years since Freud commented in *Three Essays on the Theory of Sexuality* (1905/1961) that we know too little about the human brain or the contributions of heredity to construct a viable and parsimonious biological explanation of human sexual orientation. The chance of ever doing so may be slim because there are so many different forms of heterosexuality, bisexuality, and homosexuality. In fact, there is so much variation within each group that the chances of finding any small set of variables which will account neatly both for average differences between groups with differing sexual orientations and for variations within groups approaches the vanishing point.

Nevertheless, there seem to be some commonalities in the data. Exclusive or predominant heterosexuality is most common, followed by predominant or exclusive homosexuality; bisexuality is least common. Higher levels of eroticism for bisexuals were uniformly found in those studies which examined sexual fantasies and behaviors. Bisexuals had more heterosexual fantasies, more heterosexual activity beginning sooner, masturbated more and enjoyed it more, had stronger orgasms, and were more sexually adventurous. Bisexuals studied were also more "masculine" and less "feminine" in various ways: masculinizing hormones in women with adrenogenital syndrome or exposed to DES, personality characteristics in women, an extra Y chromosome and more paraphilias in men with 47,XYY syndrome, LH feedback effect in men, and a single male INAH 3 brain nucleus. Bisexuals were not necessarily any happier, though.

This may all be just coincidence. Populations sampled are in no way comparable. To say that all but one of the studies being compared is small is an understatement. However, research hypotheses concerning relationships among bisexuality, elevated eroticism, "masculinity," and "femininity" can be easily postulated and tested. One that comes to mind: Men are more often bisexual than women. Usually true, except among swingers.

REFERENCES

Adkinsregan, E. (1988). Sex-hormones and sexual orientation in animals. *Psychobiology, 16*(4), 335-347.

Bailey, J. M., & Pillard, R. C. (1991). A genetic study of male sexual orientation. *Archives of General Psychiatry, 48,* 1089-1096.

Baldwin, J. D., & Baldwin, J. I. (1989). The socialization of homosexuality in a non-western society. *Archives of Sexual Behavior, 18*(1), 13-29.

Bell, A. P., & Weinberg, M. S. (1978). *Homosexualities: A study of diversity among men and women.* New York: Simon & Schuster.

Bell, A. P., Weinberg, M. S., & Hammersmith, S. K. (1981). *Sexual preference: Its development in men and women.* Bloomington, IN: Indiana University Press.

Bieber, I., Dain, H. J., Dince, P. R., Drellich, M. G., Grand, H. G., Gundlach, R. H., Kremer, M. W., Rifkin, A. H., Wilbur, C. B., & Bieber, T. B. (1962). *Homosexuality: A psychoanalytic study.* New York: Basic Books.

Blumstein, P. W., & Schwartz, P. (1976). Bisexuality in women. *Archives of Sexual Behavior, 5*(2), 171-181.

Breslow, N., Evans, L., & Langley, J. (1986). Comparisons among heterosexual, bisexual, and homosexual male sadomasochists. *Journal of Homosexuality, 13*(1), 83-107.

Bressler, L. C., & Lavender, A. D. (1986). Sexual fulfillment of heterosexual, bisexual, and homosexual women. *Journal of Homosexuality, 12*(3/4), 109-122.

Brownfain, J. J. (1985). A study of the married bisexual male: Paradox and resolution. *Journal of Homosexuality, 11*(1/2), 173-188.

Carrier, J. M. (1985). Mexican male bisexuality. *Journal of Homosexuality, 11*(1/2), 75-85.

Clarke, I. J. (1977). The sexual behavior of prenatally androgenized ewes observed in the field. *Journal of Reproduction and Fertility, 49*, 311-315.

Coleman, E. (1985). Integration of male bisexuality and marriage. *Journal of Homosexuality, 11*(1/2), 189-208.

Dixon, D. (1985). Perceived sexual satisfaction and marital happiness of bisexual and heterosexual swinging husbands. *Journal of Homosexuality, 11*(1/2), 209-222.

Dörner, G., Doecke, F., Goetz, F., Rohde, W., Stahl, F., & Toenjes, R. (1987). Sexual differentiation of gonadotrophin secretion, sexual orientation and gender role behavior. *Journal of Steroid Biochemistry, 27*(4-6), 1081-1087.

Dörner, G., Rohde, W., Stahl, F., Krell, L., & Masius, W. (1975). A neuroendocrine predisposition for homosexuality in men. *Archives of Sexual Behavior, 4*, 1-8.

Ehrhardt, A. A., Evers, K., & Money, J. (1968). Influence of androgen and some aspects of sexually dimorphic behavior in women with the late-treated adrenogenital syndrome. *Johns Hopkins Medical Journal, 123*(3), 115-122.

Ehrhardt, A. A., Meyer-Bahlburg, H. F. L., Rosen, L. R., Feldman, J. F., Veridiano, N. P., Zimmerman, I., & McEwen, B. S. (1985). Sexual orientation after prenatal exposure to exogenous estrogen. *Archives of Sexual Behavior, 14*(1), 57-77.

Ellis, L., & Ames, M. A. (1987). Neurohormonal functioning and sexual orientation: A theory of homosexuality-heterosexuality. *Psychological Bulletin, 101*(2), 233-258.

Ellis, L., Burke, D., & Ames, M. A. (1987). Sexual orientation as a continuous variable: A comparison between the sexes. *Archives of Sexual Behavior, 16*(6), 523-529.

Erwin, J., & Maple, T. (1976). Ambisexual behavior with male-male anal penetration in male rhesus monkeys. *Archives of Sexual Behavior, 5*, 9-14.

Fadem, B. H., & Barfield, R. J. (1981). Neonatal hormonal influences on the development of proceptive and receptive feminine sexual behavior in rats. *Hormones and Behavior, 15*, 282-288.

Feder, H. H. (1984). Hormones and sexual behavior. *Annual Review of Psychology, 35*, 165-200.

Ford, C. S., & Beach, F. A. (1951). *Patterns of sexual behavior.* New York: Harper & Row.

Freud, S. (1905/1961). Three essays on the theory of sexuality. In J. Strachey (Ed. and Trans.), *The Standard Edition of the Complete Psychological Works of Sigmund Freud*, Vol. 7. London: Hogarth Press.

Goode, E., & Haber, L. (1977). Sexual correlates of homosexual experience: An exploratory study of college women. *Journal of Sex Research, 13*, 12-21.

Goy, R. W., & McEwen (1980). *Sexual differentiation of the brain.* Cambridge, MA: MIT Press.

Green, R. (1985). Gender identity in childhood and later sexual orientation: Follow-up of 78 males. *American Journal of Psychiatry, 142*(3), 339-341.

Green, R., Roberts, C. W., Williams, K., Goodman, M., & Mixon, A. (1987). Specific cross-gender behaviour in boyhood and later homosexual orientation. *British Journal of Psychiatry, 151*, 84-88.

Hatterer, L. R. (1970). *Changing homosexuality in the male.* New York: McGraw-Hill.

Herdt, G. H. (1981). *Guardians of the flutes: Idioms of masculinity.* New York: McGraw-Hill.

Herdt, G. H. (Ed.). (1984). *Ritualized homosexuality in Melanesia.* Berkeley: University of California Press.

Herdt, G. (1990). Mistaken gender: 5-Alpha reductase hermaphroditism and biological reductionism in sexual identity reconsidered. *American Anthropologist, 92*, 433-446.

Hoult, T. F. (1984). Human sexuality in biological perspective: Theoretical and methodological considerations. *Journal of Homosexuality, 9*(2/3), 137-155.

Humphreys, L. (1970). *Tearoom trade: Impersonal sex in public restrooms.* Chicago: Aldine.

Imperato-McGinley, J., Peterson, R. E., Gautier, T., & Sturla, E. (1979). Androgens and the evolution of male-gender identity among male pseudohermaphrodites with *5-alpha*-reductase deficiency. *New England Journal of Medicine, 300*(22), 1233-1237.

Kinsey, A. C., Pomeroy, W. B., Martin, C. E., & Gebhard, P. H. (1953). *Sexual behavior in the human female.* Philadelphia: W. B. Saunders.

LaTorre, R. A., & Wendenburg, K. (1983). Psychological characteristics of bisexual, heterosexual and homosexual women. *Journal of Homosexuality, 9*(1), 87-97.

Lev-Ran, A. (1974). Sexuality and educational levels of women with late-treated adrenogenital syndrome. *Archives of Sexual behavior, 3*(1), 27-32.

LeVay, S. (1991). A difference in hypothalamic structure between heterosexual and homosexual men. *Science, 253*, 1034-1037.

Marshall, D. S. (1971). Sexual behavior on Mangaia. In D. S. Marshall & R. C. Suggs (Eds.), *Human sexual behavior: Variations in the ethnographic spectrum.* New York: Basic Books.

Masters W. H., & Johnson, V. E. (1979). *Homosexuality in perspective.* Boston: Little, Brown.

Matteson, D. R. (1985). Bisexual men in marriage: Is a positive homosexual identity and stable marriage possible? *Journal of Homosexuality, 11*(1/2), 149-172.

McCaghy, C. H., & Skipper, J. K. (1969). Lesbian behavior as an adaptation to the occupation of stripping. *Social Problems, 17,* 262-270.

Mead, M. (1950). *Sex and temperament in three primitive societies.* New York: Mentor Books.

Meyer-Bahlburg, H. F. L. (1977). Sex hormones and male homosexuality in comparative perspective. *Archives of Sexual Behavior, 6*(4), 297-325.

Meyer-Bahlburg, H. F. L. (1979). Sex hormones and female homosexuality: A critical examination. *Archives of Sexual Behavior, 8*(2), 101-119.

Money, J. (1985). Pediatric sexology and hermaphroditism. *Journal of Sex & Marital Therapy, 11*(3), 139-156.

Money, J. (1986). *Lovemaps: Clinical concepts of sexual/erotic health and pathology, paraphilia, and gender transposition in childhood, adolescence, and maturity.* New York: Irvington Publishers.

Money, J. (1988). *Gay, straight, and in-between: The sexology of erotic orientation.* New York: Oxford University Press.

Money, J., & Ehrhardt, A. A. (1972). *Man & woman, boy & girl: The differentiation and dimorphism of gender identity from conception to maturity.* Baltimore: Johns Hopkins University Press.

Money, J., & Ogunro, C. (1974). Behavioral sexology: Ten cases of genetic male intersexuality with impaired prenatal and pubertal androgenization. *Archives of Sexual Behavior, 3*(3), 181-205.

Morris, G. (1980). Lecture given at Illinois Institute of Technology, Chicago.

O'Neill, G. C., & O'Neill, N. (1970). Patterns in group sexual activity. *Journal of Sex Research, 6,* 101-112.

Plapinger, L., & McEwen, B. S. (1978). Gonadal steroid-brain interactions in sexual differentiation. In J. B. Hutchison (Ed.), *Biological determinants of sexual behavior* (pp. 153-218). New York: Wiley.

Reinisch, J. M. (1974). Fetal hormones, the brain, and human sex differences: A heuristic, integrative review of the recent literature. *Archives of Sexual Behavior, 3*(1), 51-90.

Reiss, A. J. (1961). The social integration of queers and peers. *Social Problems, 9,* 102-120.

Ricketts, W. (1984). Biological research on homosexuality: Ansell's cow or Occam's razor? *Journal of Homosexuality, 9*(4), 65-93.

Saghir, M. T., & Robbins, E. (1973). *Male and female homosexuality.* Baltimore: Williams & Wilkins.

Van Wyk, P. H. (1984). A critique of Dörner's analysis of hormonal data from bisexual males. *Journal of Sex Research, 20,* 412-414.

Van Wyk, P. H., & Geist C. S. (1984). Psychosocial development of heterosexual, bisexual, and homosexual behavior. *Archives of Sexual Behavior, 13*(6), 505-544.

Weinberg, M. S., & Williams, C. J. (1974). *Male homosexuals: Their problems and adaptations.* New York: Oxford University Press.

West, D. J. (1977). *Homosexuality re-examined.* Minneapolis: University of Minnesota Press.

Wolf, T. J. (1985). Marriages of bisexual men. *Journal of Homosexuality, 11*(1/2), 135-148.

Dexterity and Sexuality: Is There a Relationship?

John A. Hamill, MA

San Francisco

SUMMARY. In all the recent research on sexuality, one striking analogy that has been largely overlooked is that of sexuality and dexterity. This article is a parallel synthesis of the current knowledge of these two subjects. Although there does not seem to be a causal relationship between these two traits (a particular dextral tendency does not imply any associated sexual tendency, or vice versa), a short description of past attitudes and beliefs concerning left-handedness illustrates the historical similarity of social bias against homosexuality. Second, a discussion of the current scientific information on dexterity and sexuality reveals how these tendencies are in fact analogous. Finally, the article questions how society can maintain its discriminatory policies against homosexuality when it is no more a distinctive trait in human nature than left-handedness.

One of the never-ending moral, clinical, and legal discussions centers on the causes and effects of homosexuality and what should be the proper social response. Politicians, scholars, theologians, and other "experts" have expounded their theories, even "cures," but no consensus has been reached. In fact, there is no agreement on what constitutes homosexuality. Is it a chosen lifestyle, a learned

---

Correspondence may be addressed: 140 Douglass Street, San Francisco, CA 94114.

[Haworth co-indexing entry note]: "Dexterity and Sexuality: Is There a Relationship?" Hamill, John A. Co-published simultaneously in *Journal of Homosexuality* (The Haworth Press, Inc.) Vol. 28, No. 3/4, 1995, pp. 375-396; and: *Sex, Cells, and Same-Sex Desire: The Biology of Sexual Preference* (ed: John P. De Cecco, and David Allen Parker) The Haworth Press, Inc., 1995, pp. 375-396. Multiple copies of this article/chapter may be purchased from The Haworth Document Delivery Center [1-800-3-HAWORTH; 9:00 a.m. - 5:00 p.m. (EST)].

behavior, a psychological disorder, or a phase one outgrows? Is one born that way or is it due to an overbearing mother? These disparate views are the origin of all the theories on the causes of homosexuality. *The importance of the argument is that much of our legal and social attitudes on homosexuality rest largely on what we believe are its causes and its effects.*[1,3,6,29,47]

If one believes homosexuality is a chosen lifestyle, that one chooses to be gay or straight, then one could argue that it is immoral behavior because it has been traditionally condemned by Judaism, Christianity, and Islam. Therefore, it is something one should not do, just as one should not lie, steal, or kill. If one believes it is an undesirable learned behavior, one that can become addictive like drugs, then the politicians and moralists can argue for tighter controls on what youth can see and learn and pass laws prohibiting homosexual activity. Our current moral, social, and legal attitudes reflect a combination of these two perspectives.

How can we look at homosexuality to help us analyze it objectively? If we are looking for the etiology of homosexuality, aren't we really looking for the causes of human sexuality? What is the origin of hetero-, homo-, and bisexuality? What else is similar, from a scientific point of view, to being homosexual? An analogy could provide a neutral point from which controversial subjects can be discussed dispassionately. Homosexuals, just like heterosexuals, are not limited to any one race, culture, nationality, or religion. They can be of either gender, any age, or come from any economic class. There are explanations for all of these categories, and none are analogous to homosexuality. Homosexual behavior has been observed in many species, so it is not unique to humans.

But is homosexuality a totally unique characteristic? Dexterity, like sexuality, is a mysterious facet of human, and animal, behavior. As in sexuality, there are many theories on the etiology of right-, left-, and ambidexterity. Some investigators consider it to be a biological trait, while others hold it to be the result of social influences, or even birth stress.[2,30,46,48]

There is no closer analogy to homosexuality than left-handedness. The percentage, distribution, and developmental patterns of each in the human population are strikingly similar, and both have at various times been labeled pathological, sinful, or criminal behavior. Even theories and measures developed by psychiatrists and psychologists to correct the "abnormal" tendencies of left-handers and homosexuals have followed parallel paths. As a result, both groups have been the objects of much historical social pressure and discrimination.

HISTORICAL ATTITUDES TOWARDS LEFT-HANDERS

To better understand the analogy, we need to compare how left-handedness and homosexuality have been viewed historically. While the social stigma associated with homosexuality is well known, the current and past perceptions of left-handedness are not. At present, many would scoff at the idea of discriminating against a left-handed person. However, there is a bias toward right hand use in everyday life. Though right-handers are mostly unaware of this, the prejudice is omnipresent to the left-hander.

In some countries, official sanctions against left-hand use still prevail. Writing with the left hand, once forbidden in many American schools, is still discouraged or even prohibited in the schools of Germany, Sweden, Greece, Russia, and the former and current communist countries around the world. To this day, Communist China maintains that it has no left-handers or homosexuals, both of whom are viewed as capitalist degeneracies. Left-hand prohibitions are strictly enforced in Moslem countries where social custom prohibits using the left hand for any publicly acceptable social purpose, especially eating. The nations of Africa and the Indian subcontinent also pursue this policy in varying degrees.[5,10] In Western cultures, however, the moral and physical restrictions concerning the use of the left hand are slowly dissipating.

One source of the prejudice can be traced to the widespread association the left hand has had with the cleansing of the excretory functions. For hygienic purposes, the designated hand that was used for cleaning the genital and anal areas could not be used for community eating or social greeting. This taint found its way into the moral values and religious dogma of many cultures. For instance, the ancient Romans considered left-handed people immoral.

Though it is not a sin in Christianity to be left-handed, there are over 100 Biblical references in which the right hand is made the symbol of things noble, praiseworthy, or desirable.[5,8,16,30,33] For instance, it is at the right hand of God where the "saved" shall sit, while the "condemned" will be at His left hand. The Bible does not have one honorable reference to the left hand. Islam and Judaism echo the Bible in their praise of the right hand. Additionally, in medieval Europe, witchcraft practices were associated in part with the use of the left hand. As a result, many left-handers were hanged or burned at the stake as witches.

Historically, the world-wide social attitudes towards left-handers have not been positive. Left-handers have been frequently categorized as perverse, morally depraved, and even connected with the devil.[5,10,23] At other times more "compassionate" attitudes judged them to be clumsy, incompetent, and unreliable people who were to be pitied for their unfortunate condition.[8,33] To this day the word "left" has the connotation of "sinister," from a Latin word meaning both left and evil, thereby including anything that is devious. Thus, the most common historical approach has been to assume that left-handedness represented a sign of some moral, mental, or physical aberration in the individual.

CLINICAL STUDIES OF LEFT-HANDERS

Around the turn of the nineteenth century two prominent psychologists, Cesare Lombroso[19,23,40] and Wilhelm Fliess,[19,20,23] gave clinical reinforcement to the negative attitude towards left-handers. They taught that some maladjustment in the sinistral personality caused degenerate conditions, associating it with homosexuality, incest, and perversion.

One relatively recent proponent of this school of thought was Abram Blau.[9] In 1946, Blau concluded that left-handedness represented an arrest of emotional maturation due to "infantile psychoneurosis." He believed that sinistrality was nothing more than an expression of "infantile negativism," akin to contrariety in feeding, elimination, and general perversity. Blau asserted that left-handedness could be easily traced to a lack of love and attention by the mother. His psychiatric studies of left-handed children and adults bore out, to him, the theory of maternal rejection in early infancy, of early emotional troubles, and of a negativistic attitude in adulthood.

Blau even developed a personality profile for left-handers in which they were portrayed as compulsive, obstinate, parsimonious, and generally deficient mentally and physically. However, Blau contended that since left-handers were also artistic and individualistic, they could be an asset to society if directed along socially acceptable lines. He emphasized the desirability of retraining the ambidextrous and left-handed to conform to the use of the right hand. He expected that this would prevent the child from acquiring sinistral character traits and from suffering the stigma and disadvantages of being left-handed in a right-handed world.

In addition, studies of left-handers in prisons and mental institutions reinforced the perception that left-handers tended to be more lunatic, neurotic, and criminally inclined than the average person.[5,19,23] Other research showed that there was a higher incidence of physical affliction among left-handers.[8,16,23,33] There were more mentally retarded, stutterers, dyslexic, epileptics, and other physical deficiencies among them than in the population as a whole.[16,19,23,48] Left-handedness was seen as a vice that occurred concomitantly with mental, moral, and physical impairments in the individual. Therefore, clergy, doctors, teachers, and parents colluded to suppress any tendency a child might have to use the left hand. In an atmosphere where left-handedness was thought of as a deliberate and contagious perversity, can one imagine the chances of a left-handed teacher finding employment?

These negative beliefs were so entrenched that many left-handers themselves, as many homosexuals do today, assimilated the social view that they were not normal, were somehow inferior, and even prone to immoral and criminal tendencies. Thus, many hid their "affliction" rather than subject themselves to being singled out as freaks.

CURRENT ATTITUDES ON LEFT-HANDERS

Recent clinical studies have shown that the use of one hand over the other is not a consciously acquired habit.[5,27,38,41,48] In addition, there is overwhelming evidence that left-handedness is not inherently related to any physical or mental impairment of the individual, nor is it more conducive to "immoral" behavior than right-handedness. On the contrary, only in those whose "natural" left-handedness has been suppressed is a higher incidence of mental and physical problems found. It has been determined that it is the suppression of left-handedness, in a person who has such a tendency, that facilitates the development of neuroses, stuttering, epilepsy, and other disabilities.[5,10,23]

Blau's ideas regarding left-handers are largely rejected today by both psychologists and psychiatrists. However, Blau's views show striking parallels to many present attitudes and beliefs concerning homosexuality and the societal need to prevent it. Concerns about "normal" and "abnormal" development seem to have permeated research. Thus, many psychologists and psychiatrists assumed, a priori, that left-handedness was an aberration from normal right-handed development, just as many others still assume that homosexuality is an aberration from normal heterosexual development.

While the etiology of dexterity is still debated, the question of right- or left-handedness is no longer a question of normal versus abnormal development, but of equally valid alternate forms of development. It is widely recognized that dexterity is set before school age.[5,27,38,41] Today we are approaching a stage, at least in Western countries, where children are no longer forced to write with their right hand. It is recognized that the suppression of this tendency constitutes unjustifiable and harmful interference. Since the use of the left hand in public is no longer deemed offensive in Western culture, a child can freely develop in a healthy and natural manner, without the social pressure concerning which hand to use.

However, even in many Western countries, a prevalent pedagogical attitude is still to press for right-handedness, especially in those who are ambidextrous.[5,10] If the child "fails," then the child is allowed to continue with the left hand. In many schools pupils are not taught to write with the left hand, only permitted. The left-handed pupil needs more help, not less, in order to master social and technical behavior that has evolved for the use of the right hand. This attitude can still cause left-handers to suffer from a secret shame of being different.

What has caused the overall Western societal change in attitude concern in left-handedness, but not homosexuality? First of all, our society was never as emotionally attached to the proscriptions against left-handedness as it was to those against homosexuality. Granted, the social impact of each is vastly different. People have always been much more interested and mystified by sexuality than by dexterity. In addition, dexterity usually involves individual behavior. Sexuality involves behavior between individuals. Society has always had a higher interest in controlling behavior between people. This interest is reflected by the much heavier emphasis that religions place on sexual rather than dextral conduct. Also, it is now more widely accepted that dextral tendency seems to be a predisposition in the individual. Society seems to recognize that one cannot be faulted for being left-handed, now generally considered a natural inclination. However, homosexuality is not generally viewed as either a predisposition or a natural inclination. Homosexuality is still widely regarded, contrary to the evidence, as a voluntary perversity, a "life style" which one has chosen, damned by many current religions, and considered criminal behavior in many countries.

ANALOGY

Nature of Dexterity and Sexuality

Dexterity is a combination of the individual's orientation and behavior. Dextral orientation is the tendency to have greater ability and strength in one hand than in the other. Dextral behavior, however, is the expression of the use of one hand over the other. The difference is that one can behave contrary to one's tendency.

A person's sexuality, as in dexterity, is the combination of orientation and behavior. Sexual orientation, however, expresses itself as the degree of the physical attraction that one has to either the same or the opposite sex. Sexual behavior is the expression of sexual contact with one sex or the other. Again, the difference is that one can act contrary to one's tendency.

What is critical to understand is that the orientation is not a conscious preference. The "feeling" of this disposition is beyond the individual's control.[5,44] No one chooses which sex one will find more attractive; no one chooses which hand will be more dexterous. At no point in life do people decide that they will be hetero-, homo-, or bisexual, or right-, left-, or ambidextral in their tendency. Behavior, however, is a conscious choice of expression which can be controlled by the individual or environment. One does not have to act according to one's tendency; the behavior can be either expressed or suppressed. A right-handed person can write with the left hand, but not with the same ease. A heterosexual can have a homosexual affair, but it will not have the same emotional impact. Unless one is ambidextrous or bisexual these situations will be awkward and feel "unnatural."

Circumstances can force or encourage individuals to act contrary to their natures. Persons of heterosexual tendency may engage in homosexual behavior in situations such as prisons where there is no physical outlet for their natural tendency. Homosexual persons may try to hide or suppress their orientation and may engage in heterosexual behavior when there is no acceptable social outlet for their tendency.[32] For example, it would be very hard to find individuals in the Islamic World to admit that they are either left-handed or homosexual today.

The range of sexuality and dexterity must be viewed as a continuum between their extremes. Only those who are mainly ambidextrous or bisexual are actually in a natural position to "choose" which tendency they want to express. However, present social pressures will usually preclude this choice, favoring heterosexual and right-handed behavior. Those who are equally inclined to either tendency can function fully within society's norms. Their left-handed or homosexual tendencies can be suppressed to the point where they may discount or perhaps never realize their existence. Not until social pressures favoring heterosexuals and right-handers dissipate will we know the true proportion of bisexual and ambidextral people. It has been observed that the number of behaviorally left-handed and ambidextrous people has risen where left-handedness has ceased to be a social disgrace.[5,10,16,19,23]

Distribution and Percentage Patterns

The percentage and distribution patterns of both tendencies seem to be parallel. Neither left-handers nor homosexuals are readily distinguishable from the rest of the population. Estimates are difficult to gauge, especially for homosexuality, since so many people would be reluctant to admit such a tendency. However, most statistics show that both these tendencies seem to be predominant or exclusive in approximately five to ten percent of the population.[5,8,13,16,24,29,30,35] Furthermore, it seems that about 20 to 30 percent of the population shares some degree of bisexuality or ambidexterity.[5,23,35]

Left-handedness and homosexuality seem to have always been the minority tendency everywhere throughout recorded human history. There is no conclusive evidence that either of these two tendencies has ever been shared by a majority, regardless of whether these tendencies have been promoted or discouraged by a culture.[23,24,48] These factors could be interpreted as indicating that environmental settings do not play a large or determinant role in the incidence of either tendency. However, in some instances, cultures have encouraged bisexual or ambidextrous behavior, as in some societies of Ancient Greece and of New Guinea for bisexuality, and some periods of Ancient China for ambidexterity.[5,10,23] Unfortunately, there is no information as to whether the incidence of homosexual or left-handed tendency increased accordingly. Almost all of the studies examine behavior exclusively, but, as has been noted, behavior can be heavily influenced by the culture. There is no record of any culture encouraging exclusive homosexual or left-handed behavior.

Another curious similarity is that both orientations seem to be more prevalent in men than in women. Statistics indicate that twice as many men as women are homosexual or left-handed.[5,10,24,33,36] However, it is the reverse when it comes to ambidexterity and bisexuality. Women seem to be more likely than men, as a group, to tend towards ambidexterity and bisexuality.[5,33,36,55] Whatever the actual figures may be, it should be noted that left-handedness and homosexuality seem to share similar distributive trends among the population. In other words, there are as many left-handed and ambidextrous people as there are homosexual and bisexual people.

These distribution patterns lead to the question of what is "normal." Because left-handedness and homosexuality are in the minority, some maintain that they must be "misprints" or "aberrations" of nature. To consider this question we must look at three general biological distribution patterns proposed by Vilma Fritsch.[23] The first biological distribution pattern is present on a roughly 50-50 basis throughout the population, such as the ratio of males and females. Clearly, being male is not an aberration of being female, or vice versa. To be male or female is largely a matter of natural randomness. The second pattern is the ratio of the presence or absence of "essential" characteristics. Thus the absence of these characteristics constitutes a handicap; it will cause some impairment in the functioning of the individual. For instance, genetic blindness, deafness, lameness, or retardation are obvious handicaps, the result of a "misprint" of nature.

Dexterity and sexuality provide an example of the third pattern. Here the distribution lies somewhere between the first two examples. Since these characteristics are not present on a roughly equal basis in the population, they cannot be explained by the operation of randomness. Apart from this, the proportion of the minority tendencies is too great for them to be simply treated as "misprints" in the process of heredity. This is even more evident when one considers the percentage of ambidextrals and bisexuals. Additionally, as will be discussed later, left-handed and homosexual tendencies do not affect the physical or mental functions of the individual; therefore, they cannot be associated with those characteristics that are handicaps. In essence, they seem to be alternate patterns of development.

Pattern of Development of Dexterity and Sexuality

The pattern of development is similar for both orientations. The orientations seem to be present at the very early stages of development, and studies by Gieseke, Ludwig, Freud, and Kinsey show that in a group of children, one will always find a larger proportion of left-handed usage and homosexual behavior than in a group of adults.[10,22,27,35,41] The percentages of behavioral left-handedness, homosexuality, ambidexterity, and bisexuality, decline as a group ages. One proposal to explain this is that in the course of growth, the child seems to pass through a series of stages in which there is an alteration between right and left hand dominance, and between homosexual and heterosexual behavior.[22,23,26,27] Another explanation is that this is a function of the potentially ambidextrous or bisexual child responding to the cultural saturation of heterosexuality and right-handedness.

There are those who subscribe to a genetic origin for both orientations. One significant difficulty with this theory is that genetically identical twins will not necessarily develop identical sexual or dextral tendencies. Though the genetic pattern does not exactly follow that of dominant and recessive genes, such as blue or brown eyes, limited studies do not exclude the possibility that sexuality and dexterity display some unique inheritance pattern. For instance, studies reported by Claire Porac and others found that 80% of identical twins are same-handed, and that there is a higher concordance of left-handedness among identical twins than among fraternal twins.[16] Similarly, in a study published in December 1991 in the *Archives of General Psychiatry,* Michael Bailey and Richard Pillard found 52% of identical twin brothers of homosexual men were also homosexual, compared to 22% of fraternal twins and 11% of genetically unrelated adoptive brothers. These patterns are the type that geneticists claim demonstrates a significant genetic basis. The closer the relation between individuals, the higher the concordance should be. If these tendencies were purely a matter of choice then the concordance for the tendencies among the different types of siblings should be about the same. However, if these tendencies were purely a matter of biology, then the identical twins should have 100% concordance. Pillard states that whatever the other non-genetic factors are in forging the orientation, they must come into play early in the pattern of development of the individual, since the orientation seems to be set at an early stage.

In addition, genealogical studies done by David Rife, Paul Bakan, and reported by Clare Porac determined that if both parents are right-handed, about 90 percent of the children will become right-handed; if one parent is right-handed, about 80 percent of the children will become right-handed; and if both parents are left-handed, about 50 percent of the children will still turn out right-handed.[16,23,48]

It would be interesting to see how a similar genetic study on sexuality would compare, if such a study could be carried out today. Our current society is not sufficiently open to the subject to make any such study meaningful. However, preliminary results in the sexual development of children raised by lesbian mothers indicate that they infrequently develop homosexual tendencies.[11] Also, there are other preliminary studies indicating that homosexuality runs in families. This allows for the possibility that sexuality may follow a similar inherited distribution pattern as dexterity.

Though these patterns do not follow "standard" genetic laws, a genetic trend heavily favoring right-handedness and heterosexuality seems to develop. This trend could be regulated by a dominant factor that ensures the great majority becomes right-handed and heterosexual. This would explain the constant minority distribution of left-handers and homosexuals that is found throughout time. The obvious causative explanation, in the case of sexuality, is that such a factor ensures the continuity of the human race. This does not mean that procreation will only occur through heterosexuals, for many homosexuals are also parents. An inheritance pattern could partially explain the reported rise of homosexuality in societies which are very repressive and force greater numbers of homosexuals to marry and have families, thus potentially increasing the percentage of homosexual children.[12]

Additionally, in order to explain homosexuality's role in the preservation of the species, sociobiologists have suggested that it may be one biologically influenced way of providing individuals freed from direct family obligations. These additional adults could thus be an important asset to the welfare of the members of the extended family.[57]

Dexterity could also have a purpose in the preservation of the species. As has been mentioned before, societies with primitive hygienic methods needed separate functions for each hand. This raised the health standard and survival rate in the community. In addition, as we will see later, dexterity is linked to cerebral dominance between the right and left sides of the brain. The different sides of the brain handle interpretation of spatial and verbal functions. Thus, by diversifying abilities amongst its population, the species is strengthened for environmental survival.

Psychological Comparisons

The question is then raised of whether there are any demonstrable psychological differences in those who share these tendencies. Psychological comparisons demonstrate that, apart from the tendencies themselves, there are no distinctions between healthy left-handers and homosexuals and the population as a whole.[4,11,23] Though most can accept this conclusion concerning left-handers, very few would believe this to be true of homosexuals. The reason is the method of research used in the past. The same methods that "discovered" the psychotic status of left-handers also "discovered" a similar status in homosexuals. By studying and analyzing homosexuals who needed psychopathological treatment and criminals in penal institutions, a pathological "homosexual character" evolved and was fed to society.

While the suppression of left-handed behavior could induce a variety of primarily physical impairments, such as stuttering or epilepsy, the suppression of homosexual behavior could induce a variety of primarily mental problems.[51] Studies show that homosexuals can be as "mentally healthy" and well adjusted as heterosexuals when a representative sample of homosexuals, not just criminals and psychopathological individuals, is studied.[32]

Studies in parent-child relationships are varied and inconclusive; they cannot support the assumption that pathological parent-child relationships are determinants of homosexuality or left-handedness.[32,48] Parents cannot be blamed for "causing" homosexuality in their children any more than for "causing" left-handedness. Aside from the sexual-object orientation, there is no scientific evidence that homosexuals differ in any consistent psychological way from their heterosexual counterparts.[32] Apart from being a member of a minority, it is no impairment or handicap to be either left-handed or homosexual. Such people can be just as healthy physically and mentally, as long as they are not forced to act against their nature. Thus, psychological studies have failed to demonstrate that homosexuality or left-handedness is a pathology.

Physiological Comparisons

Many studies have been done to determine if there are any biological differences between homosexuals and heterosexuals, or between right-handers and left-handers. Only recently have studies revealed any physiological differences between homosexuals and heterosexuals. A study by Simon LeVay revealed that the size of some brain cells in the hypothalamus are different between homosexuals and heterosexuals.[37] This organ controls some of the body's most vital functions, including sexual behavior. Another study by Dick F. Swaab and M. A. Hofman also noted differences between homosexuals and heterosexuals in the size of the brain cells in a different part of the hypothalamus.[52] These cells also seem to link sexual orientation as well as gender itself to brain structure. These findings are being interpreted by some as potentially setting the stage for a physiological basis for sexual orientation.

Otherwise, no other studies on homosexuals have revealed evidence to demonstrate any other physiological differences to distinguish them from heterosexuals.[3,37,44] In addition, no adverse physiological effects have been identified with homosexuality. Homosexuals cannot be visually distinguished physically from heterosexuals. A common misconception prevalent in our society is that gays and lesbians are nevertheless recognizable because they are respectively more "effeminate" or more "masculine" in their physical appearance. However, "masculinity" or "femininity" cannot be used as differentiating criteria between homosexuality and heterosexuality, and have nothing to do with physiology.

Investigators of dexterity have also provided evidence of a physiological distinction in the brain. It is widely accepted that the cause of dexterity must be sought in the brain. The left side of the brain is dominant in right-handed people. However, left-handedness seems to be less regularly associated with the dominance of either side of the brain.[19,31,59] Studies concerning cerebral dominance show that right-handed people use the right side of the brain for spatial functions such as handling and interpreting three-dimensional objects and images. The left side is used for verbal functions such as speaking or writing. Left-handed people have these functions reversed in their brains.[13,48] Jerre Levy and Sandra Witelson contend that since behavioral differences are reversed when brain organization is reversed, this constitutes strong evidence that brain organization and dexterity are genetically determined.[3,38,39,58] In addition, studies by McCormick and Witelson found significantly more left-handers among homosexuals than heterosexuals.[43,58] They believe that this indicates that homosexuality could be linked to left-handedness, since the brain organization of left-handed people differs from that of right-handed people.

Otherwise, other research on dexterity has determined that there are no significant physiological differences between the hands which would make one more dominant than the other. There is no apparent physical reason why one hand should be more skillful or stronger than the other. There is no physiological difference between the right hand of a right-hander and the right hand of a left-hander. The variance in dexterity therefore does not appear to constitute a visible physical difference.[23,27,41] Thus, the only physiological differences between the tendencies appear to lie in the brain.

Cerebral Dominance

Since homosexuality and left-handedness were defined by many psychiatrists and psychologists as a pathology, many different attempts were carried out in order to "cure" people to the norm. However, efforts to change sexual or hand orientation, from prayer to electro-shock treatment, have been not only questionable but damaging to the mental and physical health of the individual.[21,23,33,49] At most, these methods suppress behavior; they do not change the orientation. Thus, psychology and psychiatry have failed to demonstrate that either of these orientations is a condition or a preference that can be reversed through therapy.

One possible way to change an orientation seems to be through the extreme method of brain surgery.[5,12] Studies have discovered the specific location in the brain of the sexual tendency centers.[25,32,50] By removing these cells, the sexual tendency can be destroyed, thus leaving the individual with no sexual tendency at all. In effect, the individual has been neutered mentally but can still be coached to behave as a heterosexual. Animal studies provide a good deal of evidence for a biological basis for both orientations. In experiments done on animals, the paw tendency or sexual tendency can be reversed or expanded by making a circumscribed lesion in the brain, or by careful manipulation of the hormone levels in the newborns.[1,3,5,6,28,29,37]

The discovery that both dexterity and sexuality are regulated by specific parts of the brain accentuates the implausibility that environmental factors could play a significant role in the development of the tendencies. The inner workings and developmental patterns of the brain are not likely to be arranged or determined by cultural conditions. An individual's behavior, however, can be easily influenced by cultural factors.

Predisposition

Experiments by Judd Marmor with lower animals and primates suggest the possibility that humans may be born with a hidden predisposition to their sexuality.[42] He adds that recent studies have revealed that there may be certain genetic differences between homosexuals and heterosexuals. Other research by John Money, Neil Carlson, G. Dörner, and Lee Ellis corroborates Marmor's theory.[12,14,15,18,44,45] Studies on animals indicate that before birth, the brain is programmed by hormones which predispose the individual toward a certain sexual orientation.[3,11,28,29,58] This research has indicated that sexual tendency is primarily linked to differences in brain/hormone interactions. The amount of prenatal androgen at the critical period of brain differentiation appears to predispose males to heterosexuality and females to homosexuality, whereas their lack seems to predispose males to homosexuality and females to heterosexuality.[4,25,53] Bisexual tendencies would be the result of intermediate amounts of androgen. Thus, the most likely explanation of the origins of homosexuality, bisexuality, and heterosexuality is that certain dispositions are implanted in the brain from the fetal stage which predispose the establishment of any of the three conditions.

As with sexuality, it is almost universally accepted today that dexterity is a phenomenon whose cause must be sought in the brain. The idea has evolved that children are born with a dextral predisposition, that the tendency is innate, set during fetal development.[5,6,23,29,38] It has been proposed that differing concentrations of estrogen in male and female fetuses might have generalized effects on either the left or right side of the body. Compelling data has emerged to support the theory that dexterity is programmed in some way by sex hormone levels in the developing fetus.[3,28,30,38,39,58] This would also explain the higher levels of homosexuality in left-handers because of some association among early hormonal events.[58] We thus have the parallel possibility that prenatal brain/hormone interactions may be the common source for both tendencies. Most scientists now believe there is compelling evidence that dexterity has a significant biological basis. In addition, the growing body of evidence points to a similar biological source for sexuality.

CONCLUSION

Whether the etiology of the tendencies is biological or psychological, or a combination of the two, the analogy reveals that homosexuality is no more a distinctive trait in human nature than left-handedness. In addition, there is no rational basis for condoning repressive attitudes against these tendencies and behaviors. While much prejudice against left-handers has dissipated in Western cultures, the prejudice against homosexuals has not. This negative perception is so ingrained that even rational arguments have yet to take much effect with either political or religious organizations.

An example of this is the continuing policy of the U.S. Government concerning homosexuals in the military. A 1988 United States Defense Department report prepared to determine if homosexuals are security risks and deserving of exclusion from the military concluded that "studies of homosexual veterans make it clear that having a same-gender or an opposite-gender orientation is unrelated to job performance in the same way as is being left- or right-handed." The report goes on to suggest that the military should begin the systematic integration of lesbians and gay men in its ranks, just as it did with black soldiers in the 1950s.[17] However, the military disregarded its own report, because it believes the "homosexual character" is incompatible with the military and would be detrimental to the morale of the troops. Yet, as stated in the Defense Department's report and by many other studies, homosexuals and left-handers are as diverse in character, lifestyle, politics, and religion as are heterosexuals and right-handers.[4,7,32,54,56] There is no evidence of such a thing as a homosexual or left-handed "personality."

Left-handedness has gradually become more socially acceptable, partially because it is generally recognized that it has no adverse physical or moral effect on the individual. Therefore, does similar evidence for homosexuality mean that we should accept it, along with left-handedness, as an alternate and natural form of human development?

Contrary to popular misconceptions, no causal relationship has ever been established between moral or cultural decline and acceptance of homosexuality or left-handedness.[4,34,56] Ancient China preferred the left side without any cultural or moral decay.[5,10,23] Ancient Greece idealized homosexual love without a decline in family structure or military power. The Roman Empire fell more than a century after it had banned homosexual marriage. The acceptance of left-handedness or homosexuality has no direct correlation to the decline in cultural sophistication, moral values, economic viability, or military power of any civilization. In fact, many individuals who possess these tendencies have had great impact in the development of our civilization. Arguably two of the most creative geniuses humanity has ever produced, the models for the "Renaissance Man," Leonardo da Vinci and Michelangelo, were by coincidence left-handed homosexuals.

One tragic result of intolerant attitudes against homosexuals falls on children. As a child becomes aware of his or her homosexual tendencies, a deep sense of isolation and anguish ensues. The main source of security and support for any child, the family, suddenly becomes its major barrier. Homosexual children have no support network or role models to help them understand their emotional and sexual development. On the contrary, they live under the constant fear of being exposed as "perverts." Should they be identified as gay or lesbian by their families or peers, they are subject to physical and verbal abuse. Families and schools not only ignore the needs of its homosexual children, they support an attitude of homophobia which encourages the ostracism of its own children. The homosexual child needs more help, not less, in order to overcome the terrible stigma of being different in a culture that insists on the norm. This is a major factor in the high incidence of runaways and teenage suicide among homosexual teenagers.

The scientific evidence has failed to support the claims that homosexuality and left-handedness are pathological, contagious, or reversible orientations. In addition, there is growing evidence that neither orientation is chosen, and both are subject to biological influences at early stages of development. Society has nothing to fear from adopting an accepting attitude toward these orientations. On the contrary, a positive attitude would be beneficial for it would avoid creating conditions that harm and alienate a significant portion of the population. The measure of a society is not only how it treats its disadvantaged minorities, but whether it creates them. It is time to adopt a rational stance and question the values which dictate that only heterosexual and right-handed behavior is acceptable, normal, and moral.

REFERENCES

1. Angier, Natalie. (1991, September 1). The Biology of What It Means to be Gay. *New York Times*, pp. E-1, E-4.
2. Bakan, P., Dibb, G., & Reed, P. (1973). Handedness and Birth Stress. *Neuropsychologia, 11*, 363-366.
3. Barinaga, Marcia. (1991, 30 August). Is Homosexuality Biological? *Science, 253*, 956-957.
4. Barnett, Walter. (1973). *Sexual Freedom and the Constitution.* University of New Mexico Press.
5. Barsley, Michael. (1966). *The Other Hand.* New York: Hawthorne Books.
6. Begley, Sharon, & Gelman, David. (1991, September 9). What Causes People to Be Homosexual? *Newsweek*, p. 52.
7. Bell, Alan P., & Weinberg, Martin S. (1978). *Homosexualities.* New York: Simon and Schuster.
8. Birnbaum, Jesse. (1991, April 15). The Perils of Being a Lefty. *Time*, p. 67.
9. Blau, Abram. (1946). The Master Hand. American Orthopsychiatric Association, Inc., New York. In: Barsley, Michael. (1966). *The Other Hand.* New York: Hawthorne Books.
10. Bliss, James, & Morella, Joseph. (1980). *The Left-handers Handbook.* New York: A&W Visual Library.
11. Brody, Jane E. (1978, March 8). New Scientific Studies on Human Sexuality. *Modesto Bee.* (article reprinted from the *New York Times*).
12. Carlson, Neil R., Physiology of Behavior. In: Gengle, Dean, & Murphy, Norman C. (1978, November 1). An Emerging Model of the Origin of Sexualities. *Advocate*, pp. 15-21.
13. Cromie, William J. (1978, January 22). Male and Female Brains are Different. *San Francisco Chronicle*, World, p. 47.
14. Dörner, G., & Hinz, G. (1968). Induction and prevention of male homosexuality by androgen. *Journal of Endocrinology, 40*, 387-388.
15. Dörner, G. (1986). Systemic Hormones, Neurotransmitters, and Brain Development. In: Murray, Linda. (1987, April). Sexual Destinies. *Omni*, pp. 100-128.
16. Duncan, Don. (1991, January 27). Out There In Left Field. *San Francisco Examiner*, pp. D-13, D-14.

17. Dyer, Kate. (1990). *Gays in Uniform: The Pentagon's Secret Reports*. Alyson.

18. Ellis, Lee, In: Winokur, Scott. (1987, April 27). Theory of the '80s: Gays born, not bred. *San Francisco Examiner*, p. 1.

19. Fincher, Jack. (1977). *Sinister People: The Looking-Glass World of the Left-Hander*. New York: Putnam.

20. Fliess, Wilhelm. (1954). *Letters to Wilhelm Fliess from Freud: The Origins of Psycho-Analysis*. New York: Basic Books.

21. Frank, Jerome. (1972). Treatment of Homosexuals. *National Institute of Mental Health Task Force on Homosexuality*. DHEW Publication (HSM) 72-9119, pp. 63-68.

22. Freud, Sigmund. (1953). Three essays on the theory of sexuality. In: *The Standard Edition of the Complete Psychological Works of Sigmund Freud*. London: Hogarth.

23. Fritsch, Vilma. (1968). *Left and Right in Science and Life*. London: Barrie and Rockliff.

24. Gebhard, Paul H. (1972). Incidence of Overt Homosexuality in the United States and Western Europe. *National Institute of Mental Health Task Force on Homosexuality*. DHEW Publication No. (HSM) 72-9119, pp. 22-29.

25. Gengle, Dean, and Murphy, Norman C. (1978, November 1). An Emerging Model of the Origin of Sexualities. *Advocate*, pp. 15-21.

26. Gesell, Arnold. (1928). Infancy and Human Growth. In: Fritsch, Vilma. (1968). *Left and Right in Science and Life*. London: Barrie and Rockliff.

27. Giesecke, Minnie. (1936). The Genesis of Hand Preference. *Society for Research in Child Development*. National Research Council. New York: Kraus reprint, 1973.

28. Gooren, Louis. (1990). The Endocrinology of Transsexualism: A Review and Commentary. *Psychoneuroendocrinology, 15*, 3.

29. Gorman, Christine. (1991, September 9). Are Gay Men Born That Way? *Time*, pp. 60-61.

30. Hardyck, C., & Lewis, P. (1977). Left-Handedness. *Psychological Bulletin, 89*(3), 385-404.

31. Herron, Jeannie, Editor. (1980). *Neuropsychology of Left-handedness*. New York: Academic Press.

32. Hooker, Evelyn. (1972). Homosexuality. *National Institute of Mental Health Task Force on Homosexuality*. DHEW Publication No. (HSM) 72-9119, pp. 11-21.

33. Jackson, John. (1905). *Ambidexterity*. London.

34. Katz, Robert L. (1972). Notes on Religious History, Attitudes, and Laws Pertaining to Homosexuality. *National Institute of Mental Health Task Force on Homosexuality*. DHEW Publication No. (HSM) 72-9119, pp. 58-62.

35. Kinsey, Alfred C. et al. (1948). *Sexual Behavior in the Human Male*. Philadelphia: Saunders.

36. Kinsey, Alfred C. et al. (1953). *Sexual Behavior in the Human Female*. Philadelphia: Saunders.

37. LeVay, Simon. (1991, August 30). A Difference in Hypothalamic Structure Between Heterosexual and Homosexual Men. *Science, 252,* 1034-1037.

38. Levy, Jerre. (1976). A Review of Evidence for a Genetic Component in the Determination of Handedness. *Behavior Genetics, 6*(4), 429-53.

39. Levy, Jerre. (1978, July 4). In: Feet, Sex and Body Development. *San Francisco Chronicle.*

40. Lombroso, Cesare. (1911). Crime, its causes and remedies. Boston: Little, Brown and Co. In: Fincher, Jack. (1977). *Sinister People: The Looking-Glass World of the Left-Hander.* New York: Putnam.

41. Ludwig, Wilhelm. (1932). Rechts-Links-Problem im Tierreich und beim Menschen. In: Giesecke, Minnie. (1936). The Genesis of Hand Preference. *Society for Research in Child Development.* National Research Council. New York: Kraus reprint, 1973.

42. Marmor, Judd. (1972). Notes on Some Psychodynamic Aspects of Homosexuality. *National Institute of Mental Health Task Force on Homosexuality.* DHEW Publication No. (HSM) 72-9119, Appendix C, pp. 78-79.

43. McCormick, Cheryl, Witelson, Sandra, & Kingstone, Edward. (1990). Left-Handedness in Homosexual Men and Women: Neuroendocrine Implications. *Psychoneuroendocrinology, 15,* 69.

44. Money, John. (1972). Pubertal Hormones and Homosexuality, Bisexuality and Heterosexuality. *National Institute of Mental Health Task Force on Homosexuality.* DHEW Publication No. (HSM) 72-9119, Appendix B, pp. 73-77.

45. Money, John. (1988). *Gay, Straight, and In-Between: The Sexology of Erotic Orientation.* New York: Oxford University Press.

46. Perelle, Ira, & Ehrman, L. (1982). What is a Left-Hander? *Experientia, 38,* 1256-58.

47. Perlman, David. (1991, August 30). Brain Cell Study Finds Link to Homosexuality. *San Francisco Chronicle,* p. 1.

48. Porac, Clare, & Coren, Stanley. (1981). *Lateral Preferences and Human Behavior.* New York: Springer-Verlag.

49. Portland Town Council. (1976). *A Legislative Guide to Civil Rights.*

50. Scheflin, Alan W., & Opton, Edward M. (1978). *The Mind Manipulators.* New York: Paddington Press.

51. Schur, Edwin. (1972). Sociocultural Factors in Homosexual Behavior. *National Institute of Mental Health Task Force on Homosexuality.* DHEW Publication No. (HSM) 72-9119, pp. 30-41.

52. Swaab, D. F., & Hofman, M. A. (1990, December). An Enlarged Suprachiasmatic Nucleus in Homosexual Men. *Brain Research, 537,* 141.

53. Timnick, Lois. (1978, November 1). Homosexuals: Many Types, Many Causes. *Los Angeles Times.*

54. Tripp, C. A. (1975). *The Homosexual Matrix.* New York: McGraw-Hill.

55. Walster, Elaine, & William, G. (1978, September 29). A New Look at Love. In: *The Sacramento Union.*

56. Weinberg, George. (1972). *Society and the Healthy Homosexual.* New York: St. Martin's Press.

57. Wilson, Edward. (1978). *On Human Nature*. Harvard University Press.

58. Witelson, Sandra. (1991). Neural Sexual Mosaicism: Sexual Differentiation of the Human Temporo-Parietal Region for Functional Asymmetry. *Psychoneuroendocrinology, 16,* 131.

59. Zangwill, Oliver. (1960). Cerebral Dominance and its Relation to Psychological Function. *The Henderson Trust Lectures,* No. 19. Edinburgh: Oliver and Boyd.

Policing "Perversions": Depo-Provera and John Money's New Sexual Order

Daniel C. Tsang, PhD (precand.), MA

University of California, Irvine

SUMMARY. The use of the drug Depo-Provera (medroxyprogesterone acetate [MPA]) in the treatment of sexual minorities, such as sadomasochists, transvestites, sexually active children and teenagers, and adults sexually attracted to minors, is the latest development in a long tradition of dangerous and crude experimentation by psychiatrists and clinical psychologists with biodeterministic and reductionist views of human sexuality. Among them is clinical psychologist John Money, whose zealous advocacy of such treatments ignores or downplays critical issues of ethics, informed consent, and the side effects of the drug. The U.S. Food and Drug Administration has failed to effectively regulate such uses of Depo-Provera. Public outcry, more stringent regulation, and a new acceptance of the rights of

---

Daniel C. Tsang edited *The Age Taboo: Gay Male Sexuality, Power and Consent* (Boston: Alyson, 1981) and the journal *Gay Insurgent*. He achieved PhD precandidacy in political science at the University of Michigan, Ann Arbor, where he also earned two master's degrees. He teaches a politics of sexualities course at the University of California, Irvine, where he is also a social sciences bibliographer. He is a research associate at the Center for Research and Education in Sexuality at San Francisco State University. He also directs the Lesbian and Gay Declassified Documentation Project.

Correspondence may be addressed: 380 Main Library, P.O. Box 19557, University of California, Irvine, CA 92713. e-mail: dtsang@uci.edu.

[Haworth co-indexing entry note]: "Policing "Perversions": Depo-Provera and John Money's New Sexual Order." Tsang, Daniel C. Co-published simultaneously in *Journal of Homosexuality* (The Haworth Press, Inc.) Vol. 28, No. 3/4, 1995, pp. 397-426; and: *Sex, Cells, and Same-Sex Desire: The Biology of Sexual Preference* (ed: John P. De Cecco, and David Allen Parker) The Haworth Press, Inc., 1995, pp. 397-426. Multiple copies of this article/chapter may be purchased from The Haworth Document Delivery Center [1-800-3-HAWORTH; 9:00 a.m. - 5:00 p.m. (EST)].

397

sexual minorities are necessary to forestall the imposition of a repressive, new sexual order.

Since the nineteenth century, psychiatry and clinical psychology have policed sexual behavior that previously either was ignored or fell within the domain of law enforcement. According to Michel Foucault (1978) the sexual mission of psychiatry and clinical psychology, which at times has taken on the character of purity crusades, has been carried out in two ways. First, it has silently favored heterosexual monogamy and the family, a form of sexual behavior not scrutinized by professionals or scientists as long as it operates within prescribed boundaries. Second, for some sexualities, including homosexuality, it has resorted to the "implantation of perversions," the multiplication of forbidden sexualities for the purpose of exposure, control, and, in some cases, outright suppression.

In the early twentieth century the medical interventions into "perverse sexualities" took on the form of what Elliot Valenstein (1986) has called "great and desperate cures" to which the so-called sexual psychopaths and offenders were involuntarily subjected. These include the use of surgery for testicular castration and transplants, the destruction of particular areas of the hypothalamus, and the removal of the frontal lobes of the cerebral cortex (e.g., Banay & Davidoff, 1942). According to Valenstein, the same factors that promoted these drastic sexual "therapies" are still part of mainstream psychiatry and clinical psychology. Today, however, the favored treatment is to drug the brain rather than excise parts of it.

In his *Gay American History* (1976, pp. 129-207), historian Jonathan Katz has chronicled and abstracted the horrifying variety of medical treatments conducted on homosexuals from 1884 to 1974. Sylvere Lotringer (1988), in his book *Overexposed: Treating Sexual Perversion in America,* documents, sometimes from the anguished perspective of the sex offender, the frightening lengths to which modern-day "helping professionals" will go to manipulate, control, and suppress one's sexual fantasies. His composite stories illustrate the proliferation of sex offender treatment programs that attempt to prescribe "cures" for societally tabooed sex, including pedophilia.

Among the "cures" is the drug, known by its trade name, Depo-Provera, which has been used in the United States as a means of suppressing certain sexual behaviors for over two and a half decades. Depo-Provera is a synthetic hormone manufactured by the Kalamazoo, Michigan-based Upjohn Company. Its chemical name is medroxyprogesterone acetate (or MPA). The drug has often been administered to men arrested for or convicted of a sex offense involving children. The treatment is usually given while the accused is in prison or on probation, parole, or even out on bail.

Because biochemistry is a relatively new field of study, little is known about the complex interactions and effects of hormones on brain functioning. Natural hormones are substances which are conveyed by the blood to an organ to stimulate it either to act or to secrete another hormone. Androgens, for example, are secreted by the tissues of the testicles in the male and, in both sexes, by the adrenal gland located at the top of the kidney. In males the androgens stimulate the growth of pubic and facial hair, the deepening of the voice, the development of muscle tissue, the distribution of fat, and the development of the genitals ("Androgen," 1986). Androgens are a class of hormones (Thomas, 1989). It is incorrect to call them "male hormones" since they are also present in females.

Depo-Provera is classified as an "antiandrogen." In the case of men incarcerated for sex offenses, Depo-Provera is administered to block the release into the blood stream of one of the androgens, testosterone. Testosterone is believed to govern the intensity of a putative male sex drive. In adult males the prolonged use of Depo-Provera can reduce the testosterone level to that of the prepubertal boy (Money, 1979a, p. [1]; 1987b, p. 220). Testosterone is a derivative of still another hormone, progesterone (sometimes called the "pregnancy hormone")–hence the chemical name (i.e., medroxy-*progesterone* acetate).

One national survey of juvenile and adult sex offender programs and providers found that out of 643 treatment programs for sex offenders, 14% of the adult programs and 6% of the juvenile programs regularly used Depo-Provera (Knopp, Rosenberg, & Stevenson, 1986, pp. 9, 14). As a "treatment" for sex offenders, the drug is usually administered on a weekly basis by intramuscular injection into the buttocks, sometimes in massive doses, up to 500 milligrams or more, depending on a subjective judgement of the survival strength of the person's inclination to repeat the forbidden sexual behavior (Money, 1987b, p. 221). In comparison, when used as a contraceptive on women, the recommended dosage is 150 milligrams every *three months* (Vaid, 1985, p. 8). The non-Depo form of the drug, Provera, marketed as a tablet, is "not well absorbed in the gut and is not satisfactory for the treatment of paraphilia," according to Money (1987b, p. 221).[1] The strength of this inscrutable tendency is determined either through the inmate's self-report or measured by devices attached to the inmate's penis to detect minute changes in circumference and length while he views photographs of his *object d'amour,* or by assaying every few months testosterone levels in the blood. Treatment may be continued for a period of two to three years.

In addition to its use for preventing men from having sex with minors, the drug has been used on children who are considered sexually precocious (see below). But more attention has been devoted to its use on men convicted of rape or attempted rape. Instead of imprisonment, such men are sometimes sentenced to undergo Depo-Provera treatment during probation or parole (Tempest, 1983; Abrams, 1985; McFarland, 1986). Such drug therapy for rape cases, however, goes against the feminist view of rape as a crime involving violence and domination of women, and assumes rape to be primarily a sexual act (Vaid, 1985, p. 9). Feminists would argue that reducing the "libido" would do nothing to reduce the threat of violence. With sexual desire supposedly reduced or erased, murder might well be a more likely outcome. Another dubious assumption is that rapists are "abnormal, oversexed men" (ibid.), thus discounting the effect of a chauvinistic culture on the crime.

Depo-Provera is more widely used as a contraceptive for females; it is marketed in more than 90 countries and used by an estimated 30 million women worldwide (Cimons, 1992a). Although approved for restricted use as a contraceptive in some countries (e.g., Veitch, 1984), its use in the United States for birth control had been banned by the Food and Drug Administration (FDA) until late 1992 because of a correlation with uterine and breast cancer (e.g., Minkin, 1981). However, in late October 1992 the FDA approved its use as a contraceptive, downplaying or discounting any adverse effects (Cimons, 1992b; Leary, 1992). Groups such as the National Women's Health Network, the National Latina Health Association, and the National Black Women's Health Project remained adamantly opposed to FDA approval because of persistent doubts about its safety and the documented risk increase for breast cancer in women under the age of 35 during the first four years of use (Cimons, 1992a; Hilts, 1992; *Ms.* Editors, 1993). Dr. Sidney Wolfe, director of consumer advocate Ralph Nader's Health Research Group, called the FDA action "reckless." He noted: "Just because a drug has been in use for a long time doesn't mean it is safe" (cited in Cimons, 1992a, p. A11). Whether or not its prolonged use in men is also carcinogenic remains as yet unknown.

Despite the then FDA ban, the drug had been promoted as a contraceptive on Indian Reservations in the United States by the Indian Health Service (U.S. Congress, 1988b; Swenson, 1987, p. 3). So many gynecologists in the San Francisco Bay Area were privately prescribing Depo-Provera that the National Women's Health Network filed a class action lawsuit against the drug's manufacturer, Upjohn Company, in the 1980s (Fraser, 1985, p. 19). In drug trials in the United States, some 1,100 Detroit-area women, including inner-city drug addicts, those with mental impairments, and others awaiting sterilization, received Depo-Provera from 1971 to 1974. Over 100 of them reported abnormal vaginal bleeding (Haenlein, 1983a, p. A8).

Upjohn has aggressively marketed it to women, especially in Third World countries, producing sales of about $100 million a year (Hilts, 1992; Minkin, 1981; "One Shot Too Many," 1983, p. 12; Swenson, 1987, 1988; cf. McDonough, 1988). With Depo-Provera's approval as a contraceptive in the United States, Upjohn, which is about to lose patent protection on three other major products, stands to gain another $100 million in annual sales ("Upjohn," 1992). In 1983, Upjohn made Ralph Nader's top ten Corporate Hall of Shame list for its campaign to gain governmental approval to market the drug in the United States (United Press International, 1983).

Ethical concerns have been raised about the high rate at which women in the Third World, compared with the industrialized world, have been injected with this suspected carcinogen. Tonga, for example, has the highest rate of usage in the world of Depo-Provera as a birth control method, but it probably has the most inadequate monitoring of its usage, calling into question whether there was really informed consent (Parsons, 1990, pp. 106, 109).

In Hong Kong, it was being injected into Vietnamese refugee girls and women to prevent pregnancy, reportedly without their full, informed consent. In 1989, 539 (or 37%) of the new Vietnamese cases seen by Hong Kong's Family Planning Association were injected with Depo-Provera (Davies & Howells, 1990; Howard, 1990). And in Nepal, almost 60% of the women receiving Depo-Provera complained of side effects (Acharya et al., 1978, p. 9).

Prior to October 1992 the FDA had approved the drug in the United States only to treat certain inoperable cancers of the endometrium (cervical lining) and the kidneys, even though it causes cancer in beagles and monkeys. Through a glaring loophole in the law, it could also be used in the "individualized practice of medicine" (Vaid, 1985, p. 7). This is because any drug already on the market for any approved use, with the authorization of any physician, can be prescribed for any other use, without further FDA approval or regulation, but subject only to "personal liability for an unorthodox use" (Adkinson, 1983, p. [1]). According to the national registry of drug prescriptions, National Disease and Therapeutic Index, some 3,000 prescriptions for Depo-Provera were written between October 1982 and September 1983 to treat "sexual deviation" (cited in Vaid, 1985, p. 8).

Legislation to permit the use of Depo-Provera by the government on rapists has been approved in Oregon (Haenlein, 1983b, p. A8; Vaid, 1985, p. 8). But Connecticut's prison system (Vaid, 1985, p. 8) has rejected its use, citing uncertainty about its safety. In 1994, Florida citizens were debating a Senate bill to mandate Depo-Provera treatment on rapists and other sex offenders (see debate on *Sonya Live!* 1994).

Beginning in 1966, clinical psychologist John Money and two physicians at Johns Hopkins Hospital in Baltimore, Maryland, were the first researchers in the United States to use Depo-Provera on "sex offenders" (Money, 1970, p. 165; Boodman, 1992), even though the drug had not been approved by the FDA for that purpose. The FDA viewed Money and his colleagues' use to be the "individualized practice of medicine," and refused to monitor it (Meyer, 1983). The FDA maintained its position even though

Money could not practice medicine, since he was a clinical psychologist and not a psychiatrist. Similarly, Johns Hopkins' Joint Committee on Clinical Investigation, which is the hospital's internal review board, refused to get involved, and decided that the Hopkins team was not doing a "clinical investigation" subject to oversight (Hendrix, 1983). Whether called patient care or research, drug treatment continued, and in 1984, 192 men were treated with the drug at Money's Biosexual and Psychohormonal Clinic (also called Sexual Disorders Clinic), 20% of whom were incarcerated in prison, and the rest (80%) were on parole or probation (Vaid, 1985, p. 8). Another account placed a third of the "outpatients" there as "pedophiles" (Gardner, 1984).

In 1985, Ralph Nader's Public Citizen Litigation Group (Glitzenstein et al., 1984) pressured Johns Hopkins Hospital to seek official FDA permission to conduct a research study on the use of Depo-Provera to control sexual behavior. The Hospital obtained from the FDA an Investigational Exemption for a New Drug (IND), which permitted the "research" use of Depo-Provera. With an IND, there are supposed to be more stringent reporting and control requirements for such uses of a drug (Vaid, 1985, p. 8). However, the formal results of that "study" are as yet unknown. Money's colleague, psychiatrist Fred Berlin, admitted that he refuses to conduct double-blind studies because of the risk such a study would pose to children (Cardinal's Commission, 1992, Appendix C, p. 62).

An Upjohn Company spokesman, Joseph Galligan, told an investigative newsletter that Upjohn was not interested in marketing the drug as therapy for sex offenders for two reasons: (1) "We just don't feel it's worth the time and expense that would be required to have the drug approved." (2) "When administration of a drug becomes a condition of sentence or parole, you're taking the issue beyond the normal medical practice of prescribing medicine." Galligan added, "If Upjohn continued to be active in [these] studies . . . we could be construed as encouraging the inappropriate prescribing of a non-approved drug" ("Depo-Provera," 1984, p. 3). Nonetheless, Upjohn continues to supply the drug to Johns Hopkins.

Besides Johns Hopkins, other Depo-Provera treatment programs (apart from private physicians' offices) have included: the Sex Offender Unit, Oregon State Hospital (Salem); New Hampshire State

Hospital (Concord); Isaac Ray Center (Chicago); Gender Clinic, University of Texas Medical Branch (Galveston); Northwest Treatment Associates (Seattle, Washington); Rosenberg Paraphilia Treatment Clinic (Galveston); Ka Cor Associates (San Diego, California) (Vaid, 1985, p. 8); Atascadero State Hospital (California) (Kiersch, 1990); Rush Presbyterian St. Luke's Medical Center (Chicago) (Foreman, 1984, p. 24); St. Luke's Institute (Suitland, Maryland); Servants of the Paraclete Center (Jemez Springs, New Mexico); and "antiandrogenic treatment" at the Vermont Treatment Program for Sexual Aggressors, a legislature-mandated program treating sex offenders in prison and in the community (Pithers, Martin, & Cumming, 1989, p. 298). The Isaac Ray Center, St Luke's Institute, and Servants of The Paraclete Center are sites where Catholic priests accused of having sex with minors are treated (Cardinal's Commission, 1992, p. 35; Money, 1988, p. 179; "Priestly Sins," 1992, p. 22).

Worldwide, doctors are prescribing other chemically castrating drugs for sexually taboo behavior, such as cyproterone acetate (CPA), norhydroxyprogesterone caproate, oestrone, oestrogen, progesterone, and the tranquilizer benperidol (Herrmann & Beach, 1980, p. 182). In Canada, although Depo-Provera has not been officially approved for use to treat sexual "anomalies," Pierre Gagné of Quebec's Sherbrooke Hospital has been prescribing it since 1974 (Gagné, 1981). It is also used at the Clarke Institute of Psychiatry in Toronto by S. J. Hucker (1985). Elsewhere in Canada, CPA, which is unavailable in the United States (Berlin, 1983, p. 105), has been used extensively at the Sexual Behaviors Clinic of the Royal Ottawa Hospital and the University of Ottawa (Bradford, 1988, p. 199). It has also been used at Calgary General Hospital (Belanger, 1981). In Europe, the predominant medication is CPA (Herrmann & Beach, 1980, p. 182). Proponents claim that it is superior to Depo-Provera, although it has been linked to testicular atrophy (Langevin, 1983, p. 59). In Germany, the Division for Sex Research at the University of Hamburg stopped the routine use of antiandrogens as a sex offender treatment because of the serious effects on the bones and liver. According to its director, Gunter Schmidt, "the use of anti-androgens only is justified in special cases of sex offenders, for very short periods, to be able to get the psychotherapeutic contact begun" (Schmidt, 1989, p. 7). In the United Kingdom, a similar drug, Goserelin (also known by its trade name, Zolandex), was ordered to be used on a 25-year-old male patient *without his consent* in order to "modify his attitude towards women" ("Mental Patient," 1988). One writer subsequently described this collaboration of state, judiciary, and the medical establishment as "lynch mobs in white coats" (Levin, 1988).

The list of effects and side effects associated with Depo-Provera when used on males reads like a phantasmagoria of medical symptoms, including: increased appetite and weight gain of 15-20 pounds, fatigue, mental depression, hyperglycemia, impotence, abnormal sperm, lowered frequency and intensity of thoughts/ erections/ejaculations, lowered ejaculatory volume, insomnia, nightmares, dypsnea (difficulty in breathing), hot and cold flashes, loss of body hair, nausea, leg cramps, irregular gall bladder function, diverticulitis, aggravation of migraine, hypogonadism, elevation of the blood pressure, hypertension, phlebitis, diabetic sequelae, thrombosis (leading to heart attack), and shrinkage of the prostate and seminal vessels (Hucker, 1985; Bradford, 1983, p. 163; Brooks, 1983, p. 4; Langevin, 1983, p. 58).

The consent form that has been used by The Johns Hopkins Hospital Clinic warns of the following dangers:

> Depo-Provera is a hormone which is similar to those contained in birth control pills. Therefore, the risk of developing blood clots may exist. Depo-Provera has been found to increase the frequency of malignant breast tumors (breast cancer) in female beagle dogs, and of uterine cancer in female monkeys. There have been no reports of this drug causing cancer in men. (Consent Form, 1989, p. [78])

Although the form does state that the "most common" side effects are weight gain and higher blood pressure, no mention is made of the World Health Organization data (cited in Minkin, 1981, p. 52) showing the increase in cancer in Thai women in a location where over half have used the drug.[2] Neither is any mention made of the reason Depo-Provera had been banned as a contraceptive in the United States. In the paragraph preceding the statement quoted, patients are warned of "less common side effects," including nightmares, cold sweats, hot flashes, sexual impotence, muscle cramps, and "a tendency to become easily fatigued." It does not inform the patient that hypertension is often an irreversible side effect or that atypical sperm might result and produce malformed offspring (Brooks, 1983, pp. 3-4). Nor is it disclosed that Hopkins researchers have never undertaken any controlled, double-blind, scientifically-sound studies of Depo-Provera. It also fails to disclose that the medical school's internal review committee withdrew its approval of the drug's experimental use in the early 1980s (Adkinson, 1983). Additionally, no mention is made as well that as a substitute for rigorous research, sex offenders are paraded before the press as "success stories" (Kobren, 1984). Nor is the potential patient told that the Connecticut Department of Corrections has rejected the drug's use on inmates because of "real concerns" about its safety (Brooks, 1983).

It has been widely touted that those who take the drug lose their interest in having sex. Women who have taken the drug as a contraceptive have also complained about a loss of "sex drive" ("Limp Libidos," 1981). In males, Depo-Provera does lessen the frequency of erections and ejaculations. In the words of John Money (1988, p. 233), "[i]t . . . induces a period of sexual quiescence in which the feeling of sex drive is at rest. The patient 'has a vacation' from his or her sex drive." Money's former colleague, psychologist Paul Walker, echoes Money when he states that Depo-Provera just "provides a vacation from sex and sexual fantasizing until these men learn to do it right" (Foreman, 1984). But this cannot be an enjoyable vacation. One can well imagine that a drug that produces depression and lethargy, leaving the person with a general feeling of bodily dysfunction, would reduce interest not only in sex but in being alive.

It is naive to believe that hormones are more basic in shaping sexual desire and behavior in human beings than personal experience and social norms. With the evolution of the human brain, the control that hormones have over sexual desire and behavior has arguably been progressively relaxed. At this point in the evolution of the human brain and of civilization, it is impossible to isolate the influence of hormones in shaping our sexuality from the influence of personal experience (see, e.g., Vines, 1994).

The belief that human sexuality is determined by hormones,

however, has been zealously propagated by John Money. He headed the "psychohormonal unit" in John Hopkins' medical school, even though he never earned a degree in medicine. *Psychology Today,* however, has called Money the "Doctor of Sexology" (Holden, 1988). At Hopkins, he also was associated with its surgical program for transsexuals, which was shut down in 1979 after a study revealed surgery alone did nothing for the patient's emotional adjustment (Mitzel, 1981, p. 22). Since the 1960s, he has zealously promoted the use of Depo-Provera in the treatment of paraphilias (his neologism for sexual perversions), among which he includes pedophilia, ephebophilia, cross dressing, voyeurism, and sado-masochism (Money, 1988, pp. 179-180).

Money's strenuous advocacy of Depo-Provera as a means of eliminating forbidden forms of sexual behavior is anchored in his general view of human sexuality. Money has spent a long career writing about and even occasionally studying the causes of human sexual behavior. According to Ruth Doell (1990, p. 121), a biologist:

> Money's view of what a human being is . . . is that of an advanced ape, one whose behaviors, primed by prenatal hormonal exposure, reflect his primate inheritance. Not that we don't inherit much from our primate ancestry. We do. But Money ignores the intervening several million years of evolution of the human brain since we parted from the great apes, which have allowed the development of a quite different mode of behaving at the conscious level.

Money does not seem to believe that human beings are able to exercise any discretion over their sexual behavior, including the decision to be abstinent. Although he endlessly declares that his theories are interactionist, that is, they embrace both biological and social factors, he reiterates his belief that prenatal hormone exposure is the *primary* determinant of the character of our sexual desires, including the adult sexual interest in children and other so-called paraphilias. Early social conditioning is considered secondary.

For example, Money is pleased that the Catholic Church is injecting Depo-Provera into wayward priests accused of being "pedophiles" or "ephebophiles." He asserts:

> This adoption of a biomedical treatment is the thin edge of a wedge that may have far-reaching consequences on Vatican sexology . . . It gives official recognition to the proposition that sexual behavior is not attributable exclusively to the morality of good and evil, righteousness and sin. Repentance, prayer, and penance alone are not sufficient for the governance of paraphiliac sexuality, even among those in holy orders. Nor are punishment and imprisonment. (Money, 1988, p. 179)

Money and his colleagues have not been shy to rush to the press and claim success for their biochemical treatment, even without conducting any controlled studies. As far back as 1982, they were publicly proclaiming success in curbing the "sexual appetite" of pedophiles and exhibitionists treated with Depo-Provera. Money and his colleague Fred Berlin told *Science News* that they had identified a cluster of biological abnormalities in such sex offenders. They claimed such findings called into question the idea that early life experiences alone lead to deviancy in adulthood. They reported that 20 of their subjects had unusual brain scans that showed cortical atrophy, unusual brain electrical activity, and significantly higher levels of testosterone and pituitary hormones. Seventeen of the twenty patients were able to avoid illegal sexual behaviors, in one case for 15 years ("Curbing Sexual Appetite," 1982).

In an article headlined "Is Sexual Deviance a Biological Problem?" *Psychology Today* (1983) similarly reported that Money and Berlin had "discovered a surprising number of physiological abnormalities" in the sex offenders they treated, and were "now launching more detailed studies of brain metabolism with new PET (positron emission tomography) scanner equipment," with an aim of identifying "key biological differences between the sexes and among those with different sexual preferences." The magazine predicted that Money and Berlin's research "could lead to a new theory of sexual desire, drive, and behavior, and do much to promote a more humane approach to sex offenders" (McAuliffe, 1983).

In Toronto, Canada, as a defense witness in the 1979 indecency trial of the Pink Triangle Press and the editors of the now defunct Canadian gay liberation monthly *The Body Politic* for publishing an essay on pedophilia, Money testified that it is biology that determines pedophilia, not the environment. Pedophilia, Money told the court, "is a condition which develops within the person and it's an internal complex developmental process that takes place and it's not a simple response to the act of reading one piece of material" such as the *Body Politic* article (cited in Adelman, 1981, p. 319). Asked by the prosecutor why he would not condone pedophilia, Money replied incongruously, "[b]ecause of its disparity in the equilibrium" ("The Body Politic Trial," 1979, p. 99).

Professor Doell has discussed Money's biological fatalism (1990, p. 123), pointing out:

> The most that biology can be shown to determine in humans is a capacity for sexual behavior which each of us can integrate into the experiences of our childhood and adolescence to come to some conclusion as to what is in our own best interests with respect to sexual behavior. This is in contrast to Money's statement . . . that self conscious decision plays no role in developing homosexual behavior.

Money's theories of sexuality are heterosexist. They assume that heterosexual reproduction is the biological *sine qua non* of human gender and sexuality. Over a period of thirty years, he has tediously litanized the "immutable and irreducible" sex differences (e.g., Money, 1988, p. 54): "They are specific to reproduction: men impregnate and women menstruate, gestate, and lactate." Forms of sexuality that preclude reproduction, including homosexual behavior, are categorized as sexual perversions or paraphilias. Homosexual pedophilia and pederasty, in Money's system of thought, are particularly perverse not only because the man/boy contact itself precludes reproduction, but also because it undermines the possibility of the boy in the future performing his biologically-mandated, heterosexual mission—impregnation. These so-called pedophiles and pederasts have no control over their condition, for "[p]edophilia and ephebophilia are no more a matter of voluntary choice than are left-handedness or color blindness," according to Money (1987a, p. 6). He further acknowledges, despite his advocacy of Depo-Provera as a treatment for these sexual differences, that "[t]here is no known method of treatment by which they can be effectively and permanently altered, suppressed, or replaced. Punishment is useless" (ibid.). He even goes so far as to argue that they are "unnatural" and irrelevant to evolution: "There is no satisfactory hypothesis, evolutionary or otherwise, as to why they exist in nature's overall scheme of things" (ibid.). But, condescendingly, he advises, "[o]ne must simply accept the fact that they do exist, and then, with optimum enlightenment, formulate a policy of what to do about it" (ibid.). He told a reporter he would like to see all convicted sex offenders offered a "choice" between incarceration and placement in a halfway house that provided Depo-Provera treatment. Discounting fears of a "Brave New World," Money proclaimed, "We've been doing it ever since we invented alcohol in ancient Egypt" (Colen, 1975). Money even gained the support of the embattled then-director of the Kinsey Institute, June Reinisch, who told a Bloomington, Indiana, public radio station that Depo-Provera should be used to rehabilitate nonviolent sex criminals because it helps "individuals to stop their obsessive behavior . . . [and] return to a normal and healthy sex life with their wives" (Jackson, 1984).[3]

Money's "enlightened" policy is clearly far from benign. After reducing human beings to sexual robots, Money can justify all manner of reprogramming for those who do not operate within the social norms. Since the social norms are treated as brute reality, it is the robots that must change. Obviously, since robots cannot change themselves, the reprogramming must be done for them by the self-appointed guardians of heterosexual privilege.

Money also advocates the early detection and treatment of "potential" sex offenders, especially for young boys who have engaged in taboo sex, or for girls with an early onset of puberty. Money admits that he did not consider Depo-Provera dangerous because "it had been used a great deal in pediatric endocrine health care with children who were getting into puberty too early, from as early as 18 months up to six years of age" (Money, 1991, p. 11). According to Money, his "patients" at the clinic are usually aware of their "problem" by age 13 (Gardner, 1984). A 15-year-old girl was treated at the clinic with Depo-Provera for "periodic psychosis of puberty," which included incoherent speech, insomnia, and hallucinations (Berlin, Bergey, & Money, 1985). It is nothing short of outrageous that at his clinic, girls as young as one year old reportedly have been treated with Depo-Provera, in an attempt "to retard the onset of incredibly early adolescence" (Mitzel, 1981, p. 22). Today, such girls and boys would be labelled child perpetrators (see Okami, 1992). Given the rhetoric about protection of children, it is ironic that they have become the newest guinea pigs in the war against taboo sex. Psychologist Toni C. Johnson coined the term "mini-perps" to describe these children. When questioned by this author, she admitted that the "little ones," who are "sexual all the time," have been treated with the drug Clonidine, rather than Depo-Provera, to control their sexual behavior (Johnson, 1991; see also Johnson, 1988).

Ironically, Money's advocacy of Depo-Provera occurs at the same time as he readily passes himself off as a friend and supporter of adults sexually attracted to minors. As indicated above, he testified for the editors of the *Body Politic,* defending their publication of an essay on pedophilia. He wrote a favorable introduction to Theo Sandfort's *Boys on Their Contacts with Men* (1987). Sandfort's publisher, Global Academic Publishers (a pro-pedophilia press), has also brought out a collection of essays by Money (1992). In addition, he has been sought out and interviewed favorably by pedophile movement publications such as *Paidika* (Money, 1991) and *OK* (Cobelens, 1991), both based in the Netherlands. Even the New York City-based *NAMBLA Bulletin* featured him on the cover and reported his comments supportive of man/boy love in the *Paidika* interview (Andriette, 1991). Whether Money is being disingenuous, merely opportunistic, or acting out of guilt is a question that is beyond the scope of this paper. But one might speculate that his behavior might not be so different from that of a nineteenth-century missionary who saw himself on a quest to save the lost souls of "savages" and who enjoyed mingling with them. After all, Money probably believes he has the "pedophile's" best interests in mind.

In order to disguise his role of sexual policeman and master reprogrammer, Money sounds what is intended to be a compassionate note in offering his magical chemical cures. In the case of pedophilia, Money tries to convince the patient that the suppression of the behavior in question will free him from the tyranny of those awful impulses and thereby enable him to take his rightful and satisfying place among the husbands and fathers of the world. As *60 Minutes* correspondent Ed Bradley remarked in a program on Depo-Provera and the Hopkins' role, "the treatment is controversial, but the doctors say that Depo-Provera can actually help control the behavior of men like those you are about to meet, men who suffer from hormonal imbalances that they say make them fall victim to their own unbearable urges" (Bradley, 1984, p. 2). Or as an *Omni* interviewer wrote about Money's work, "The shared principle of all paraphilias, says Money, is that they represent tragedy turned into triumph. The tragedy is the defacement of the ordinary lovemap" (Stein, 1986, p. 80), that is, the failure to perform one's heterosexually mandated mission. The triumph "is the rescue of lust from total wreckage and obliteration. The new map gives lust . . . a second chance but at a price: that 'saintly' love and 'sinful' lust are separated" (ibid.). Money has asserted that the use of antiandrogens like Depo-Provera "really depends on how much humanitarian concern you have for people that are in trouble. Are you willing to do something to try and help them?" he asked rhetorically (Money, 1991, p. 11).

This sanctimonious note of compassion about perverts being given a "second chance" is found in a memorandum Money addressed to the Maine House Judiciary Committee. In this two-page memorandum, Money (1979b) declares he has "no hesitation" in recommending the use of Depo-Provera, and asserts that it is "by far the most effective method known":

> There is now available for sex offenders a form of treatment that enables them to self-regulate their pathological behavior (paraphilia) instead of being the victims of it. Without treatment, they are as much the victims of their pathology as untreated epileptics are victims of their epileptic seizures. The new treatment combines the use of medication, a hormone, an anti-androgen, to induce a time-limited antisexual effect, with the use of counseling to enable the person to take advantage of the hormonal reduction in sex drive in order to begin and maintain a new pattern of sexual life.

This quote summarizes his argument for the use of Depo-Provera. With the propensity simultaneously to inform, shock, entertain, and advise in detached and macabre scientific jargon, Money's main defense for the use of the drug is that it is preferable to surgical castration, which had been facing constitutional challenges for "cruel and unusual punishment." Depo-Provera treatment is preferable not because of the obvious brutality of castration, but because castration does not really get rid of behavior. In what comprises two thirds of the memorandum, he explains why castration does not work. The memorandum is accompanied by a treatment protocol (Money, 1979a) for the use of Depo-Provera. The protocol varies little from that published as an article (Money, 1987b) and later as an appendix in Money (1988). Money also has stated, even though he lacks medical training, "I don't think it's my business to refuse to treat" someone who volunteers for hormonal therapy. However, he has not treated anyone since his retirement (Money, 1991, p. 12).

Does Money's paternalistic concern for the welfare of sex offenders settle the ethical questions involved in using Depo-Provera for inmates in prison hospitals and those under the custody of the courts? This question arises since it is foolish to claim that prisoners can freely give informed consent to submit to treatment if doing so is a condition of their earlier release and probation (Tsang, 1989, p. [5]). In fact, in *People v. Gauntlett,* the Michigan Supreme Court found that requiring Depo-Provera treatment as a condition of probation was "unlawful," because Money's program was still experimental. Ironically, the case involved Roger A. Gauntlett, an heir to the Upjohn fortune (Melella et al., 1989, pp. 228-229). A congressional report, noting that some prison administrators have proposed using the drug on all inmates to control violence and homosexual activity, concluded that "[s]uch broad and general use of the drug might meet the Supreme Court's test for cruel and unusual punishment: 'shocking to the conscience of reasonably civilized people'" (U.S. Congress, 1988a, p. 43). Yet Money (1977, pp. 122) cavalierly dismisses this ethical issue with these words: "That is a specious argument, if not a vindictive argument, for being in jail is a fact of life for a prisoner just as being in a hospital is for a patient. The facts of our lives shape all of our judgments, including those of informed consent." The cynicism of this statement is not surprising when we recall that its author believes that the concepts of choice and will are pre-scientific. Money has elsewhere also evaded this ethical issue by claiming that sex offenders are not usually forced into treatment by the law: "Usually, when someone is in trouble with the law it is their lawyer who recommends that they come to the clinic"! (Money, 1991, p. 12).

Money's colleague at Johns Hopkins who continues to direct the clinic, Fred Berlin, echoes this cynicism when he argues that if Depo-Provera "is effective, as it often seems to be, then it is difficult to see why a person should be denied the opportunity to take it just because he is on probation or perhaps even incarcerated" (Berlin & Krout, 1986, p. 25). Berlin also dismisses any concern about the drug's side effects by stating they are comparable to those of birth control pills, which can cause blood clots in the legs, leading to a stroke or pulmonary embolism. Berlin believes that pharmacological therapy helps take the edge off a person and lessens his sexual preoccupation. He admits that the clinic, which has treated over 600 patients, does not rely much on behavioral therapy (Cardinal's Commission, 1992, Appendix C, pp. 61, 62, 64). Testifying in the trial of a Pennsylvania man whom he treated at his clinic after the man was charged with receiving child pornography, Berlin blamed the man's past sexual behavior on the body's high production of a hormone that "fuels the sex drive" (Muir, 1985). Berlin believes that there is a biological predisposition to sexual orientation, implying that sexual attraction is not under our conscious control (ibid., p. 62).

Berlin (1981, p. 1516) has further claimed that such psychotropic drugs are "not given to control attitudes and behaviors such as those concerning political beliefs or personal affiliations. They are not 'mind controlling.' Rather they may be given to help a person whose thinking is clearly out of touch with reality." He continues, "antiandrogenic medications are given with the intent of increasing rather than decreasing a person's capacity for self control." He also has argued, "it is difficult to see how helping a willing patient to be better able to free his mind from obsessional cravings and ruminations about unacceptable forms of sexual behavior, could be considered any form of 'mind control'" (Berlin, 1989, p. 236). That argument is misleading, according to forensic attorney John T. Melella et al. (1989, p. 277), for Depo-Provera affects one's thought processes by inhibiting the chemical messenger that stimulates the production of androgen. "This in turn inhibits the offender's sexual fantasies" (ibid.). Melella et al. conclude that convicted felons still retain rights to procreate, refuse intrusive medical treatments, and generate ideas, all rights violated by the use of involuntary antiandrogen treatment. Informed consent, as applied to research subjects, requires (1) that the person be told the risk and benefits of the procedures, (2) that he understand what he is told, and (3) that he be allowed to refuse participation without any threat of punishment. The Money/Berlin protocol for informed consent fails on all three counts.

First, it does not name all the physical risks, including all the short-term side effects. Money himself dismisses the side effects and claims that they "might have occurred without the treatment anyway" (Money, 1991, p. 11).

Second, it does not inform the person of the very high likelihood he will resume the forbidden behavior as soon as he is free to do so without the threat of punishment. He is not told that when Depo-Provera "is discontinued, allowing the sexual appetite to heighten or return, behaviors engaged in to satisfy that appetite are also likely to be reinstituted" (Berlin & Meinecke, 1981, p. 607). Back in 1975 Money boasted that Depo-Provera could free a sex offender of his compulsion, by turning down the "thermostat" on his sex drive. However, "[t]he nice thing about the thermostat analogy . . . is you can turn (the sex drive) back up again," he added (Colen, 1975). Data from Money's own clinic indicate that when medication is discontinued, patients "relapse" in most cases (Berlin, 1983, p. 110).[4]

Finally, despite Money's insistence that patients give "completely informed consent" (Money, 1991, p. 12), the language of the treatment protocol, which is signed by the patient as evidence of being informed, is likely beyond the understanding of the prisoner, as in the following example (Money, 1988, p. 234): "The size of the maintenance dosage is judged on the basis of the patient's subjective report of how well the paraphilic imagery and ideation is under control, together with the lowered blood level of testosterone." One can imagine the terror and confusion of the person who is facing a sentence of several years on a charge of child molestation and who knows that submission to treatment is his only hope for probation or a short sentence, trying to decipher this language and weigh the consequences of his consent. One physician, Dr. Sidney Wolfe, of the Health Research Group, calls this a travesty: "It makes a mockery of the whole concept of informed consent when your option is to go to jail or get injected with a carcinogen that can increase the risk of heart attack . . . It's human experimentation" (Engel, 1983, p. A5). The American Civil Liberties Union (ACLU) has also protested that inmates are, in effect, being "coerced" to participate in any Depo-Provera treatment program (U.S. Congress, 1988a, p. 43). Judicial clarification expected in 1992 failed to materialize. In November 1992 the U.S. Supreme Court refused to decide whether sex offenders could be required to undergo therapy as a condition of staying out of jail if the therapy required the offender to acknowledge guilt denied at trial. This let stand a 1991 Montana Supreme Court ruling that outlawed such forced therapy (Greenhouse, 1992a, p. A15; 1992b, p. A10). Prison psychologist Nicholas Groth and his colleagues do admit that "[b]asically treatment is coercive–the offender, realizing the social and legal consequences of disclosure does not self-refer. Therefore, treatment must be confrontative" (Groth et al., 1982, p. 142).

The veiled threat of incarceration appears in the informed consent form that has been used at the Johns Hopkins Hospital: "Even if you are in this treatment program as a condition of probation, you are still not obligated to take Depo-Provera. If you are receiving counseling here as a condition of probation and you fail to adhere to your agreed-upon appointment schedule, we will notify your Probation Officer that you have been noncompliant" (Consent Form, 1989, p. [79].) The patient is thereby reminded that the word of the medical authorities could send him to prison. Dr. Berlin himself admitted on the Phil Donahue Show that "[i]f a man misses an injection the court is notified. Any noncompliance is notified" ("Depo-Provera," 1983, p. 17). Although he is willing to send his patient back to jail, Berlin has also told a reporter that jail is not the appropriate punishment for some sex offenders, because there "is a moral issue of whether it is right to punish someone for not controlling that which they cannot control. Even if someone else is hurt" (Tempest, 1983, part I, p. 12).

Resistance to treatment is no secret to those who prescribe or advocate the use of Depo-Provera. Dr. Judith Becker, professor of psychiatry and psychology at the University of Arizona College of Medicine, who has treated hundreds of sex offenders, concedes that "many men stop taking" Depo-Provera because of its side effects (Boodman, 1992). Nonetheless, the former (dissenting) member of then Attorney General Edwin Meese's Commission on Pornography continues to recommend its use, most recently when consulted by the Chicago Archdiocese Cardinal Joseph Bernadin's Commission on what to do with priests who are sexually attracted to teenage boys. According to the commission report, Becker recommends the use of Depo-Provera on priests with multiple "victims" (Cardinal's Commission, 1992, Appendix C, p. 57).

Even compliance with the protocol is no guarantee of avoiding prison, as Ray Latham found out. As an outpatient at Money's clinic, and an unrepentant boy lover, Latham, who opted for Money's program so that he could get probation for having had consensual sex with boys, eventually realized that "at age 66, I needed [Depo] like a hole in the head" (cited in Mitzel, 1981, p. 22). He later made the mistake of "bragging" to his Johns Hopkins Depo counselor about helping turn around the life of a teenage runaway. There was no sexual contact. But his counselor promptly informed his probation officer, his probation was revoked and he was sentenced to 16 years' imprisonment (Latham, 1981; Mitzel, 1981, p. 22). As Groth and his colleagues have argued, "[a]lthough confidentiality may be appropriate when treating non-criminal behavior, it is not appropriate when dealing with the child sex offender. . . ." (Groth, Hobson, & Gray, 1982, p. 144). Berlin claims to be against mandatory reporting laws for child sexual abuse (Berlin, 1988). He asserts that his patients have "voluntarily" come to Johns Hopkins in Maryland to receive treatment because Maryland, unlike other states, requires therapists to report sexual abuse only after a child is examined (Berlin, 1989, p. 238). But clearly, as a court-referred convicted sex offender in Maryland, Latham forfeited his right to confidentiality. Berlin justifies exposing Latham, stating that Latham "hadn't done anything sexually wrong, but he was uncooperative. There was no evidence that he had become sexually involved. . . . But it was only a matter of time" (Weiss, 1984, p. A9). Latham (1984) remained unrepentant, declaring that he would continue speaking out, even if it meant sacrificing his last chance for freedom by submitting to Berlin and confessing, "I am one of the sick," a step he resolutely refused to take.

It is a travesty of justice that any human being under the law is subjected to coercive treatment that severely reduces brain function and could eventually result in death from cancer (at least among women). It is a barbaric practice that cries for reform when we recall that some of the men subjected to such cruel treatment are punished for having sex with teenagers who encouraged, consented to, and enjoyed the sexual encounter. The same system that savages their adult partners makes these young people feel they are victims of their own sexual desires and enjoyment.

"This combination of judicial ignorance and medical zeal has frequently had catastrophic results, and sometimes lethal ones," writes a critic of such treatment (Levin, 1988). In England some three decades ago, computer inventor and World War II codebreaker Alan Turing was imprisoned for illegal homosexual sex.

> He was 'sentenced' by a judge whose vocation should have been burning witches, and 'treated' by a doctor who would have been more at home diagnosing his patients' ailments by examining the entrails of a freshly killed chicken, to a course of hormonal injections which were supposed to correct his abnormal sexual propensities. (ibid.)

In the end, Turing committed suicide, another victim of a system that considers homosexuals, highly talented or not, to be sex fiends or sex addicts. That the medical profession, whose members have each taken the Hippocratic Oath, should allow itself to be misled by sexological moralists is a bitter irony. In fact, "[h]istorically, physicians who have used biological intervention to treat criminals have tended to exaggerate both the dangerousness of the deviant person's behavior and the social benefit that comes from eradicating it. At the same time, they have often underestimated the harm the treatment imposes on the offender," declared an editorial in the *American Journal of Psychiatry,* which also called for the development of ethical guidelines for the use of antiandrogen drugs (Halleck, 1981, pp. 642-643). This perspective is echoed by a Canadian study of the construction of "dangerousness" about sex offenders, noting that "our present knowledge of the biomedical and behavioral effects of antiandogenic (sic) drugs is very imperfect," raising important ethical issues (Webster et al., 1985, p. 55). Bancroft (1989, p. 721) similarly notes that

> [a]lmost all the evidence of the efficacy of these pharmacological agents [like Depo-Provera] is of an uncontrolled kind and therefore cannot be regarded as conclusive. . . . The use of drugs to control sexual offenses is therefore still of uncertain value. This is of particular relevance when using them for social control, when it is necessary to be more certain of such effects before using drugs as an alternative to imprisonment. In addition, the potentially irreversible side-effects . . . pose major ethical problems when used in this context.

As psychiatric abuse critic Thomas Szasz (1987, p. 171), has observed:

> By separating church and state, religion was deprived of its power to abuse the individual and the state was deprived of one of its major justifications for the use of force. The upshot was a quantum jump toward greater individual liberty such as the world had never seen. By separating Psychiatry and the State, we would do the same for our age: At one fell swoop, psychiatry would be deprived of its power to abuse the individual and the State would be deprived of one its major justifications for the use of force. The result would be another major advance for individual liberty–or, perhaps, the advent of another system of justificatory rhetoric and persecutory practice, replacing both the religious and psychiatric systems.

The ease with which the public, politicians, media, police, social workers, therapists, the Church, and the medical establishment are aroused to moral panic over pederasty and pedophilia in particular suggests a refusal to accept children as sexual beings. Instead of poisoning alleged offenders with Depo-Provera, or imprisoning them, the diversity of our sexualities must be accepted. A minimal first step would be to reform our age of consent laws (while retaining sanctions against coercive or violent acts) so that young people will no longer be "jail-bait" or sexual outlaws but recognized as human beings with the capacity to say not only "no" but also "yes" to sex.

It is also surely time, as Professor Valenstein has argued, for more effective regulation of dangerous medical interventions. Valenstein remains unconvinced that a professional ethics code alone will be sufficient, for "[i]t is rare that codes of conduct apply unambiguously to the specific cases under dispute. Physicians who can be shown in retrospect to have caused great harm can always claim to have been motivated by the noblest of goals and the highest ethical principles" (Valenstein, 1988, p. 436). Valenstein's view "is that in most cases the undesirable effects of reasonable regulation and restraint have been exaggerated, certainly when compared to the cost of the unbridled use of dangerous treatments. Ultimately, some effective regulation will have to be instituted" (Valenstein, 1988, p. 437). Federal regulations should be changed to bar such experimentation under the guise of individualized patient care. Until restrained by the state or public outcry, Money and his sex police are, indeed, parading like "lynch mobs in white coats," with no qualms about using sexually active children, adults who love minors, transvestites, S&M practitioners, and pederasts as guinea pigs in their quest for a biologically determined new sexual order.

In short, John Money (cf. Money, 1986, p. 17) has found his vocation, having left the religion of his childhood in New Zealand, to become, even in retirement, the misguided missionary zealot of Depo-Provera in his Brave New World.

AUTHOR NOTE

The author thanks Urvashi Vaid, a past executive director of the National Gay and Lesbian Task Force, Washington, D.C., for generously sharing voluminous files of her research on Depo-Provera while she was at the ACLU National Prison Project; Mark McHarry and John Earl for additional research assistance; and finally but not least to John De Cecco for providing his insightful analysis of John Money's prolific output.

NOTES

1. Lotringer (1988, pp. 136-137) reports the case of a "pedophile" given 100 milligrams a day who rejected the treatment "because I was getting sick" and then pinched himself to prevent erections when tested.

2. Later WHO studies show the risk of breast cancer to be no greater than that associated with birth control pills (Cimons, 1992a; "Depot-Medroxyprogesterone Acetate," 1993).

3. Reinisch's position would undoubtedly make Alfred Kinsey–a scientist who studied rather than condemned sexual behavior–roll over in his grave.

4. However, Berlin was later to claim there was only a 5% recidivism rate (that is, those who "reoffend" and were caught) among his patients (Cardinal's Commission, 1992, Appendix C, p. 61).

REFERENCES

Abrams, L. J. (1985). Sexual offenders and the use of Depo-Provera, *San Diego Law Review, 22*, 565-586.

Acharaya, A., Shrestha, M., & Fisher, A. (1978). *An assessment of the Depo Provera program.* Kathmandu, Nepal: Family Planning and Maternal Child Health Project.

Adelman, H. (1981). Publicizing pedophilia: Legal and psychiatric discourse, *International Journal of Law and Psychiatry, 4*, 311-325.

Adkinson, N. F., Jr. (1983, July 26). Letter to S. M. Wolfe, Director, Public Citizen Health Research Group, Washington, DC. 4 pages. (Adkinson was acting chair, Johns Hopkins Joint Committee on Clinical Investigations.)

Andriette, B. (1991). Major American sex researcher speaks out for man/boy lovers: Dr. John Money makes strongest statements yet in *Paidika* interview, *NAMBLA Bulletin, 12*(7), 3, 5.

Androgen (1986). *The New Encyclopaedia Britannica,* vol. 1, *Micropaedia* (pp. 393-394). 15th edition. Chicago: Encyclopaedia Britannica.

Banay, R. S., & Davidoff, L. (1942). Apparent Recovery of a Sex Pyschopath after Lobotomy, *Journal of Criminal Pyschopathology, 4*, [59]-66.

Bancroft, J. (1989). *Human sexuality and its problems* (2d. ed.). New York: Churchill Livingstone.

Belanger, J. (1981, November 26). 'Temporary castration' for sex offenders. *San Francisco Chronicle*, p. 58.

Berlin, F. S. (1981). Ethical use of antiandrogenic medications, *American Journal of Psychiatry, 138*(11), 1515-1516. (Letter.)

Berlin, F. S. (1983). Sex offenders: A biomedical perspective and a status report on biomedical treatment. In J. G. Greer & I. R. Stuart (Eds.), *The sexual aggressor: Current perspectives on treatment* (pp. 83-123). New York: Von Nostrand Reinhold.

Berlin, F. S. (1988). Laws on mandatory reporting of suspected child sexual abuse, *American Journal of Psychiatry, 145*(8), 1039. (Letter.)

Berlin, F. S. (1989). The paraphilias and Depo-Provera: Some medical, ethical and legal considerations, *Bulletin of the American Academy of Psychiatry and the Law, 17*(3), 233-239.

Berlin, F. S., Bergey, G. K., & Money, J. (1985). Unusual case: Periodic psychosis of puberty, *Medical Aspects of Human Sexuality, 19*(1), 194.

Berlin, F. S., & Krout, E. (1986). Pedophilia: Diagnostic concepts, treatment and ethical considerations, *American Journal of Forensic Psychiatry, 7*(1), 13-30.

Berlin, F. S., & Meinecke, C. F. (1981). Treatment of sex offenders with antiandrogenic medication: Conceptualization, review of treatment modalities, and preliminary findings, *American Journal of Psychiatry, 138*(5), 601-607.

Body Politic Trial: In the Courtroom, The (1979, February/March). *Centerfold,* pp. 94-103.

Boodman, S. G. (1992, March 17). Does castration stop sex crimes? *Washington Post,* p. WH7.

Bradford, J. M. W. (1983). The hormonal treatment of sexual offenders, *Bulletin of the American Academy of Psychiatry and the Law, 11*(2), 159-169.

Bradford, J. M. W. (1988). Organic treatment for the male sex offender. In R. A. Prentky & V. L. Quinsey (Eds.), *Human sexual aggression: Current perspectives* (pp. 183-192). New York: New York Academy of Sciences. (Series: *Annals of the New York Academy of Sciences, 528.*)

Bradley, E. (correspondent). (1984). Depo-Provera, *60 Minutes, 16*(44). Transcript of program.

Brooks, R. J. (chairman). (1983, October 4). Report of the Depo-Provera Study Group. Hartford: Connecticut Department of Corrections. 9 pages.

Cardinal's Commission on Clerical Sexual Misconduct with Minors, The. (1992, June). *Report to Joseph Cardinal Bernadin, Archdiocese of Chicago.* [Chicago: The Archdiocese.]

Cimons, M. (1992a, June 20). FDA panel backs contraceptive's approval, *Los Angeles Times,* p. A14.

Cimons, M. (1992b, October 30). FDA Approves 3-month shot for contraception, *Los Angeles Times,* pp. A1, A11.

Cobelens, G. (1991, September/October). Interview: John Money, een seksuoloog in de tegenaanval, *OK* (33), pp. 20-21.

Colen, B. D. (1975, November 30). Drug for sex offenders called success, *Washington Post,* p. B3.

Consent Form of The Johns Hopkins Hospital Sexual Disorders Clinic. (1989). Table 5.2 in G. W. Barnard, A. K. Fuller, L. Robbins, & T. Shaw, *The child molester: An integrated approach to evaluation and treatment* (pp. [78-79]). New York: Brunner/Mazel.

Curbing sexual appetite. (1982, October 23). *Science News,* p. 270.

Davies, S. T., & Howells, B. (1990, April 1). A controversial contraceptive, *Sunday Morning Post Magazine* (Hong Kong), p. 21.

Depot-Medroxyprogesterone Acetate (DMPA) and Cancer: Memorandum from a WHO meeting. (1993). *Bulletin of the World Health Organization, 71*(6), 669-676.

Depo-Provera: A shot to the system. (1984, March). *Institutions Etc., 7*(3), 1-4.

Depo-Provera Therapy for Rapists. (1983). Cincinnati, OH: Multimedia Entertainment. (Series: Donahue Transcript, 09073.)

Doell, R. (1990). Review of J. Money, *Gay, straight, and in-between: The sexology of erotic orientation* (New York: Oxford University Press). *Journal of Homosexuality, 19*(4), 121-125.

Engel, M. (1983, July 18). Giving sex offenders drug spurs concern, *Washington Post*, pp. A1, A5.

Foreman, J. (1984, March 5). Drug may help sex offenders, *Boston Globe*, pp. 21, 24.

Foucault, M. (1978). *The history of sexuality, Vol. 1*. New York: Pantheon Books.

Fraser, L. (1985, October 9-16). The deadly riddle of Depo-Provera, *San Francisco Bay Guardian*, pp. 9, 11, 19, 29.

Gagné, P. (1981). Treatment of sex offenders with medroxyprogesterone acetate, *American Journal of Psychiatry, 138*(5), 644-646.

Gardner, J. (1984, June 24). Offering help for sex offenders, *Philadelphia Inquirer*, pp. 1K, 6K.

Glitzenstein, E. R., Schulz, W. B., & Morrison, A. B. (1984, March 15). Letter to M. Novitch, Acting Commissioner, Food and Drug Administration, Rockville, MD. 5 pages. (The authors are attorneys for the Public Citizen Litigation Group.)

Greenhouse, L. (1992a, March 3). Supreme Court roundup: Legality of therapy requirements to be addressed, *New York Times*, p. A15.

Greenhouse, L. (1992b, November 4). High Court drops case on forcing sex offenders to undergo therapy, *New York Times*, p. A10.

Groth, A. N., Hobson, W. F., & Gary, T. S. (1982). The child molester: Clinical observations. In J. R. Conte & D. A. Shore (Eds.), *Social work and child sexual abuse* (pp. 129-144). New York: The Haworth Press, Inc. (*Journal of Social Work & Human Sexuality, 1*[1-2]).

Haenlein, J. L. (1983a, August 21). Contraceptive produces bitter controversy, *Oakland Press*, pp. A1, A8.

Haenlein, J. L. (1983b, August 21). Drug use on sex offenders, *Oakland Press*, pp. A1, A8.

Halleck, S. L. (1981). The Ethics of antiandrogen therapy, *American Journal of Psychiatry, 138*(5), 642-643. (Editorial.)

Hendrix, T. R. (1983, September 29). Letter to S. M. Wolfe, Director, Public Citizen Health Research Group. 2 pages. (The author is Chairman, Joint Committee on Clinical Investigation at Johns Hopkins University.)

Herrmann, W. M., & Beach, R. C. (1980). Pharmacotherapy for sexual offenders. In T. A. Ban & F. A. Freyhan (Eds.), *Drug treatment of sexual dysfunction* (pp. 182-194). Basel: S. Karger. (Series: Modern Problems of Pharmacopsychiatry, 15.)

Hilts, J. (1992, June 20). Panel urges contraceptive's approval, *New York Times*, p. 6.

Holden, C. (1988, May). Doctor of sexology, profile: John Money, *Psychology Today*, pp. [44]-48.

Howard, T. A. (1990, February 12). Use of Depo-Provera should be carefully scrutinized, *South China Morning Post* (Hong Kong). (Letter.)

Hucker, S. J. (1985). Management of anomalous sexual behavior with drugs, *Modern Medicine of Canada, 40*(2), 150-153.

Jackson, J. (1984, February 11). Sex advisors? *Gay Community News*, p. 5. (Letter.)

Johnson, T. C. (1988). Child perpetrators–Children who molest other children: Preliminary findings, *Child Abuse and Neglect, 12*, 219-229.

Johnson, T. C. (1991, October 20). Remarks responding to a question at her presentation on Sexuality in Children: From Normal to Pathological, at the meeting of the Society for the Scientific Study of Sex, Western Region, held at Yamashiro Restaurant, Hollywood, California.

Katz, J. (1976). *Gay American history: Lesbians and gay men in the U.S.A.* New York: Thomas Y. Crowell.

Kiersch, T. A. (1990). Treatment of sex offenders with Depo-Provera, *Bulletin of the American Academy of Psychiatry and the Law, 18*(2), 179-187.

Knopp, F. H., Rosenberg, J., & Stevenson, W. (1986). *Report on nationwide survey of juvenile and adult sex-offender programs and providers.* Syracuse, NY: Safer Society Press.

Kobren, G. (1984, April 10). A profile of the child molester: Sex offenders "go public" at hospital seminar, *Los Angeles Times*, part VI, p. 12. (*Baltimore Sun* dispatch.)

Langevin, R. (1983). *Sexual strands: Understanding and treating sexual anomalies in men.* Hillsdale, NJ: Lawrence Erlbaum Associates.

Latham, R. (1981, May 27). Letter to NAMBLA, New York. 3 pages.

Latham, R. (1984, July). Not ashamed of being a boy-lover, *Gay Paper* (Baltimore).

Leary, W. E. (1992, October 30). U.S. approves drug used by injection for birth control, *New York Times*, pp. A1, A9.

Levin, B. (1988, September 5). Lynch mobs in white coats, *Times* (London), p. 10.

Limp Libidos. (1981, November). *Mother Jones, 6*(9), 37.

Lotringer, S. (1988). *Overexposed: Treating sexual perversion in America.* New York: Pantheon Books.

McAuliffe, Sharon (1983, March). Is Sexual deviance a biological problem? *Psychology Today*, p. 84.

McDonogh, R. T. (1988). Depo-Provera in the First World, *Hastings Center Report, 18*(4), 44.

McFarland, L. (1986). Depo-Provera therapy as an alternative to imprisonment, *Houston Law Review, 23*, 801-819.

Melella, J. T., Travin, S., & Cullen, K. (1989). Legal and ethical issues in the use of antiandrogens in treating sex offenders, *Bulletin of the American Academy of Psychiatry and the Law, 17*(3), 223-232.

Mental Patient Facing "Chemical Castration." (1988, August 9). *Times* (London), p. 3.

Meyer, H. M., Jr. (1983, December 16). Letter to S. M. Wolfe, Public Citizen

Health Research Group. 2 pages. (The author is Director of FDA's National Center for Drugs and Biologics. The letter was signed by an aide, P. Parkmen.)

Minkin, S. (1981, November). Nine Thai women had cancer, *Mother Jones, 6*(9), 34-39, 50, 52.

Mitzel (1981, 27 November/December 18). An unholy alliance of medicine and law: Chemical castration increasingly inflicted on boy-lovers, *Gay News* (Philadelphia), pp. 21-22.

Money, J. (1970). Use of an androgen-depleting hormone in the treatment of male sex offenders, *The Journal of Sex Research, 36*(3), 165-172.

Money, J. (1977). Issues and attitudes in research and treatment of variant forms of human sexual behavior. In W. H. Masters, V. E. Johnson, & R. C. Kolodny (Eds.), *Ethical issues in sex therapy and research (1,* 119-132). Boston: Little, Brown.

Money, J. (1979a, April 2). Antiandrogenic and counseling treatment of sex offenders, memorandum on Johns Hopkins Medical Institutions letterhead. 3 pages.

Money, J. (1979b, April 4). Memorandum, to Committee on Judiciary, House of Representatives, State of Maine. 2 pages.

Money, J. (1986). *Venuses penuses: Sexology, sexosophy and exigency theory.* Buffalo, NY: Prometheus Books.

Money, J. (1987a). Introduction. In Theo Sandfort, *Boys on their contacts with men: A study of sexually expressed friendships* (pp. 5-7). Elmhurst, NY: Global Academic Publishers.

Money, J. (1987b). Treatment guidelines: Antiandrogen and counseling of paraphilic sex offenders, *Journal of Sex & Marital Therapy, 13*(3), 219-223.

Money, J. (1988). *Gay, straight and in-between: The sexology of erotic orientation.* New York: Oxford University Press.

Money, J. (1991). Interview: John Money, *Paidika* (Amsterdam), *2*(3), 2-15.

Money, J. (1992). *The Adam Principle.* Elmhurst, NY: Global Academic Publishers.

Ms. Editors (1993 January/February). Is Depo Provera safe? *Ms.,* pp. 72-73.

Muir, C. (1985, August 3). Probation given in pornography case, *The Patriot* (Harrisburg, PA), p. A3.

Okami, (1992, February). Child perpetrators of sexual abuse: The emergence of a problematic deviant category, *The Journal of Sex Research, 29*(1), 109-130.

One Shot Too Many. (1983, March). *The Progressive,* pp. 12-13.

Parsons, C. D. F. (1990). Drugs, science, and ethics: Lessons from the Depo-Provera story, *Issues in Reproductive and Genetic Engineering: Journal of International Feminist Analysis, 3*(2), 101-110.

Pithers, W. D., Martin, G. R., & Cumming, G. F. (1989). Vermont Treatment program for sexual aggressors. In D. R. Laws (Ed.), *Relapse prevention with sex offenders* (pp. 292-310). New York: Guilford Press.

Priestly Sins (1992, October 7). *Oprah: The Oprah Winfrey Show.* Transcript. Livingston, NJ: Burrelle's Information Services.

Schmidt, G. (1989). Interview: Gunter Schmidt, *Paidika* (Amsterdam), *2*(1), 2-9.

Sonya Live! (1994, March 15). Transcript #505. [Available on NEXIS.]

Stein, K. (1986, April). Interview: John Money, *Omni, 8*(7), [78]-80, 82, 84, 86, 126, 128, 130-131.

Swenson, S. (1987). Depo-Provera: Loopholes and double standards, *Hastings Center Report, 17*(5), 3-4.

Swenson, S. (1988). Sara Swenson replies, *Hastings Center Report, 18*(4), 44-45. (Reply to letter.)

Szasz, T. (1987). Justifying coercion through religion and psychiatry, *Journal of Humanistic Psychology, 27*(2), 158-174.

Tempest, R. (1983, September 17). Sex offender issue: Drugs or jail term, *Los Angeles Times,* part I, p. 1, 12.

Thomas, C. L. (Ed.). (1989). *Taber's cyclopedic medical dictionary* (16th edition). Philadelphia: F. A. Davis. Entries for *androgen, depo-provera, hormone, medroxyprogesterone acetate, progesterone,* and *testosterone.*

Tsang, D. C. (1989, March 22-25). *Ethical Dilemmas in Sex Research and Therapy.* Paper presented at the Annual Meeting of the Society for the Scientific Study of Sex, Western Region, Marina Del Rey, California.

United Press International. (1983, December 22). Corporate "Hall of Shame": Nader lists 10 firms that he says flout public interest, *Boston Globe.*

Upjohn to Try Again to Get Contraceptive Depo-Provera Cleared. (1992, June 11), *Wall Street Journal,* p. B9.

U.S. Congress. (1988a). Office of Technology Assessment. *Criminal justice, new technologies and the Constitution.* OTA-CIT-366. Washington, DC: U.S. Government Printing Office. (Chapter 4: New Technologies for Correctional Supervision.)

U.S. Congress. (1988b). House of Representatives. Committee on Interior and Insular Affairs. Subcommittee on General Oversight and Investigations. *Use of the drug, Depo Provera, by the Indian Health Service.* Serial No. 100-33. Washington, DC: U.S. Government Printing Office.

Vaid, U. (1985, Summer). Depo-Provera: Blessing or curse? *ACLU National Prison Project Journal* (4), 1, 7-9.

Valenstein, E. S. (1986). *Great and desperate cures: The rise and decline of psychosurgery and other radical treatments for mental illness.* New York: Basic Books.

Valenstein, E. S. (1988). The history of lobotomy: A cautionary tale, *Michigan Quarterly Review, 27*(3), 417-437.

Veitch, A. (1984, April 12). Contraceptive injection drug sanctioned: Minister relents on Depo-Provera but backs experts' stringent precautions on use, *The Guardian* (London), p. 2.

Vines, G. (1994). Raging hormones: Do they rule our lives? Berkeley: University of California Press.

Webster, C., Dickens, B., & Addario, S. (1985). *Constructing dangerousness: Scientific, legal and policy implications.* Toronto: Centre of Criminology, University of Toronto. (Series: Research Report, 22.)

Weiss, K. (1984, March 28). Drug reduced urges but didn't fix attitudes, *The Montgomery Journal* (Maryland), pp. A1, A9.

CONCLUSION

Sexual Expression:
A Global Perspective

David Allen Parker, MA
John P. De Cecco, PhD

SUMMARY. Current research into possible biological bases of sexual preference has failed to produce any conclusive evidence. These studies omit the influence of psychological and sociological factors on sexual expression. They conflate the individual with his or her behavior. An argument against the dichotomization of sexual expression on the basis of the individual's biological sex or that of his or her partners concludes this paper.

As this collection of papers has shown, the search for purely biological determinants of sexual preference is fraught with shortcomings. It conflates biological sex with gender and gender with sexuality, it reduces a given sexual preference to specific behaviors and further reduces those behaviors to biological processes, and it accepts and reinforces society's whimsical moral judgements, cate-

[Haworth co-indexing entry note]: "Sexual Expression: A Global Perspective." Parker, David Allen and John P. De Cecco. Co-published simultaneously in *Journal of Homosexuality* (The Haworth Press, Inc.) Vol. 28, No. 3/4, 1995, pp. 427-430; and: *Sex, Cells, and Same-Sex Desire: The Biology of Sexual Preference* (ed: John P. De Cecco, and David Allen Parker) The Haworth Press, Inc., 1995, pp. 427-430. Multiple copies of this article/chapter may be purchased from The Haworth Document Delivery Center [1-800-3-HAWORTH; 9:00 a.m. - 5:00 p.m. (EST)].

gories, and proscriptions regarding sexuality. It is no wonder, then, that in spite of the zeal shown by researchers and the availability of sophisticated equipment and methodology over the past decade, the search for biological markers of sexual preference has failed to produce any conclusive evidence. The studies themselves compete for the right to lay claim to the causes of sexual preference and employ disparate branches of scientific and medical inquiry in their attempts to do so. And for the most part, they omit the intensity of personal history, social setting, and culture as co-determinants of sexuality.

Certainly, as biological organisms, any and all of our behaviors must have biological correlates, but that does not mean that those correlates *determine* our behavior. In fact, one of the maxims of scientific research is, "correlation is not causation." We are more than biological organisms; we are creatures shaped by experience, emotion, time, and circumstance, and in turn we re-shape ourselves for our needs and goals. Sexuality can be reduced to neither a purely biological state nor a purely psychosocial one. Any plausible explanation of sexual expression would have to include all of its components. But most importantly, any explanation of sexuality must assign primacy to the individual.

For no matter how constrained we are by biology, personality, or culture, each of us chooses to express our sexuality in our own unique way based on our individual needs, desires, understanding, and motivation. Over the course of a lifetime a single individual will likely express different components of her or his sexuality to varying degrees, for example, more or less sexual or nonsexual, dominant or submissive, active or passive. Over time that same individual may be more or less accepting or rejecting of cultural mores of not only with whom to have sex, but also of what attributes to be prized in partners. And over the course of a lifetime, the individual's sexual activity will wax and wane. Sexuality is rarely static.

Even one's sexual preference may change over time. Many adults who engage in homosexual sex started their lives as avowed heterosexuals, but somehow changed. Individuals who are attracted to both males and females may find themselves being sexual with persons of only one sex. Sexually active individuals, regardless of their usual choice of partners, may choose to be abstinent. As with all components of sexual expression, sexual preference can be fluid.

Homosexual sex between incarcerated individuals provides the classic example of the flexibility of our sexual expression. Unfortunately, the researchers that have studied sexuality in this setting created a special category in their attempts to explain it which they called "situational" or "facultative homosexuality" and which summarily dismisses the "real homosexuality" involved as an unnatural byproduct of the lack of availability of members of the opposite sex. But this narrow explanation has led investigators away from the real opportunity for learning in such settings. Rather than focussing on the limitation of choice, researchers should consider instead the individual's *willingness* to choose *in spite of* limited options. Perhaps then, rather than merely propagating the stereotype that homosexuality results from some inability to perform proper heterosexual sex, "situational homosexuality" could provide us with some insights into the natural flexibility of human sexual expression and the need for it.

This case does provide excellent insights into the common misconceptions built into the deterministic theories of sexual expression. First, investigators operate from the faulty notion that homosexual and heterosexual sex, aside from the biological sex of the participants, somehow differ. Secondly, these purported differences are the focus of the research rather than the far more numerous similarities that exist in individual sexual expression regardless of the biological sex of those involved. Thirdly, these differences are used as a rationale for numerous static partitionings of sexual expression on the basis of biological sex. Finally, as we mentioned before, most explanations fail to incorporate our natural flexibility as a part of their models of sexuality.

If science wishes to understand the multiplicity of human sexual expression, it must abandon society's notion of heterosexual reproductive monogamous sex as the standard of sexual expression. It must abandon the search for differences in sexual expression between men and women and it must abandon the static categories of homosexuality, bisexuality, and heterosexuality in favor of conceptualizations that allow for the fluidity of sexual expression.

A reconceptualization of sexuality is called for in the sexological studies. Rather than a conception of sexuality dichotomously rooted either in the biological sex of the individual or that of the individual's sexual partners, we propose a new conceptualization that assimilates the notions of biological sex and partner choice into a broader framework of "sexual expression." Sexual expression as conceived here is rooted in the individual, allows for any sexual expression without conflating them with the individual, and allows the individual to change at any given moment in time. And, most importantly, it emphasizes the similarities rather than the differences between individual sexual expressions.

For surely the similarities far outnumber the differences. Regardless of its details, sexuality is a biological, emotional, psychological, and social experience for each of us. We seek to give and receive pleasure, love, excitement, companionship, adventure, and so on. Our sexual desires and behaviors are all equal. Until sexological studies cease to create dividing lines in favor of adopting a more global perspective, the bases of sexual expression will remain a mystery.

Glossary

A A A A A A A

AC–*See* anterior commissure.

ACTH–*See* adrenocorticotropic hormone.

adaptation–The process by which organisms change over generations to best suit their environment.

adrenal gland–Either of the pair of organs located near the kidneys that produces hormones (*see* Figure 4, p. 280).

adrenocorticotropic hormone (ACTH)–A hormone that stimulates the adrenal gland (*see* Figure 4, p. 280).

adrenogenital syndrome–A condition in which the adrenal glands over-produce androgenic hormones which in females promotes the development of male genital structures and secondary sex characteristics; in males, genital development may be disrupted prenatally.

afferent connections–Specialized nerve cells that direct impulses from the body to the brain (compare efferent connections).

AI[S]–*See* androgen insensitivity syndrome.

allele–One of the various forms of a particular gene that can occupy a particular location on a chromosome.

amenorrhea–A complete or near complete absence of menses.

amniotic fluid–The fluid that surrounds the fetus within the amniotic sac in the mother's womb.

[Haworth co-indexing entry note]: "Glossary." Co-published simultaneously in *Journal of Homosexuality* (The Haworth Press, Inc.) Vol. 28, No. 3/4, 1995, pp. 431-446; and: *Sex, Cells, and Same-Sex Desire: The Biology of Sexual Preference* (ed: John P. De Cecco, and David Allen Parker) The Haworth Press, Inc., 1995, pp. 431-446. Multiple copies of this article/chapter may be purchased from The Haworth Document Delivery Center [1-800-3-HAWORTH; 9:00 a.m. - 5:00 p.m. (EST)].

431

androgen–The generic name for compounds that encourage the development or maintenance of male sex characteristics (e.g., testosterone).

androgen insensitivity syndrome (AIS)–A condition in which a genetically male (e.g., XY) individual is partially or completely insensitive to androgens; complete insensitivity results in the development of female external genitalia.

androphilia–Recurrent attraction to males.

androstenedione–An androgenic hormone produced by the adrenal glands.

anterior commissure (AC)–A bundle of nerve cell fibers that connects portions of the temporal and frontal lobes on the right side of the brain to the corresponding region on the left side (*see* Figures 1, 3, & 4, pp. 278-280).

anti-estrogen–Any substance that inhibits estrogen.

aversion therapy–A therapeutic approach to behavior modification which attempts to alter a given behavior by associating it with an unpleasant stimulus.

axon–Part of a nerve cell that transmits information away from the cell to other cells.

azoospermia–A condition in males in which there is a complete or nearly complete lack of sperm in their semen.

B B B B B B B

bed nucleus of the stria terminalis (BNST or BST)–A group of nerve cells in the hypothalamus that surrounds the stria terminalis as it passes through the preoptic and anterior areas of the hypothalamus (*see* Figures 3, p. 279 & 4, p. 280).

berdache–The name given to North American Indians who laid claim to the gender associated with the opposite sex; they often cross-dressed and had sexual relationships with partners of their own sex.

biphilia–Recurrent attraction to both females and males.

BNST–*See* bed nucleus of the stria terminalis.

bolus–A large, rapid infusion.

BST–*See* bed nucleus of the stria terminalis.

bulbourethral gland (also called Cowper's gland)–Either of a pair of glands in the internal male genitalia (*see* Figure 2, p. 95).

C C C C C C C

CAH–*See* congenital adrenal hyperplasia.

California Personality Inventory (CPI)–A measure used to assess personality.

callosum–*See* corpus callosum.

cerebral cortex–The outermost region of the brain thought responsible for higher brain functioning (*see* Figure 1, p. 278).

chi-square (X^2)–A statistical measure used to determine the significance of data.

chromosome–A structure in the cell that carries the genes.

circadian rhythm–The natural daily fluctuation of many biological phenomena (e.g., hormonal levels).

commissure–Dense group or bundle of tissue.

concordant–Sharing the same trait.

congenital–Acquired prenatally.

congenital adrenal hyperplasia (CAH)–A condition in which the adrenal glands under-secrete some hormones, but over-secrete androgens causing varying degrees of ambiguous genitalia.

control [subjects]–In an experiment, an individual or group of individuals considered to be representative of the larger population, with whom the other subjects are compared.

corpus callosum–A group of fibers mostly interconnecting the cortical hemispheres of the brain (*see* Figures 1, p. 278 & 3, p. 279).

cortex–The outer portion of an organ.

cortical–Relating to a cortex.

cortisol–*See* hydrocortisone.

Cowper's gland–*See* bulbourethral gland.

CPI–*See* California Personality Inventory.

critical period–Hypothetical periods during which the brain becomes "male-like" or "female-like" due to a respective over- or under-exposure to androgens.

curvilinearity–A statistical measure used to determine the significance of data.

D D D D D D D

dendrite–Part of a nerve cell that receives information from other cells.

deoxyribonucleic acid (DNA)–A complex molecule that carries the hereditary information.

depo-provera–A long-lasting injectable form of medroxyprogesterone acetate.

DES–*See* estrogen diethylstilbestrol.

dihydrotestosterone–A hormone with the same effects as testosterone.

dipsomania–An acute and recurring craving for alcoholic drinks.

discordant–Not sharing the same trait.

dizygotic (DZ)–Having different alleles for a given gene.

dizygotic twins (also called fraternal twins)–Twins originating from two separate eggs.

DNA–*See* deoxyribonucleic acid.

dominant–The expression of one allele over another (compare recessive).

dorsomedial nucleus–A cluster of nerve cells in the hypothalamus (*see* Figure 4, p. 280).

Down's syndrome–A congenital syndrome in which the individual may suffer mental retardation and a variety of physical abnormalities caused by a defect in the replication of the 21st chromosome.

DZ–*See* dizygotic.

E E E E E E E

EB–*See* estradiol benzoate.

efferent connections–Specialized nerve cells that direct impulses from the brain to the body (compare afferent connections).

endocrine system–A system of glands and organs that produce, receive, and manipulate many substances including hormones.

ephebophilia–Recurrent attraction to teenagers.

epididymis–A structure on the outer surface of the testis that connects it to the vas deferens (*see* Figure 2, p. 95).

estradiol–The most potent naturally occurring estrogen.

estradiol benzoate (EB)–An estrogenic substance usually given as an injection.

estrogen–A substance that promotes estrus and development of secondary sex characteristics (*see* Figure 4, p. 280).

estrogen diethylstilbestrol (DES)–A non-steroidal estrogenic substance usually given orally or as an injection.

estrus–That portion of the ovarian cycle during which most mammals are sexually receptive.

F F F F F F F

fallopian tube–Either of a pair of structures of the internal female genitalia that moves the egg from the ovary to the uterus (*see* Figure 3, p. 96).

follicle-stimulating hormone (FSH) (also follicular stimulating hormone)–A hormone produced by the pituitary that promotes the growth of hormone-producing cells in the testis and ovary (*see* Figure 4, p. 280).

fornix–A bundle of fibers that connects structures in the left and right hemispheres of the brain (*see* Figure 4, p. 280).

47 XYY syndrome–*See* XYY syndrome.

46 XX–Normal human female chromosomal pattern.

46 XY–Normal human male chromosomal pattern.

fraternal twins–*See* dizygotic twins.

frontal lobe–The front area of the brain (*see* Figure 2, p. 279).

FSH–*See* follicle-stimulating hormone.

G G G G G G G

gamete–A mature egg in women; a mature sperm in men.

gender transposition–Crossing over from a male to a female gender or from a female to a male gender.

gene–The functional unit of the chromosome that effects inheritance by specifying the structure of certain proteins or by regulating the activity of other genes.

genome–The genotype of an individual; with respect to a population, the alleles of all the genes contained by the individuals who comprise the population.

genotype–The genetic make-up of an individual.

gland–A multi-cellular structure in the body that secretes compounds (e.g., hormones).

glans clitoris–The erectile tissue capping the body of the clitoris (*see* Figure 3, p. 96).

glans penis–The head of the penis (*see* Figure 2, p. 95).

glucocorticoid–Steroids or steroid-like compounds that regulate glucose metabolism and influence immune functions (e.g., cortisol).

gonad–A reproductive gland that produces gametes and secretes hormones; in men, the testis; in women, the ovary (*see* Figures 1, 2, & 3, pp. 94-96).

gonadectomy–Removal of a gonad.

gonadotropin–A hormone produced by the pituitary that promotes gonadal growth and functioning (i.e., FSH & LH).

granulosa–The outer layer of the ovarian follicle.

gynephilia–Recurrent attraction to women.

H H H H H H H

hCG–*See* human chorionic gonadotropin.

hermaphrodite–An individual possessing both testicular and ovarian tissue.

heterotypic–Of a different type.

heterozygote–An individual possessing different allelic genes at corresponding locations on similar chromosomes (compare homozygote).

hijras–The name given to males in India who undergo emasculation and assume a third gender role; they often have sex with males.

homozygote–An individual possessing the same allelic gene at corresponding locations on similar chromosomes (compare heterozygote).

hormone–A chemical substance produced by one organ and carried to another through the blood stream.

human chorionic gonadotropin (hCG)–A hormone that stimulates ovarian production of estrogen primarily during the first 12 weeks of pregnancy.

hydrocortisone (also called cortisol)–A glucocorticoid primarily produced in the adrenal cortex.

hypogonadism–Deficient secretion of hormones by the testis or ovary usually due to inadequate gonadotropin production.

hypothalamus–The region of the brain under the thalamus that is comprised of different types of nerve cells and that primarily regulates the endocrine system by means of its connections with the pituitary gland (*see* Figures 1, 3, & 4, pp. 278-280).

I I I I I I I

identical twins–*See* monozygotic (MZ).

imprinting–A type of learning that takes place in response to experience during an early and restricted period of biological readiness.

INAH 1, 2, 3, or 4–*See* interstitial nuclei of the anterior hypothalamus.

index [case]–An individual who is the contact source for bringing another individual into an experiment or study.

intermediate nucleus (also called INAH 1 & SDN)–*See* interstitial nuclei of the anterior hypothalamus.

interstitial nuclei of the anterior hypothalamus (INAH 1, 2, 3, 4)– Groups of cell nuclei in the human hypothalamus (*see* Figure 4, p. 280).

in utero–In the womb.

J J J J J J J

K K K K K K K

Kinsey scale–A six-point scale developed by Alfred Kinsey et al. (1948) that ranks individuals from exclusive homosexuality to exclusive heterosexuality on the basis of sexual behavior and fantasy.

L L L L L L L L L L L L L L

labia–Part of the external female genitalia (*see* Figure 3, p. 96).

lateral ventricle–A fluid-filled cavity in the brain (*see* Figure 3, p. 279).

Leydig cells–Cells found in the testes and believed to produce testosterone.

LH–*See* luteinizing hormone.

LHRH–*See* luteinizing hormone releasing hormone.

lordosis–A term used in animal research which refers to the arching of the back in order to facilitate penetration during copulation (compare mounting).

luteinizing hormone (LH)–A pituitary hormone that stimulates testosterone secretion by the testis in males and, in females, estrogen and progesterone secretion by the ovaries which triggers ovulation (*see* Figure 4, p. 280).

luteinizing hormone releasing hormone (LHRH)–A hormone produced in the hypothalamus that causes the pituitary to secrete both FSH and LH (*see* Figure 4, p. 280).

M M M M M M M

magnetic resonance imaging (MRI)–A radiological method of examining internal parts of the body.

mammillary body–A structure in the hypothalamus that receives a bundle of fibers from the fornix and projects fibers to the thalamus (*see* Figure 4, p. 280).

massa intermedia (MI)–A small mass of grey tissue interconnecting the left and right halves of the thalamus (*see* Figure 1, p. 278).

medroxyprogesterone acetate (MPA)–A compound with effects similar to those of progesterone.

menarche–The start of menstruation.

MI–*See* massa intermedia.

Minnesota Multiphasic Personality Inventory (MMPI)–A measure used to assess personality.

monozygotic (MZ)–Denoting twins derived from a single fertilized egg who are thus genetically identical.

morphology–A field of biology that focuses on the structure and form of plants and animals.

mounting–A term used in animal research which refers to the position of the animal on top during copulation (compare lordosis).

MPA–*See* medroxyprogesterone acetate.

MRI–*See* magnetic resonance imaging.

Mullerian duct–A structure in the embryo that develops into the uterus and part of the vagina in females and that mostly disappears in males (*see* Figure 1, p. 94).

Mullerian regression hormone–The hormone that causes the Mullerian duct to regress in males.

mutation–A change in the hereditary components of a cell perpetuated by subsequent replications of that cell.

MZ–*See* monozygotic.

N N N N N N N

natural selection–The interaction between organisms and their environments which determines their ability to successfully reproduce.

neonatal–Immediately after birth.

neuron–A nerve cell.

nucleus–A group of cells.

O O O O O O O

occipital lobe–The rear area of the brain (*see* Figure 2, p. 279).

oestradiol–*See* estradiol.

oestrogen–*See* estrogen.

optic chiasm–The site where the optic nerves cross (*see* Figure 4, p. 280).

ovarian follicle–The structure in the ovary that contains an egg.

ovarian theca cells–The cells that form the walls of egg-containing ovarian follicles; the inner layer of the theca cells is the primary source of estrogen.

ovariectomy–Removal of an ovary.

ovary–Either of the pair of female gonads (*see* Figure 3, p. 96).

P P P P P P P

P–*See* progesterone.

paraphilia–Any recurrent attraction involving nonhuman objects, nonconsenting partners, or mental or physical pain inflicted on oneself or one's partner(s).

paraventricular nucleus (PVN)–A group of cells in the hypothalamus near the third ventricle; this nucleus contains a variety of cell types, most prominently very large neurons whose processes terminate in the posterior hypothalamus (*see* Figure 4, p. 280).

parietal lobe–The center area of the brain (*see* Figure 2, p. 279).

pedophilia–Recurrent attraction to children.

perinatal–Around the time of birth.

phenotype–The observable expression of the interaction between genotype and environment.

pituitary [gland]–The primary endocrine gland that secretes hormones that regulate many other endocrine glands, including the gonads and adrenals; it is connected with and regulated by the hypothalamus (*see* Figures 1, p. 278, & 4, p. 280).

placenta–The organ that unites the fetus with the mother's womb and allows metabolic exchange.

planum temporale–A part of the temporal lobe thought to influence language functions (*see* Figure 3, p. 279).

POA–*See* preoptic area.

posterior hypothalamic area–The area of the hypothalamus between the dorsomedial nucleus and the mammillary bodies.

posterior nucleus–An imprecise term used to designate either the entire region of the posterior hypothalamus between the dorsomedial nucleus and the mammillary bodies, or the largest group of identifiable cells within that region (*see* Figure 4, p. 280).

postnatal–After the time of birth.

Prader-Willi syndrome–A congenital syndrome characterized by mental retardation and lack of development during puberty.

prenatal–Before birth.

preoptic area (POA)–The portion of the hypothalamus that is in front of the suprachiasmatic nucleus.

preoptic nucleus–Any of a number of so-identified cell clusters in the preoptic area.

progesterone (P)–An ovarian anti-estrogenic steroid hormone that stimulates the uterine changes that are necessary for the implantation and growth of a fertilized egg (*see* Figure 4, p. 280).

progestin–The generic term for a compound that mimics any or all of the actions of progesterone.

prolactin–A hormone that stimulates the production of breast milk (*see* Figure 4, p. 280).

prostate gland–In males, a gland that secretes part of the ejaculatory fluid (*see* Figure 2, p. 95).

pseudohermaphrodite–An individual with the gonads of one sex but genitals with some features of the opposite sex.

PVN–*See* paraventricular nucleus.

Q Q Q Q Q Q Q

R R R R R R R

recessive–The suppression of one allele by another (compare dominant).

refractory period–A short period immediately after a response before a second response is possible.

reproductive success (RS)–The passing on of genetic material to future generations.

ribonucleic acid (RNA)–A complex molecule that influences cell replication and function.

RNA–*See* ribonucleic acid.

RS–*See* reproductive success.

S S S S S S S

SCN–*See* suprachiasmatic nucleus.

SDN–*See* sexually dimorphic nucleus.

SDN-POA–*See* sexually dimorphic nucleus of the preoptic area.

secondary sex characteristics–Characteristics that develop as a result of pubertal hormone levels; for instance, breast development and the widening of the hips in females, and the increased hairiness and lowered voice pitch in males.

seminal vesicle–Either of a pair of folded glands connected to the ejaculatory duct that secretes one of the components of semen (*see* Figure 2, p. 95).

seminiferous tubule–A structure in the testis where sperm is manufactured.

sexually dimorphic–A structure or function that differs on the basis of biological sex.

sexually dimorphic nucleus (SDN) (also called INAH 1 & intermediate nucleus)–*See* interstitial nuclei of the anterior hypothalamus.

sexually dimorphic nucleus of the preoptic area (SDN-POA)–A nucleus in the preoptic and anterior portions of the rat hypothalamus that is larger in males than in females; its function is unknown as it can be destroyed without any observable effect.

spayed–*See* ovariectomy.

spermatazoa–Sperm.

splenium–The hind part of the corpus callosum (*see* Figure 1, p. 278).

steroid–Any of a group of several substances with a specific molecular structure including many of the hormones.

stria terminalis–A band of nerve cell fibers that interconnects the hypothalamus and other brain structures.

suprachiasmatic nucleus (SCN)–A group of cells located on each side of the hypothalamus just above the optic chiasm; this nucleus is believed to influence circadian and other biological rhythms (*see* Figure 4, p. 280).

supraoptic nucleus–A nucleus in the hypothalamus located above the optic nerves (*see* Figure 4, p. 280).

T T T T T T T

T–*See* testosterone.

"tearoom"–Slang term for a men's restroom.

temporal lobe–The side area of the brain (*see* Figure 2, p. 279).

testicular feminization syndrome (TFS or Tfm) (also complete AIS)– A syndrome in which the body becomes feminized at puberty due to an absence of normal androgen receptors and the natural derivation of estrogen from the testes; the external genitalia are unambiguously female at birth and the individuals are most often reared as females.

testis–Either of the pair of male gonads (*see* Figure 2, p. 95).

testis determining gene–A gene on the Y chromosome that stimulates sexual differentiation.

testosterone (T)–A hormone primarily produced in the testis which promotes secondary sex characteristics (*see* Figure 4, p. 280).

testosterone propionate (TP)–A form of testosterone frequently used in animal research.

tetrachoric correlation–A statistical measure used to determine the significance of data.

TFS–*See* testicular feminization syndrome.

thalamus–An ovoid mass of grey matter in the brain that serves as a relay station for information travelling in either direction between the cerebral cortex and other areas of the brain and spinal cord (*see* Figure 1, p. 278).

third ventricle–A fluid-filled cavity in the brain (*see* Figure 3, p. 279).

thyroid gland–One of a pair of endocrine glands located in the neck that is regulated by the hypothalamus and pituitary (*see* Figure 4, p. 280).

thyroid-stimulating hormone (TSH)–A pituitary hormone that stimulates thyroid hormone production and secretion (*see* Figure 4, p. 280).

TP–*See* testosterone propionate.

TSH–*See* thyroid-stimulating hormone.

t-test–A statistical measure used to determine the significance of data.

U U U U U U U

urogenital sinus–Part of the undifferentiated prenatal genitalia (*see* Figure 1, p. 94).

V V V V V V V

vas deferens–The duct that carries the sperm from the testis to the urethra (*see* Figure 2, p. 95).

ventromedial nucleus–A nucleus in the hypothalamus (*see* Figure 4, p. 280).

W W W W W W W

Wolffian duct–A structure in the embryo that develops into the vas deferens in men and mostly disappears in women (*see* Figure 1, p. 94).

X X X X X X X

X^2–*See* chi-square.

X chromosome–The female chromosome.

XYY syndrome–A chromosomal abnormality in males in which an extra Y chromosome is present.

Y Y Y Y Y Y Y

Y chromosome–The male chromosome.

Z Z Z Z Z Z Z

zygosity–The allelic makeup of an individual with respect to a particular gene (*see* both heterozygote and homozygote); or in the case of twins, whether they were derived from a single zygote (homozygotic) or separate zygotes (dizygotic).

zygote–The single cell with a full complement of chromosomes resulting from the union of a sperm and an egg.

Index

Achilles, 307
Acquired immune deficiency
        syndrome (AIDS), 176
    epidemic of, 2,8,248
    homosexuals' immunological
        susceptibility to, 317
Acquired immune deficiency
        syndrome victims
    hypothalamic anatomy of, 292,
        293-294,329
    testosterone levels of, 329
Adaptation, 150,205-206,210
    definition, 431
Additive genetic variance, 125
Adolescents
    bisexual male, as prostitutes, 363,
        364
    homosexual, suicide by, 392
Adrenogenital syndrome, 97-98,263,
        365-367,369
    definition, 431
Advocate, 6,7,110,199
Alexander the Great, 24
Alleles, 123
    definition, 431
    epistatic interactions of, 123
    gene frequency of, 124
Allen, Laura, 5-6
Altruism, of homosexuals, 176,
        187-194
    relationship to religiousity,
        192-193
Ambidexterity. *See also*
        Left-handedness
    in ancient China, 383,392
    prevalence of, 383
Ambisexuality, 100-101,109

American Civil Liberties Union,
        opposition to Depo-Provera
        therapy, 416
American Journal of Psychiatry,
        418-419
American Psychological Association,
        2,24-25*n*.
Anal intercourse
    medical investigations of, 36,60
    nineteenth-century attitudes
        towards, 36
    as preferred homosexual sexual
        practice, 41
Analogy, human-animal, 33-34,49,241
Andrin, 45
Androgen insensitivity syndrome
    complete, 97,261-263,444
    definition, 432
    partial, 261
Androgens. *See also* Testosterone
    definition, 432
    effect on mammalian sexual
        behavior, 359
    effect on prenatal sexual
        differentiation, 310,390.
        See also Prenatal hormonal
        hypothesis, of sexual
        orientation
    as homosexuality treatment, 249
    as masculinizing hormone, 3,399
        in female animal models,
            346-347
    prenatal stress-related decrease of,
        270
    as secondary sex characteristic
        inducing agents, 215
Androgy, 13
Androphilia, 306-307
    definition, 432

criticism of developmental stage
   theory, 203
gender concepts of, 233*n.*
Feminization
   androgen insensitivity-related,
      261-263
   of genetic males, 359
Fetus, sexual differentiation of, 359.
      See also Prenatal hormonal
      hypothesis, of sexual
      orientation
Fitness. *See also* Inclusive fitness
   Darwinian theory of, 35
Fliess, Wilhelm, 378
Florida, Depo-Provera use in, 402
Follicle-stimulating hormone (FSH)
      levels
   definition, 435
   in homosexuals, 249,251,254,
      256-257
   in lesbians, 254
Food and Drug Administration
      (FDA), Depo-Provera
      approval by, 400-401,4
      02-403
"Fop," 167
46,XX chromosomal pattern, 93
46,XY chromosomal pattern, 93
47,XYY syndrome, 367,369
Freud, Sigmund, 5,92
Freudian psychology, 19

Gagne, Pierre, 404
Gall, Franz Joseph, 40,43
Galligan, Joseph, 403
Gall wasps, Kinsey's research with,
      206-207
Gauntlett, Roger A., 413
Gay activism, 176
Gay activists, attitudes towards
      sociobiology, 199
Gay American History (Katz), 398
Gay and Lesbian Alliance Against
      Defamation, 12

Gay community, activism of,
      176,199
Gay liberation movement, 2,71-72
Gender
   classification of, 80-81,82-83
   feminist concept of, 233*n.*
Gender identity
   historical transformations of, 167
   imprinting of, 165
   prenatal hormonal hypothesis of,
      295
   Western concept of, 159
Gender inversions, 68-71
Gender roles
   cultural variations in, 363-364
   of homosexuals, 14-15
Gender systems, cultural variations
      in, 67-68
Gender transpositions, 158,436
Gene frequency, 124
Genes
   definition, 436
   for homosexuality, 6,13-14,116,
      132,133-134,155,305,
      308-309,348
   indirect expression, 162
   invariant, 123
   paternal, methyl groups of,
      123-124
   relationship to behavior, 308
   variant, 123
Genetic architecture, 122
Genetic constitution, 122
Genetic factors
   in handedness, 385,386
   in homosexuality, 5,115-145,218,
      390
      interaction with environmental
         factors, 161-162, 163,
         164-165,201,308-309
Genetic markers, of homosexuality,
      gay community's attitudes
      towards, 200
Genetic models, 116,126-128
   social implications of, 140

as biological "aberration," 211,
238,306,307-308
body-mind duality theory of,
79-80
causation, 62
lack of consensus regarding,
375-376
as central nervous system
hermaphroditism, 306
as choice, 16-19,352-353,375-376
classification of, 81-82
constant vs. periodic, 45
as cross-gender behavior, 13-14,
23,45,68-69
definitional problems in, 32,
157-161
development of concept of, 345
distinguished from gender
inversion, 68-71
essentialist-constructionist debate
concerning, 166-167,
177-179
eugenic theory of, 38-39
evolutionary adaptive benefits of,
185-187
facultative, 12-13,429
familial factors in, 3-4,5,37-38,
115,385-386
general conception of, 19-24
genetic factors in. *See* Genetic
theories, of homosexuality
and sexual orientation
as group identity, 22-23
as inappropriate femaleness, 69
incidence, 154,165
as intersex, 306
Kinsey scale rating of, 100
as learned behavior, 376
legal prohibition of, 81,376
naturalness of, 159
as normal developmental pattern,
383-384
obligatory, 12,13
parental factors in, 385,387
prevalence, 369,382-383

relationship to mutational
equilibrium, 208
psychiatric theory of, 39
as psychopathology, 81,116,
386-387
biological arguments for,
210-211
eugenic theory of, 38-39
historical background, 304
during nineteenth century,
34-35
religious prohibition of, 16,376
situational, 158,429
social attitudes towards, 376
historical background, 304
stigmatization of, 352-353
suppression of, 387
tests for, 83-85
as third gender, 13,20,22,68,
81-82,239
treatment of
of Alan Turing, 418
with antiandrogens, 404-405,
418-419. *See also*
Depo-Provera
with aversion therapy, 211
with hormonal therapy, 47,
51*n*.,84-85,242,249,
309-310
surgical, 42,51-52*n*.,85,398
Homosexual research subjects
recruitment of, 120-121
sexual orientation determination
of, 117-119,131-133,255
Homosexuals
androphilia of, 306-307
anthropometric measurements of,
43-44
children of, homosexuality of,
385,386
classification as bisexuals, 358
female characteristics of, 34
femininity of, 13,388
early research in, 49-50
relationship to plasma

Oregon, Depo-Provera use in, 402
Origin of the Species (Darwin), 150
Ovarian cycle, hormonal regulation of, 313-314
Ovarian hormones, effect on sex-related behavior, 229-231
Ovary
embryonic development of, 94-95,96
sexual differentiation of, 241
Overexposed: Treating Sexual Perversion in America (Lotringer), 398
Ovotestis, 241
Ovulation, luteinizing hormone surge in, 347

Paidika, 411
Panchreston, 157
Paradigms, 62
Paraphilia
definition, 441
Depo-Provera therapy for, 400, 407,412
Parental factors, in homosexuality, 385,386
Parental manipulation, 107-108
of children's celibacy, 174-177
of children's homosexuality, 178
Parent-child relationships, of homosexuals, 387
Parenthood, by same-sex couples, 169-70
Parent-offspring studies, of homosexuality, 129,142*n*.
Path models, genetic, 127
Pederasty. *See also* Pedophilia
Depo-Provera therapy for, 420
nineteenth-century attitudes towards, 36
as obstacle to reproduction, 409
Pedigree analysis, 6

Pedophilia
definition, 441
John Money's theory of, 408-409
publications supportive of, 408-409,411
treatment of, 398
with Depo-Provera, 399,403, 407-408,411-412,415-416
Peer review, of scientific journal articles, 330-333
Penis
of homosexuals, size and shape of, 43,44,60
of rats, muscular control of, 227
People v. Gauntlett, 413
Perversion, homosexuality as, 36.
See also Psychopathology, homosexuality as
ethological theory of, 48
psychiatric theory of, 41
Petitio principii, 158-160
Phenotype, 162
definition, 93,441
environmental influences on, 122
expression in twins, 101-103
genetic-environmental co-determination of, 163
homosexuality as, 116
nature-nurture equation of, 124-125
negative selection of, 186
permanent, 122-123
Phenotypic plasticity, 162-163
Phil Donahue Show (television program), 416
Phrenology, 40-41,43
Piaget, Jean, 203
Pillard, Richard, 3-4
Pink Triangle Press, 408-409
Pituitary gland, anatomy of, 278, 280,281
Planum temporale
definition, 281,441
sexual dimorphism in, 318, 319-320

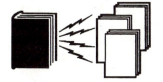

Haworth
DOCUMENT DELIVERY
SERVICE

This new service provides a single-article order form for any article from a Haworth journal.

- *Time Saving:* No running around from library to library to find a specific article.
- *Cost Effective:* All costs are kept down to a minimum.
- *Fast Delivery:* Choose from several options, including same-day FAX.
- *No Copyright Hassles:* You will be supplied by the original publisher.
- *Easy Payment:* Choose from several easy payment methods.

Open Accounts Welcome for ...
- Library Interlibrary Loan Departments
- Library Network/Consortia Wishing to Provide Single-Article Services
- Indexing/Abstracting Services with Single Article Provision Services
- Document Provision Brokers and Freelance Information Service Providers

MAIL or *FAX* THIS ENTIRE ORDER FORM TO:

Haworth Document Delivery Service
The Haworth Press, Inc.
10 Alice Street
Binghamton, NY 13904-1580

or **FAX:** (607) 722-6362
or **CALL:** 1-800-3-HAWORTH
(1-800-342-9678; 9am-5pm EST)

PLEASE SEND ME PHOTOCOPIES OF THE FOLLOWING SINGLE ARTICLES:
1) Journal Title: _____
   Vol/Issue/Year: _____ Starting & Ending Pages: _____
   Article Title: _____
   _____

2) Journal Title: _____
   Vol/Issue/Year: _____ Starting & Ending Pages: _____
   Article Title: _____
   _____

3) Journal Title: _____
   Vol/Issue/Year: _____ Starting & Ending Pages: _____
   Article Title: _____
   _____

4) Journal Title: _____
   Vol/Issue/Year: _____ Starting & Ending Pages: _____
   Article Title: _____
   _____

(See other side for Costs and Payment Information)

COSTS: Please figure your cost to order quality copies of an article.

1. Set-up charge per article: $8.00

              ($8.00 × number of separate articles) _____

2. Photocopying charge for each article:

              1-10 pages: $1.00 _____

              11-19 pages: $3.00 _____

              20-29 pages: $5.00 _____

              30+ pages: $2.00/10 pages _____

3. Flexicover (optional): $2.00/article _____

4. Postage & Handling: US: $1.00 for the first article/

              $.50 each additional article _____

            Federal Express: $25.00 _____

            Outside US: $2.00 for first article/

              $.50 each additional article _____

5. Same-day FAX service: $.35 per page _____

              GRAND TOTAL: _____

METHOD OF PAYMENT: (please check one)

❑ Check enclosed   ❑ Please ship and bill. PO # _____

        (sorry we can ship and bill to bookstores only! All others must pre-pay)

❑ Charge to my credit card: ❑ Visa;   ❑ MasterCard;   ❑ American Express;

Account Number: _____ Expiration date: _____

Signature: *X*_____

Name: _____ Institution: _____

Address: _____

       _____

City: _____ State: _____ Zip: _____

Phone Number: _____ FAX Number: _____

MAIL or *FAX* THIS ENTIRE ORDER FORM TO:

Haworth Document Delivery Service	**or FAX:** (607) 722-6362
The Haworth Press, Inc.	**or CALL:** 1-800-3-HAWORTH
10 Alice Street	(1-800-342-9678; 9am-5pm EST)
Binghamton, NY 13904-1580	